angel

*f 8*

URAL MOUNTAINS

D0718930

Perm

■ Sverdlovsk
*(Ekaterinburg)*

Kostroma

KAMA

oslavl
● Rostov Veliki
Pereslavl Zalesski
exandrov
**Gorki**
*(Nizhni Novgorod)*

Kazan

Vladimir-Suzdal

Simbirsk

OKA

la

VOLGA

URAL

Orenburg
*(Samara)*

Saratov

● Voronezh

Guryev

kov

■ **Volgograd**
*(Tsaritsin/Stalingrad)*

DON

ASTRAKHAN

Caspian Sea

Taganrog
● Rostov-on-Don
Azov

zov

Novorossisk

CAUCASUS MOUNTAINS

GEORGIA

Derbent
*(Derband)*

Batum

Baku

● Yerevan
*(Erivan)*

E Y

I R A N

Ian McLeod
Strachur
1984

# HOLY RUSSIA

Red Square, Moscow

# Holy Russia

An Historical Companion
to European Russia

## FITZROY MACLEAN

WEIDENFELD AND NICOLSON   LONDON

ISBN 0 297 77489 1

Printed in Great Britain by Butler & Tanner Ltd,
Frome and London

For Charlie, this
brief introduction
to a large country

# Holy Russia

The Russian revolution, when it comes, will be the more terrible because it will be proclaimed in the name of religion. Russian policy has melted the Church into the State and confounded heaven and earth: a man who sees a god in his master scarcely hopes for paradise, except through the favours of the Emperor.

MARQUIS DE CUSTINE, *La Russie en 1839*

'Do you know?' he began almost menacingly, leaning forward in his chair with his eyes blazing and holding up the first finger of his right hand, evidently without realizing he was doing it. 'Do you know who are the only god-fearing people on earth, whose destiny it is to regenerate and save the world in the name of a new god and who alone have been entrusted with the task of preserving Life and the Word? Do you know who these people are and what they are called?'

'Judging by your manner, I suppose I must conclude, and the sooner the better, that you are referring to the people of Russia.'

DOSTOYEVSKI, *The Possessed*

With the mind Russia cannot be grasped,
Nor can she be measured by any ordinary standards.
Russia is different,
To be believed in with unquestioning faith.

F. I. TYUTCHEV (1866)

# Contents

# Illustrations

ILLUSTRATIONS

# Maps

# *Acknowledgements*

My thanks to Major General Lord Cathcart for the story on p. 116; to Mr Michael Vyvyan for his most useful and enlightening comments on my manuscript; to Miss Alex MacCormick, Mr Michael Graham-Dixon and my secretary, Mrs Macpherson, for their patient help with the text; and to my son Jamie for allowing me to use his excellent photograph of the Winter Palace on p. 81, so much better than those I took of it myself.

F.M.

# *Note on Dates*

Having at long last adopted it, the Russians retained the old or Julian calendar until 1918, when it was finally abandoned in favour of the new or Gregorian calendar, used in most other Christian countries. In the eighteenth century the old system was eleven days behind the new, twelve in the nineteenth, and thirteen in the twentieth. It is thus that what we all think of as the October Revolution occurred, in fact, on 7 November. However, to avoid confusion, I have given the new-style dates throughout.

F.M.

# *Preface*

The first two volumes of what has now become a trilogy concerned Central Asia and the Caucasus. My original intention had been to leave it at that. But I very soon realized that what I had written would be incomplete without some account of Russia and of the Russians, the race which in the long run was to dominate both regions.

In writing this third volume, I have become increasingly conscious of the direct relevance of Russia's historical development, not only to that of her neighbours, but also to much that is happening in Russia today. More even than most countries, present-day Russia is hard to understand without some knowledge of her history. Almost everything, one soon finds, is rooted in the past.

Like its predecessors, this is not a book for the expert. I have begun it with a necessarily brief outline of Russian history and gone on to describe Moscow, Leningrad and a number of other Russian towns and cities, concentrating on those which seemed to me to possess the greatest historical significance and retain the greatest number of links with their past. Once again, I hope that what I have written may be of some use to intending travellers to the Soviet Union.

F.M.

# 1 *The Origins*

THE EARLY HISTORY of Russia, like that of most countries, is confused and obscure. For centuries the vast plain that is now European Russia was the stamping-ground of a kaleidoscopic collection of tribes, who, owing to their own nomadic and aggressive tendencies and the absence of natural barriers, overran each other and were in turn overrun in a constantly shifting pattern of races and, for want of a better word, civilizations. 'Their names,' wrote Edward Gibbon, with evident distaste, 'are uncouth, their origins doubtful, their actions obscure. Their superstition was blind, their valour brutal and the uniformity of their public and private lives was neither softened by innocence nor refined by policy.'

Of these unprepossessing nomads, the first of whom we have much knowledge are the Scythians and the even more shadowy Cimmerians. The Scythians, who held sway in southern Russia as early as the seventh century BC, seem to have come from further east and to have been of Iranian origin. Their neighbours on the northern shores of the Black Sea were the colonies of Greek settlers, who in much diminished form have survived there to this day, and it is, one suspects, partly to Greek skill or at any rate influence that we owe the superb cups, torques and scabbards of Scythian gold now displayed in Leningrad and Kiev.

From the Greek historian Herodotus, who visited Scythia in the fifth century BC, we learn of the Scythian habit of drinking the blood of their enemies, flaying them, scalping them and sewing the scalps together to make cloaks for themselves. They also, it seems, took vapour baths, throwing hemp-seed on red-hot stones to produce the vapour, 'for they never,' adds Herodotus, 'by any chance, wash their bodies with water.' He tells, too, of their obsessive fear of foreign influence, quoting the example of two famous Scythians killed by their fellows for adopting Greek habits. Early in the first century of our own era, the Scythians appear to have made way for a fresh wave of invaders from the east, like them of Iranian origin, the Sarmatians and the Alans. Of these, the Alans, when in their turn displaced, fell back on the Caucasus, where, as the Ossetians, they have survived ever since.

In the third century came the Goths, a collection of Germanic tribes, who poured into south Russia from the north-west, only to be driven out again a century or two later by the Huns, a tribe of Turkish or Mongolian origin, who towards the end of the fourth century swept in from the east, pushing the Goths back westwards across the frontiers of the Roman Empire. The Huns, some of whom eventually settled in Hungary, were followed in their turn by wave upon wave of invaders from the east, mostly, like them, of Turkish or Mongolian origin: Avars, Khazars and Pechenegs or Patzmacs. In the forests of the north, where Leningrad, Novgorod and Moscow are today, the Finno-Ugrians, likewise of Asian origin, had come to rest. It is not until the ninth century that we at last find, in what is now southern Russia, signs of a more settled population, and it is at this moment in time that most historians seek to fix the beginnings of Russian history.

The race or tribe who, abandoning their nomadic habits and turning to agriculture, eventually settled in the fertile plains of southern Russia was the Slavs and, more particularly, the Eastern Slavs. Who were the Slavs and where did they come from? According to most authorities they can first be reliably identified as a separate race or tribe in the fifth century of our era. By then they were living in the Northern Carpathians and the valley of the Vistula under Hun overlordship and it is no doubt in the train of the Huns that they first reached what is now southern Russia and the Ukraine. Following the death of the great Hun leader Attila in 453 and the subsequent collapse of Hun power, there ensued a wide dispersal of the various races subject to the Huns and it was during the next century or so that the Slavs, who had hitherto spoken a common Slav language, split up into three main groups: the Western Slavs, who in due course became Poles, Czechs or Slovaks; the Southern Slavs, who, pushing down into the Balkan Peninsula, became Serbs, Croats and Slovenes; and the Eastern Slavs, who, remaining roughly where they were, became in the long run Russians.

It was the lure of trade as much as anything that led the Eastern

Slavs to settle where they did, trade and the ready-made system of inland communications furnished by the great rivers of Russia, which run for the most part north and south, while their tributaries flow east and west, thus forming a network of waterways which covers practically the whole of European Russia. Taking advantage of this, they helped their latest overlords, the Khazars, a tribe of Turkish nomads whose rulers, though not Jewish by race, had curiously enough embraced Judaism, to establish a regular trade route from the Baltic to the Black Sea and Byzantium. From mere trading centres, Kiev and Novgorod (literally 'New Town') became prosperous cities. From hunting and fishing and the purely pastoral life of nomads a gradual transition now took place to agriculture and permanent settlement.

The Khazars had once controlled a vast area of territory reaching from the Urals to the Dnieper. But in the first half of the eighth century, following their defeat by the Arabs, their power had begun to decline, a process accelerated by a new and desperate struggle with the latest wave of invaders from the east, the Pechenegs, and by this time with the Eastern Slavs themselves, who had chosen this moment to turn against their suzerains. Freed from Khazar suzerainty, but also deprived of the protection which it afforded them, the Eastern Slavs now began to look elsewhere for support.

They did not have far to look. This was the age of Viking conquest and expansion, which in a century or two took the Norsemen to France, to Sicily, to the Hebrides and, as we now know, to North America. Setting forth from their bases in Scandinavia, half pirates and half merchant-adventurers, they had already pushed down from the Baltic into the region of the Upper Volga, whence they moved eastwards and southwards in the direction of the Sea of Azov. It was only natural that the Eastern Slavs, feeling isolated, should turn for help to these dynamic newcomers 'from across the sea', to whom many of them were already paying a regular tribute of white squirrel skins.

From an early Russian chronicler we learn that in 862 the people of Novgorod on the River Volkhov, or at any rate some of the people of Novgorod, appealed to the Varangians, as their Norse neighbours were known, to take them in hand and help order their affairs. 'Our land,' they are reported as saying, 'is great and rich. But there is no order in it. Come and rule over us.' The Norsemen, it appears, responded readily to the invitation, and, after a preliminary reconnaissance, the Varangian Prince Rurik, or Roderick, hitherto ruler of South Jutland, having first successfully overcome any actual or potential opposition, established himself in Novgorod and became the founder of the first Russian ruling dynasty, the Rurikids. Or so it is said. For at this stage of their history the Russians could neither read nor write and Nestor, the earliest of the Russian Chroniclers, who eventually recorded these events, was not born until a couple of centuries later.

According to the Chronicler, Rurik died in 879. On his death, his brother-in-law, Oleg, also a Varangian, assumed the title of Prince of Novgorod as Regent for Ruril's young son, Igor. Oleg was to play a decisive part in early Russian history. Marching rapidly south, he captured Smolensk and then, pushing on to Kiev on the Dnieper, managed, by a stratagem amounting, some might say, to treachery, to capture and kill its rulers, his fellow Varangians, Askold and Dir, seize the town and make it his capital. Kiev, he announced, was to be 'the Mother of Russian Cities'.

It was thus that by 882, only three years after Rurik's death, Oleg had become the ruler of an area reaching from Novgorod to Kiev, some eight hundred miles from north to south and four hundred miles from east to west, while Kiev had come to be the capital of a more or less unified Eastern Slav state, to which the Varangians gave the name Rus. Or such, once again, is the story. For both the origins of the new state's name and the respective parts played in its foundation by Norseman and Slav have long been the subject of impassioned controversy, which, considering the slenderness of the evidence available, is likely to continue indefinitely. One thing seems clear: it was only a matter of time before the Varangian ruling class became increasingly assimilated to their more numerous Eastern Slav subjects.

Russia, it has been said, was born on the route between two seas – the Black Sea and the Baltic. Oleg was above all a trader and Kiev, his capital, the centre of a far-flung trading organization. His chief concern was to keep his trade routes open. For the next thirty years, until his death in 912, he fought, with this aim in view, one campaign after another, battling with the Khazars and Pechenegs and, 'with horse and ship', even raiding Byzantium – or, as the Vikings preferred to call it, Micklegarth – until in the end the Byzantines were obliged to buy him off with a commercial treaty highly favourable to Kiev. Little wonder that his deeds are to this day celebrated in Russian legend and song.

Rurik's son Igor, who succeeded Oleg, seems to have been a good deal less successful, both as a statesman and as a military leader. He finally met his death at the hands of a tribe known as the Drevlians, from whom he was seeking, unsuccessfully, to extort double tribute. This left the field open for his widow Olga, a Slav by birth and reputedly a woman of great beauty, considerable wisdom and utter ruthlessness, whose regency, according to the Chronicler, was marked by a number of much-needed reforms.

After the founding of Kievan Rus, the most important event in early Russian history was the adoption, towards the end of the tenth century, of Orthodox Christianity as the religion of the new state in place of the lively but somewhat confused pagan beliefs that had preceded it. Of great importance, too, was the fact that Christianity, when it came, came not from Rome but from Byzantium, from the Eastern and not from the Western Church.

For a considerable time now there had been numerous contacts between Kiev and Byzantium. Each spring the Grand Prince of Kiev would make his way, with an armed retinue known as a *druzhina* and a flotilla of vessels carrying cargoes of furs, honey and slaves, down the Dnieper and across the Black Sea to Constantinople, varying this procedure with an occasional raid on his trading partners if he thought that his rights had in any way been infringed. From these expeditions the Russians brought back with them, not only Byzantine gold, silk, wine and spices, but, in the long run, Byzantine ideas. As early as the ninth century there had been signs of Christian influence in Kiev. Then, in the year 957, Princess Olga went on a pilgrimage to Constantinople, from which she returned a fervent Christian, indeed, as things turned out, a future saint. Given her strength of character, it seemed likely that the whole country would quickly follow her example. But despite, or possibly because of, her proselytizing zeal, her own son Svyatoslav, the reigning Grand Prince, remained resolutely pagan.

Svyatoslav was first and foremost a warrior, 'stepping,' the Chronicler tells us, 'lightly, like a panther.' His interests were in the main military. With his large, well-trained, well-organized *druzhina*, already assuming the character of a future aristocracy, he carried fire and sword into his neighbours' territory, battling with Khazars and Bulgars, challenging Byzantium, and vastly extending his country's frontiers, while leaving his mother to carry on the government at home. 'On his raids,' writes the Chronicler, 'he carried with him neither wagons nor kettles, but cut off small strips of horseflesh, game or beef, and ate it after roasting it on the coals. Nor did he have a tent, but he spread out a piece of saddle-cloth under him and set his saddle under his head.' At heart he was a conservative. 'How can I change my religion?' he would ask in his bluff, soldierly way, when urged to become a Christian. 'Why, my friends in the *druzhina* would laugh at me.' And he would go off again to fight the Bulgars or whoever needed fighting at that particular moment.

By 967 he had defeated the Khazars and the Volga Bulgars and brought the entire course of the Volga under Russian control. Setting out again from Kiev in 968, he first defeated the Bulgars on the Danube and then, pressing on across the Balkans, threatened Constantinople itself. Seriously alarmed, the Byzantine Emperor of the day, also no mean warrior, counter-attacked and in the end Svyatoslav was forced to withdraw. Returning to Russia with a small retinue in the summer of 971, he was, as chance would have it, ambushed and killed near the cataracts of the Dnieper by a band of marauding Pechenegs who turned his skull into a drinking cup with a mocking inscription engraved upon it.

A prolonged period of fratricidal strife now followed between Svyatoslav's sons, at the end of which he was succeeded by his third son Vladimir, the only one of several brothers to survive this particular dispute.

It was Vladimir who gave Kievan Rus the character of a real state or, perhaps it would be more accurate to say, a confederation of principalities. In 988 he married Anna, sister of the co-Emperors of Byzantium, Basil and Constantine, and in the process became converted to Christianity. Formally renouncing the old pagan beliefs on his own behalf and on behalf of his subjects, he now smashed all the heathen idols he could lay hands on and declared Christianity the official, indeed the obligatory, religion of Kievan Russia, enforcing it with a ruthlessness worthy of his sainted grandmother. For this he, too, was in due course canonized and today a great statue of him, bearing a massive bronze cross, looks pensively out across the Dnieper.

But, saint though he was, Vladimir seems to have lost none of his zest for life or interest in the affairs of this world. He proved a highly effectual ruler, who recast the civil administration, did much for education and erected a number of handsome public buildings in and around Kiev. In addition to his imperial consort, he is said to have kept no fewer than eight hundred concubines, more than two for every day of the year, and is described by a knowing German chronicler of the period as *fornicator immensus et crudelis*. He also enjoyed an occasional drink and, previous to his conversion to Christianity, had, according to the chronicler, rejected a Moslem proposal that he and his people should embrace Islam, on the grounds that Russians must have strong drink. *Rusi est vesele piti*, he declared, in rhyming couplets, *Bez nego ne mozhet biti* – 'Russians are happier drinking. They just cannot live without it.' Taken all in all, it seems by no means inappropriate that eight centuries later, the Empress Catherine the Great, who shared many of his tastes and inclinations, should have instituted in his honour a much coveted order of knighthood, the Order of Vladimir, to be awarded for distinguished public and private services of one kind or another.

Whatever the spiritual benefits derived by Kievan Rus from the advent of Orthodox Christianity (and they were no doubt considerable), there can be no question as to its immense political significance or its civilizing effect. Russia now became part of Christian Europe (though markedly of its eastern sector) and, as a result of ever closer contacts with Byzantium, was henceforward increasingly opened up to Byzantine influence and Byzantine culture. With Christianity came literacy and the Cyrillic alphabet, devised for the Russians by St Cyril and his brother St Methodius, while Kiev's splendid Christian churches could confidently bear comparison with their counterparts in Constantinople.

The death of St Vladimir in 1015 was followed by yet another disputed succession. His eldest son, Svyatopolk the Accursed, managed without much difficulty to eliminate three of his brothers, including St Boris and St Gleb, who offered no resistance whatever, thereby earning martyrs' crowns. But a fourth, more effectual brother, Yaroslav the Wise, was too quick for him. Escaping in time, he raised an army, defeated Svyatopolk, despite the support given to the latter by Boleslaw the Brave, the by no means disinterested King of Poland, and successfully established himself in Kiev. This he now made into an even finer city, adding yet more beautiful buildings to those built by his father. He it was who built there the great Cathedral of Saint Sophia, as well as the cathedral of the same name in Novgorod. His reign also saw the foundation of the Monastery of the Caves, a famous centre of scholarship and learning, where a start was eventually made by the monk Nestor with the chronicling of Russian history.

Under Yaroslav, Kievan Rus became a powerful and important state, linked by marriage to several of the royal houses of Europe. Yaroslav himself married the daughter of the King of Sweden, Harold Hardrada; his three daughters became Queens of France, Norway and Hungary; and his sons married one Byzantine and three German princesses. Embassies were exchanged. Trade flourished and soon Kiev had become an even more important commercial centre.

The economy of Kievan Rus was by this time firmly founded on agriculture. By comparison with the bleak forest regions of the north, both soil and climate were reasonably favourable. For the most part the land was farmed by *smerdi*, or 'stinkers', free peasants owning their land, stock and farm implements. There were also *zakupi*, agricultural labourers, who worked for hire, but remained legally free. Finally there were the *kholopi* or slaves, who had either voluntarily surrendered or had been in one way or another deprived of their freedom.

Among his other achievements, Yaroslav in 1034 decisively defeated the Pechenegs, for so long a thorn in the flesh of Russia. These now migrated for the most part to the Balkans, adding yet another element to the mixture of races who had already made their home there. Less successful was an attempt made by Yaroslav in 1043 to capture Constantinople, an ambition which, attractive though it was, the Russians were now to abandon for several hundred years.

Taken together, the reigns of Vladimir and of Yaroslav the Wise, covering, as they did, three quarters of a century, marked the peak of the cultural, economic and political development of Kievan Rus, already an acknowledged European power. As a city, Kiev could now bear comparison with any in Western Europe. During these seventy-five years, there was even an element of democracy in its system of government. Neither Vladimir nor Yaroslav ruled as an absolute monarch. Nor was Russia, at this stage, a single unified state so much as a confederation of principalities in each of which the nobles or *boyars*, as the members of the Prince's *druzhina* had come to be called, enjoyed a considerable measure of independence, while a *veche* or council of all adult male citizens (the word derives from the same root as *soviet*) had powers to appoint or dismiss a ruling prince and decide whether or not to go to war.

But this relatively happy state of affairs was not destined to last for long. The Russians seemed constitutionally incapable of settling the question of the succession to the throne without an interval of rivalry and civil war. This was at least partly due to an unusually complicated and impracticable system of inheritance which seems not to have been based on the law of primogeniture, but to have provided that on a prince's death the succession should pass sometimes to his sons, sometimes to his brothers, one after the other, and in certain circumstances even to his nephews.

It is thus scarcely surprising that Yaroslav the Wise should have been in effect the last Grand Prince to rule, even loosely, over the whole of Kievan Rus. On his death in 1054, a fierce struggle for the succession broke out, as it had done on the deaths of his father and grandfather. While Yaroslav's sons fought each other for the control of Kiev, the confederation over which their father had presided quickly dissolved into its component parts.

To make matters worse, Yaroslav was no sooner dead, than a new nomad tribe of Turkish origin, even fiercer and more bloodthirsty than the Pechenegs, and variously known as the Kipchak, the Cumans or the Polovtsi, now swept into Russia, burning towns and villages and massacring the inhabitants. Beginning in 1061, their raids continued at yearly intervals for over a century and a half. Soon foreign trade fell off and prosperity declined. Instead of uniting against the common enemy the individual princes continued to fight among themselves, while the inhabitants, whenever they could, took refuge in the woods and forests. Nor was this all. In the north-west new enemies were now emerging – the Teutonic Knights in Livonia, the Lithuanians and the Swedes – while from the south-west the Hungarians were starting to push their way eastwards.

A final attempt to rally the princes and reunify Russia in the face of these various threats was made in the reign of Vladimir Monomakh. Elected Grand Prince of Kiev at the age of sixty in 1113, Vladimir was the son of a younger son of Yaroslav the Wise by a daughter of the Emperor Constantine Monomakhos of Byzantium, from whom he seems to have inherited not only his second name but also a measure of Byzantine moderation and state-craft. His wife, as it happened, was the daughter of Harold of England, who had sought asylum abroad after her father's defeat by William the Conqueror. He himself was an experienced military commander. In 1103, before his accession, he had led a united Russian army to victory against their common enemies and after he came to the throne he ruled wisely and well for some twelve years over most of Kievan Russia, maintaining law and order with reasonable success. After his death, however, fierce fighting quickly broke out between his sons and grandsons. The Polovtsi resumed their encroachments on Russian territory, driving the Russians off the Lower Dnieper with disastrous effects on their trade with Constantinople. And the decline of Kiev continued apace.

With the decline of Kiev, power in Russia passed elsewhere. Fleeing before the nomad invaders, great numbers of Russians had moved into the forest regions of the north, hitherto inhabited in the main by Lithuanians and Finno-Ugrians. 'The history of Russia,' as Professor Klyuchevski so pertinently observes, 'is the history of a country which colonizes itself.' By the beginning of the thirteenth century two strong new Russian principalities had emerged in place of Kiev: Novgorod and Vladimir-Suzdal. This movement northwards of population and power to a bleak, remote region, isolated both from Byzantium and from Western Europe, was in the long run to prove of the greatest consequence in Russia's cultural, economic and political development. Hunting, fishing and forestry became the main support of the economy, while agriculture, conducted on some kind of communal basis, again became secondary. Exactly what form this sharing of land, labour and produce took, has long been a matter of controversy. But it is clear that the land was held collectively and that the peasants who worked it had certain obligations to the *mir* or *obshchina*, as the village community was known.

Of Kiev's successors, Novgorod (*Gospodin Veliki Novgorod*, 'Lord Novgorod the Great', as its citizens liked to call it) had by this time long ceased to pay tribute to Kiev and already held sway over an area greater in extent than the whole of the rest of Russia. Both Novgorod and Pskov, the second city of the principality, which in due course was itself to gain a measure of independence as 'the Younger Brother of Novgorod', were by now larger than any other cities in Russia. In Novgorod a kind of democracy pre-

Suzdal

vailed. Here power resided first and foremost with the *veche* or
assembly of its citizens, which was summoned by the great bell
of St Sophia and which elected both the Prince and the Archbishop.
To the Prince it was made clear on his election that, if at any time
he incurred the displeasure of his subjects, he would be 'shown
the way out of Novgorod'.

In contrast to the agricultural economy of Kiev, Novgorod's
power and prosperity were largely based on its trade in furs from
the forests of the north. In pursuit of trade, its merchants or boyars
(in time the two became synonymous) ranged far and wide, exploiting the forests, subjugating the inhabitants and constantly opening
up fresh markets. From the quantities of Arab coins found at one
time or another in Novgorod it is evident that their trade extended
at least as far as the Middle East.

Bordering on Novgorod to the east was Rostov-Suzdal, lying
between the Oka and the Upper Volga, likewise a land of forests
sparsely populated by indigenous Finnish tribes and more recently,
as we have seen, by Russians fleeing before the onrush of the nomad
invaders. By the end of the eleventh century Rostov-Suzdal had
become an independent principality and was formally bestowed by
Vladimir Monomakh of Kiev on his son Yuri Dolgoruki ('Long-in-
the-Arm'). To the existing Russian settlements at Suzdal
and Rostov were now added the new towns of Vladimir, Yaroslavl and Moscow. In Rostov-Suzdal, in contrast to Novgorod, the
monarchic principle prevailed over the democratic. Here it was
the princes who conquered the new territories, forded or bridged
the rivers and built new cities, thus imposing their authority
on the people. Here there was little talk of any *veche*.

On the death of Yuri Dolgoruki in 1157 his son, Andrei of Bogolyubovo, a man of considerable force of character, established himself as Prince of Suzdal. Disregarding the claims of his brothers
and the murmuring of the nobles, he made Vladimir his capital
in place of Suzdal, embellished it with fine stone churches, notably
the Uspenski Cathedral or Cathedral of the Assumption, and fortified it against all comers. Nor was this all: Andrei had ambitions
beyond the frontiers of his own principality. Having raised a powerful army, he attacked first Novgorod and then, in 1169, Kiev,
capturing and sacking the former capital and eventually returning
home to Vladimir laden with loot and with the title of Grand
Prince.

In the course of his reign Andrei made both friends and enemies. In 1175 he was assassinated by the latter, acting in collusion with his wife, and his place taken by his brother Vsevolod, another great warrior, who like him dominated the Russian scene and whose proud boast it was that he could 'splash the Volga dry with his oars and empty the Don with his helmets'. On Vsevolod's death, however, came the usual quarrel over the succession between his various sons and nephews with, inevitably, disastrous results for the principality.

While some Russians fled northwards from Kievan Rus, others had sought refuge in the south and south-west. Just as the Russian migration north-eastwards had led to the foundation of Suzdal-Vladimir, so the movement of Russian population south-westwards from Kiev to the lands west of the Dnieper produced the independent principalities of Galicia and Volhynia. Of these the larger, Volhynia, extended west of Kiev from the foothills of the Carpathians into what is now White Russia, while Galicia, stretching along the northern slopes of the Carpathians, bordered on Volhynia to the south. Owing to their geographical position and common border with neighbouring Poland and Hungary, both Galicia and Volhynia were brought into closer contact with the West than were the other Russian principalities. The Russian word for borderland is *ukraina* and from this comparatively late removal to a new borderland came in due course a fresh sub-division of the Eastern Slavs into Great Russians, Little Russians (or Ukrainians) and White Russians, corresponding on the present-day map of the Soviet Union to three separate Soviet Republics: Russia proper, the Ukraine and White Russia. It need scarcely be said, however, that not all Polish historians would necessarily accept this somewhat simplistic view of the ethnic origins of the Ukraine.

At the end of the twelfth century, Volhynia and Galicia, which were usually allotted to one or other of the younger Russian princes, were briefly united under Prince Roman Mstislavich of Volhynia. But not for long. Real power lay with a Council of Boyars and in the end Volhynia-Galicia fell a victim to its own turbulent aristocracy and to the aggressive tendencies of its Polish, Lithuanian and Hungarian neighbours, not to mention the still ever-present Polovtsi. Meanwhile, though few seem to have suspected it, a worse enemy than the Polovtsi was waiting eagerly in the wings.

While the descendants of Rurik were pursuing their individual interests and bickering ineffectually among themselves, a new and formidable phenomenon had arisen a couple of thousand miles further east. In the year 1154 a son had been born to Yesugei Bagatur, a lesser Mongol or Tartar chieftain, who gave the child the name of Temuchin. This, Temuchin, of his own accord, later exchanged for the more impressive appellation of Jenghiz Khan or Ruler of the World. Having first achieved complete ascendancy over his own tribe and then over the rest of Mongolia, Jenghiz next made it his business to build up the most formidable and best organized military machine the world had ever seen. He then set out to give substance to the name he had assumed. 'The greatest joy a man can know,' he declared with engaging frankness, 'is to conquer his enemies and drive them before him. To ride their horses and plunder their goods. To see the faces of those who were dear to them bedewed with tears and to clasp their wives and daughters in his arms.' Having successfully invaded Northern China in 1213, he next turned west and, sweeping triumphantly across Asia, arrived ten years later at the frontiers of Europe. (For a fuller account of Jenghiz Khan and the Mongols, see my book *To the Back of Beyond*, chapter 3.)

The arrival of the Mongols before their gates seems to have taken the Russians completely by surprise, 'No one knows for certain,' wrote the Chronicler of the day, 'who they are or whence they come, or what their language is, or race, or faith. But they are called Tartars.' The first people to feel the impact of the new arrivals were, ironically enough, the Polovtsi, who, fleeing before the invading hordes, plaintively appealed for help to their old enemies the Russians. Without fully realizing what they were taking on, the Russians agreed to come to their aid and the two opposing armies met in 1223 on the River Kalka, near the Sea of Azov. In the ensuing battle, the Mongol cavalry wreaked terrible slaughter. The flower of the Russian army was annihilated and the Prince of Kiev crushed to death under the boards on which the triumphant Tartars had spread their victory feast.

For the Mongols this first assault had been no more than a reconnaissance in strength. On Jenghiz's death in 1227 his vast empire passed to his sons and grandsons, who, like him, were impelled by the same insatiable lust for conquest. Ten years later, in 1237, while other Mongol armies launched offensives in other directions, his grandson Batu, Khan of the Golden Horde and ruler of the

Vladimir, St Dimitri

Vladimir, Golden Gate

Pereslavl, Goritski Monastery

Zagorsk, Cathedral of the Assumption

western sector of the Mongol Empire, embarked on the conquest nor merely of Russia, but of all Europe.

Hurling their cavalry across the Volga in December 1237, the Mongols first attacked the Russian town of Riazan, burning it down and massacring the inhabitants. Then Kolomna. Then Moscow. Then Vladimir. In the spring of 1238, they moved on Novgorod, but, with the thaw, were checked by its marshy approaches and withdrew southwards to the country of the Lower Volga and the Don. A year later they were back, ravaging the north-east. Then in 1240, after regrouping, they turned south again, overrunning Pereyaslavl and Chernigov, and, after a great battle, capturing and utterly destroying Kiev itself. Five years after this the Pope's emissary, Fra Giovanni de Plano Carpini, records that in Kiev barely two hundred houses were left standing and that the country around was still strewn with the skulls and bones of the dead. 'We found,' he wrote, 'lying in the fields, countless heads and bones of dead people.'

Batu now advanced further west, conquering Volhynia and Galicia, crossing the Carpathians, and overrunning Hungary and Poland. Soon the Mongol Empire stretched from Peking to the gates of Vienna. But, just when it seemed that nothing could stop the Mongols from reaching the Atlantic, events suddenly took a different turn. In Bohemia the Mongol advance was temporarily checked by more resolute resistance than they had met hitherto. Then, early in 1242 the news reached Batu that back in the Mongol capital of Karakorum his Uncle Ogetai, who had succeeded Jenghiz as Kakhan or Great Khan, was dead and that he himself must return there for the *kurultai* or assembly which was being held to elect a successor.

By the time Batu came back to Russia, his armies' advance westwards had lost much of its impetus. He decided to make a halt. Withdrawing to the Lower Volga, where the fertile steppe meets the Trans-Caspian desert, he established his headquarters near the mouth of the river at a place simply called Sarai or Encampment. Thence it was later moved upstream to a new site not far from the future city of Stalingrad and for a couple of hundred years served as the permanent capital of the Golden Horde.

Most of European Russia now became an integral part of the Mongol Empire. Mongol rule was absolute. Heavy tribute was exacted and any attempt at rebellion was put down with extreme ferocity. Apart from this, the conquerors did little to disturb the Russian way of life, preferring for their own part to stay on the steppe with their horses and cattle. Having not yet embraced Islam, they were tolerant in matters of religion and in general left the Russians to rule over their own principalities and collect their own taxes, always provided that the tribute due from them was punctually paid and that the ruling prince did homage to the Khan at Sarai and, on occasion, to the Great Khan at Karakorum.

Meanwhile Russia's northern neighbours, the Swedes, Danes and Germans, had taken advantage of her misfortunes to encroach still further, the Swedes seizing what is now Finland, the Danes Estonia and the Germans colonizing the country near the mouth of the western Dvina and the Niemen. The Pope, too, who in 1229 had forbidden all commerce with the Russians as enemies of the True Faith, continued, jointly with the Holy Roman Emperor, to encourage various orders of Teutonic Knights to establish themselves in Livonia or Latvia on the Baltic.

With time the Russians adapted themselves to their new situation. In Suzdal-Vladimir, Prince Yaroslav, the son of Vsevolod, had soon rebuilt his cities. He was careful, however, to pay regular homage to Batu Khan at Sarai and to the new Kakhan at Karakorum. Yaroslav's son Alexander ruled over Novgorod. Though Novgorod had not in fact been conquered by the Tartars, Alexander had likewise prudently preferred to submit and pay protection-money to his powerful neighbours, strongly advising his fellow-princes to do the same.

This strengthened his position and left him free to meet the danger which threatened his principality from the north and west. In 1240 he fell on the Swedes who had invaded Novgorod by way of Finland and utterly defeated them on the River Neva, not far from the present site of Leningrad, thereby gaining the proud title of Alexander Nevski. Two years later, in 1242, he inflicted a decisive defeat on the German Knights of the Sword in Livonia. He then pushed on to Pskov, again routing the Germans in a no less famous battle fought on the ice of Lake Peipus. In 1245 he gained yet another victory, successfully driving the Lithuanians out of his principality.

On the death of his father Yaroslav, Alexander became in his turn Prince of Vladimir, being duly confirmed in this title by his Tartar suzerains. By conciliating the Tartars rather than resisting them, he was able, not only to fight off his country's other enemies, but also to keep in being much that would otherwise have been destroyed. In 1263 he died, on his way back from one of his periodical visits to the Tartars, and was buried at Vladimir. In a score of years Alexander had firmly established himself as a Russian national hero. For his victories over the Teutonic Knights and for his part in saving Russia from Roman Catholicism, he was in due course to be canonized by the Orthodox Church. Later again, in 1942, to celebrate the seven-hundreth anniversary of these same victories, his remote successor Generalissimo Stalin, in his turn hard-pressed by the Germans, instituted a high Soviet military decoration in honour of his saintly, princely and likewise extremely shrewd predecessor.

The Russians were to live under the Tartar yoke for another two and a half centuries. The effect of Tartar suzerainty on Russia's development as people has been variously estimated. It is true that in some ways there was less contact than might have been expected between conquerors and conquered, that the Russians clung to their own way of life and that, largely thanks to realists like Alexander Nevski, the spirit of Russian patriotism was preserved through the centuries. On the other hand, there was a good deal of intermarriage between members of the Russian and Tartar ruling classes, while the Russians, already strongly influenced by Byzantium, were now inevitably more than ever cut off from the civilizing influences of the West. No less inevitably were they exposed during this period to Tartar influences and ideas, notably to the concept of a centrally controlled and highly regimented autocracy, based on the unquestioned obedience and subordination of the individual to the state, a concept which they were quick to adapt to their own requirements and certain features of which have survived in one form or another until the present day.

An important result of the years of Tartar domination was the rise of the relatively new and hitherto relatively unimportant little town of Moscow to be the chief seat of power in Russia. Founded a hundred years earlier by Prince Yuri Dolgoruki and hitherto part of Suzdal-Vladimir, Moscow first became a separate principality in the second half of the thirteenth century under David, the youngest son of Alexander Nevski. It was to be ruled over by his descendants for more than three hundred years. Henceforward, whether because of its geographical position at the centre of Russia's river-borne trade-routes, or of the wisdom and longevity of its rulers, or simply because it suited its Tartar overlords to promote its interests at the expense of its neighbours, the territories of the new principality grew year by year in extent and importance until in the year 1328 Prince Ivan Kalita, or Ivan the Moneybag, of Moscow was formally recognized by the Tartars as Grand Prince. This title now became in practice the prerogative of Moscow, which quickly swallowed up the principality of Vladimir of which it had once been part. It was Ivan Kalita, too, who obtained from the Tartars the right to collect the tribute on their behalf, in return for which he was always ready to help suppress any insurrection against them. This had the advantage of keeping them out of his territories, while by good administration and the prosperity thus engendered he managed to attract to his principality large numbers of desirable and enterprising settlers. Simultaneously Moscow became the seat of the Orthodox Metropolitan, who, as it happened, was a staunch supporter of Prince Ivan, and it was not long before the official titles of both Grand Prince and Metropolitan included the pregnant phrase *Vseya Rusi*, 'of All Rus', or, as it later came to be translated, 'of All the Russias'.

Of particular significance is the close co-operation henceforth maintained between Church and State, between Grand Prince and Metropolitan. From now onwards this was to be fundamental to Russian government and whenever, owing to youth or any fault of character on the part of the reigning prince, there was a lack of firm government from the throne, the need was almost invariably supplied by the spiritual leaders of the day. Like their political counterparts, these made it their business to keep in with the Tartars, while never missing an opportunity of promoting the secular interests of Moscow. During the reign of Ivan Kalita's weak son Ivan the Red (1353–59) and the minority of the latter's son Dmitri, St Alexius, at that time Metropolitan, practically governed Muscovy, ably supported by St Sergius of Radonezh, who combined great spiritual gifts with unusual force of character. Founder of the famous Monastery of the Trinity and St Sergius at Zagorsk, fifty miles north of Moscow, he was known to subsequent generations as the Builder of Russia.

On coming of age, young Dmitri Ivanovich was in his turn confirmed by the Tartar Khan in the title of Grand Prince and, taking over the conduct of affairs, governed vigorously, strongly asserting

Moscow's ascendancy over the other Russian principalities and, where necessary, imposing his will on them by force of arms. Nor was this all. Despite their conciliatory attitude to their Mongol overlords, the Russian Grand Princes had long included in their supplications an appeal to the Almighty to 'take away the Tartars', a prayer that 'the candle', in other words the consciousness of Russia's nationhood, 'might not go out'. So long as the Tartars stayed strong and united, their prayer remained a prayer and they continued to pay tribute and do their best to conciliate their Tartar suzerains. But now things began to change. In the Golden Horde a struggle for power had broken out between rival Tartar factions, the supreme authority being at this moment claimed by the former Vizir, Mamai Khan. At the same time a new political and military force had arisen in the north-west. With the decline of Kiev, most of the Dnieper basin had passed under Lithuanian control. Under their Grand Prince Jagiello, the Lithuanians had built up a sizeable empire which was now beginning to encroach more and more on Muscovite territory until soon it extended from the Baltic to the Black Sea. In 1370 they even laid siege to Moscow, which in the event was only saved from capture by the newly fortified walls of the Kremlin.

It was against this confused background that in 1377, for the first time for a hundred and forty years, fighting broke out between Russians and Tartars. Some time before, certain bands of Tartar dissidents, worsted in their own internal struggles, had established themselves in the north, near the Oka and Sura rivers, where they lived by plundering the nearby Russian settlements. Learning of this, Prince Dmitri of Moscow and the Princes of Riazan and Nizhni-Novgorod sent troops out to drive them off. Confronted with Russian resistance, the various Tartar factions again joined forces and heavily defeated the Russians on the Piana River, a tributary of the Sura. To this the Russians responded by laying waste the nearest Tartar settlements. Soon a regular Russian-Tartar war had broken out. By now Mamai Khan had successfully established himself as Khan of the Golden Horde and in 1378 marched against the Russians, determined to crush what he not unnaturally regarded as a rebellion. The Tartars had already over-run Riazan and Nizhni-Novgorod and were advancing on Moscow, when Prince Dmitri, marching out to meet them, defeated them decisively on the Vozha River.

Clearly Mamai could not afford to accept such a defeat at the hands of a subject prince. Assembling his forces, he concluded a treaty with Prince Jagiello of Lithuania by which both agreed to attack Dmitri simultaneously in September 1380. Dmitri in his turn now began to look around for allies, but with little success. Fear of Tartar vengeance still acted as a powerful deterrent. The Prince of Riazan had done a deal with the Horde. Tver, Suzdal and Nizhni-Novgorod would not commit themselves either way. Lord Novgorod the Great prevaricated. In the end Dmitri found that he could only count on his own resources. But these, fortunately, were considerable, amounting, according to some accounts, to 200,000 or even 400,000 men. In August, having received the blessing of the good St Sergius, he took the initiative and marched out of Moscow at the head of his army, determined not to wait for Mamai to attack him, but rather to bring him to battle before he could join forces with his Lithuanian allies.

The Russian and Tartar armies met on 8 September 1380 at Kulikovo, the Field of the Snipe, an expanse of flat marshy ground on the right bank of the River Don. At first the battle, which was a fierce one, went against the Russians. Many of their leaders were killed and Dmitri himself was severely wounded. Disaster threatened. Then, at the critical moment, the Russians threw in additional reserves which the Tartars did not know they possessed. This turned the tide. Mamai was forced to flee and Dmitri won the day.

For the Russians the cost of victory had been heavy. 'It was,' wrote the Chronicler, 'terrible and pitiful to see Christian corpses lying like stooks of hay by the banks of the great Don. And for three days the River Don flowed blood.' Nor had the Tartars, in the words of the Russian prayer, been 'taken away'. They were still very much there, waiting for a chance to avenge their defeat and reassert their authority. But something at least had been achieved. By his victory at Kulikovo, Dmitri, who now assumed the title of Donskoi, Prince of the Don, had destroyed the legend of Tartar invincibility, rallied the Russians and restored Russian morale. Henceforth, the Russians could be certain that the candle which they prayed should not go out would never be extinguished. There was another thing. By acting as he did, Dmitri had firmly and finally established Moscow's claim to the leadership of All Russia.

Dmitri of the Don was thirty at the time of his victory. He was to live for another nine years. During these years he was to see the roles once more reversed and much, though not all, of what he had fought for swept away. In 1382 Mamai was superseded as Khan of the Golden Horde by Toktamish, a leader of an altogether different calibre. Once again the Tartars came surging across the steppe. Moscow was sacked and burned, the remainder of the principality devastated and vast numbers of Russians were carried off into captivity. Dmitri was obliged to resume his payments of tribute and even surrender his own son as a hostage to the Tartars.

In the next twenty years there was to be only one major cause for satisfaction for the Russians: the defeat by the Tartars in the year of 1399 of their former ally Prince Jagiello of Lithuania. But even this was to be of short duration. Having been converted in the interval to Roman Catholicism, Jagiello had, by a clever marriage and quick change of name, become, while still remaining Grand Prince of Lithuania, King Wladislaw of Poland. His defeat at the hands of the Tartars was no more than a temporary set-back. Appropriating the ancient Russian city of Smolensk on the Dnieper, the Lithuanians now made themselves masters of the whole of what is now White Russia, while the Poles, for their part, took possession of Galicia. For Moscow the presence on its south-western borders of what was in effect a rival Russian empire, by now more or less free from the Tartar yoke, posed acute domestic as well as external problems, problems further aggravated by the continuing division of the Eastern Slavs into three branches, all slightly differing amongst themselves: Great Russians, Ukrainians and Belorussians.

Worse still, Moscow was once more under pressure from the east. The great Tartar leader Tamerlane, who saw himself (not without reason) as a reincarnation of Jenghiz Khan, had, after reaching Riazan, suddenly turned back, leaving Moscow un-scathed. But in 1408, after his death, a fresh Tartar army under Edigei, the Vizir of the Golden Horde, had laid siege to Moscow, devastating the surrounding country and extorting fresh tribute. This had been in the reign of Dmitri's son Vasili I. Under pressure from both east and west, Vasili now sought a way out of his difficulties by marrying the daughter of Prince Vitovt of Lithuania and concluding an uneasy peace with his father-in-law, who, on Vasili's death in 1425, became the guardian of the latter's ten-year-old son, Vasili Vasilievich the Dark (or Blind).

Vasili II reigned from 1425 until 1462. His long reign was, in the well-chosen words of Professor Sergei Fyodorovich Platonov, 'very turbulent and unfortunate', being largely taken up by a bitter struggle over the succession with his own great-uncle and some cousins. This lasted for twenty years, Moscow changing hands frequently in the process. Vasili himself had a hard time, being defeated and captured by the Tartars and blinded by his political opponents. And yet, for Russia, Vasili's reign held an element of hope. For one thing his eventual victory over his uncle helped to establish a more rational principle of inheritance – from father to son rather than from brother to brother. And, for another, though the Russians were scarcely united, the Tartars were by now even more disastrously divided amongst themselves. Toktamish, the ambitious Khan of the Golden Horde, who had so easily brought Dmitri of the Don to heel in 1382, had, as we have seen, been impudent enough to challenge the great Tamerlane. The defeat which Tamerlane inflicted on him at Tatartub on the River Terek in the Northern Caucasus in 1398 not only disposed of Toktamish. It broke the power of the Golden Horde for good (see my book *To the Back of Beyond*, chapter 5). Henceforward it began to disintegrate. By the middle of the fifteenth century Sarai was no longer all-powerful. The Crimea had become a separate Khanate under the Nogai Tartars and other independent Khanates had been set up at Kazan and Astrakhan on the Volga.

Yet another important development took place in the reign of Vasili II, in the realm, this time, of church affairs. A joint Council of Orthodox and Roman Catholic clergy had in 1439 assembled in Florence to proclaim the reunion under Rome of the Eastern and Western Churches, in the hope that this might somehow save Constantinople, then threatened by the Turks. But the Council's acceptance of the supremacy of the Pope was anathema to the Orthodox faithful in Russia and also to the Russian bishops. The latter now disowned and later deposed their own Metropolitan, a Greek named Isidore who had attended the Council on their behalf, and in 1448 appointed one of themselves, the Bishop of Riazan, as Metropolitan in his place. When in 1453 Constantinople finally fell to the Turks (a disaster which the Russians naturally regarded as divine retribution for having ever contemplated union with Rome), the original links which had bound the Russian Orthodox Church to Byzantium were further weakened. From now onwards Russia was more than ever cut off, not only from the West, where the Renaissance and the Reformation were soon to mark the end of the Middle Ages, but even from the remnants of Byzantine culture and civilization. By this break with Byzantium the Russian Church became to all intents and purposes a national church – the only Orthodox Church, incidentally, in a country still ruled over by an Orthodox sovereign. It was an event of which the anniversary was to be celebrated with unabated enthusiasm under Soviet auspices five hundred years later. Meanwhile the foundations of Holy Russia had been well and truly laid.

# 2 The Fore-runners

IN 1462 VASILI the Blind's son, Ivan Vasilievich, succeeded his father as Ivan III. Aged twenty-two, he was an able, ambitious, ruthless and effective man, tall and striking in appearance (women were said to swoon at the sight of him), who by the end of his long reign was to earn himself the name of Ivan the Great. Quite early in his reign he made a significant and characteristic move. His first wife having died, he married as his second wife Zoe, or Sophia, Paleologue, the orphan niece of the last Emperor of Byzantium, at the same time somewhat presumptuously assuming as his arms the Imperial Double-headed Eagle. Before coming to Moscow, Zoe had lived in Italy as a ward of the Pope and His Holiness, having helped to arrange the marriage, had hoped thereby to gain a foot-hold in Russia. But in this he was disappointed. Ivan, who had other fish to fry, remained staunchly Orthodox.

In the course of the forty-three years during which he reigned as Grand Prince of Muscovy, Ivan expanded his dominions to more than three times their original size, mainly at the expense of his Russian neighbours. Though not himself a great warrior, he usually got what he wanted by one means or another. It was to Lord Novgorod that he first directed his attention, Lord Novgorod the Great, whose far-flung dominions now reached to the Arctic Ocean and beyond the Urals. Proud Novgorod, with its rich merchants, its democratic institutions and its famous bell which called its citizens to council; Novgorod, which in the long run must control Moscow's access to the Baltic, by now a consideration of the first importance.

Moscow's relations with Novgorod had long been uneasy, as had the relationship within Novgorod between the richer and poorer classes of citizens, the former favouring a connection with neigh-bouring Lithuania, while the latter looked to Moscow for support.

This continuing class war made the principality an easy prey for its more powerful neighbours. It was a situation which Ivan exploited to the utmost. In his day Vasili the Blind had sacked Novgorod and forced its citizens to swear loyalty to him. This, not unnaturally, had caused resentment and had led its people to seek the protection of Lithuania. In 1471 the rulers of Novgorod concluded a formal treaty of alliance with Kasimir, Prince of Lithuania and King of Poland. This alignment with Lithuania was denounced by Moscow as an act of treachery. Of treachery not only to the Grand Prince, but also (for Lithuania was Catholic) to the Orthodox Church. The decision was taken to attack Novgorod at once. The campaign, which took on the character of a crusade, was a short one. No help came from the Lithuanians. Novgorod was overrun and its citizens were obliged to break off relations with Lithuania, swear loyalty to Moscow and pay an enormous indemnity.

Ivan, an autocrat by nature, had little use for democracy. He was therefore displeased to learn after his return to Moscow that party strife had once more broken out in Novgorod. Nor did he greatly welcome the constant deputations and delegations from Novgorod who kept bringing him their grievances. But one of these, as it happened, was to provide him with an opening which he naturally put to the best possible use. Normally the people of Novgorod addressed the Grand Prince of Moscow as *gospodin* or 'mister'. By a slip of the tongue, however, a member of one deputation happened to address him as *gospodar* or 'sovereign', the form used by slaves when speaking to their masters. Ivan at once seized on the opportunity, insisting that the people of Novgorod must in future use this form of address on all occasions, thereby confirming their subservience to him. This was too much for the democratically minded citizens of Novgorod, who utterly refused to humiliate themselves in this way. At which Ivan, declaring that they were double-dealers and had gone back on their word, promptly laid siege to their city and demanded its unconditional surrender.

Isolated and disarmed, the people of Novgorod had no choice. In January 1478 they accepted Ivan's terms, sealing their oath of loyalty to him by kissing the Cross. The great bell which had been used to summon the meetings of the *veche* was now removed to Moscow, and Novgorod, as an independent principality, ceased to exist. Not long after, its remaining territories were also annexed to Moscow.

But there was more to come. Twelve months later there were signs of resentment in Novgorod, of resistance to the new order, of revived hankerings after democracy and independence. This gave Ivan the chance he was waiting for. Large numbers of the 'better people' of Novgorod, says the Chronicler, were now arrested and executed as being unreliable and the remainder deported to the east, their lands being confiscated and distributed amongst dependable Muscovites, specially imported from Moscow for the purpose. At the same time, 'the lesser people', in other words the workers and peasants, were organized in tax-paying communes on the same lines as their counterparts in Moscow. As an additional measure of precaution, Novgorod's trade with Western Europe was cut off and its long-established colony of German merchants arrested and sent back to Germany. Thus vanished one of Russia's last remaining links with the West. It was a pattern that, over the years, was to recur more than once in the course of Moscow's dealings with its neighbours.

For the time being Pskov, Novgorod's 'younger brother', was allowed to retain an appearance of independence. The Prince of Tver, on the other hand, who had readily helped Ivan to discipline Novgorod, was now imprudent enough to seek in his turn to establish friendly relations with Lithuania. On learning of this, Ivan at once invaded Tver and in 1485 annexed it. The neighbouring Princes of Rostov and Yaroslavl, for their part, simply handed over their principalities to the Grand Prince and were given in return the status of boyars or ordinary nobles. The Princes of Ryazan, being Ivan's own nephews, agreed to let him rule Ryazan on their behalf.

Thus, by one method or another, Ivan contrived to bring under his own authority the greater part of northern Russia. Catholic Lithuania-Poland, it is true, with its vast Russian-populated territories, still loomed large on his western horizon. But at least its expansionist tendencies had for the moment been contained, though its eastern borders were still uncomfortably close to Moscow itself and a preventive war, which Ivan fought against the Lithuanians towards the end of his reign, proved indecisive.

There remained the Tartars. With the progressive fragmentation of the Golden Horde, Ivan's natural policy was to play off the rival

Tartar Khans one against the other. This was not difficult. The Khan of Kazan, the Khan of the Crimea and the Khan of the Golden Horde were by this time all at each other's throats. Ivan now concluded an alliance with the Khan of Kazan, who, by a reversal of their previous roles, soon became his vassal. He also enlisted the help of Mengli-Ghirei, Khan of the Crimea, against Akhmet, Khan of the Golden Horde. The latter he now felt able to treat with studied contempt, deliberately refusing to render him homage or pay him tribute.

Eventually, in 1480, Akhmet, provoked beyond endurance, marched on Moscow to demand payment of the tribute to him. Ivan marched out to meet him and the two armies came face to face on the Ugra River. There they remained throughout the summer and autumn of 1480, exchanging abuse and occasional volleys of arrows, but without in fact attacking each other. Ivan's failure to engage the enemy brought him some criticism from his more bellicose subjects. But this he ignored and with the first snows Akhmet withdrew without having achieved his purpose. Not long after he was killed in an affray with some other Tartars, generally thought to be in Ivan's pay. His sons met a similar fate and not long after the Golden Horde ceased to exist, destroyed in the end by the Khan of the Crimea.

Thus by 1480 Moscow had ceased to be a vassal of the Tartars and Ivan, by nature no warrior, had achieved this object without fighting a single battle. He had also, in a score of years, by means other than war, enormously increased the standing and prestige of the Grand Principality of Muscovy or Moscow and strongly asserted its claim to all-Russian sovereignty. Almost imperceptibly Muscovy had become the largest country in Europe. But when in 1486 the Holy Roman Emperor sent to offer Ivan the title of King, he declined it abruptly. 'We,' he wrote in reply, 'have been sovereign in our land from our earliest forefathers, and our sovereignty we hold from God.'

For Russia Ivan had better things in store than the title of King, flung to him contemptuously by a Hapsburg Emperor. By marrying Sophia Paleologue (whom he later relegated to a nunnery) and assuming as his arms the double-headed eagle, he had taken a first step towards declaring himself successor to the Emperors of Byzantium. The Russians call Constantinople Tsargrad, the Imperial City. For them it has always held a special fascination, mystic, dynastic and, latterly, strategic. If Byzantium, now fallen to the Turks, had been the second Rome, why should Moscow not become the third Rome? A direct apostolic succession had already been devised for the Russian Orthodox Church. With the help of obliging genealogists, an interesting new family tree was now produced for the Grand Princes of Moscow, tracing their line of descent back via Rurik to Prussus or Prus, a long-lost brother of the Roman Emperor Augustus and ancestor both of the Prussians and (even more conveniently) of the Russians. To the grand-princely orb, crown and sceptre were attributed a more than princely provenance. And now, more and more frequently, in official and semi-official documents and declarations, the word 'Tsar', directly derived from 'Caesar', began to be used with reference to the Grand Prince of Muscovy.

By this time, too, Ivan was beginning to surround himself more and more with the outward and visible manifestations of imperial pomp. With the decline of the Tartars there were fresh contacts between Russia and the outside world and in the train of his Byzantine bride Ivan had imported a number of Greek and Italian craftsmen and architects whom he now used to make Moscow a capital worthy of an emperor by endowing it with a succession of fine new fortresses, cathedrals and palaces. By these, and notably by the famous Aristotle Fioravanti, were built, between 1485 and 1495, the massive red brick walls and towers of the Kremlin, which the vicissitudes of the ensuing five centuries have left largely unchanged. It was Fioravanti, too, who built the new Uspenski Cathedral, in which all future Tsars were to be crowned, the Arkhangelski Cathedral, in which they were buried, and the Granovitaya Palace, where they lived.

In this new and splendid setting, within his massive new fortress walls, the ruler of Russia now held court, held it in greater state than previously and to the accompaniment of a new etiquette and new formal rules of procedure primarily designed to isolate him and make him less generally accessible. And with the court came, not unnaturally, courtiers and court intrigue.

Though Ivan III was by nature an autocrat and ruled autocratically, a *Boyarskaya Duma* or Council of Nobles was established during his reign and endowed with certain limited executive functions. Selected on various intricate hereditary and genealogical principles, well calculated to cause confusion, this worked sufficiently well so long as it was controlled by an autocratic monarch. Any weakening of the autocracy, on the other hand, was liable to lead to feuding among rival nobles and, in the ultimate analysis, to anarchy. As a safeguard against any such event, Ivan took further steps to strengthen his own position and bolster the autocracy by bringing into being a new class of *pomeshchiki* or serving land-owners, who, in return for a grant of land, rendered certain services, usually military, to the state. These he used to colonize Novgorod, rewarding them with the estates of any of the natives whom he regarded as unreliable. The *pomeshchiki*, for obvious reasons, he knew he could count on.

The institution of private property, with its emphasis on the rights of the individual and other built-in political safeguards, played no great part in mediaeval Muscovy. Everything that mattered belonged to the state. As *gospodar* or sovereign, the Grand Prince personally possessed the territories he ruled over and could dispose of them as he liked. Thus, by making grants of land to the *pomeshchiki*, he was bringing into being, not a hereditary aristocracy or a territorially based ruling class of the kind that was emerging elsewhere in Europe at the time, but rather a land-holding bureaucracy, whose local tenure of land and power depended entirely on the whim of the monarch and whose children could be certain that both would be taken away from them unless they made themselves at least as useful to him as their fathers had done.

Nor were the boyars now very much better off. Hitherto they had enjoyed the right to leave the country at will and transfer their allegiance, should they so wish, to another principality. But with Moscow's rise to paramountcy ever fewer options were open to them short of downright treachery, so that they, too, were beginning to fall, like everyone else, under the all-embracing control of the autocracy.

Ivan the Great died in 1505, leaving the principality which he had inherited well on the way to becoming a national state. He was succeeded by his son, Vasili III. Very much his father's son, Vasili's first care was to complete Ivan's work as 'Assembler of Russia'. In Ivan's day the ancient principality of Pskov had retained, under a Muscovite governor, some vestiges of independence. Vasili quickly put an end to them. In 1510 the bell that summoned the local *veche* was removed to Moscow; three hundred leading families were deported and an equal number of entirely dependable Muscovite

Inside the Kremlin: Ivan Veliki

The Kremlin, Moscow

colonists sent to take their place. Not long after, in 1517, Vasili seized the person of his own cousin, the Prince of Riazan, and annexed his principality. Once again a precautionary exchange of population ensued, designed to obviate any possibility of insurrection or revolt. The same method was used wherever it seemed necessary and by 1523 the territories of all the remaining subject princes had finally been absorbed by Moscow; in other words, had become the property of the Grand Prince to dispose of as he chose.

Against Lithuania Vasili scored an important success by seizing Smolensk. He also sought, as his father had done, to lure away as many Russian princes as he could from their allegiance to Lithuania. From the Tartars he suffered, it is true, some minor depredations, but in general managed to buy them off or otherwise get rid of them, in his turn successfully avoiding any major confrontation.

Vasili enjoyed power. He wielded it absolutely, surrounding himself with people who did as they were told. 'He holds,' wrote Baron von Herberstein, twice Ambassador of the Holy Roman Empire to Moscow, 'unlimited control over the lives and property of all his subjects. None of his councillors has enough authority to dare oppose him or even to differ from him ... they openly declare that the Prince's will is God's will ... all the people consider themselves to be *kholops*, that is slaves of their prince.' Just as the Grand Prince personally owned the land, so the people, whatever their station in life, were his personal vassals. During Vasili's reign the phrase 'Tsar and Autocrat by the Grace of God of All Russia', used tentatively in Ivan's day, appeared regularly after his name on formal proclamations and documents of state. Meanwhile, work continued on the Kremlin and on the further beautification of the capital; there were more contacts with the outside world; and the foreign colony or German Quarter, as it was known, grew in size and importance.

Like most autocrats, Vasili III did not hesitate to use his power for his own private purposes. Tiring of his wife Solomonia, he forced the ecclesiastical authorities to let him divorce her so that he could marry the beautiful Polish Princess Helen Glinskaya, who in 1530 bore him a son, Ivan Vasilievich. On Vasili's death three years later, Princess Helen assumed the regency on behalf of little Ivan and, with the help of her lover, Prince Obolenski, ruled firmly and well, quelling domestic feuds, fighting off the Swedes and Lithuanians and, as an additional measure of precaution, casting her own and her children's uncles into jail, where they died. So capable a woman was, however, bound to make enemies and in 1583 Helen died, poisoned, it was said, by some dissident boyars.

There ensued a decade of utter chaos. No regent was appointed. The autocracy was in abeyance. The boyars, instead of attempting to govern, simply fought amongst themselves, the two main factions being led by the Belski and Shuiski families respectively. While nominally recognizing little Ivan IV as their sovereign, in practice they ignored or insulted him, openly pillaging his palace and often leaving him without proper food or clothing. The treatment he received at their hands during these impressionable years left its mark on the young prince. It also taught him a number of useful lessons.

By 1544, Ivan, now fourteen, was already showing signs of knowing his own mind. Calling the principal boyars before him, he harangued them from the throne. Many of them, he said, were guilty, but he would only punish one, the chief offender, Prince Andrew Shuiski. Whereupon Prince Andrew, the most powerful man in Russia, was forthwith arrested and executed. The new Tsar had made his mark. In 1547, on reaching the age of seventeen, Ivan announced his intention of marrying Anastasia, the daughter of a minor boyar, whom he personally picked from a parade of several hundred virgins. Later that same year he had himself crowned as Tsar of all Russia in the Uspenski Cathedral in the Kremlin, the first of his dynasty to assume this title at his coronation.

Though later to be known as the Terrible, Ivan began his reign by decreeing, under the influence of two wise and moderate personal advisers, Sylvester, a priest, and Adashev, a young country gentleman, a series of much needed legal, administrative and military reforms, introducing military service for the gentry and setting up a standing army in place of the temporary levies which were all that had existed hitherto.

Ivan's new army, in particular his well-trained, well-led *Streltsi* or 'Sharp-shooters', armed with muskets and supported by artillery, was to prove of the greatest value in the war against the Tartars on which he now embarked. In 1552, after a siege of six months, he stormed and captured the great Tartar stronghold of Kazan on the Upper Volga, using, for the first time in Russian history, gunpowder to blow up the enemy's fortifications. Kazan was subsequently looted and burned, the Khan taken prisoner and baptized a Christian, and his Khanate abolished. What remained of the old

Tartar city was then destroyed and a Russian city built in its place, the surviving Tartar inhabitants being relegated to the outer suburbs. It was to celebrate this victory that on his return to Moscow Ivan built the astonishing Cathedral of St Basil on the Red Square, with its cluster of multi-coloured onion domes.

Four years later Ivan took Astrakhan at the mouth of the Volga, the stronghold of the Nogai Tartars, another offshoot of the Golden Horde. This gave him control of the whole course of the river from Moscow to the Caspian, and the Volga, so vital to the fortunes of Muscovy, became in truth a Russian river. Only the Crimean Tartars, who from 1475 were to be under the suzerainty of the Sultan of Turkey, still survived as a continuing irritation to Moscow.

By his victories over the Tartars Ivan opened up vast new areas to Russian colonization, notably Siberia. The earliest inhabitants of Siberia known to history had been the Samoyeds, a Finno-Ugrian people who found their way there from the plains of Mongolia in the third century BC. Later came various Turkic tribes, Kirghiz and Uigurs, followed in the thirteenth century by the Tartars. By the end of the fifteenth century a Tartar Khanate had been established with its capital at Kashlyk or Sibir, a settlement on the Irtysh River from which Siberia was to take its name. By this time the Russians were expanding rapidly. Early in the sixteenth century their forces had reached the River Ob. By the middle of the century they had made contact with the Siberian Tartars and in 1555 we find Yadiger, the Tartar Khan of Siberia, sending envoys to Moscow and agreeing to pay an annual tribute of one thousand sable skins to the Grand Duke of Muscovy. Three years later, in 1558, Ivan authorized Grigori Stroganov, founder of the famous family of merchant-adventurers, to establish a first settlement and trading-post on the Upper Kama River. This was considerably extended ten years later by Yakov Stroganov. A dozen years later, in September 1581, the Cossack Hetman Yermak, with the encouragement of the Stroganovs, set out with a force of 840 men to cross the Urals and conquer fresh territories for the Tsar in the region that lay beyond them. Twelve months later he was besieging the Tartar Khan Kuchum in his capital and shortly after this, in October 1582, Yermak entered Sibir in triumph, while Kuchum sought refuge in the steppe.

But the Russians did not have it all their own way: Kuchum counter-attacked. In 1584, in the fighting that ensued, Yermak was

St Basil's Cathedral, Moscow

drowned as he tried to escape across the Irtysh River and, following their leader's death, his troops withdrew from the territories they had occupied. It was not long, however, before fresh bands of frontiersmen took their place, pressing on through the Urals with the vigorous moral and material support of Moscow.

Encouraged by Ivan's early successes, there had been those among his advisers who urged him to complete his conquests in the east by rooting out the Crimean Tartars once and for all, but by the late 1550s his eyes were set on the Baltic and the possibilities it offered of trade and other openings to the west. 'The shores of the Baltic', he said, 'are of silver; its waters of gold.' In 1553 Richard Chancellor, an English merchant-adventurer, had reached Archangel at the mouth of the Dvina and had been well received by the Tsar, who three years later granted a first charter to the Muscovy Company. in 1558 Ivan attacked the Livonian Order of Knights, the weakest of his enemies in the west. But, although he won some initial successes against the Knights, by this time far past their prime, he also aroused the hostility of Sweden and Lithuania-Poland, with whom he now became involved in a prolonged, bloody, expensive and unrewarding struggle.

In the year 1560 Ivan's wife Anastasia died, by poison, he suspected, or witchcraft. Simultaneously his nature seemed to undergo a sudden change. His childhood memories had left him with little reason to love the boyars. Hitherto he had done no more than arrange for the elimination by one means or another of individual nobles who had incurred his displeasure. Now he unleashed against them as a class the full force of his pent-up hatred. His old advisers were discarded and replaced by relays of toadies and boon companions who quickly disappeared in their turn. Only Prince Kurbski, one of his principal advisers at the beginning of the reign, was quick enough to defect to Lithuania, whence he conducted an acrimonious correspondence with the Tsar. Soon terror, suspicion, treachery and delation were rife everywhere.

The purge (to use a present-day term) took a little time to get going. In 1564 the Tsar gave it a new and dramatic twist. At the very end of December he left Moscow and suddenly reappeared fifty miles away at Alexandrov, near the famous Monastery of the Trinity and St Sergius. Thence, in January 1565, he sent word to Moscow announcing to his subjects that he had renounced the tsardom because of the treachery of the boyars, the Church and the great and powerful in general. He bore, he said, no grudge against the ordinary people, who, like him, had been betrayed by the unspeakable boyars.

This startling move quickly produced the desired effect. Before long a deputation of solemn-faced laymen and clerics arrived at Alexandrov to beg him to reconsider his decision and resume the burden of government. After listening to what they had to say, he agreed to do so. But on his own terms. First of all, he said, he wanted the traitors to be properly punished. Secondly, he proposed to set up his own private Oprichnina (from the word *oprich*, meaning 'apart'), an instrument of civil and military government with practically unlimited powers and responsible only to himself.

Once established, the Oprichnina, an institution which in one form or another and under one name or another has survived in Russia until the present day, became a state within a state. Soon it controlled half Russia, the other half being ultimately left to the nominal control of a puppet prince, a recently baptized Tartar, contemptuously picked for the purpose. It had its own court, its own headquarters and its own government departments through which it ruled whole cities and districts, notably the former estates or *votchini* of the great boyar landowners, as though they were conquered territories. It also had its own, or rather the Tsar's own, select corps of several thousand *Oprichniki*, as they came to be called, whose task it was to destroy the Tsar's enemies and the enemies of the state.

Clothed in black, riding black horses and carrying at their saddle-bows a severed dog's head as their symbol, the *Oprichniki* brought terror wherever they went, torturing, murdering, massacring and burning. Some were simply minor landowners whom Ivan used to eradicate the great nobles. But others were well enough born and, given the opportunity, liked nothing better than massacring the lesser gentry. It was a question of aptitude and inclination. Not that the *Oprichniki* themselves were ever quite safe from their master's sudden whims and suspicions. They, too, were frequently purged. The system, in short, was a flexible one. 'Sorting folks out', Ivan used to call it in his jocular way.

There was nothing haphazard about Ivan's campaign against the boyars. In fact it formed part of a carefully thought out plan, designed to strengthen the autocracy and give it a firmer social and organizational basis. Continuing a process which had been begun under his grandfather, he deliberately set out to destroy the existing concept of *mestnichestvo* (under which each boyar was installed for all time in his own inherited position), and at the same time build up, as a powerful counter-balance to the boyars, the *pomeshchiki* or serving landed gentry, whose tenure of the land granted to them by the state was made dependent on their service to the state, whether civil or, more usually, military. What is more (and this was a master-stroke), he extended this same all-important condition to the boyars, by now deprived of the right to move abroad or transfer their allegiance elsewhere. 'The chief nobility,' wrote Giles Fletcher, the English Ambassador, 'were equalled with the rest.' Their local territorial base was weakened or destroyed. And all, as Baron von Herberstein so perceptively pointed out, became the *kholops* or slaves of the Tsar.

In this manner Ivan created a centralized service-state in which each class was bound by bonds of compulsory service to the central autocracy, and which at the same time provided a framework for a centrally controlled civil and military administration. Nor was this all. A *pomeshchik* needed peasants to work his *pomestie* or estate. In previous reigns the peasant's freedom of movement had already begun to be restricted. Now, to guarantee the *pomeshchiki* the labour they needed, further limitations were placed upon it. The first fateful steps had thus been taken towards the introduction of actual serfdom. The first steps, too, towards total central control.

Despite occasional differences with the clergy (in which the clergy invariably came off worst), Ivan was in his own rather strange way a deeply religious man and also a strong upholder of the doctrine of the Third Rome. After the executions he had ordered had been carried out, he would always see to it that lists of his victims were promptly passed on to the monasteries, so that the monks might pray for the peace of their souls. He was also an enthusiastic composer of church music, some examples of which still survive. At Alexandrov he even set up, in competition with neighbouring Sergievo, a kind of private monastery with himself in the role of Abbot, where bouts of torture worthy of the Spanish Inquisition would alternate with prayers, bell-ringing and prolonged prostrations, from which he would emerge with bleeding forehead. As was perhaps to be expected, the Orthodox hierarchy did not take a uniformly favourable view of these activities. Indeed Philip, the Metropolitan of Moscow and All Russia, went so far as to denounce Ivan in public. For this the Tsar had him arraigned before a court of fellow clerics and subsequently strangled in his cell by Malyuta, or 'Boy' Skuratov, the Chief of all the *Oprichniki*. Two Archbishops of Novgorod went the same way, one being stitched into a bearskin and hunted to death by a pack of hounds. So did an unspecified number of monks, whose monasteries, for good measure, the *Oprichniki* also looted.

But perhaps the Oprichnina's most spectacular exploit was the destruction of Novgorod in 1570. Always a suspicious man, Ivan had somehow got it into his head that his own subjects in Novgorod were hatching some treachery with the Poles. To punish them for this he accordingly had their city sacked and more than sixty thousand of its people massacred in an orgy of killing which lasted for five weeks. He also devastated Tver and a number of other places he passed through on his way there.

Often Ivan, who was far from squeamish, would invent new methods of torture which he himself would try out in person. Thus in Moscow on 25 July 1570 he personally presided over the final dismemberment and boiling alive of a number of prisoners who had already been severely tortured. But, again, this did not prevent him from paying out considerable sums for prayers to be said for the souls of his victims – a practice of which his eventual successor, Generalissimo Stalin, who gave up praying quite early in life, is said to have expressed laughing disapproval, adding that in Ivan's place he would have used the time to massacre even more boyars.

In the event, the long, costly campaign in the north-west as well as the zeal which Ivan displayed in disciplining his own subjects did little good to the promising military machine which he himself had built up twenty years earlier. In 1571 Devlet-Ghirei, the Tartar Khan of the Crimea, actually succeeded in burning most of Moscow to the ground, taking back with him to the Crimea many thousands of Russian prisoners. But the shock may have been salutory, for when Devlet-Girey Khan attacked Moscow again the following year, he was himself decisively defeated. The Russian commander on this occasion was Prince Michael Vorotinski, who had already distinguished himself twenty years earlier at the capture of Kazan. But, to a ruler of Ivan's temperament, two such military successes in twenty years were more than enough and he personally helped to stoke the fire over which Prince Michael was burned alive.

It was during Ivan's reign that another new and characteristically Russian phenomenon first came into prominence. Preferring a relatively free and adventurous life on the outer fringes of Russia's fast expanding empire to what was becoming an increasingly precarious and oppressive existence at its centre, thousands of Russians (townsmen, peasants and freebooters) simply moved to the southern and eastern steppes. Known as Cossacks, from a Tartar word meaning 'horseman', and grouped together in armed bands under their own atamans or hetmans, they led the semi-nomadic life of frontiersmen in any country and at any period in history, hunting, marauding and plundering. With their nearest Russian or Tartar neighbours they lived on terms of alternate intimacy and hostility, bickering or interbreeding, as the fancy moved them. From outlaws, they developed in time into irregular military units with an independence and a character all of their own.

In the north-west, meanwhile, the Livonian war, which was to last in all for twenty-five years, continued to drag out its weary course. Livonia itself and the Livonian Order had long since disintegrated and for another ten years or so Swedes, Russians and Lithuanians fought inconclusively over its remains. In 1576, however, Stephen Batory, a born military leader, became King of Poland and Lithuania and at once launched a vigorous offensive against northern Russia. Ivan's forces were in a state of disarray and the central provinces of Russia, largely owing to his own policies, badly depopulated. Having recaptured Polotsk, which had been taken by the Russians in 1553, Stephen Batory was able to carry the war deep into Russian territory. Only the heroic defence of Pskov saved the Russians from total disaster. By a peace signed in 1582, Ivan gave up all the Lithuanian territory he had captured and abandoned his claims to Livonia. A year later, in 1583, the Swedes, exploiting Moscow's temporary weakness, took back the strip of territory which the Russians had won from them on the Gulf of Finland and formally annexed Estonia. Ivan's imaginative attempt at a break-through to the sea had failed disastrously. But Russia needed an outlet to the Baltic and the task which he had set himself would be taken up again by his successors.

Early in 1584 Ivan died. Sir Jerome Horsey, a local agent of the Muscovy Company, has left a lively account of his end. 'The Emperor,' he writes, 'began grievously to swell in his cods, with which he had most horribly offended above fifty years together, boasting of a thousand virgins he had deflowered and thousands of children of his begetting destroyed.' Day after day he would have himself carried to his treasure-chamber, there to fondle certain precious stones which he believed had the power to heal him, though his soothsayers and the spiders which they used as a method of divination held out but little hope. In the end, death came to Ivan at the chess-board. 'He sets his men,' writes Horsey, '(all saving the King, which by no means he could make stand in his place with all the rest upon the plain board) ... the Emperor in his loose gown, shirt and linen hose faints and falls backwards. Great outcry and stir; one sent for *aqua vita*, another to the apothecary for marigold and rosewater and to call his ghostly father and the physician. In the mean he was strangled and struck dead.'

Different historians have made different assessments of Ivan's achievement and personality. In Stalin's day, for example, a quite new appreciation was shown of the progressive character of his social engineering. From the point of view of Russia, however, his most important achievement was probably the creation of a standing army and the use he made of it to break the power of the Tartars. His early victories opened the way for the eventual conquest of much of Siberia and it is for these early victories that he is above all remembered in Russian song and legend.

No less necessary from Russia's point of view was the outlet to the west which he strove to secure. Though in the end he failed to break through to the Baltic, his contacts with western countries (he even proposed marriage to Lady Mary Hastings, a cousin of Queen Elizabeth I of England and the daughter of Lord Huntington or, as Ivan chose to call him, 'the Prince of Tintun') and his encouragement of Richard Chancellor and other western merchant-adventurers successfully paved the way for future trade and other contacts with the west. Soon English ships were plying regularly to Archangel.

To form a balanced judgement of Ivan's character and of the internal policies which gained him the epithet Terrible, or, more properly, Formidable, is not easy. Russia in his day was not (any more than it was in Stalin's day or is now) an easy country to govern. Nor did he begin his reign under very auspicious circumstances. The fact that he achieved so great a degree of ascendancy and control and introduced such radical reforms marks him out as one of the handful of revolutionary leaders who in their different ways have, over the centuries, in spite of all obstacles changed the face of Russia and the course of Russian history. Nor do his excesses seem altogether to have alienated the Russian people, who, as so often happens, rather liked the eccentric, dramatic side of his character, his arbitrariness and unaccountability (he once had an elephant cut to pieces for refusing to bow to him), his sudden rages, his repeated marriages (he married at least six more wives after Anastasia), his taste for debauchery and strong drink, and the open-handedness with which he dealt out punishment to all and sundry, but particularly to the great nobles. 'I think,' wrote Henry Lane, a British merchant then in Muscovy, 'no prince in Christendom is more feared of his own than he is, nor yet better beloved.'

A woodcut of Ivan by a contemporary artist shows a somewhat piratical-looking character with a pointed beard, wearing his hat on the side of his head, with his bushy hair sticking out all round. The eyes look directly at you and the mouth, as some of his victims must have noticed, has an unnervingly sardonic twist. By creating the Oprichnina, tailor-made to serve what he regarded as a necessary purpose, Ivan established, it is true, a dangerous precedent, though by constantly purging its personnel (a method successfully used by several of his successors) and in the end abolishing it altogether, he wisely made certain that it never became dangerous to him. Inevitably he became with time the victim of his own insidious suspicions, destroying in the end not only the turbulent, treacherous boyars, but much also that he himself had brought into being: his army, his country's prosperity and finally his own eldest son, Ivan Ivanovich, whom in a moment of irritation he killed with an all too well directed blow of his steel-pointed staff, leaving Russia to be ruled over on his death by his sickly, pious, feeble-minded second son, Fyodor, with, as next heir, Dmitri, the child of his seventh and more than dubious marriage to a certain Maria Nagaya. 'God,' wrote Sir Jerome Horsey, with considerable prescience, 'hath a great plague in store for this people.'

# 3 *Troublous Years*

THOUGH HE WAS NOT, it appears, entirely indifferent to bear-baiting, young Tsar Fyodor's chief interests seem to have been bellringing and elaborate church ritual. But as his face was set in a perpetual simper, his precise reactions to what was going on around him may not always have been very easy to fathom. From the start of his reign, however, it was reasonably clear that, whoever else governed Russia, it would not be he. For a few months following his accession, the regency was held by his maternal uncle, old Nikita Romanov. After which, on the latter's death, power passed to and remained with Boris Godunov, the brother of Fyodor's wife Irina.

Whether or not Boris, a minor boyar of Tartar origin, was an actual member of the Oprichnina, he certainly had close connections with it, having married Maria, the daughter of Maliuta Skuratov, the notorious Chief *Oprichnik*, who personally strangled the Metropolitan Philip and whose house in Moscow is still pointed out to the curious. An able, quick-witted, ambitious young man, Boris had during the dangerous last years of Ivan's reign somehow managed to win and keep the confidence of the old Tsar, whose son, as we have seen, had married his sister.

From his connections by marriage and from experience gathered during the declining years of the last reign, Boris, who, though illiterate, was far from stupid, had managed to acquire a good working knowledge of the methods by which Ivan had achieved and retained power. It could even be argued that he possessed some elements of statesmanship. Certainly his approach was rather saner and considerably more subtle than Ivan's, while he consistently kept his ultimate purpose firmly in view.

Seeing a serious threat to his personal position in a move made early in the new reign by the Metropolitan Dionysius and a group of disaffected boyars, including the Shuiski family, to persuade

Fyodor to divorce Irina, Boris at once took rapid and resolute action. He promptly banished the boyars, amongst them the Shuiskis, to the most unpleasant place of exile he could devise, and simultaneously replaced the Metropolitan Dionysius by an Archbishop called Job who, he had good reason to believe, would suit him better. He then himself formally assumed the Regency. With Job's appointment, the Church became Boris's close ally, an alliance which was further consolidated when by a clever stroke of diplomacy he arranged for the Metropolitan of Moscow to be promoted to Patriarch and for his friend Job to become the first incumbent of the Patriarchate.

As a matter of general policy, Boris continued to build up the smaller landowners or *pomeshchiki* at the expense of the remaining great nobles, at the same time binding the peasants ever more closely to the soil, so as to give them what soon amounted to the status of serfs. He also continued the colonization of Siberia, so successfully begun in the previous reign. In the closing years of the century a series of Russian forts were built in strategic positions: Tyumen on the River Tura in 1585; Tobolsk two years later; Tara on the Irtysh in 1594, and Narym on the Ob in 1596. In 1604 Tomsk was founded and not long after the Russians reached the River Yenisei.

In addition to this, Boris revived the war in the north-west, defeating the Swedes and recouping some of Ivan's losses on the Baltic. Nor did he neglect contacts with the west. Indeed he even sent a few young Russians to be educated abroad, one of whom became a Church of England clergyman, but none of whom returned, despite determined Russian efforts to have them extradited. Last, but not least, Boris was careful to establish an efficient internal security system, which marked a considerable advance on Ivan's Oprichnina and enabled him to plant agents and informers in the households of any potential enemies or rivals.

Under this efficient and relatively benevolent dispensation it was not long before a measure of peace and prosperity returned to Russia, and the Russian people found in the resulting benefits what was tactfully described as 'consolation after the sorrows of the past'. This happy state of affairs they attributed partly to the prayers of pious Tsar Fyodor, and partly, when they stopped to think, to the administrative ability of his Regent. But there was, as usual, more, and worse, trouble ahead.

On the accession to the throne of Tsar Fyodor (who, like his murdered brother Ivan, was Ivan the Terrible's son by his first wife, Anastasia) his two-year-old half-brother and heir, Dmitri Ivanovich, the son of Ivan's seventh wife, Maria Nagaya, had been sent with his mother and her brothers to the little town of Uglich on the Volga. There they were kept under strict supervision by the local Governor, a certain Bityagovski, whose instructions were to see that they caused no trouble. This was in 1584. Seven years later, at about noon on 15 May 1591, when little Dmitri was nine and still heir to the throne (for Fyodor had had no children), Maria Nagaya, hearing a scream in the courtyard of the house in which they were living, rushed out to find her son dying from a knife wound in the throat. At this her immediate reaction was to accuse Bityagovski of murdering the little prince. Egged on, or so it was said, by Maria and her brothers, a crowd now assembled and killed Bityagovski, his son and ten others.

When news of these disquieting events reached Moscow, the decision was taken to set up a Committee of Enquiry, which, after due deliberation, reported that Prince Dmitri had in fact knifed himself by mistake and that Maria Nagaya and her brothers had deliberately incited the crowd to murder the innocent Bityagovski. As a result of this Maria was sent to a convent, where she took the name of Marfa, and the rest of her family were exiled. There were, however, those who said that little Prince Dmitri had in fact been murdered on the orders of Boris Godunov.

Not long after a daughter was born to Fyodor's wife (and Boris's sister) Irina. But the child lived for less than two years. Soon after her death Fyodor's health began to fail and in January 1598, leaving no other children, he died. With him the line of Ivan Kalita was, after almost three centuries, finally extinguished. In his will he had named Irina as his successor, but she showed no great wish to ascend the throne, retiring soon after to the Convent of Novo-devichi on the outskirts of Moscow, where she hastened to take the veil and where the apartments she occupied can still be seen. Moscow, for the moment, was without a Tsar.

In these circumstances, the duty of convoking a *Zemski Sobor* or Territorial Assembly to choose a Tsar fell upon Boris Godunov's old friend, the Patriarch Job. There were at this stage two candidates in the running: Boris himself and Fyodor Nikitich Romanov, the son of Nikita Romanov, the former Regent and a cousin of Tsar

Fyodor's through his mother, Anastasia. The Assembly, a gathering of clergy, nobles and merchants, was convoked in February. Job gave his support to Boris; Boris was elected and, after a proper show of reluctance, accepted the nomination.

In the following September Boris was duly crowned Tsar. A contemporary portrait shows us a shrewd-looking personage of a markedly Asiatic cast of countenance with the high cheekbones and drooping moustaches of the Tartar, looking out obliquely from under the Tsar's glittering diadem. Around his neck, over his heavily jewelled vestments, he wears a heavy gold cross and carries, with due ceremony, the Imperial Orb and the Sceptre with its great double-headed eagle. One is thus left in no doubt as to the exalted position which he is fortunate enough to occupy.

There were, as was only to be expected, those who claimed that the election had not been fair and that, in order to achieve a favourable result, Boris had resorted to bribery, threats and even murder. Whether or not this was so, the new Tsar, once elected, certainly lost no time in removing any possible rivals or trouble-makers from circulation. Fyodor Nikitich Romanov, his principal competitor, was despatched to a distant monastery and there enrolled as a monk under the name of Philaret, while numerous nobles, Bielskis, Shuiskis and Golitsins, who might sooner or later have proved troublesome, were all sent as far away as possible. After which Boris, with his usual blend of realism and far-sightedness, but without the innate confidence of an hereditary monarch, resumed the far from easy task of governing Russia, a task to be made even more difficult during the next three or four years by a series of bad harvests, followed by famine and widespread unrest.

Nor were these Boris's only troubles. In 1603, from south-western Russia and Poland, came a disquieting story, which gathered credence as it spread, that little Prince Dmitri Ivanovich had not really been killed on that May morning twelve years earlier in the courtyard at Uglich; that he was in fact still alive, now aged twenty-one; and that the King of Poland, Sigismund III, was helping him raise an army of Poles and Cossacks with which he was preparing to march on Moscow in order to evict the usurper Godunov and lay claim to his just inheritance.

Alarmed, Boris officially informed the King of Poland that the young man must be a false Dmitri, in all probability a run-away monk called Gregory Otrepyev, who should on no account be given any encouragement. But the King of Poland, for his part, preferred to accept the version retailed by the Pretender, who was accordingly allowed to continue his activities unmolested, indeed given every possible encouragement. It was thus that in the autumn of 1604 the Pretender, who clearly believed himself to be Dmitri, left his headquarters at Sambov with such troops as he had collected and started to march on Moscow. At first he met with little opposition, but then, having failed to join up, as he had hoped, with some Don Cossacks who had come over to his side, he was defeated and driven back by a superior Russian force. He did not, however, let this first defeat deter him. In April 1605, with a much increased force, drawn for the most part from Cossacks, disaffected frontier troops, banished boyars, and escaped serfs, he set out once more for Moscow. And in April, just as he was advancing on the capital, came the astonishing news that Tsar Boris Godunov had died.

It was now, in the words of one authority, that Russia began to fall apart. Small wonder that the ensuing fifteen years or so came to be known as *Smutnoye Vremya* or the Time of Trouble. On Boris Godunov's death, which may or may not have been due to natural causes, his young son Fyodor succeeded him as Tsar, while power passed in effect to Fyodor's mother, the unpopular and not very gifted daughter of the notorious *Oprichnik* Skuratov. But not for long. Glad to get their own back on Boris Godunov, even posthumously, the great boyars rallied openly to the Pretender. Led by Prince Vasili Shuiski, who twenty years earlier had borne public witness to little Dmitri's death, they swore eternal loyalty to his reincarnation. Impressed by this, a mob of frenzied Muscovites stormed the Kremlin and murdered young Fyodor and his mother. A week later the Pretender (whose identity has to this day never been finally established) entered the capital in triumph as 'the true Tsar Dmitri'. Here he was joined by Marfa the Nun, in other words, Maria Nagaya, the mother of the murdered Prince, who, emerging from her convent, at once recognized him as the son whose death she herself had witnessed fourteen years earlier.

For the great nobles who had helped to bring it about, the arrival in Moscow of the Pretender's army was not, however, quite the happy event they had hoped for. Many of the disaffected Cossacks, escaped serfs and others who swelled its ranks liked the boyars no better than they liked the Godunovs and had entirely different aims in view. Belatedly realizing his mistake, Prince Vasili Shuiski now decided that it would be as well to issue a fresh statement to the effect that Prince Dmitri was indeed dead and that the present claimant could be nothing but an impostor. But in vain. This time Shuiski was not believed and quickly consigned to jail as a liar.

The reign of the false (or, according to some authorities, the true) Dmitri was short but eventful. For so shadowy a personage he showed considerable initiative and independence. The Poles had supported him on the understanding that he would spread Catholicism and Polish influence in Russia. But, once installed, he made it clear that he was staunchly Orthodox and had no intention of furthering Polish interests or of yielding an inch of Russian territory to Poland. His first step on arrival was to appoint a new Patriarch, the Archbishop of Riazan, and then have himself crowned Tsar. He next recalled from exile the Nagois, Romanovs and other families banished by Boris and did what he could to instil new life into the Council of Boyars.

But in the long run the Polish connection was to count against him. In particular his marriage to Marina Mniszech, the beautiful daughter of an impoverished Polish nobleman, was used to stir up feeling against him among the people of Moscow, who were already complaining that his manners and way of life were not sufficiently regal. He was, they noticed, short, sturdy and red-haired, with a wart on the side of his nose; walked through the streets without a bodyguard and, unlike most monarchs, rarely took a siesta after luncheon. As usual, the trouble-makers were a group of disaffected boyars, led once again by the egregious Prince Vasili Shuiski, who had most mistakenly been released from prison. Early on the morning of 17 May 1606 a mob stirred up by the conspirators burst into the Kremlin and murdered the Pretender, barely a year after his accession, after which his remains were burned and, as though to emphasize his end, the ashes fired from the mouth of a cannon in the general direction of Poland.

Two days later Prince Vasili Shuiski had himself proclaimed Tsar, not by the *Zemski Sobor*, but by a crowd which he himself had collected for that purpose on the Red Square. Once on the throne, Vasili, who was clearly a far from estimable character, did his best to ingratiate himself with his fellow-conspirators and with the other great boyars by making wild promises, dwelling at length on his own ancient lineage and encouraging a new cult centred round the remains of little Prince Dmitri, which had recently been brought to Moscow from Uglich and were now conveniently found to possess miraculous qualities. But Vasili, perhaps not surprisingly, failed to win the confidence of the population, particularly in the provinces, where feeling against him, against Moscow and against all that went on there was growing daily stronger. In the end disgruntled boyars, small landowners, Cossacks, townsmen, peasants, slaves and serfs all rose simultaneously against him, finding a leader for the occasion in one Ivan Bolotnikov, an escaped serf or slave, who had once served as a helmsman on a Turkish galley and who, calling on his fellow-slaves and serfs to kill their masters and seize their possessions, their wives and their daughters, now embarked on a long, hot summer of burning, massacring, pillage and rape. Finally, in the autumn of 1606, Bolotnikov marched on Moscow. By this time he was beginning to lose the support of some of his more moderate followers. Defeated by Vasili's troops, he fell back on Tula, where his army was slowly starved into surrender. He himself, meanwhile, had disappeared without a trace, having first set a notable precedent for peasant revolt.

The flames of Bolotnikov's rebellion had barely died down when in 1607 a fresh pretender appeared on the scene, to be known to history as the Second False Dmitri or the Thief of Tushino. Claiming identity, not only with the original little Prince Dmitri who had died at Uglich, but also with the First False Dmitri who was well known by all concerned to have been killed the year before and his remains blown from the mouth of a cannon, the new Pretender quickly won widespread support. Recruiting an army from the Poles and from what remained of Bolotnikov's and the First Pretender's forces, he now marched in his turn on Moscow, where, in the summer of 1608, he virtually besieged Tsar Vasili Shuiski in the Kremlin. Setting up a rival court in the suburb of Tushino, he was joined there by the beautiful Marina Mniszech, who without any difficulty recognized him as her late husband. Meanwhile between Tushino and the Kremlin a constant two-way traffic had now grown up, those who changed sides most regularly being known as *pereleti* or 'birds of passage'.

By this time most of central Muscovy had declared for the new Pretender and Shuiski's position was rapidly becoming desperate. By offering to cede Karelia and other Russian territories to Sweden he managed to induce the Swedes to lend him their support. But this only produced a declaration of war from the Poles, who in the autumn of 1609 laid siege to the great fortress of Smolensk and then marched on Moscow, driving the defeated Russians before them.

The *pomeshchiki* and the people of Moscow had by now had as much as they could bear of Tsar Vasili Shuiski. In July 1610 they rose against him in strength and dethroned him, though without any very clear idea as to whom they should put in his place. After some confused deliberations, the assembled boyars and clergy eventually decided to offer the throne to Wladislaw, son of King Sigismund of Poland, only to be told that the fiercely Catholic King Sigismund, whose troops were now garrisoning most of Moscow, while he continued to besiege Smolensk, wanted it for himself, wanted, in other words, to make Russia a mere dependency, a province of Catholic Poland, where the Counter-Reformation was at its height. Having thus explained his attitude and shortly after that captured and destroyed Smolensk, Sigismund then returned to Warsaw, there to await developments. To the boyars in their dilemma, in that bleak December of 1610, even the news that the Second False Dmitri had been murdered by one of his own followers while out hunting brought little consolation. In Pskov, meanwhile, yet another pretender had appeared, sometimes known as the Third False Dmitri.

But now, after the long years of unrelieved chaos and disaster, came at last signs of a national revival. From Hermogen, the aged Patriarch of Moscow, went out on Christmas Day 1610 a call to the Russian people to rise against the Poles. Hermogen himself was immediately arrested by the Polish garrison of the Kremlin, but his summons had not fallen on deaf ears. Soon patriotic Russians from different walks of life, including many of the small gentry, were marching on Moscow from all over the country, collecting reinforcements as they went and utterly determined to drive out their Polish oppressors. On reaching Moscow, they were joined by many of its citizens and at Easter 1611 laid siege to the Kremlin with its garrison of Poles. They were, however, thrown back and heavily defeated.

For the Russians the outlook was now bleaker than ever. The Poles held Moscow and Smolensk; the Swedes had seized Novgorod; in Russia there was no government of any kind. But still something was stirring. Though the Patriarch Hermogen had in the end been silenced and not long after had died, the remnants of the Orthodox clergy continued to egg on the faithful against the Catholic Poles and against their Russian collaborators. In all this a leading part was played by the Archimandrite Dionysius and the monks of the Troitsko-Sergyevski Monastery, who, after successfully withstanding a prolonged siege, continued to act as a focus of national resistance.

It was now that from Nizhni Novgorod on the Volga and its mayor, Kuzma Minin, a prosperous local cattle-dealer and butcher, came in September 1611 a fresh call to resistance and a proposal to raise a new national militia. Funds and volunteers were collected and, despite the inevitable disputes and dissensions, a force was raised which was then placed under the command of Prince Dmitri Pozharski, a local boyar with at least a modicum of military experience.

During the winter of 1611 to 1612 more funds were raised and more volunteers flocked in from other parts of Russia to join the nucleus of a national army which had now come together in Nizhni Novgorod. In the spring of 1612 Pozharski moved his force, not to Moscow, but to the old town of Yaroslavl on the middle Volga, 150 miles north of the capital. There he assembled a *Zemski Sobor*, which at his suggestion assumed formal responsibility for the civil and military government of Russia.

Pozharski's original plan had been to elect a new Tsar before attempting to move against Moscow. But in July he received information that King Sigismund of Poland was proposing to reinforce the Polish garrison in the Kremlin, now under siege by an independent force of Cossacks, and, on learning this, decided to march on the capital without further delay. On reaching Moscow, he found the situation more than usually complicated by the attitude of the Cossacks, some of whom made a determined attempt to assassinate him, while others, under Prince Trubetskoi, seemed half-disposed to join him. In the middle of all this, the Polish reinforcements arrived and at once attacked Pozharski, while the Cossacks for the most part simply stood by and looked on. In the end, however, after a savage struggle, Pozharski's troops managed, on 22 October 1612, with some help from the Cossacks, to fight off the Polish reinforcements and establish themselves in the mercantile quarter of Kitaigorod, less than half a mile from the Kremlin. Four days later the Polish garrison surrendered to Pozharski and Moscow was once more free and in Russian hands. It was to celebrate this badly needed victory that the great Kazan Cathedral was in due course erected on the Red Square, only to be torn down again three hundred years later in the outburst of anti-clericalism which followed the November Revolution.

Muscovy, meanwhile, was still without a Tsar. In February 1613 the widely representative *Zemski Sobor* which had been summoned to choose one elected Michael Romanov, the sixteen-year-old son of Fyodor Nikitich Romanov – in other words, of the Metropolitan Philaret. The Romanovs, though of noble birth, were not one of the great boyar families, but through his father's cousin Anastasia, wife of Ivan the Terrible and mother of Tsar Fyodor, the new Tsar could claim a tenuous connection with the former dynasty. He also profited from the reflected prestige of his father Philaret. Banished as a dangerous rival by Boris Godunov fifteen years earlier and forced to take Holy Orders, Philaret had continued to play a prominent part in Church and public affairs. He had been made Patriarch by the Second False Dmitri and had later been one of those sent to offer the throne of Russia to the Polish Prince Wladislaw. For the time being, however, he was a prisoner in Poland, where he was held hostage by King Sigismund.

The country in which the young Tsar Michael now somewhat hesitatingly assumed power was in an appalling state. In not much more than thirty years the clock had been set back for generations. Moscow and most other towns had been sacked and burned several times over. The countryside had been devastated and crops, livestock and houses destroyed. By famine, foreign invasion, massacre and disease, the population, according to one estimate, had been reduced from fourteen millions to nine. The treasury was empty. The national economy was on the brink of collapse. Any administrative machinery had long since disappeared, leaving a total vacuum. Bands of armed marauders roamed everywhere. The boyars, in so far as they could be called a ruling class, had destroyed themselves by their bickering. The peasantry were fast being reduced to serfdom. Such hope as there was of ultimate recovery lay once again in the smaller landowners, the *pomeshchiki* (or *dvoryane*, as they were now beginning to be called), who of recent years had emerged as the most stable and politically active element of the population.

If the new Tsar was to retrieve the situation, it was essential that he should, for a time at any rate, continue to enjoy the support and co-operation of the *Zemski Sobor*. Though this still included the Boyars' Council, it was now dominated in the main by the *pomeshchiki* and for a short time Russia enjoyed a roughly representative system of government. At first the Assembly met constantly, debating and deciding such issues as war and peace, law and order and public finance. After that it met at less frequent intervals. It represented, one is forced to concede, a concept of government which in the long run was never really to take root in Russia.

A revealing light is cast on these developments and on the Russian view of parliamentary government by the great Russian historian, Professor V. O. Klyuchevski. 'Popular representation,' he wrote in 1882, 'arose in our country, not in order to restrict the central authority, but in order to strengthen it. Herein lies the difference between it and Western European representation.' And again: 'The National Assembly, which at first constituted an element of support to the new dynasty, became less indispensable to it as the position of the dynasty became stronger.'

The opening years of the new reign were largely taken up with the task of restoring or trying to restore peace at home and abroad. The country was still in turmoil, offering tempting opportunities for marauding bands of Cossacks and other potential troublemakers. Thus it was, for example, that a certain Cossack hetman named Zarutski now joined forces with Marina Mniszech and her four-year-old son by the Second False Dmitri (known to some as Tsarevich Ivan but to others as the Little Thief) and with them set out at the head of his band of Cossacks for Astrakhan at the mouth of the Volga, where it was his intention to set up a free Cossack state under the protection of the Shah of Persia. This proved easier said than done. In the event Zarutski was finally brought to bay on the Ural River, his force was dispersed, he and little Ivan were summarily executed and the beautiful Marina, her brief but dramatic career at an end, was sent to prison. In a sense, however, Zarutski was a forerunner and his venture, though unsuccessful, a sign of the times and an indication to others of what, with boldness and a little luck, could be done in the vast no man's land of the southern steppes. From the White Sea and the Dnieper to the gates of Moscow other Cossack bands ranged freely, while parties of Polish and Lithuanian marauders continued to plunder and devastate the countryside. But in due course these, too, were put down and order of a kind was restored.

The Russians, meanwhile, remained at war with both Poland and Sweden. Indeed the Swedes were still occupying considerable parts of Russia, notably Novgorod. But in the end agreement was reached with Sweden, the disputed territories were re-allocated and peace was finally signed in 1617. The Poles, for their part, had as yet not abandoned their designs on the Russian crown, to which both King Sigismund and his son still laid claim. They were also still in possession of Smolensk and several other Russian towns and were holding prisoner large numbers of Russians, including the Metropolitan Philaret, the father of the new Tsar. Twice, in 1617 and 1618, Polish armies advanced on Moscow, but failed to take it. In the end peace was also patched up with Poland, the fate of Smolensk left in suspense and the Russian prisoners, including Philaret, were at long last repatriated.

Philaret returned to Moscow in the summer of 1619, six years after his son's accession to the throne. He was at once consecrated Patriarch in succession to Hermogen who had died in 1612 but had not yet been replaced. He also assumed the title of Grand Sovereign, thus making himself coequal with his son. From now until his death in 1633, it was he who governed Russia. This he did wisely and firmly, though under extremely difficult conditions.

One problem which by this time had begun to confuse and bedevil Russian life was that of serfdom and the serfs. Clearly, the conditions prevailing in seventeenth-century Russia did not make for stable agriculture. Inevitably the peasant population was restless and unsettled. Quite apart from an innate Russian urge to move about, it was understandable that in times of famine, civil strife and foreign invasion the peasants should have felt tempted to exchange their burnt-out homesteads for more attractive accommodation elsewhere, to start off in search of better wages and better employers or simply to leave the land altogether for the freebooting life of a Cossack. For the landowner and in particular for the small landowner, now of considerable political significance, it became increasingly important, if they were to survive economically, to restrict the peasant's freedom of movement and bind him more closely than ever to the land. There were even cases in which it might suit a man to be a serf. A free peasant was liable to conscription and taxation. A serf was not. By becoming a serf, a free peasant, a townsman or even a member of the gentry could evade both taxes and conscript duty.

With the years, a confused body of laws and restrictions had grown up concerning taxation, land-tenure and a peasant's obligations to his landlord or employer. Now, at long last, a proper census of lands and population was held and legislation passed which was designed to tie the peasant to the land on which he worked and ensure the regular collection of taxes. From a loose mutual arrangement between master and man, serfdom, by a series of laws passed in the course of Tsar Michael's reign, and in particular by the subsequent *ulozhenye* of 1649, became a regular national institution readily enforceable by law. An institution which, it is true, enormously increased the power and central control of the state, but which for the next two hundred years and more was to be at the root of most of Russia's internal troubles.

Michael was not by nature an empire-builder. Apart from an unsuccessful attempt to recapture Smolensk in 1633, he showed little anxiety to extend or even to restore Russia's European frontiers. Even when in 1637 the semi-independent Cossacks of their own initiative captured the strategically important Tartar (or rather Turkish) town of Azov at the mouth of the Don and invited him to send troops to help them hold it, he procrastinated for four years and then informed them that he could give them no help. At which the Cossacks sacked the town and then returned what was left of it to the Turks. In Siberia, on the other hand, the Russians continued to advance. Subduing the nomadic tribes they encountered beyond the Yenisei, they pushed forward for another thousand miles to the Lena, building more forts as they went forward. Yeniseisk was founded in 1618, Krasnoyarsk in 1628 and Yakutsk on the Lena in 1632. In 1639, just fifty-seven years after Yermak's capture of Sibir, they reached the Sea of Okhotsk and so gained a foothold on the Pacific.

Over the next forty or fifty years the Russians consolidated and extended their conquests, subduing the Buryat Mongols in the area of Lake Baikal and pushing northwards and eastwards to the Arctic Circle and the Bering Straits. In 1653 the Cossack Hetman Yerofei Khabarov reached the Amur River and established himself there. By this time, however, they were beginning to encroach on Chinese territory and the country occupied by Khabarov was restored to China under the Treaty of Nerchinsk in 1689.

Michael Romanov died in the summer of 1645 and was succeeded by his sixteen-year-old son, Alexis the Gentle, who, like his father, was anything but self-assertive. Possibly because of this, his reign was marked by a variety of rebellions. During the next thirty years the hardship inflicted on the Russian people by the growth of serfdom, penal taxation, the devaluation of the currency and corruption in high places led to a series of risings and riots in Moscow, Novgorod and Pskov, all of which were put down with extreme savagery.

Even the Orthodox Church was not immune from upheaval. For the last couple of centuries it had not thrown up many new ideas. 'Reasoning', a prominent Russian divine had declared, 'is the mother of all lusts.' But now the consecration in 1652 of the Patriarch Nikon was to mark the beginning of a prolonged period of schism and unrest. Nikon, a peasant turned monk, possessing exceptional ability and force of character, first met Tsar Alexis while Abbot of a monastery on the White Sea. Falling strongly under Nikon's influence, the young Tsar brought him to Moscow and within five or six years had made him Patriarch, bestowing on him over and above that great office the added power and prestige conferred by the title of Grand Sovereign, once held by his grandfather Philaret. Thus, when two years later Alexis reluctantly left to take part in the newly resumed war against Poland, it was the Patriarch who, as a matter of course, took his place as ruler of Russia.

Nikon, in the words of a contemporary, now started to 'stand high and ride far'. A giant of a man, his manner became increasingly imperious and overbearing. On the River Istra, outside Moscow, he built as his 'Holy Kingdom' the Monastery of the New Jerusalem. He had decided, amongst other things, that the Russian Church had fallen into obscurantism and error and needed bringing back into line with the older and purer usages of Greek Orthodoxy. Not only did he introduce new service books: he also decreed that in future all Orthodox churches should have five domes; that the Sign of the Cross should be made, not with two fingers, but with three; that a change should be made in the hitherto accepted spelling of the name of Jesus; and finally that one word should be omitted from the Creed. These foreign innovations, as Nikon's reforms were inevitably regarded, encountered frenzied opposition from the so-called Old Believers who at once prepared to give battle in defence of what they, as good Russians, had always held to be the true Orthodoxy. The fact that Byzantium might have thought otherwise did not impress them. Indeed the express approval which

Nikon now received for his reforms from the Patriarch of Constantinople in 1655 only made his opponents angrier.

In the course of his career, Nikon had not unnaturally made a great many enemies, in the Church, amongst the boyars and in the Tsar's own family. Together they combined to turn Alexis against him. The word went round that he was the Antichrist. Soon relations between Tsar and Patriarch became strained and in 1658 the break came. But, though Nikon left Moscow, he continued to cling to the Patriarchate, stoutly maintaining that Church must come before State. A solution was not reached until 1666 when a Church Council, while formally approving and accepting Nikon's reforms, deposed him from his high office and banished him to a distant monastery for the rest of his life.

Meanwhile the *raskol* or schism which he had provoked continued unabated. So strongly did the monks of the Solovyetski Monastery, far away near the Arctic Circle, feel on the subject that they withstood an eight-year siege by regular troops rather than give in, while in 1662 the fiery young Archpriest Avvakum (or Habbakuk) readily suffered martyrdom for his beliefs. He died in a cause which to many Russians has always been sacred: unrelenting resistance to outside ideas. Even today the schism still persists, as visitors to the Church of the Old Believers in Moscow can see for themselves.

In another quarter, meanwhile, more trouble was brewing. In the south-west, as we have seen, the situation had long been fluid and unstable. Since the Union of Lublin in 1569 the southern half of Lithuania, including Volhynia, Podlachia and the territory of Kiev, had been an integral part of the Kingdom of Poland, the remainder being constituted a separate principality under the Polish crown. This boded ill for the large Russian population of the territories in question which, it will be observed, included Kiev, the Mother of Russian cities and the cradle of the Russian nation. Nor was it long before the Russian Orthodox population of these territories was under severe pressure from the Church of Rome, while the Russian peasantry had to endure even worse treatment from the big Polish landowners than they would have suffered at the hands of Russian boyars.

Moving into the Ukraina or Russian border-lands along the Dnieper, the Polish nobles came into contact with the Cossacks, who, as we have seen, ranged freely over this whole area, making a living by plundering their neighbours, fighting the Tartars and, when they had nothing better to do, farming. Upon the arrival of the Poles, the Cossacks simply withdrew deeper into the steppes. Polish attempts to reduce them to serfdom, form them into regular Polish military units or stop them from attacking the Tartars failed utterly. On the contrary, the worse the Poles treated the Russian peasantry, the bigger became the flow of fresh volunteers to the Cossacks and the harder the Cossacks became to deal with. Soon what amounted to an independent Cossack state had been set up in the Ukraine.

So long as the Poles were fighting the Russians for Smolensk, they had little time to devote to the Cossacks. But in 1638, diverting strong forces to the Ukraine, they embarked on a methodical drive against the Cossacks, depriving them of their independence, massacring them in large numbers and reducing the rest to serfdom. This continued for ten years. Then, as sometimes happens in such circumstances, a resistance leader arose in the Ukraine. On the islands of the lower Dnieper, 'beyond the cataracts', some Cossacks had established a number of fortified settlements, known as *Zaporozhkaya Siekh* or the Stronghold Beyond the Cataracts. There they resolutely held out against all comers, taking from their stronghold the name of Zaporozhian Cossacks.

In the spring of 1648 a certain hetman, Bogdan Khelmnitski, raised a force of Zaporozhian Cossacks, and, with the help of their former enemies the Tartars, attacked the Polish army from the south. Two Polish forces were routed by him in rapid succession. The ensuing massacres, recalled to this day in Russian revolutionary folklore, were on an unprecedented scale. Cossacks, Tartars and peasants all played their part enthusiastically. The Polish gentry were hanged, burnt alive, flayed and torn limb from limb in their thousands. The Polish clergy fared no better, meeting atrocious ends on the altars of their desecrated churches. But perhaps the worst treatment of all was reserved for the Jews, who, as middle-men and factors of the Polish nobility, had no friends at all and no means of defending themselves. In this manner a pattern and a precedent were established which, on one pretext or another, were constantly to be repeated in the Ukraine during the centuries that followed.

Shocked, the Poles sent in September 1648 a fresh army against the Cossacks, consisting this time of the flower of their nobility, dressed, as was their wont, in ermine and cloth of gold. It was anni-hilated. Khelmnitski was by now master of all south-western Russia, including Galicia, master, in fact, of the whole of the Ukraine.

Right at the start of his rising, Khelmnitski had approached the Russians with a request for help. Characteristically Tsar Alexis had hesitated and in the end done nothing. Now Khelmnitski approached him again, inviting him to take the south-west under his powerful protection. Still Alexis hesitated. For Moscow much was at stake, but Alexis, as we have seen, was a gentle Tsar, who hoped, as far as was possible, for a quiet life.

By this time, however, the Poles had resumed hostilities and Khelmnitski, abandoned by his Tartar auxiliaries, was beginning to lose ground. Alexis now referred the matter to the *Zemski Sobor*, who, after discussing it for two years, from 1651 to 1653, finally took the decision to unite the south-west with Great Russia. In January 1654 this decision was confirmed at a meeting of the Ukrainian or Zaporozhian Ruda or Assembly at Pereyaslavl, which unanimously acclaimed the union by yelling 'We want to belong to the Eastern, the Orthodox Tsar!' Under the agreement that fol-lowed, the Ukraine retained the right of self-government and the right to elect the Hetman of the Cossacks, but was debarred from having direct relations with the King of Poland or the Sultan of Turkey. Three months later Alexis the Gentle, having first formally assumed the title of Tsar of All Great, Little and White Russia, declared war on Poland, while King Charles X of Sweden, also seeing an advantage to be gained from such a course, did the same.

A rapid series of victories for the new allies ensued. The Russians took Smolensk in 1654 and Vilna, Kovno and Grodno in 1655. Khelmnitski seized Lublin. And the Swedes, invading Poland, took Warsaw and Cracow. Poland seemed doomed. But in 1656 Alexis, alarmed at the speed of the Swedish advance, quickly made peace with Poland at Vilna, obtaining in return the whole of Little and White Russia. After which both Russia and Poland attacked Sweden, without, however, achieving much by it.

In 1657 the death of Hetman Khelmnitski, whose statue still stands in the centre of Kiev, gave events a new and interesting twist. Finding themselves less independent under the new dispensation than they had hoped, the Ukrainian Cossacks now rose against the

Russians, who, as was to be expected, reacted vigorously. One Cossack faction turned to Poland for help, but others opposed this, enlisting Russian and even Turkish support. While civil strife raged in the Ukraine, hostilities again broke out between Russia and the Poles, who by the end of 1660 had won back most of what they had been forced to cede four years earlier. In 1667, after ten more years of fighting, during which most of White and Little Russia was completely devastated, the Poles and Russians again made peace. This time they simply divided the whole area between them, Poland taking Lithuania and the Ukraine to the west of the Dnieper, while Russia kept Smolensk, Kiev and the Ukraine to the east of the Dnieper. Once again the dreams of a united independent Cossack Ukraine, in so far as they had ever had any substance, were doomed to disappointment. But of one thing there could be no doubt. Over the past half-century the balance of power between Russia and Poland had shifted decisively in Russia's favour.

Meanwhile there was more trouble ahead. Thanks to heavy taxation and the growing burden of serfdom, the last twenty years of Alexis' reign had been marked by a succession of local peasant uprisings, in the course of which numerous landowners and government officials had been murdered and their houses burnt down. All these risings had in due course been suppressed. But for Alexis the Gentle fate was holding something worse in store.

In the course of the year 1667 a band of Don Cossacks under the leadership of a certain Stepan or Stenka Razin, finding their opportunities limited on the Don, had made their way to the Volga and there embarked on what proved to be a highly successful career of piracy and freebooting. First they worked their way down the Volga, looting as they went, until they reached the Caspian Sea. Thence they made their way eastwards to the Ural River, where they spent the winter, and in 1668, numbering by now about two thousand, successfully attacked the Persian settlements on the Caspian from Derbend to Resht and, after amassing enormous spoils, dug themselves in for the following winter on a little island not far off the Persian shore. In the spring of 1669, laden with loot and covered with glory, Stenka Razin started back for the Don, travelling by way of Astrakhan, where the Tsar's men were too afraid to try to stop him. Already hundreds more volunteers were flocking to join him.

Stenka's next move was not against the Persians, but against those whom he regarded as the oppressors of the Russian people: landowners, merchants and government officials. He was, he would say, loyal to the Tsar; it was the rest of them he wanted to root out. In the spring of 1670, he attacked the Tsar's Governors on the lower and middle Volga. The rebellion spread like wildfire. Wherever Stenka went, he was joined by crowds of new recruits, peasants, townsmen and even the soldiers of the regiments sent against him, all joining forces in the common struggle against oppression. Tsaritsin, Astrakhan, Saratov and Samara fell to the rebels in quick succession. In town and country alike the houses of the rich were looted and burned and their owners dragged out and put to the sword. From a Cossack revolt his movement had become a national uprising. Soon Moscow itself was threatened.

It was now that the government sent against Stenka Razin a force of crack troops specially trained by foreign officers. First checking him at Nizhni Novgorod, these turned south and utterly routed him at Simbirsk. The spell was now broken. The Patriarch publicly cursed him. His fellow Cossacks refused him shelter and in the end betrayed him to his enemies. He was taken to Moscow, subjected to terrible tortures, which he bore with exemplary fortitude, and was finally quartered alive on the Red Square in June 1671. His army now broke up into scattered bands and for a time continued to fight on. But in the end they, too, were hunted down and destroyed.

The reigns of Tsars Michael and Alexis had been chaotic, but less chaotic than the period immediately preceding them. During the second half of the seventeenth century Russia was once again opened to a limited extent to foreign influences and trends. From the West came merchants, doctors, craftsmen, engineers and soldiers of fortune to train the Tsar's forces. Even Tsar Alexis had an English physician, Dr Samuel Collins, whose memoirs give a vivid glimpse of life in Russia at the time. From the Near East, too, came scholars and theologians.

As was inevitable in a nation so steeped in conservatism and so deeply convinced of its own God-given holiness and rightness and of the wrongness and depravity of everyone else, the process of assimilation was not an easy one. Under Tsar Michael a golden jug and basin had always been kept by the throne, so that after receiving a foreign ambassador in audience the Tsar might cleanse himself both ceremonially and physically from this contact with the unorthodox and the unclean. Now, as before, the attitude of the Russians towards foreigners and the fashions and ideas they brought with them remained basically ambivalent. On the one hand, they were fascinated by them, on the other, deeply suspicious of them, some more and some less. But at least the curtain showed signs of lifting, if only a little.

For the foreign colony in Moscow a new foreign quarter was now built outside the city on the River Yauza, in place of an earlier settlement which had been destroyed. It was known as Nemetskaya Sloboda or the German Settlement (or Suburb), foreigners in general being grouped under the heading *nemtsi*, meaning dumb and, by extension, German or foreign. Thence, over the years a limited number of foreign styles and foreign notions seeped slowly out into Muscovy. As far as possible dealings with foreigners were channelled through a special Diplomatic Office presided over by Russians with at least some previous experience of foreigners. For there still persisted a deep seated fear of infection or contagion from anything foreign or non-orthodox in the very widest sense of the word.

And yet, contacts were made and ideas exchanged and Russia gradually became less isolated and less cut off from the outside world. With time, European ornaments and furniture made their appearance in the houses of the richest boyars, Western-style music came to be played at state banquets and a Palace of Amusements was opened in the Kremlin. Theatrical performances, attended by the pick of Moscow society, included *Judith and Holofernes* and *Esther*, a biblical tragi-comedy set to German music and lasting for ten hours. In all this a moving spirit was Artamon Matveyev, a boyar reputedly well versed in Western ways, who discharged some of the functions of a Foreign Minister. Artamon had, as it happened, married a Miss Hamilton from Scotland. With her help he entertained in his house in Moscow in something approaching European style. He was also quite well educated and his library was said to contain books in four or five different languages. By this time, despite the dead hand of the Church, a few foreign books had begun to find their way into Russia and a badly needed start had been made with education.

Another leader of Muscovite society was Prince Vasili Golitsin, whose house the French Ambassador described as being one of the most magnificent in Europe, even going so far as to compare it to the palace of an Italian prince.

But these were only beginnings. The real opening-up of Russia to the West, the real wind of change, was yet to come.

# 4 *Pater Patriae*

TSAR ALEXIS THE GENTLE died suddenly in 1676 at the age of forty-five. By his first wife, Maria Miloslavskaya, he left two sons, Fyodor, aged fourteen, and Ivan, aged ten, and an older daughter Sophia. By his second wife, the young and beautiful Natalia Narishkina, a connection and protégée of Artamon Matveyev, he left another son, Peter, aged four. While Sophia enjoyed normal health, both Fyodor and Ivan were sickly, Fyodor being partially paralysed and Ivan half-witted and almost blind. Little Peter, on the other hand, was as bright and as sturdy as he could be.

On his father's death, Fyodor, as eldest son, succeeded to the throne, on to which he had at his coronation to be hoisted bodily by his personal attendants. This accomplished, his mother's family, the Miloslavskis, lost no time in banishing Peter, his mother Natalia and as many as possible of her family, the Narishkins, to a safe distance from Moscow. At the same time Natalia's friend and protector, Artamon Matveyev, was dispatched to Siberia.

Six years later, in 1682, after a reign in which he played no part and which was remarkable for nothing besides the usual feuding and court intrigue, Fyodor died. Normally, if that is the word, the succession should have gone to feeble-minded Ivan. But the Miloslavskis had won few friends during their spell in power. The Narishkins, on the other hand, had made good use of their time. It was thus that on Fyodor's death Peter and not Ivan was proclaimed Tsar, on the grounds that Ivan was incapable of ruling.

Peter had the support of both Patriarch and boyars. But the Miloslavskis were not out of the fight. Unlike her little brother, Ivan's sister the Tsarevna Sophia, though far from beautiful, was anything but feeble-minded. 'She is,' wrote a contemporary

French observer, 'immensely fat, with a head as large as a bushel, hairs on her face and tumours on her legs. But in the same degree that her body is broad, short and coarse, her mind is shrewd, unprejudiced and full of politics.' And he went on to say that, although she had probably never heard of Machiavelli, his precepts came naturally to her.

With the help of her enlightened but in many respects inefficient lover, Prince Vasili Golitsin (he of the splendid palace), Sophia now not only publicly challenged Peter's right to the throne, but promptly enlisted the support of the Moscow garrison. This consisted of some twenty thousand *Streltsi* or 'Sharp-shooters', a force of doubtful discipline, well-armed and equipped and enjoying special privileges, who, when they felt like it, were liable to intervene suddenly and disastrously in the affairs of the capital.

On 15 May 1682, having been told by Sophia that the boyars had strangled little Ivan, an armed mob of *Streltsi* marched on the Kremlin with drums beating and flags flying. To convince them that there was no truth in the story of Ivan's assassination, Natalia, accompanied by Artamon Matveyev, who had by now returned from Siberia, at once brought both Ivan and Peter out on to the Red Staircase of the Kremlin Palace to show the *Streltsi* that both Princes were alive and well. Indeed, half-witted though he was, little Ivan himself personally announced that he had not been strangled.

But by now the soldiers' blood was up. Bursting into the palace, they hacked to pieces any of the Narishkins they could find before the eyes of Peter and his mother, after which for the next three days they ranged through the city, tracking down and doing to death all the Narishkin supporters they could lay hands on in accordance with a list provided for this purpose by Princess Sophia. Another victim of their blood-lust was the unfortunate Matveyev who, in spite of all Natalia's efforts to save him, was hacked to pieces in front of her.

Power, for the time being, rested with the *Streltsi* and with their ambitious commander, Prince Khovanski. After erecting a special monument to commemorate their latest exploits, they next insisted that henceforth Ivan should reign jointly with Peter and that Sophia, who had given them ten roubles each, should be Regent in place of Natalia. These proposals were promptly put into effect and Sophia took up residence with little Ivan in the Kremlin, whence, making the most of her opportunities, she proceeded to rule the country. Her first act of policy was a bold one. Hearing rumours that Prince Khovanski was thinking of having her and the two little Tsars murdered and making himself Tsar in their place, she had him and his son arrested and executed. This damped the enthusiasm of the *Streltsi* and not long after their monument celebrating the massacre of 15 May was taken down.

Natalia, meanwhile, taking Peter with her, had gone to live outside Moscow near the village of Preobrazhenskoye, not far, as it happened, from the German Settlement. Peter, who a few months earlier had seen a number of his relatives massacred before his eyes and had himself narrowly escaped death, was now ten. Henceforward his education, hitherto rudimentary, was to be mainly practical in character. His mother was not afraid of foreigners and from the foreign craftsmen and experts in the German Suburb he picked up all kinds of useful knowledge. He also became used at an early age to meeting foreigners and working with them.

Already Peter's chief passion was for the arts of war, 'the games of Mars and Neptune', as he called them. With the local boys, peasants' sons and nobles' sons alike, he would play endlessly at soldiers. The games they played became, as he and his friends grew older, more serious and realistic, reaching the point at which, in due course, he was able to form the nucleus of two famous Russian regiments, the Preobrazhenski and Semyonovski Guards. In this, too, the foreigners from the German Settlement could help. From Dutchmen, Scots and Germans he avidly learned the elements of mathematics, gunnery and fortification as well as of sailing and navigation, the latter on the lake near Yaroslavl in an old English-built sailing-boat, which he was later to call the father of the Russian fleet. A close friend and boon companion was General Patrick Gordon, a soldier of fortune from Aberdeen, who in his time had served with the Holy Roman Emperor, the Swedes and the Poles. At Preobrazhenskoye Peter also seems to have learned a good deal about life in general, acquiring on his visits to the German Settlement a taste for strong drink and, as soon as he was old enough, a mistress, Anna Mons, the pretty flaxen-haired daughter of a German wine-merchant. When he was seventeen, a well-born wife, Eudoxia Lopukhina, two years older than he was, was found for him by his mother, but relegated by him to a convent so soon that she scarcely had time to bear him a baby son.

The massive Princess Sophia, meanwhile, having assumed the title of Autocrat, was, with the help of Prince Golitsin, governing Russia energetically, though with only limited success. A campaign against the Crimean Tartars, with her inefficient lover in command, ended in disaster. In the Far East, too, where the Russians had now reached the Pacific, a clash with the Chinese forced them to withdraw from the Amur River valley. None of which helped to enhance Sophia's popularity. Worried at the way things were going, she now seems to have hatched a plot to declare herself Empress, seeking once again the support of the *Streltsi*.

It was thus that one night in August 1689 a report, never in fact confirmed, reached Preobrazhenskoye to the effect that a force of *Streltsi* were on their way to kill Peter. Peter, pulled out of bed, threw himself on to a horse and galloped off through the forest in his nightshirt to the Monastery of the Holy Trinity at Sergievo. Here he was later joined by his mother, by some leading boyars, who by now had had enough of Sophia, and by a considerable number of troops, including the regiments which he himself had raised, some *Streltsi* and a number of other regiments.

For the teenage boy the emotional shock, coming on top of so much else, must have been a severe one. But the incident served to bring matters to a head. It also showed Peter how much support he enjoyed and where various loyalties lay. In order to force an issue, he now summoned Sophia to explain her conduct and in particular to tell the truth about her dealings with the *Streltsi*. At the same time he called a meeting of boyars. It was clear by now that public opinion was on Peter's side and against his sister. The Patriarch and the boyars openly declared themselves against the Regent and the *Streltsi* followed suit. Without further ado, Sophia was sent to the Convent of Novodevichi on the outskirts of Moscow, Golitsin was arrested and banished and a number of their supporters were executed. Although Peter's poor half-witted brother Ivan did not die for another seven years, there could no longer be any question as to who was now Tsar.

At first, Peter, still only seventeen, did not take over the government of the country, leaving this to his mother, while he continued to drill his private army which, now fully equipped and armed, was well on the way to becoming a regular military force. It was not until his mother Natalia's death in 1694, followed two years later by that of his half-brother and nominal co-Tsar Ivan, that he finally took up the reins of power. Powerfully built and almost seven feet tall, he already gave an impression of enormous energy and strength.

As things turned out, the new Tsar did not have to wait long for an opportunity to display the military expertise which he had acquired over the years on the playing fields of Preobrazhenskoye. Russia had now been at peace with Poland for thirty years. Under a treaty signed in 1656, King John Sobieski of Poland had agreed to the permanent surrender of Kiev to the Russians in return for active Russian support against the infidel Tartars and their Turkish suzerains. Here, should one be needed, was a ready-made pretext for an attack on either Tartars or Turks. Accordingly, following the failure of Prince Golitsin's attempted invasion of the Crimea, Peter decided to try another approach to what could by now be called the Eastern Question.

First making a feint against the Crimea to conceal his real intentions, in the spring of 1695 Peter struck in strength against Azov, his purpose being to gain effective control of the steppes of the Don valley. But Azov was strongly fortified and the Tartar garrison, who put up a determined resistance, was able to receive supplies and reinforcements by sea. With the approach of autumn the town was still holding out. Peter now realized that what he needed were ships with which to blockade Azov. Characteristically he spent the winter building up a fleet of suitable craft. By March 1696 they were ready. Sailing down the Don, he returned to the attack and this time Azov, encompassed by sea and by land, fell to the Russians.

From this early naval victory sprang, in no small degree, the concept of a strong Russian navy. This appealed powerfully to Peter's imagination and henceforward bulked large in his plans for the future. Without loss of time work was put in hand. New shipyards were built at Voronezh and elsewhere, foreign experts were imported, Russians were trained in shipbuilding and it became the duty of peasants, townsmen and nobles alike to contribute by taxes and other means to the cost of the Tsar's new navy.

Linked with this project was another equally ambitious one: to form a Grand European Alliance, drive the Turk from Europe and win Constantinople – Tsargrad – for the Christians, in other words for Russia. With this object in mind, Peter launched in the spring of 1697 an Embassy Extraordinary to Germany, Austria, Holland,

Great Britain, Poland, Venice and the Vatican, accompanying it himself under the somewhat unconvincing alias of Corporal Peter Mikhailov of the Preobrazhenski Guards.

Peter's embassy evoked universal curiosity, but little response to the proposals it put forward. On the other hand it was certainly not a waste of time. No Tsar had ever left Russia before. Peter, by the time he came back, had seen a great many new people and new places and learned a great deal about a great many things. Breaking away from his companions, he spent four months working as an ordinary shipwright in Amsterdam and four more in the English Government Shipyard at Deptford. While in England and Holland, always keen to pick up new ideas, he visited innumerable museums, factories and other institutions of one kind or another, and in his spare time did what Sir Christopher Wren estimated as £350 worth of damage to the house he rented from John Evelyn, ruining the lawn, scratching and smearing the walls, smashing the furniture, using the pictures for target practice and pushing the wheelbarrow, by which he was fascinated, backwards and forwards through the hedge. 'Right nasty' was the impression he and his companions made on those who had to minister to them. The young Tsar even attended a debate in the House of Commons. 'How agreeable,' was his comment afterwards, 'to hear the sons of the fatherland tell the truth so plainly to the King. We must learn that from the English.' But it was a lesson which, if ever learnt, did not in the event sink in. Despite his enthusiasm for Western efficiency and Western technology, Peter remained Russian to the core. 'We shall need Europe for a few decades,' he said to a friend, 'and then we can turn our backside to her.'

Peter was now twenty-six. A portrait, painted during his stay in England by Sir Godfrey Kneller, shows him as a tall, dark, strongly built, good looking young man, dressed in the armour of the period with, over it, a splendid ermine-lined robe. In the background, Sir Godfrey, no doubt at his patron's behest, has painted a ship of the line under full sail. The Tsar carries his Marshal's baton in a challenging manner and the same challenge is reflected in his slightly protuberant grey-green eyes. All in all the portrait gives a strong impression of energy and drive. A young man, one would say, in the American phrase, who is going places.

While in Vienna, on his way back to Russia, Peter received in the summer of 1698 the news that in his absence the *Streltsi* had mutinied. Their mutiny, it appeared, had been promptly and murderously crushed. But even so he decided to cut short his journey and hurry home as fast as he could. He was by now full of reforming zeal.

Driving straight to his own favourite country retreat at Preobrazhenskoye, he first summoned the members of his Court and of the great noble families and informed them that in future they would shave their beards like civilized noblemen in Western Europe and wear shorter, Western-style coats in place of their long traditional kaftans. Where necessary, he himself, with the help of his court jester Turgenyev and of a large pair of shears, personally enforced his own commands. He was utterly determined to get the nobles under control. *Mestnichestvo*, the archaic system under which each noble was bound to his own hierarchical position or rank, had in theory been abolished twenty years earlier. Peter now gave it the coup de grâce.

The Tsar next turned his attention to the mutiny of the *Streltsi*. This had aroused his deepest suspicions and he was inclined to think that it had not been severely enough dealt with. As a first step he ordered a fresh investigation of the mutiny's origins. In the course of the autumn and winter almost two thousand more *Streltsi* were tortured by every conceivable means and in the end executed, some by the Tsar himself, their mangled bodies being left hanging in the Red Square and elsewhere as a warning to other potential trouble-makers.

Before being finished off, many of the mutineers were forced to confess. By a fortunate coincidence, their confessions all pointed in the same direction: to the Convent of Novodevichi, now housing the one-time Regent, the Tsar's chunky half-sister, Princess Sophia. A scapegoat had been found. On the Tsar's orders the Princess was now shorn as a nun, placed under even closer restraint, and the bodies of three dead *Streltsi* were put to dangle outside the window of her cell. After which the corps of *Streltsi*, which Peter had in any case always regarded as an old-fashioned and reactionary institution and the repository of all the ideas he disliked most, was finally disbanded and its few surviving members were dispersed to Siberia and other remote areas.

These early reforms were followed in due course by a whole series of others. Hitherto the Russians, curiously enough, had reckoned the date of the month from the creation of the World, believed to have been completed on the first of September some 7207 years earlier. Now, having given the matter some serious thought and duly celebrated the New Year of 7208 on the first of September 1699, Peter decreed that, as in other Christian countries, the calendar should in future run from the birth of Christ and the year start on the first day of January. Unfortunately, by adopting the Julian Calendar, then going out of use in most Western countries, instead of the Gregorian, he created a fresh time-lag with the West which was to last for another couple of hundred years.

As time went by, Peter also intervened with characteristic vigour and impatience in the realms of government administration (both local and central), of education, of public finance, of industry, of Church affairs and, needless to say, of the army and navy. In each he set his subjects working harder than ever before and over each he established more firmly than ever his own personal control. He also brought into being, somewhere round the turn of the century, a new police department known as the *Preobrazhenski Prikaz* and specifically responsible for dealing with political offences and misdemeanours.

'Faced,' wrote Stalin two centuries later, 'with the more advanced countries of the West, Peter the Great went feverishly to work to build factories and mills in order to supply his army and improve his country's defence. It was a characteristic attempt to break out from a framework of backwardness.' Peter was not the first, nor the last, ruler of Russia to be confronted with the problem of his country's relative backwardness or to attempt to solve it by a revolution from above.

If Russia was really to be westernized and brought up to date, it seemed to Peter, as it had seemed to some of his more farsighted predecessors, that what she needed most was an outlet to the West, an outlet which could only be achieved by breaking through to the Baltic Sea. On his way back from his European tour, he had made friends with Augustus, the new King of Poland and Elector of Saxony. In him and in King Christian of Denmark he found ready allies for an attack on the power which stood between him and the Baltic: on Sweden, where Charles XII, a boy of barely eighteen with a reputation for irresponsibility, had recently ascended the throne. In the summer of 1700 the formal conclusion of peace with Turkey removed a potential threat to Russia's rear. In August an army of 40,000 Russians under the Prince de Croy set out for the Gulf of Finland, where they laid siege to the Swedish fortress of Narva.

Young Charles XII of Sweden was at this stage still an unknown quantity. He did not remain one for long. On the outbreak of war, he first struck hard at Copenhagen, forcing the Danes to sue for peace. Then in November, in a snowstorm, he rounded on the Russians at Narva, utterly defeated them and forced them back in total confusion to the River Narova. There being only one bridge over the river, many panic-stricken Russians tried to swim across and were drowned. Only Peter's own Preobrazhenski and Semyonovski Guards stood firm and, acting as a rearguard, eventually withdrew in good order, leaving the much less numerous Swedes in possession of Peter's fortified camps and of all his artillery. Peter himself having apparently lost his nerve, was by this time far away. He clearly still had a lot to learn both about the art and the practice of war.

But, for all this, Peter was not easily put off. Within weeks of his defeat at Narva, he had started to assemble a bigger and better army organized on more modern lines and was having the church bells from all over Russia melted down to cast several hundred fresh cannon to replace those he had lost. More foreign experts were called in. For conscripts (and almost every Russian was now liable for service of one kind or another) the period of service was twenty-five years and the discipline uniformly ferocious. In his own Guards Regiments he built up a well-trained and dependable *corps d'élite*, officered entirely by nobles and constituting a kind of Praetorian Guard. To pay for all this, the scale and scope of both direct and indirect taxation were sharply increased.

It was now Charles's turn to blunder. Instead of following up his advantage against the Russians and hitting them again even harder while they were weak, he let himself become involved in a prolonged campaign against his third enemy, King Augustus, and, in Peter's pregnant phrase, he 'got stuck in Poland'.

This gave the Tsar the time he needed to reorganize his forces and also some scope for manoeuvre. While one Russian army threatened the Swedes in Poland, another made for Estonia, Livonia and the Gulf of Finland and there, bit by bit, established itself, moving gradually nearer to the mouth of the River Neva. First, in 1701 and 1702, came some successful Russian cavalry raids under Alexander Menshikov, a resourceful young man of humble origin, said by some to have been a pastrycook's assistant, with whom Peter, though he normally preferred women to men, maintained an intermittent homosexual relationship and whom he ultimately made a Prince and a Field-Marshal. Then in the autumn of 1702 Peter himself joined his northern army, captured the important Swedish stronghold of Nöteborg (later renamed Schlüsselburg or Key Fort) on the Neva and, pressing on down the river in the spring of 1703, took the fortress of Nyenschanz at the junction of the Okhta and the Neva.

It was here, on a small, marshy, windswept island in the Neva known as Hare Island, that were laid in May 1703 the foundations of the future fortress of St Peter and St Paul and, round it and across the river from it, on even marshier gound, those of the improbably sited city that was to bear Peter's name and be his Western-style capital and his window on Europe – St Petersburg (now Leningrad).

Peter now had a fortified foothold on the Baltic. This he hastened to exploit and consolidate. By the autumn of 1703 ships were being built in large numbers on nearby Lake Ladoga and a naval base for the new Baltic Fleet had been established on the island of Kronstadt, commanding the Gulf of Finland and the approaches to St Petersburg. In 1704, four years after his first disastrous set-back, there followed the capture by the Russians of Narva and of two or three other strong-points well suited to protect their Baltic foothold both by sea and by land.

So far, so good. But there was another side to the coin. By his ruthless and impatient reforms of Church and State, by the savage jolts he had administered to nobility, clergy and peasantry alike, by the intolerable degree of taxation which he had inflicted on every section of the population to pay for his military adventures, Peter had severely tried the patience and endurance of the long-suffering Russian people. In short he had come very close to shaking the whole machine to bits. Financial and administrative chaos, long a feature of the Russian scene, now reached danger level. The Tsar had incurred the hostility both of the Orthodox clergy and, to an even greater degree, of the Old Believers. In 1705 there was a rebellion in Astrakhan against 'boyars and foreigners', followed by a rising among the Bashkirs beyond the Volga. Finally and worst of all, there was once more serious unrest amongst the Cossacks in the Ukraine and on the Don.

In the autumn of 1707 this unrest turned to open insurrection. The Don and its Cossacks still afforded asylum and a future of sorts to those who needed it most, fugitives from justice and runaway serfs. These were at the bottom of the trouble and, even though such newcomers were not particularly welcome to the established Cossack bands, all Peter's efforts to secure their surrender were unsuccessful. Peter now responded by sending a detachment of troops to the Don to hunt them out. But these proved no match for the Cossacks and were annihilated. Soon the whole area of the Don was aflame.

Nor was this all. There was trouble brewing in the Ukraine. In Poland, Peter's ally King Augustus had by now been badly beaten and forced to abdicate and the victorious Swedes, still undefeated, were preparing to march in strength against Moscow. Just what the outcome of the impending conflict would be, was anything but clear. Such at any rate was the view of Ivan Mazeppa, for twenty years Hetman of the Ukrainian Cossacks, who, in order to secure his position in any event, had for some time been in secret correspondence with Peter's old enemy Charles XII of Sweden. Clearly there was a serious risk that, at a moment when Moscow was threatened with an attack by the Swedes, the Ukrainian Cossacks would join the Don Cossacks in a combined insurrection the like of which had never been seen.

Peter had at all costs to secure his rear. He first sent a strong force, which he could ill spare, to put down the Cossack rising on the Don. He next charged Mazeppa with treachery. Somehow Mazeppa managed to clear himself to the Tsar's satisfaction and, having done so, quickly executed those who (with good reason) had denounced him as a traitor. Soon he would appear in his true colours, but not yet. The outlook meanwhile was scarcely encouraging and at times even Peter is said to have seemed depressed.

Charles XII launched his attack early in 1708, advancing through Poland at the head of an army 40,000 strong, while 16,000 more Swedes under General Loewenhaupt marched south from Livonia to join him with additional supplies, artillery and ammunition. After taking the Russian-held town of Grodno, Charles continued his advance in the direction of Smolensk, defeating the Russians whenever he encountered them. Peter now expected him to attack Smolensk, but, instead, before reaching it, he turned south into the Ukraine with the evident intention of joining forces with Mazeppa.

This gave Peter his opportunity. General Loewenhaupt had failed to catch up with the main Swedish force before Charles turned south towards the Ukraine. Before he had time to do so, Peter attacked him on the River Sozh and heavily defeated him, inflicting terrible casualties on him and capturing the entire Swedish baggage train. At the same time further south Alexander Menshikov struck hard at Mazeppa, of whose treachery there could no longer be any doubt. Escaping almost alone, Mazeppa now joined Charles; in the Ukraine any other potential insurgents took cover; and the danger of a rising, for the time being at any rate, receded.

To Charles of Sweden the campaign of 1708 had brought few successes. He had, it is true, reached the Ukraine and there gone into winter quarters to the east of Kiev. But the rising he had been promised by Mazeppa had never materialized. He could have little hope of receiving either supplies or reinforcements. And now, with winter coming on, he found himself entirely surrounded by Peter's armies.

In the spring of 1709, after trying unsuccessfully during the winter to break out in the direction of Moscow, Charles decided to leave his winter quarters and lay siege to the Russian fortress of Poltava on the Vorskla River, some two hundred miles southeast of Kiev. Poltava was a Russian border strong-point, originally built as an outpost against the Turks and Tartars. Its possession, he calculated, would provide him with a base for further operations and at the same time put him within reach of another potential ally – the Sultan of Turkey.

But Poltava did not prove as easy a nut to crack as Charles had hoped. The Russian garrison put up a gallant defence and the Swedes were beginning by now to suffer from a shortage of supplies and ammunition. As a result, the siege dragged on inconclusively for several weeks and this gave Peter time to come to the relief of the beleaguered garrison.

It was thus that on the morning of 8 July 1709 the Swedish army, by now numbering no more than 30,000 men, encountered a Russian army of 42,000 men in battle at Poltava. By midday the battle was over. Half Charles's army had been killed or captured. The remainder were in full retreat to the Dnieper, where Menshikov was lying in wait for them. Charles himself, badly wounded, was somehow brought across the Dnieper and carried to safety in Turkish territory.

Historically, Peter's decisive victory at Poltava was of the greatest importance. It put Russia in the front rank as a military power. And, though formal recognition of this was only to follow later, it also in fact established Russian supremacy in north-eastern Europe. As Peter himself put it, 'The final stone has now been added to the foundations of St Petersburg.'

Charles was not, however, the man to admit defeat. Having taken refuge in Turkey, he soon persuaded the Sultan to declare war on Russia. Peter was glad to accept the challenge. To drive the Turk from Europe (which included the Crimea) had always been one of his ambitions. Already he saw Russia as the natural protector of the Orthodox Christians under Turkish rule in the Balkans and elsewhere. In the spring of 1711, without much preparation, he marched south at the head of an army of 40,000 men. But the local Orthodox Christians did not rise, as he had been told they would. Nor did any help come from Poland. On the River Pruth the Russians, who had not had an easy approach march, encountered a Turkish force of no less than 200,000 men, which quickly surrounded them. If they were not to surrender or be wiped out, their only hope was to negotiate and this the Sultan, much to their relief, agreed to do. In return for the surrender of Azov, which Peter had taken from them with so much trouble fifteen years earlier, the Turks made peace and allowed the rather crestfallen Russian army to go home. Once again Peter had suffered a set-back in the south. But at least he was now free to direct his full attention to the north.

Here he was more successful. In 1714 his new Baltic Fleet heavily defeated the Swedish navy and the Russians occupied the Aland Islands and actually threatened Stockholm. During the years that followed Peter, in alliance with the Danes and Germans, continued operations on the southern shores of the Baltic. Having in 1717 visited Paris to try to enlist the help of Louis XV, he next opened direct peace negotiations with the Swedes. But these broke down on Charles's death in 1718 and hostilities continued for another three years, the Russians invading Sweden by sea and devastating it as far as Stockholm. Finally in August 1721, just twenty-one years after the beginning of the war, a treaty of peace was signed at Nystad, under which, though it surrendered most of Finland, Russia acquired Ingria and part of Karelia and the Baltic coast from Riga to Viborg, including most of what is now Estonia and Latvia.

In the end Peter, who despite a severe attack of gout, danced on the table during the ensuing victory celebrations, had done what he set out to do. He had broken the power of Sweden and given Russia a firm foothold on the Baltic and a window open on the West. To mark this achievement, he now assumed the title of Emperor of All Russia, while, in addition to the imperial title, the newly created Senate conferred on him the styles of 'the Great' and of 'Pater Patriae'.

But Peter had not finished. No sooner was the Northern War at an end, than he declared war on Persia. Having got what he wanted in the north, his thoughts and ambitions were now turning southwards and eastwards, to the Caspian and beyond it, to Central Asia and India. An earlier attempt to take the Khanate of Khiva, hundreds of miles away beyond the Caspian, had ended in disaster. This time he was more successful. After a Russian force from Astrakhan had occupied the Persian-protected Khanates of Derbend and Baku, the Shah agreed to negotiate and in 1723 ceded to Russia the whole western seaboard of the Caspian. To Peter's 'window on the West' had now been added a 'window on the East'.

For more than a quarter of a century Peter had kept his country continuously at war. At the same time he had shown himself utterly determined to force through the programme of reforms he had set himself at the beginning of his reign. Their purpose was to Westernize and modernize Russia and fit it for its new role as a great power. To achieve this, he had to have the men and money necessary to raise and keep in being a modern army, navy and administrative machine. To this end every Russian from the greatest noble downwards was forced in one capacity or another into the service of the state. Simultaneously the burden of taxation grew by leaps and bounds. A standing army had already replaced the *Streltsi* and the haphazard feudal levies of the past. Even the nobles were now obliged to serve in regular regiments, usually the Imperial Guards. By the end of Peter's reign his army numbered 200,000 regular troops and 75,000 or more Cossacks, while the navy he had created could now boast as many as 48 large warships and 800 smaller vessels, with a complement of 28,000 sailors. Instead of serving in the army, the peasants, now tied more closely than ever to the land, paid taxes. By now ninety per cent of the population were serfs of one kind or another. The nobility and gentry were, for their part, liable to a lifetime of service either in the army or in some other branch of the government service, being forbidden even to marry until they had attained the standard of education Peter considered necessary for them. No one could escape the call of duty.

At the same time, the ramshackle machinery of government which Peter had inherited from his predecessors was ruthlessly recast and reformed. Under a new Table of Ranks the government service, both civil and military, was divided into fourteen different grades. All candidates, regardless of social standing, entered the service of the state at the lowest grade, promotion being by merit. The result was not, however, as beneficial as it might have been, for a new, all-encompassing bureaucracy and a new and stultifying snobbery of rank, which in some respects have survived to this day, soon replaced the old snobbery of birth and inherited wealth.

In 1708, in a drastic attempt at decentralization, the whole country was divided up into eight enormous regions, to be known as *guberniyi* or governments, each with its own Governor, their number being later increased to twelve. But this reform gave rise to as many problems as it solved. Preferring to govern with the advice, when he needed it, of an inner circle of personal friends, Peter had long since ceased to convoke the old Council of Boyars. Soon the lack of any effective central authority made itself felt. During the war with Turkey a Council of Nine had been set up to conduct affairs in the Tsar's name and serve as a supreme court of justice. In 1711 this body was reconstituted as the Senate and entrusted with the overall supervision of the different governments, whose Governors were made directly responsible to it.

In 1718 there followed a reconstruction of the central administration. In place of the old system of *Prikazi* or Chancelleries, originally set up in the days of Ivan the Terrible or even of Ivan the Great, a number of Ministerial Colleges were established, each responsible for a different field of government – finance, foreign affairs, the army, the navy, commerce and so on – and presided over, not by a single minister, but by a board of twelve with collective responsibility. Finally in 1722 Peter brought into being a peculiarly Russian institution, a special Procuratorship-General, under a Procurator-General, required to act as 'the eye of the sovereign', to supervise, in other words, the actions of all other government bodies, including the Senate, and to 'find out secretly, denounce and expose' any misconduct on the part of any servants of the government. For all classes discipline was strict. Thus in 1715 two erring senators were flogged and had their tongues branded and their property confiscated.

The Orthodox Church, needless to say, did not escape Peter's reforming zeal any more than any other national institution. Resolutely obscurantist and firmly entrenched in ancient tradition, it stood for much that he disliked. It had also opposed many of his reforms. Since the death of Adrian in 1700 he had deliberately neglected to appoint a new Patriarch. 'Here is your Patriarch!' he exclaimed, thumping his own chest, when a deputation of clerics invited him to appoint one. In 1721 he formally abolished the Patriarchate and set up in its place a Holy Synod directly subject to the Senate (and, through the Senate, to the Procurator-General). At the same time the monastic orders were briskly brought into line. Henceforward there would be little danger of any serious conflict between Church and Crown.

Peter also approached the problem of Russian economic and industrial development with the same relentless energy as everything else, establishing factories manned mainly by serf labour, setting up state monopolies and pouring public money into innumerable different enterprises. In this he was helped by his usual group of cronies who greatly enriched themselves in the process. While the methods he adopted did little to promote private enterprise or healthy economic growth and the results achieved were often disappointing, the fact remains that by the end of his reign Russia had her own state mining and manufacturing industries. In this field, as in so many others, a pattern was set during Peter's reign which was to cast its shadow far into the future.

For education, finally, Peter showed boundless enthusiasm, founding the Academy of Sciences, launching the first Russian newspaper, arranging for the translation of foreign books, setting up a number of technical and other schools which he forced his subjects to attend and even attempting by means of special books of etiquette and much careful rehearsal to drum into the Russian ruling class the elements of good manners, ballroom dancing and polite conversation, as practised in the West. 'I belong,' ran the inscription on his private seal, 'to those who seek knowledge and are willing to learn.' He was no less determined that others should learn too. But, for all the energy and enthusiasm with which Peter pushed them through, these measures only touched a tiny proportion of the population. Their effect was thus in the long run to drive a further wedge between a now superficially Westernized upper class and the still profoundly backward masses over whom they ruled.

Meanwhile, during the whole of the time that he was fighting his wars and pushing through his programme of reforms, Peter had been pressing on with the project which meant as much to him as any of his other great undertakings and in a sense summed up and symbolized the whole of his achievement: the creation in the north, on the shores of the Baltic, on land won in battle from the enemy, of what he called his paradise, his window open on Europe, a truly Western capital and base for his fleet, worthy of the great empire he had brought into being: the creation of the city that bore his name. In his frenzied haste to see it finished, vast numbers of labourers were sent north under appalling conditions to drain and clear the inhospitable marshland on which he had chosen to build it. And when they died by tens of thousands of cold and hardship and disease, tens of thousands more were sent to take their place, so that work could go on without interruption. It was a project that in treasure as well as in human lives and suffering cost as much as any of his campaigns.

But to Peter all this was secondary, so long as he achieved his object. And achieve it he did, installing government departments in new public buildings, forcing his reluctant nobles to build themselves fine new town houses and, from the little house he had built for himself on the banks of the Neva, personally supervising the growth of the city until the day came when he was finally able to move the Court and the seat of government to the new capital, to St Petersburg. A St Petersburg which did not yet possess the full splendour which it was to achieve in the course of the next hundred years, but which was already recognizable as a Western, a European city and a fitting capital for the newest of the great European powers: Russia, as the old Muscovy was now renamed.

In 1722 Peter reached the age of fifty. He had by this time brought the Swedish war to a victorious conclusion and had by his Persian campaign prepared the way for a future Russian thrust eastwards and southwards into Asia. His new capital was built. He had given effect to the bulk of his reforms. The Senate, his own creation, had named him Pater Patriae, Imperator, Maximus. But

Winter Palace

Tauride Palace

St Isaac's Cathedral

Kunstkamera

in one direction the outlook was less reassuring. As so often before in Russian history, there was no obvious heir to the throne.

After discarding his first wife, Eudoxia Lopukhina, Peter had taken their son Aleksei away from her. But the boy had grown up to hate his father and had stubbornly resisted the latter's spasmodic efforts to make a European of him. Instead, with the support and encouragement of the more conservative elements at Court, who saw in him at least some hope for the future, Aleksei had gone out of his way to prove himself a Muscovite to the core and, when offered the choice of mending his ways or renouncing the succession, had chosen the latter alternative. Fleeing the country, he had next, to his father's rage and disgust, taken refuge with the Emperor Charles VI in Vienna. But in 1718 Peter had lured him back to Russia and on his return imprisoned him in the new Fortress of St Peter and St Paul. Despite a promise 'before God and his judgement seat' to 'cherish him like a son', he now had him tortured, interrogated and eventually charged with high treason, alleging that he and certain associates were involved in a plot against his person. At the ensuing trial Aleksei had been found guilty and (for there could be no other sentence) condemned to death. Two days later, however, before the sentence could be carried out, the Tsarevich had died in his cell from the effect, apparently, of the tortures he had undergone, inflicted, according to the Guard Book, in his father's presence. Peter, at bottom an emotional man, is said by some authorities to have wept bitterly at his son's funeral. By others, perhaps more convincingly, it is said that on the following night he gave a great dinner and ball at Prince Menshikov's palace on Vasilievski Island. It is even possible, for we are concerned with a character, and a country, quite out of the ordinary, that both stories are true.

Alexei had left a son of three by Sophia Charlotte of Wolfensbüttel, the German princess his father had forced him to marry. Meanwhile, as long ago as 1707 Peter had himself secretly remarried, his second wife being a Baltic servant-girl called Martha, a name which, on leaving the employment of the Protestant pastor for whom she worked and formally embracing the Orthodox faith, she had changed to Catherine. Catherine, a woman of great tact, ability and above all good sense, had first fallen into Russian hands during the Northern War and, having originally shared the bed of Prince Menshikov, had later been passed on by him to the

Tsar. A contemporary portrait shows a round, pudgy little face with a rosebud mouth and shrewd, lively eyes above a low-cut and extremely well-filled bodice. In Catherine Peter found not only a mistress but a companion who swore, drank and rode like a man and who also understood and could cope with his internal conflicts, his moods and passions and rages which of late had become increasingly hard to control.

By Catherine, who had accompanied him on his Turkish campaign of 1711 and whom he officially married in 1712, Peter had no less than eleven children, only two of whom, however, survived early childhood: the Princesses Anna and Elizabeth. In 1724, he himself crowned her Empress, only to find, not long after, that she, too, like most of those around him, was involved in every kind of plot and intrigue. He also discovered at about this time that she had taken a lover, her chamberlain, William Mons, the brother of his own earlier mistress, Anna. With this particular situation he dealt in a characteristically rough and ready way, having his rival's head cut off and placed in a jar of surgical spirit in the Empress's bedroom.

In 1722, in a belated attempt to provide for the future and thus ensure that his own achievements were not swept away on his death, Peter had changed the law of succession so as to give himself and those who came after him the right to nominate their own successors, regardless of dynastic ties. But, as things turned out, it was not vouchsafed to him to take advantage of this convenient, if somewhat arbitrary measure. In the autumn of 1724 he caught cold while trying to save some soldiers in danger of drowning in the estuary of the Neva. As autumn turned to winter his health deteriorated; early in the New Year he took to his bed; and on 28 January 1725 he died in agony, having with his last breath sought desperately but unavailingly to name his successor.

'A great man,' wrote Solovyev, 'is always and everywhere the representative of his nation.' Whether you accept this somewhat sweeping aphorism or not, it undoubtedly deserves careful consideration, especially where Russia is concerned. In the narrow context of Peter's own reign it might at first sight seem hardly applicable. Indeed it might appear that he had, almost single-handed, dragged his mediaeval, Moscow-bound subjects into Europe. But, regarded as part of the wider sweep of Russian history, the succession of shocks and jolts which he administered to these same subjects, however sudden and violent, fall into place as no more than one, though an important one, in the series of such upheavals which through the centuries have marked the various stages of Russia's development as a nation. Upheavals that on a smaller, domestic scale also tend to mark the private life of many individual Russians, in whom an innate love of drama, sudden violent changes of mood, bouts of deep depression and despair followed by spasms of frantic action, somehow exist side by side with the quieter, more solid Russian qualities of patience, perseverance, endurance and endeavour.

Many of Peter's policies and reforms can thus be seen as part of a continuing process which had begun before him and has continued ever since. What particularly distinguished them was the breakneck speed and utter ruthlessness with which they were put into effect. Innovation at such a pace and on such a scale soon turns to revolution or, as the present rulers of Russia would say in their own Marxist jargon, the accumulation of quantitative changes produces a change of quality. Something of the kind had already occurred under several of Peter's predecessors, notably Ivan the Terrible, and it is surely no mere accident that, under his eventual successor, Generalissimo Stalin, another energetic reformer, especial stress should have been laid by Soviet historians on the progressive character of Peter's achievements and the vigorous, forward-looking manner of their accomplishment.

In Peter the latent revolutionary tendencies of the Russian people found full expression, as did the strange dichotomy, the apparent contradiction that exists between their essential Russianism and their bursts of enthusiasm for foreign fashions and inventions and institutions. What is certain is that, thanks to his own naturally revolutionary character and to his utter refusal to let anything whatever stand in his way, Peter's reign marks a watershed in Russian history, a watershed between the Middle Ages and modern times, between the remains of feudalism and increasing state control, between Russia's former secondary role and its new role as an emergent world power. A watershed for which, as things turned out, there was to be no real parallel for another two hundred years, when many of the trends which he initiated were carried through to their ultimate, their logical conclusion and he himself was to be hailed in retrospect as 'the first Bolshevik'.

# 5 *Monstrous Regiment*

*The Monstrous Regiment of Women*
JOHN KNOX

A PERIOD OF CONFUSION had ushered in the reign of Peter the Great. He left a legacy of equal confusion behind him. His own failure to nominate an heir compounded this. At the time of his grandfather's death, the ten-year-old Peter Alekseievich, son of the unfortunate Tsarevich Aleksei, was the only surviving male member of the Romanov family. He was therefore a strong claimant to the succession. On the other hand, there were those who maintained that it had been Peter's intention to leave the throne to one of his daughters or to his niece Anna, while yet others claimed that he had wished his widow Catherine to succeed him. His last words, interrupted by death, had left the question wide open.

Realizing the dangers of uncertainty and delay, Menshikov, essentially a man of action, lost no time in settling the issue in a sense favourable to himself. With the active support of the Imperial Guards, who, in the power vacuum left by Peter's death, were to play an ever more important part in Russian affairs, Catherine, though without any legal claim to the throne, was then and there proclaimed Empress, while Menshikov himself, her former lover and patron and now her most loyal subject, became her closest adviser. A year later, in 1726, Menshikov and five others established themselves as a Supreme Privy Council, endowed, as its name indicated, with supreme power and designed to replace the existing autocracy by what in effect would be an oligarchy.

Catherine, who did not allow her accession to the throne to temper her enjoyment of life, died in 1727 after a reign of only two years, her vigorous constitution finally undermined by reckless indulgence in the pleasures of one kind or another to which her position as Autocrat now gave her even readier access. Meanwhile Menshikov, who, as usual, had ideas of his own on the subject, had persuaded her to nominate the little Tsarevich, Peter Alekseievich, as her heir, at the same time further securing his own position by arranging a marriage between the future Tsar and his own daughter Maria. On young Peter's accession as Peter II, the twelve-year-old Tsar went to live with Menshikov, who perhaps not unnaturally now assumed that he had nothing more to worry about.

Here he was wrong. In Prince Ivan Dolgoruki, a scion of the old aristocracy, the former pastrycook's assistant had a formidable rival. In a matter of months Prince Dolgoruki had managed to win the favour of the young Tsar; had persuaded him to exile Menshikov and his whole family to Siberia; and had in his turn arranged a marriage between the Tsar and a member of his own family, Princess Catherine Dolgoruki. But he too was doomed to disappointment. On the occasion of his coronation, the young Emperor, now fifteen, was allowed to give full rein to his various appetites. He fell ill, then caught the smallpox and in January 1730, on the very day appointed for his marriage to the hand-picked Princess Dolgoruki, died without making a will.

Undaunted, the Dolgorukis sought to remedy this unhappy omission by forging one for him after the event, nominating his bride-to-be as successor to the throne. But this deceived no one; the Dolgorukis had missed their opportunity; and power passed once more to the Supreme Privy Council, who, after some deliberation, decided to offer the crown, not, as might have been expected, to one of Peter the Great's daughters, but to his niece Anna, the daughter of his half-brother and one time co-Tsar Ivan and widow of the Duke of Courland. Their hope was that Anna, whose claims to the throne were weak and whose lot in Courland as Dowager Duchess had not been particularly enviable, would prove that much easier to deal with. Simultaneously they presented her with a set of conditions, severely curtailing her powers in their own favour. But this did not suit the rest of the nobles, many of whom, determined to improve their position, were assembled in Moscow. With the support of the Imperial Guards, more active than ever in their new political role, they greeted Anna on her arrival in that city with boisterous demands that she should set aside the conditions imposed on her by the Privy Council and rule henceforth as Autocrat.

To these suggestions Anna, a sly, unprepossessing woman of thirty-seven, responded positively and with alacrity, publicly tearing up the offending document with her own hands, abolishing the Supreme Privy Council and beheading or exiling several of its leading members. At the same time she granted a good number of the nobles' other demands, relieving them of many of the restrictions and obligations imposed on them by Peter the Great. But it was no more her intention to put herself in the hands of the nobles than of the Privy Council. Instead, she chose her advisers from a small circle of personal friends, mostly Germans, who had come with her from Courland and who promptly made common cause with the noble German families already established in the Baltic provinces and with those other Germans raised to high office by Peter the Great, thus creating what quickly became an all-pervading German mafia. Of these the most influential and also the most noxious was her favourite, Ernst-Johann Biron or Bühren, a worthless and second-rate character, whose cruelty and boundless rapacity astounded even the Russians.

Anna's reign was not a happy period for the Russian people. She herself was almost exclusively occupied with the frenzied pursuit of pleasure, balls, masquerades and hunting parties succeeding each other without interruption. For her private entertainment, the Empress surrounded herself with a collection of half-wits, dwarfs and misshapen freaks, while her palace gardens were lavishly stocked with every kind of living creature, ready for her to kill with her own hands whenever the whim took her. Affairs of state she left for the most part to Biron, who in return saw to it, by means of punitive taxation, that she was kept provided with plentiful funds. Disliking the Russians as much as they disliked him and fully realizing his own unpopularity, he instituted a far-reaching system of espionage, delation and denunciation which resulted in widespread arrests and executions. In the field of foreign affairs, this period was marked by no outstanding successes. Russia, allied with Austria, intervened in Poland, relinquished Peter the Great's conquests on the Caspian and fought a long and not very rewarding war against the Turks.

Perhaps not surprisingly, Anna's end, like that of her predecessor, was hastened by her own debauchery. She died in 1740, ten years after her accession to the throne, having nominated as her successor her niece's son, Prince Ivan of Brunswick-Bevern, who at the age of three months was now proclaimed Tsar Ivan VI. At the same time Anna had appointed Biron as Regent. But to many influential Russians this was unacceptable and once again the Imperial Guards intervened. With the help of the Preobrazhenski Regiment, Biron was arrested, and sent to Siberia and little Tsar Ivan's mother, Anna Leopoldovna, made Regent in his place.

It soon became apparent, however, that the new Regent's entourage was even more solidly German than his aunt's had been. This in turn was found intolerable and again the Guards stepped in. With the help of the French Ambassador, who, as was only to be expected, shared the general dislike of German influence, a plot was hatched in the course of 1741 to put Peter the Great's younger daughter Elizabeth on the throne. 'Little Mother,' said the officers and guardsmen in their approach to her, 'we are ready; we are only waiting for your orders.' And Elizabeth, an easy-going, good-natured woman with no particular ambition to ascend the throne, but not wishing to appear disobliging, agreed. It was thus that on the night of 7 December 1741 Elizabeth rode over to the barracks of the Preobrazhenski Guards in St Petersburg and thence, by torchlight and with a company of that regiment as escort, to the Imperial Palace, where, without serious disturbance, little Ivan, now a year and a half old, and his mother were arrested and Elizabeth was proclaimed Empress of All Russia.

Once again the Imperial Guards and their nobly born officers had had their way. 'After all the pains which had been taken to bring this country into its present shape,' wrote Daniel Finch, the British Minister in St Petersburg, 'I must confess that I can yet see it in no other light than as a rough model of something meant to be perfected hereafter, in which the several parts do neither fit nor join, nor are well glued together . . . .' His comment, in the circumstances, seems fair enough.

A fine figure of a woman with all her mother's peasant sensuality, Elizabeth Petrovna was not politically minded. As daughter of Peter the Great, she lost no time in declaring amid universal enthusiasm that it was her intention to bring back her father's mode of government. But by now neither she nor those around her any longer had a very clear idea of what this amounted to. In practice she was more interested in fine clothes, parties and young men and having the soles of her feet tickled. 'Inclined to be fat, but is very genteel and dances better than anyone I ever saw,' was the comment of the British Minister's wife. 'Extremely gay,' she added, 'and talks to everybody.' Elizabeth's wardrobe is said to have contained fifteen thousand dresses. In Daniel Finch's telling phrases, the Empress had 'not an ounce of nun's flesh about her'. Perhaps the best known of her many lovers was a Ukrainian Cossack and former choirboy named Aleksei Razumovski, an easy-going character whom she raised to the rank of field-marshal and for whom she built a splendid palace. Rather more active politically were Ivan Shuvalov, another of her favourites, and his cousins Peter and Alexander, who threw themselves into public life with considerable gusto.

The government of the country Elizabeth left on the whole to the Senate, which in her reign, contrary to its original purpose, assumed legislative as well as administrative functions. This made it harder for any one individual to become too powerful and, though, like her predecessors, Elizabeth had favourites, they were for the most part as easy-going and as uninterested in politics as the Empress herself. Every now and then, for reasons of state, an attempt would be made by her political advisers to supplant one of her lovers by another. But usually the insatiable Empress would simply welcome the new lover without discarding the old. By comparison with those of her predecessors, her reign was domestically a relatively quiet one and afforded Russia a much needed opportunity to recover from the experiences of her recent past.

Under Elizabeth, French influence replaced German; French became the language of the Court; and the Empress set out, at enormous expense to the Exchequer, to turn St Petersburg into a second Versailles, the Winter Palace being one of her more notable architectural achievements. To her, too, must go the credit for founding Moscow University, and for giving proper encouragement to the great Michael Lomonosov, the famous man of learning who helped to make this possible.

In Europe, Russia's role had by now greatly increased in scope and its intervention on the side of Austria and France in the Seven Years' War came near to being decisive. Certainly the invasion of East Prussia and the occupation of Berlin in 1760 by Russian troops were long to be remembered by the inhabitants of that city. Indeed it had scarcely begun to fade when drastically refreshed just 185 years later. Fortunately for Frederick II of Prussia, by this time face to face with disaster, indeed actually contemplating suicide,

Elizabeth died on Christmas Day 1761. On Frederick, at any rate, the lesson had not been wasted. '*Après moi,*' he wrote in his political testament, '*les souverains de la Prusse auront bien raison de cultiver l'amitié de ces barbares.*'

The reason for the sudden change in foreign policy which followed Elizabeth's death lay in the person and character of her successor. Almost twenty years earlier, quite soon after her accession, Elizabeth had appointed as heir to the throne her nephew, Karl Peter-Ulrich, Duke of Holstein, the son of her sister Anna Petrovna, Duchess of Holstein. Peter, then fourteen, had been brought to Russia in 1742, received into the Orthodox Church as Grand Duke Peter, and publicly proclaimed heir to the throne. On the recommendation of Frederick the Great of Prussia, then still an ally, he had been married three years later to the sixteen-year-old Princess Sophia Augusta of Anhalt-Zerbst, another German princess who had in her turn been received into the Orthodox Church and rebaptized Catherine Alekseyevna.

Peter Ulrich, who now ascended the throne as Peter III, and at once made peace with Prussia, was both physically and intellectually a poor specimen. He was drunk for much of the time and, though a grandson of Peter the Great, felt himself a German at heart with no love for Russia or the Russians. His dominating passion was a fanatical admiration for Frederick I of Prussia; what is more, he said so to anyone who cared to listen and even wore Prussian decorations in preference to Russian. His bride Catherine, on the other hand, though not strictly beautiful, was bursting with charm, shrewdness, energy and intelligence and, though German to the core, quickly transformed herself into an enthusiastic Russian. Before long she had become one of the liveliest characters at Court, joining enthusiastically in every kind of activity and intrigue. Indeed for a time she was even in the pay of the British Ambassador, Sir Charles Hanbury-Williams. In 1754 she had produced a son, the Grand Duke Paul, whose paternity (on which depended the subsequent legitimacy of the House of Romanov) has always been a matter for conjecture. The view of many experts, including Catherine herself, was that Paul was the son of Prince Sergei Saltykov, the first of her countless lovers, but as he grew older, the little Grand Duke, whose mother disliked him intensely, was found to bear a confusing resemblance to his official father.

The latter was universally detested. His infatuation for Frederick

Stroganov Palace, Leningrad

the Great, his decision to make peace with Prussia just as Russia was winning the war, and his manifest enthusiasm for all things German were regarded as disgraceful. So was his equally evident distaste for everything Russian. Among the guards, whom he jeered at as Janissaries, the nobles and the Orthodox clergy he made innumerable enemies. He also soon began to talk of divorcing his wife and marrying his mistress. This suited no one. A conspiracy was accordingly hatched to overthrow him and put his wife on the throne in his place, a conspiracy in which, needless to say, Catherine herself played a prominent part. In this she was ably supported by her latest lover, Count Grigori Orlov, to whom she had borne a son two months earlier, and by his four enterprising brothers, all, like him, serving officers in the Imperial Guards.

Soon all necessary preparations had been made and on the morning of 28 June 1762 Catherine left the Palace of Peterhof outside St Petersburg, where she had been living apart from her husband, and presented herself to the Izmailovski and Semyonovski Guards. Prompted by the brothers Orlov, these readily swore allegiance to her, after which she was duly proclaimed Empress and Autocrat by the Archbishop of Novgorod. A vast body of soldiery now gathered in front of the Winter Palace. This greatly assisted the dignitaries within to make up their minds; a change of sovereign was found generally acceptable; and that same evening the new Empress, a splendid figure in Guards uniform and carrying a drawn sword, marched against her husband at the head of her troops.

For Peter, who had been living by himself at Oranienbaum, some twenty-five miles outside the capital, the situation was already as good as lost. He hesitated, stayed where he was, was put under arrest by the Orlovs, and on the following day abdicated. He was then removed to a neighbouring estate, where a few days later he died, strangled in all probability by Grigori Orlov's brother Aleksei, though Catherine, in her official announcement of the country's loss, attributed his demise to a haemorrhage or colic.

The minor German princess who at the age of thirty-six now assumed personal control of the Russian Empire was by any standards a remarkable woman. In addition to immense dynamism and strength of character and considerable political acumen, she possessed sufficient intellectual attainments to make her a welcome correspondent for Monsieur de Voltaire himself, though one suspects that her exalted rank may also have weighed with the great philosopher. There was another thing. Whatever may have been the calculations of those who had helped bring her to the throne, she possessed to a high degree the gift of knowing how to use able men for her own ends rather than, like her immediate predecessors, be used by them.

Having regard to the manner of her accession, however, Catherine was bound at first to take into account the likes and dislikes of the nobles who had brought her to power and whose position had in one way or another been considerably strengthened during the past thirty-odd years. During his short reign her husband had, by the Manifesto of 1762, formally proclaimed the emancipation of the nobility. These were now statutorily freed from the obligations for military and every other kind of service imposed on them by Peter the Great and, to all intents and purposes, now owned their land unconditionally. Logically, in so far as logic is relevant in the present context, this measure should have been followed by the emancipation of the serfs. But Catherine, despite the liberal principles she had learned from Voltaire and the other French philosophers, had no intention of taking such an impolitic step or of otherwise alienating the nobles. It would in any case not have been like her to allow theory or logic to interfere with practice. Her liberalism was largely an intellectual exercise. Far from emancipating the serfs, she now substantially increased the power of the nobles over their peasants. Indeed, the burden of serfdom was never more intolerable than during her reign, being extended, by the enormous grants of state land she had made to her favourites and others, to large areas of the Ukraine, the country of the Don and the Northern Caucasus.

In a rather half-hearted attempt to win the favour of the Church, she was believed for a while to be thinking of revoking another of her husband's decrees, secularizing Church property, but in fact ended up by confiscating it instead. Meanwhile one of her most serious preoccupations had disappeared when the unfortunate Ivan VI, still regarded by some as the rightful Tsar, was, after a lifetime in prison, conveniently murdered by his gaolers in his cell in the fortress of Schlüsselberg, while trying, or so it was said, to escape.

A favourite pursuit of the French philosophers of the period was the elaboration of ideal constitutions and systems of government, which, though unlikely to be put to any practical use, could be said to embody all the most fashionably rational and enlightened principles of the day. For Catherine on her new-found throne the temptation to join the ranks of the constitution-makers was irresistible. For more than a year, to the dismay of her closest advisers, she addressed herself to the task of drawing up a *Nakaz* or *Instruction*, based largely on Montesquieu's *Esprit des Lois* and intended for the use of a Legislative Commission which she summoned to Moscow in 1766 with instructions to review and recast the country's constitution and legal and administrative systems. When completed, her *Instruction* proved an impressive document, both stylistically and by the humanity and liberalism of the sentiments which it expressed. On one point, however, it was quite clear: the need to retain the autocratic character of the Russian system of government. The Commission, which consisted of five or six hundred delegates from all walks of life (except the serfs), held in a year and a half more than two hundred sessions and discussed every conceivable subject, relevant and irrelevant, without, however, arriving at any concrete conclusions. Finally, in 1769, before it had had time to make any firm recommendations, its labours were brought to an end by the outbreak of war with Turkey.

Russia's conflict with Turkey, of which the first phase was to last for five years, was part of a wider and extremely complicated pattern of international relationships, largely revolving around the problem of Poland. Poland, still so powerful barely a century before, was by this time fast approaching the end of its existence as an independent country, her affairs having been reduced, by the irresponsibility and constant bickering of its nobles and by repeated outside interference, to a state of total confusion. Old King Augustus III, himself a Russian nominee, had died in 1763 and had been succeeded, at Catherine's suggestion, by one of her former lovers, Count Stanislas Poniatowski, who, on being duly elected King of Poland by the Diet, assumed the style of Augustus IV. Although on this occasion it somehow achieved unanimity, the Diet had as a general rule become unworkable. One reason for this was the so-called *liberum veto*, under which any one member had the power to block any legislative measure. This made it in practice highly improbable that any given measure, good or bad, would ever reach the statute book.

For both Catherine and Frederick II of Prussia, who of late had come closer together, the continued discrimination practised by the Catholic Poles against their Orthodox and Protestant subjects and the Diet's stubborn refusal to remedy this provided an ever-present pretext for intervention in Polish affairs. In 1767 the despatch of a Russian military force to Warsaw and the arrest and removal to Russia of several members of the Diet produced, it is true, some concessions. It also led to the establishment of what amounted to a Russian protectorate over Poland under a Special Convention signed by the two countries in 1768. But even this did not produce the desired result. On the one hand, Catholic Confederates, formed for the defence of 'Faith and Liberty' and enjoying both French and Austrian support, made things hotter than ever for both Protestants and Orthodox, while at the same time bands of Orthodox brigands known as *Haidamaks* roamed the country, looting and burning and murdering any Catholic priests or nobles they could lay hands on. To confuse matters still further, not only Russian, but Prussian and Austrian troops now entered Poland on the pretext of restoring order.

It was at this moment, in 1768, that Turkey, egged on by her ally France, took advantage of Russia's involvement in Poland to declare war on her. Poland and Turkey at this time still had a common border in what is now the Ukraine, and Russian military action against Polish insurgents in the frontier area provided an adequate pretext for their action.

For Catherine, who had long had designs on the Sultan's European territories, whose hands were conveniently free in the West and who was by now bored with her Legislative Commission, the prospect of war with Turkey was not unwelcome. The campaign began with a series of Russian victories. Catherine's immediate aim was to gain control of Turkey's Danubian provinces with their largely Christian and Orthodox population. By the autumn of 1769 the Russian Army of the Dniester, led by Count Rumiantsev, had successfully opened up the way to the Danube and beyond, penetrating as far as the Balkan Mountains. Meanwhile the Russian navy, commanded by Peter III's probable murderer, Count Aleksei Orlov, had made its way from the Baltic to the Mediterranean and, after first stirring up revolt in the Peloponnese, had on 6 July 1770, under Admiral Elphinstone, a Scot in the Russian service, utterly destroyed the Turkish fleet in an engagement in the Bay of Chesme. At the same time another Russian army under Prince Dolgoruki had conquered the Crimea.

By 1774 the Turks had had enough of the war, the Russians likewise, and in July of that year a treaty of peace was signed between them at Kutchuk Kainardji. This gave their independence to the Crimean Tartars and to all other Tartars living on the shores of the Black Sea and the Sea of Azov, in other words, prepared the way for a Russian annexation of the areas in question. In addition to a heavy indemnity, Russia was also given Azov, the Straits of Kerch and the mouths of the Don, the Dnieper and the Bug, as well as the freedom of the Black Sea for its merchant vessels and right of access to the Aegean. Finally, and most significantly for the future, the Sultan formally recognized Russia's interest in the religious rights of his Christian subjects.

After considerable bargaining between the powers involved, a solution had also been reached in Poland. With the capture of Cracow by the Russian General Suvorov, Polish Confederate resistance had come to an end. But neither Russians, Austrians nor Prussians had withdrawn their troops from Poland. On the contrary, they had deliberately kept them there, at the same time demanding reparations for their losses and for the inconvenience to which they had been put. The reparations were in the event territorial. Under treaties signed in St Petersburg in the summer of 1772 Prussia took Pomerania and the area lying between Prussia and Brandenburg; Austria, Galicia; and Russia most of what is now White Russia. By what became known as the First Partition of Poland Catherine was, even so, left with the feeling that she had not had her fair share of the spoils.

But this was by no means the Empress's only worry. On the home front she was now facing the worst crisis of her reign. At the heart of the trouble was, once again, the deep discontent of the serf population, whose life had of late grown ever more unbearable. To make matters worse, an epidemic had broken out in 1771 which, from the Turkish front, quickly spread to central Russia. In Moscow this soon brought the life of the city almost to a standstill. In their panic the population refused to take any kind of precautions, gathering in vast crowds to pray before a favourite icon of the Virgin near the Kremlin. To stop the spread of infection, Archbishop Ambrose had the icon removed. At this the crowd set upon him and killed him and began to plunder the Kremlin. Before order could be restored, many lives were lost. And still the epidemic spread, bringing with it even worse disorder.

Violence in the meantime had flared up elsewhere. In 1771 a

rebellion broke out among the Ural Cossacks. Ruthlessly suppressed, it broke out again two years later. By this time the Cossacks
had found a leader, one Emelian Pugachov, a roving Don Cossack,
who in the summer of 1773, while Catherine was involved in Turkey and Poland, suddenly appeared on the Ural River, proclaiming
to all who cared to listen that he was her late husband Tsar Peter
III, come to fight against his wicked wife, and flying the flag of Holstein over the Cossack camp where he now held court. A born
leader, he had soon gathered round him a force of 25,000 men,
drawn from rebellious Cossacks, fugitive serfs, religious dissenters
and other discontented elements, not to mention a sprinkling of
Kazakh and Kirghiz tribesmen from the steppes, their armament
being for the most part taken from the troops sent against them.

Having captured several forts along the Ural River, Pugachov
next laid siege to the town of Orenburg, the administrative centre
of the region. Moving rapidly from point to point in true guerrilla
fashion, he appeared soon after in the Volga valley, sacking towns
and villages, burning manor-houses, and killing all the officers,
officials, merchants, priests and landowners he could find.
Wherever he went new recruits flocked to join him. The rising was
on a far larger scale than any that had preceded it.

The government had by now become thoroughly alarmed and
a substantial force was sent to crush Pugachov before it was too
late. Its commander succeeded in driving the insurgents back to
the Ural River. But, after lying low through the winter, Pugachov
re-emerged in the spring of 1774, rested and refreshed and ready
to resume operations with renewed vigour. Soon he had taken Saratov, invested Kazan, reached Nizhni Novgorod and was threatening Moscow itself.

This time Catherine, seriously disturbed, took drastic action.
Recalling Alexander Suvorov, one of her most successful generals,
from the Turkish front, she sent him against the insurgents in the
summer of 1774 at the head of a large force of picked troops. Closing in methodically on the insurgents, Suvorov inflicted savage reprisals on all who had helped them or been in any way concerned
in the rising. Again, in the face of greatly superior strength, Pugachov fell back on the Ural River. But this time the odds against
him were too great. Suvorov gave him no respite and, deserted by
most of his followers, he was eventually hunted down and finally
betrayed to his pursuers by one of his own men. After being

brought to Moscow in triumph in an iron cage, he was subjected to prolonged torture and in January 1775 publicly dismembered.

Meanwhile throughout the countryside the government's reprisals continued against all those who had taken the smallest part in the rising. Whole villages were razed to the ground and soon gallows with their dangling corpses stood everywhere as a reminder to the peasantry of the dangers of sedition. Pugachov's rising and the terrible reprisals that followed it left behind them a legacy of pent-up bitterness and hatred which nothing could eradicate and which were only to find their full expression a century and a half later. The rising also marked the end of their independence for the free Cossacks, who were now purged and reorganized under regular officers as a frontier militia.

The amply demonstrated need for a more effective system of internal security lay behind the far-reaching reform of local government upon which Catherine now embarked with the help of her latest lover, Prince Grigori Potyomkin. Fifty Governments, each with a population of between 300,000 and 400,000 and subdivided into a dozen or so smaller Districts, replaced the much larger and more unwieldy units left by Peter the Great. The fifty Governors were invested with far-reaching powers, while Governors-General, representing the Crown and directly responsible to the Senate, were put at the head of groups of two or three contiguous Governments. This system, firmly resting as it did on the alliance of the Crown with the nobles, who in practice were almost exclusively responsible for local administration, provided a solid, if rigid, basis for the autocracy and was to endure almost unaltered until 1917.

These initial measures of reform were in due course followed and supplemented by the issue in 1785 of a renewed Charter of the Nobility, giving the nobles corporate status as an officially recognized ruling class, confirming the extensive privileges and exemptions which they had won since the death of Peter the Great, and officially granting them, amongst other things, the right to travel abroad. At the same time the Empress promulgated a corresponding, though considerably less significant, Charter of the Towns. Any thought she might ever have had of emancipating or otherwise improving the lot of the twenty million or so serfs, who accounted for considerably more than half the total population of thirty-six million, had been finally driven from her head by Pugachov's rebellion.

But, serious as they were, Catherine did not for a moment allow these internal preoccupations to interfere with her far-flung ambitions in the field of foreign affairs. Here she showed herself a worthy successor to Peter the Great, for whom she felt a carefully fostered affinity and to whom she erected a monumental equestrian statue on the banks of the Neva. By the Peace of Kutchuk Kainardji she had secured much of the rich, grain-producing Black Sea steppe. To this she gave the name of New Russia and as its first Viceroy appointed her lover Prince Potyomkin, with his seat in a new capital city which he named in her honour Ekaterinoslav. Having thus secured her base, the Empress next turned her attention to a concept which had long attracted her: the creation of a revived Byzantine Empire in the Balkans under Russian control and with, as its capital, a Russian-held Constantinople. This plan, which she now elaborated with Potyomkin's help, became known as her Greek Project. Meanwhile, as a first step, she gave to her younger grandson the name of Constantine.

Following the death of Maria-Theresa of Austria and the accession to the Austrian throne of the Emperor Joseph II, friendship with Austria had effectively replaced Catherine's earlier alliance with Prussia. This had further strengthened her position with regard to Turkey. In 1783, taking prompt advantage of some internal Tartar dispute, she had actually annexed the Crimea. In view, however, of Austria's own ambitions in the Balkans it now became necessary for her, as far as that area was concerned, to carry with her new-found ally, the Emperor Joseph.

Catherine chose the most flamboyant method she could devise of demonstrating their mutual friendship. Early in 1787 she set out on a spectacular state visit to her new southern territories and to their Viceroy, Prince Potyomkin, who, though no longer her lover (their liaison, which even went to the length of a secret marriage, had only lasted a couple of years), was still in great good favour with her. On the Dnieper, Catherine was joined by another former lover, Stanislas Poniatowski, since 1763 King Augustus IV of Poland, and by the Emperor Joseph himself. After which the three sovereigns and their suites continued their joint progress in tremendous state.

The Viceroy, needless to say, was determined to impress his imperial guests and had devised for them a succession of elaborate entertainments and displays. He had in fact done much for New Russia during his viceroyalty, populating the recently annexed territories with heavily subsidized settlers from further north, providing up-to-date agricultural instruction and advice and making generous grants of land to Russian nobles who had then moved south with their serfs. The results of these impressive achievements he now proudly presented to his visitors, covering up any possible short-comings by creating along their route what have passed into history as 'Potyomkin villages', a typical example of *pokazuka*, as the Russians themselves quite openly call their not infrequent attempts at window-dressing. From start to finish Catherine saw nothing but streets of tidy, freshly whitewashed cottages and rows of happy smiling faces, loyally welcoming their Empress. But there was also a hard core of reality. At Kherson and Nikolayev Potyomkin had built forts and shipyards and at Sebastopol in the Crimea, annexed by Russia four years earlier, he had already established a naval base. Catherine's new friends were left in no doubt whatever as to Russia's naval strength in the Black Sea. Nor, for that matter, were the Turks, who had reluctantly surrendered all these rich assets to Russia twelve years earlier. They took the Empress's tour as an act of deliberate provocation (which was how they were intended to take it) and in September 1787, before she had even completed her journey, the Sultan declared war on both Russia and Austria.

It had been Catherine's intention that her Greek Project should now be put into effect. Once war had been declared, her army, supported and supplied by her Black Sea Fleet, was to sweep in triumph through the Balkans to Constantinople. But, as so often happens, things did not go entirely to plan. Unexpectedly the Turks more than held their own against the Austrians and Russians; a storm destroyed the Russian Black Sea Fleet; Potyomkin showed signs of losing heart; the Russian advance was held up for a year and a half by the Turks' stubborn defence of Ochakov on the Black Sea; and in the end this fortress was only taken at enormous cost to the Russians.

General Suvorov himself now assumed command and things began to go better. In 1790, though again at enormous cost, he stormed the great Turkish fortress of Ismail on the Danube and gained control of the main river crossings. By this time the Russian fleet had recovered from the disaster which had overtaken it and was again at sea, operating in close support of the army. For a time it seemed as though Suvorov might reach Constantinople. But by now Russia was exhausted; the Austrians had already concluded a separate peace; and the Turks, for their part, were only too glad to come to terms. By the Treaty of Jassy, signed in January 1792, Russia made do with Ochakov, the Black Sea littoral between the Bug and the Dniester, and formal recognition by Turkey of Russia's right to the Crimea.

For the time being there was no more talk of Catherine's Greek Project, though its place in her fertile imagination was soon to be taken by an even more grandiose Eastern Project, evolved by her latest lover, Count Platon Zubov. Under this ambitious plan the Russians were to strike through Persia at the Indian sub-continent, at the same time closing in on the Dardanelles by a simultaneous pincer-movement through Anatolia and the Balkans. For the present, however, it remained a plan.

More immediately, Poland held the promise of further territorial gains for Russia. In 1791 the adoption by the Polish Diet of a new and liberal constitution, influenced, it was alleged, by subversive ideas from France, since 1789 in the throes of revolution, provided a pretext for Russian intervention, at the pressing invitation, not unnaturally, of the pro-Russian faction. In May 1792 a Russian army occupied Warsaw. Simultaneously the Prussians occupied western Poland. And in 1793 the Second Partition of Poland, which in effect reduced what was left of that unfortunate country to a Russian dependency, was given the stamp of legality.

It was separated by only two years from the Third and, for the time being, final Partition. In 1794 a national insurrection, led by the Polish patriot, Tadeusz Kosciuszko, drove the Russian army of occupation out of Warsaw, at the same time inflicting heavy casualties on it. Yet again General Suvorov was sent for. Soon Kosciuszko had been defeated, Warsaw re-occupied by the Russians and a large part of the civilian population massacred. Under the partition of 1795, Prussia took the Polish territories lying between the Niemen and the Vistula, including Warsaw; Austria was given Cracow and Lublin; while Russia received the largest share of all, namely Courland and the remainder of Lithuania. As a country, Poland had ceased to exist.

Count Platon Zubov, twenty-two to her sixty-one and the last of Catherine's lovers, was anything but a good influence. Not only did he dream up wildly ambitious schemes, of which the Eastern Project was only one example. He also encouraged the Empress in the further measures of repression with which she had reacted to the French Revolution, a revolution in part brought about, ironically enough, by her one-time friends, the *philosophes*. Worse still, he went out of his way to poison the already strained relations between Catherine and her son Paul.

Having, on her husband's death thirty-four years earlier, usurped the throne which should by right have been Paul's, Catherine was now planning once more to exclude her son from the succession by nominating his son Alexander as her direct heir. But on 17 November 1796, before she could implement this latest intention, death overtook her at the age of sixty-eight and Paul, whom she had regarded, not without reason, as hopelessly incapable, became, in his turn, Tsar of All Russia.

Almost thirty years earlier, in 1767, the Legislative Commission had bestowed on Catherine, soon after she came to the throne, the title of 'the Great'. Whatever view one takes of her achievements, and there is room for more than one, it cannot be denied that her reign, in which she dominated the scene more than most monarchs, marked an important stage in Russia's rise to greatness. Under her auspices, the civilizing process, the opening-up of Russia to outside influence, begun under Peter the Great, was continued. But Catherine, unlike Peter, was no revolutionary. The advanced ideas she favoured at her accession were in fact never put into effect and by the end of her reign, following Pugachov's rising and the French Revolution, had become so abhorrent to her and to those around her that her own famous liberal *Instruction* of 1776 was in the end actually banned by the Imperial Censor. Her reforms, and in particular her reform of local administration, while possessing certain practical advantages, were in no sense original. As for the future, by refusing to face the problem of serfdom and leaving the position of the serfs worse than she found it, she bequeathed to her successors what can best be described as a time-bomb.

No less disquieting, in the long term, was the change that had come about in the status and standing of the aristocracy. By the Manifesto of 1762 and more still by the Charter of 1785 the nobles had been exempted from the greater part of their duties and obligations towards the state. But as the poet Pushkin, himself a noble, was so pertinently to explain, this is something they should in fact have regretted rather than welcomed. For now they lacked, even more than before, any solid basis for their authority, were more dependent than ever on the state for their position, provided a more tempting target than ever for the discontented and were further off than ever from constituting a proper ruling class. They, it is true, rather than the Emperor or the Empress now officially owned their own land (and the serfs who worked it). But, as Professor Pipes* has so rightly pointed out, this separation between authority exercised as sovereignty and authority exercised as ownership had come too late and too imperfectly to give them the resilience and the independence of a locally based hereditary ruling class. Worse still, with the Westernization of the Court and aristocracy, a deeper chasm than ever had been set between the aristocracy and the Russian people as a whole, between the glittering Court in St Petersburg and those 'dark masses' they bought and sold like cattle and who, in so far as they looked to anyone for salvation, looked, not to the nobles, but curiously enough to the Tsar as a possible protector and friend.

Catherine's greatness, if greatness it was, lay rather in her irrepressible, abounding, Teutonic energy, energy which stamped her mark on the life and style of her time, at any rate where the Court and nobles were concerned, which stirred up, if only to smack it down again, the intellectual life of the country, which made St Petersburg, though at enormous cost, one of the most magnificent capitals in Europe, and which in the field of foreign affairs continued, though again at heavy cost, the larger-than-life ambitions and aspirations of Peter the Great and brought Russia more extensive territorial gains than under any sovereign since Ivan the Terrible.

* P. Pipes, *Russia under the Old Regime* (London, 1974).

# 6 *Winds of Change*

PAUL, who now came to the throne at the age of forty-two, had had a strange, sad upbringing. His father, if Peter III was indeed his father, had been murdered at his mother's behest when he was eight. Thereafter Catherine had seen as little of him as possible, deliberately excluding him from her life, excluding him from public affairs, seeking to exclude him, as he must soon have realized, from the throne. Very odd-looking and mentally far from normal, he was slighted or ignored by his mother's succession of lovers. Of late he had taken to spending more and more time in the seclusion of Gachina and Pavlovsk, his estates outside the capital. With the years, Maria Fyodorovna, the German princess to whom his mother had married him, an active, affectionate, intelligent woman, found his sudden outbursts of rage ever harder to avert or control. For his eldest son, Alexander, he felt a well-merited and heartily reciprocated distrust.

His first act of state on coming to the throne was vividly symbolic of the hatred he had felt for his mother and of his deep-seated desire to reverse, as far as this was possible, every one of her policies and actions. On his orders, his father's body was now exhumed from its resting-place in the monastery of Alexander Nevski and carried in procession through the streets in its coffin to be laid next to that of his mother in the Cathedral of St Peter and St Paul. Behind it walked Peter's presumed murderer, Count Aleksei Orlov, carrying the Imperial Crown. As for Prince Potyomkin, who had died four or five years earlier, his body was, on the Tsar's instructions, disinterred and thrown unceremoniously into the common pit.

As a matter of practical politics, Paul found it harder than he had expected to undo everything his mother had achieved in the past thirty-four years. He dismissed, it is true, a few of Catherine's favourites and brought back from exile some of those she had dis-

graced. He replaced the army's comfortable old uniforms by uncomfortable new, Prussian-style uniforms. He reintroduced corporal punishment for the nobility. He restored to the serfs the right
of taking the oath of allegiance to the Crown. He considered introducing various other reforms. But he very soon made, or, in his
confused state of mind, half-made, one very important discovery.
It was not in practice possible for him to alienate the aristocracy
without simultaneously undermining his own position. The nobles,
in other words, were by now an essential support of the autocracy
and needed to be treated accordingly.

Paul's original intention on coming to the throne had been to
keep Russia out of foreign wars. Though a martinet on the parade
ground, he had no desire for military glory. His subjects, he
announced, would have a 'much-needed and deserved rest'. But
again things did not work out as he intended. His late mother's bug-
bear, the French Revolution, with, behind it, the added impetus
of Napoleon Bonaparte, was by now spreading its tentacles all over
Europe. Holland, Belgium, Switzerland, a large part of Germany
and most of Italy had already been conquered by the armies of
the Revolution and now the French were threatening Egypt and
even stirring up the Polish patriots against their oppressors. For
a time Paul held back, but in 1798 came the news that the French
had seized Malta (for whose Knights, strangely enough, he felt a
special affinity and responsibility) and in 1799, yielding to British
persuasion, he joined the Second Coalition and despatched a Russian army under General Suvorov (especially recalled from exile for
the purpose) to northern Italy to help the Austrians, whose hold
on that area was seriously imperilled.

Suvorov, who was over seventy and whose eccentricity by now
amounted almost to dementia but whose troops adored him all the
more for it, started his campaign at Verona. Russian victory now
followed Russian victory in brilliant succession: Cassano, the
capture of Milan, the action on the River Trebbia, the blood-bath
of Novi, each a more shattering blow to the revolutionary forces
of France. In a few months the great strategist had driven the
French out of Italy and was ready to invade France itself. But
Paul's Austrian allies had other views. Their Imperial War Council
insisted that the French should first be driven from Switzerland.
With the limited forces at his disposal the task imposed on Suvorov
was an impossible one. But his march across the St Gotthard Pass

and through Switzerland, the dauntless courage with which his troops fought off French attacks in the teeth of overwhelming odds and the consummate skill with which, without suffering a single defeat, he ultimately carried his whole force by way of Lake Constance to safety in Germany can be counted amongst the greatest triumphs of Russian arms.

For what had nevertheless been a set-back for the Alliance and had left the French still in possession of Switzerland, Paul, not unreasonably, blamed the Austrians. In the Low Countries, meanwhile, another Russian expeditionary force had been badly let down by the British under the Grand Old Duke of York, that epitome of Hanoverian denseness, who, having marched his men to the top of the hill, marched them down again, without regard for his Russian allies or indeed for the overall strategic concept.

Disgusted with both his allies, Paul now withdrew from the coalition. Indeed, so incensed was he against the British that, having resumed relations with France in February 1801, he now, after mutual consultation with Napoleon (by this time First Consul), instructed a force of 25,000 Cossacks to invade British India, proceeding (in the time-hallowed military phrase) by way of Khiva and Bokhara. 'Make straight for the Indus and the Ganges,' he wrote. 'I enclose,' he added in a letter to the commanding general, 'all the maps I have. My maps only reach as far as Khiva and the Amu Darya. Beyond that, it is your affair to get information as far as the English settlements.'

But by this time Paul's long-suffering subjects – at any rate the ones that mattered – had had enough. He was becoming more and more unbalanced. The utter arbitrariness with which arrests, dismissals and punishments of one kind or another were meted out had begun to pall. 'The fact is,' reported the British Ambassador, 'that the Emperor is literally not in his senses.' Despite relatively cautious beginnings, he had in the end alienated the aristocracy. He had decreed that they could once again be flogged and branded and have their nostrils slit, just like anyone else. 'In Russia,' he explained to the Swedish Ambassador, 'only he is great with whom I speak, and only while I am speaking to him.' The cessation of trade with Great Britain, the principal export market for the produce of their estates, struck the nobles as intolerable; the prospect of war with the British as even worse. The Emperor, they could now see, was really too mad to be allowed to reign. A plot was hatched to dethrone him. It had, perhaps not unnaturally, the enthusiastic support of the British Ambassador, Sir Charles Whitworth, who was later raised to the peerage for his part in it and for other public services. It also had the support of Paul's eldest son and heir, the Tsarevich Alexander, a tall, good-looking, smoothly charming young man.

Increasingly and justifiably distrustful of those around him, Paul had by this time taken up residence in the fortress-like Michael Castle. He had complete confidence in one man only, Count Peter Pahlen, the Military Governor of St Petersburg and Commander of the Palace Guard. But it was Count Pahlen, as it happened, who had personally hatched the plot against him and who, on 23 March 1801, betraying the trust placed in him, admitted the conspirators to the Palace and to the Imperial presence. The date for the execution of their plans had been chosen by the Tsarevich Alexander, who was particularly anxious that it should take place on a night when his own regiment, the Semyonovski Guards, were on duty.

What exactly happened on the night in question is not altogether clear. It is known that the conspirators had been drinking heavily to nerve themselves for whatever ordeal lay ahead of them. It is said by some that they first invited the Emperor to abdicate. What is certain is that, before leaving, they strangled him with an officer's scarf belonging to one of their number and then finished him off with a heavy malachite paperweight. '*En Russie*,' observed Madame de Staël, on learning of this, '*le gouvernement est un despotisme mitigé par la strangulation.*'

According to Professor Platonov, 'Paul's death took Alexander by surprise.' This is not altogether easy to believe, but, if true, sets yet another question-mark over the mental processes of the 'handsome and highly gifted youth' who at the age of twenty-four now ascended the throne of All the Russias and who, from his generally ambiguous and equivocal attitude, was soon to become known as the 'Enigmatic Tsar'.

Catherine had taken great care to see that her grandson, and, as she hoped, successor, received the sort of education she considered suitable for an enlightened monarch. She herself had issued a set of instructions for the Prince's preceptors, General Nikolai Ivanovich Saltykov (the younger brother of her first lover) and Frédéric-César La Harpe, a high-minded Swiss of known liberal and republican proclivities. Alexander, she prescribed, was to be trained 'in accordance with the laws of reason and the principles of virtue'. And we are told (again by Professor Platonov) that he and La Harpe looked forward to the time when serfdom would be abolished and Russia could enjoy a democratic form of government.

Good-looking and intelligent, with a slight limp and a charming, gentle, rather diffident manner, Alexander, finding himself in a difficult position between his half-mad father and his overwhelming and possessive grandmother, both of whom he treated with equal deference, had learned early in life to conceal his true thoughts. He was to find this a useful knack. From his father's untimely end, to which, as he preferred to forget, he had made his own modest contribution, he had learned another useful precept: never trust anyone.

And now his father's body, with its unpleasantly distorted features, had been discreetly removed from the Imperial Apartments in the Michael Castle and, after a suitably splendid ceremony, hurriedly committed to its sarcophagus in the Cathedral of St Peter and St Paul; and Alexander himself, after this briefly distasteful interlude, had, in accordance with his late grandmother's wishes, duly assumed, as Alexander I, the role of autocrat. For him the Michael Castle had unpleasant associations. With his attractive young wife (he, too, had been married by his grandmother at sixteen to a suitable German princess) he lost no time in moving out of its doom-laden atmosphere into the brighter, more cheerful Winter Palace, built fifty years earlier in the agreeably florid style favoured by his fun-loving great-aunt Elizabeth on the banks of the swift-flowing Neva.

Steeped in liberal and romantic ideas, the new Tsar seems, like his father before him, to have set out with the praiseworthy purpose of undoing some of the harm done by his immediate predecessor. But, like his father, and, for that matter, his grandmother, he soon found that there was a limit to what could be done without imperilling the autocracy. And the autocracy, after all, was what mattered. For ten or twelve years much patient effort was put into devising a new and more democratic constitution. But in the end Speranski, the chief constitution-maker, was accused of treasonable relations with the French and banished to Perm and the only changes actually made were the substitution of regular Ministries for the existing Colleges and the establishment of a State Soviet or Council directly responsible to the Tsar, both useful but neither of them very radical reforms, especially as the Ministers were appointed and could be summarily dismissed by the Tsar while the function of the State Soviet was purely consultative.

In foreign affairs Alexander felt that his father had over-reacted to the inevitable limitations of the alliance with Austria and Great Britain. On coming to the throne he resumed relations with Austria. He also at once gave orders for a courier to be sent after the 25,000 Don Cossacks whom his father had despatched to conquer British India, with orders for them to come back. Fortunately, by the time the courier caught up with them, they had not covered more than a thousand miles, having by now reached Orenburg on the fringes of Central Asia. But even so their journey, undertaken without proper maps, in the dead of winter, had been a painful one and, just on the way there, they had by one means or another lost a surprisingly high proportion of their total strength. At the same time the Tsar also cancelled his father's plan for the invasion of England, fortunately still only in embryo.

This change of policy on Alexander's part not unnaturally displeased Napoleon and, though for the time being the two countries remained on superficially friendly terms, it could only be a matter of time before the scale of France's conquests in Europe and the ascendancy it was establishing there made the resumption of hostilities between them inevitable.

In 1805 Russia, with Austria and Great Britain, joined the Third Coalition and Alexander (who shared his father's predilection for uniforms and parades) despatched an army under General Michael Kutusov to Central Europe to join his new allies. By the time they got there in October, Napoleon had heavily defeated the Austrians at Ulm. Kutusov accordingly withdrew to the north of Vienna, which in November was occupied by the French. Alexander, however, now ordered him to engage the enemy nonetheless. Reluctantly Kutusov did so and early in December was, with the Austrians, disastrously defeated at Austerlitz. After which the Austrians made peace and the Russians withdrew in confusion to Russia.

In July 1806 Alexander hopefully concluded an alliance with Frederick William III of Prussia. But in October 1806, before the allies could join forces, Napoleon routed the Prussians at Jena and Auerstädt and occupied Berlin and eastern Prussia as far as the Vistula. At Eylau the Russians managed to hold their own, but in

June 1807 they were badly beaten at Friedland and once again driven back to their own country, leaving the whole of Prussia in French hands.

It was now, in the summer of 1807, under the shadow of this Russian defeat, that Napoleon and Alexander met near Tilsit, alone on a raft in the middle of the River Niemen, to discuss peace terms. The idea of the two Emperors meeting in these dramatic circumstances to divide the world between them greatly appealed to the romantic side of Alexander's character. The alliance which at Alexander's suggestion they now concluded, was, however, not unnaturally, heavily weighted in France's favour, carving up Prussia and recreating Poland under the guise of a Grand Duchy of Warsaw. Both powers agreed, too, to joint action against France's old adversary Britain. From now onwards, it was decided, France would control Western Europe, while Russia dominated Eastern Europe. Russia would in particular be given a free hand in regard to Sweden and Turkey – a provision which Alexander quickly put to good use, taking Finland from Sweden and despatching Kutusov to launch an attack on Turkey's European possessions which quickly led to the Russian annexation of Bessarabia. In 1809 Alexander even went so far as to send Russian troops to fight against his former Austrian allies.

It was for many years a mystery how particulars of the secret meeting of the two Emperors reached Russia's former ally, Great Britain, now left fighting on alone, as quickly as they did. It is now believed, however, that during the talks old Count Simon Vorontsov, for many years Russian Ambassador to the Court of St James's and a rabid Anglophile, was actually sitting under the raft with his legs dangling in the water, listening to every word of the conversation, which he then promply related to his friends in London.

The Franco-Russian alliance was, in the nature of things, not likely to last. Within two or three years Alexander had begun to realize his mistake, while Napoleon, for his part, was actually preparing to invade Russia. The consequences of Napoleon's Russian campaign were to be immeasurable, not only for Napoleon, but for Russia and above all for the Russian people. Though the French attack did not take the Russians entirely by surprise, it certainly found them inadequately prepared to meet it. In the early summer of 1812 some 200,000 Russian troops under the command of General Barclay de Tolly and Prince P. I. Bagration were spread out over a long front roughly corresponding with the line of the River Niemen. Alexander had his own headquarters at Vilna, a short distance behind the front. No firm course of action had been decided on in case of a French invasion. General Barclay de Tolly, it is true, had put forward a plan of phased disengagement and withdrawal, but this had been rejected by the Tsar and nothing substituted for it.

Napoleon was quick to seize upon the opportunities offered him by the wide dispersal of the Russian forces and by their commanders' lack of any coherent strategy. Attacking in June 1812 without a declaration of war, he crossed the Niemen at Kovno with an army of 600,000 men and made directly for Vilna, thus cutting the Russian army neatly in two. At Vilna, which Alexander had evacuated shortly before, he halted for six weeks to regroup.

Belatedly, Alexander and his General Staff now realized the seriousness of the danger that threatened them. It was decided that the Tsar should return to the capital, while Barclay de Tolly assumed command in the field. For the Russians, divided as they were, a direct confrontation with a resolute and brilliantly led army which outnumbered them three to one was clearly out of the question. Barclay de Tolly accordingly fell back on Vitebsk and Smolensk, at the same time ordering Bagration to do likewise, in the hope of once again joining forces with him. Successfully avoiding any major engagements with the enemy, the two Russian armies then withdrew to Smolensk where they came together according to plan, thus preventing Napoleon from following up his initial advantage.

But this cleverly executed withdrawal met with almost universal disapproval, especially from the Emperor, who from the relative safety of his rear headquarters ordered Barclay de Tolly to stand and fight at Smolensk. This the old general now did, against his better judgement, and a fierce battle ensued in the course of which it became quite clear that the odds against the Russians were still too great. Barclay accordingly evacuated Smolensk and fell back on Moscow. Mortified by these successive Russian withdrawals, the Tsar at once relieved him of his command, replacing him by General Kutusov, whom he had previously banished but whom he now recalled from exile for the occasion.

On 16 August Kutusov, now aged sixty-seven, arrived to take over command of the retreating Russian army. Ten days later he engaged the French in a pitched battle near the village of Borodino, some seventy miles west of Moscow. In this battle 110,000 Russians fought a French army of 130,000. The battle lasted all day, the French seeking, by a series of frenzied charges, to break the Russian line, but succeeding only in pushing it back a few hundred yards. The carnage was appalling, the combined casualties amounting to about a hundred thousand, in other words more than a third of all the troops engaged. Both sides believed that they had won. At nightfall the French withdrew to their camp, leaving the Russians in possession of the battlefield. It had been Kutusov's intention to engage the enemy again next day. But when he found that he had lost half his army, he decided otherwise and resumed his retreat towards Moscow, hotly pursued by the French, who believed that by capturing the old capital they would bring the war to an end.

On reaching the outskirts of Moscow, Kutusov held a council of war. At this it was decided to abandon the city to the enemy. The inhabitants were encouraged to evacuate it while Kutusov continued his withdrawal eastwards.

It is at this stage that the war takes on a different character. 'The Emperor of Russia,' said Count Rostopchin, Governor-General of Moscow, 'will always be formidable in Moscow and terrible in Kazan. But in Tobolsk invincible.' By now even the Tsar had come round to old Barclay de Tolly's way of thinking.

Napoleon entered Moscow on 2 September. He was by this time ready to make peace. A few days later the city was set on fire and almost completely destroyed. Napoleon sought to open negotiations with the Russians. His overtures were rebuffed. Alexander was determined not to make peace so long as a single enemy soldier remained on Russian soil. In this he had the whole-hearted support of the Russian people. From a quarrel between emperors the war had become a people's war, a war of national liberation.

Napoleon's position, as he was soon to realize, left much to be desired. He was a thousand miles from any secure base, in a deserted, burnt-out city. With winter coming on, he lacked both shelter and supplies. The population was hostile. His army had no hope of receiving any reinforcements. Its morale had suffered from the long march, the slaughter of Borodino and the unfriendliness of the people; its discipline, from the opportunities for pillage. The Russians, on the other hand, amongst friends and on their own territory, were growing stronger every day. They now kept near enough to Moscow to hamper any movement by the enemy outside the city itself.

After a month in Moscow, spent partly in the Kremlin and partly in Peter the Great's old palace on the outskirts, Napoleon decided to evacuate the city. His intention was to fall back on Vilna and Smolensk and, after spending the winter there, to resume operations in the spring. The retreat of the Grand Army began in the first half of October. It was to turn into one of the great military disasters of history.

The countryside through which the French withdrew was by now bare of supplies. Though laden with loot, Napoleon's soldiers were under-nourished, thinly clad and poorly shod. Winter, as it sometimes does in Russia, came early that year, adding further to their troubles. As the French retreated, the Russians kept pace with them, small, highly mobile squadrons of cavalry and Cossacks swooping suddenly down on them, guerrilla-fashion, from across the endless expanse of snow-covered plain and disappearing again whence they had come. Left to their fate, wounded men and stragglers froze to death or were finished off by bands of angry peasants glad of a chance to revenge themselves on these invaders of their fatherland.

By the time he reached the River Berezina, late in November, Napoleon had lost almost the whole of his army. Fighting off a Russian attempt to surround what was left of it, he crossed the river and reached Vilna. But Vilna by now had nothing to offer him. Of the Grand Army of 600,000 men with which he had invaded Russia barely six months earlier, less than 20,000 remained. Leaving these survivors to follow as best they could, Napoleon himself hurried on to Paris, bent on rescuing what he could from the wreck of his fortunes.

Now that the last French soldier had been driven from Russian soil, many Russians (including Kutusov himself) thought that the war would soon be over. But the Tsar thought otherwise. This was his finest hour. He saw himself as the liberator not only of Russia but of all Europe from the Corsican upstart. In January 1813 the Russian armies, on his orders, crossed the Niemen in pursuit of the French. At the same time he called on his former allies, Prussia, Austria, Sweden and Great Britain (who for her part had never abandoned the struggle), to join him in a fresh coalition.

Napoleon, meanwhile, had, with unbelievable resilience, raised a new army and in the summer of 1813 again faced his enemies on the Elbe. But the French were by now coming to the end of their tether. After a number of hard-fought engagements in eastern Germany the decisive encounter came at Leipzig in October 1813. The battle, famous as the *Völkerschlacht*, or Battle of the Nations, lasted for four days. At the end of it Napoleon had been defeated and forced to fall back with heavy casualties across the Rhine, leaving Germany free of French troops. In December 1813, Alexander led the Allied advance into France; French resistance quickly collapsed before the overwhelming strength of the Allied armies; and on 31 March 1814 the Tsar and the King of Prussia entered Paris at the head of their victorious armies. On 11 April Napoleon abdicated at Fontainebleau. It was Alexander's moment of triumph. Back in St Petersburg the Holy Synod bestowed on him the title of Alexander the Blessed.

At the Congress of Vienna, interrupted for three months by Napoleon's escape from Elba and the fresh period of uncertainty which ended in his final defeat at Waterloo, the victorious powers met to decide the future of Europe. Here, once more, Alexander assumed a leading role. Tall, good-looking, emotional and enigmatic, with his glittering escort of Cossacks, he was widely acclaimed as the conqueror of Napoleon and saviour of Europe. With time he came to see himself more and more as an instrument of the Divine Will. Under the influence of Julie de Krudener, the seemingly pious widow of a Baltic baron, he was now going through a mystical, bible-reading phase. Indeed it was his idea that the Allied sovereigns should form a Holy Alliance under which their mutual relations were to be governed by 'the supreme truths dictated by the eternal law of God the Saviour', and 'the commandments of love, truth and peace'. They were also to 'render one another aid, support and succour'.

The first question to which the Allies were able to apply these high-sounding principles was the disposal of Poland, which under Napoleon had briefly re-emerged as a Grand Duchy. The problem was found in practice to present no great difficulty. The Tsar got the largest share, undertaking, for what that was worth, to rule over it as a constitutional monarch. Posen went to the King of Prussia and Galicia to the Emperor of Austria. As for the Allies' undertaking to afford each other mutual succour and support, reconfirmed at Troppau in 1820, this was used henceforward to justify the joint suppression throughout Europe of any manifestation of liberal thought or principles and to ensure as far as possible the maintenance everywhere of the status quo.

Nor, though he did a certain amount for education and founded several universities, were Alexander's domestic policies very much more enlightened. Ever since his accession he had been haunted, like his father and grandmother before him, by the bogy of the French Revolution; his subsequent experience of Napoleon had done nothing to reassure him. The reforming zeal and liberal principles imbibed from Frédéric La Harpe were things of a distant past. Already in 1812, Michael Speranski, his relatively liberal Secretary of State, had been sent to Siberia and the greater part of his proposals for a constitution consigned to the scrap-heap. Power now passed more and more into the hands of Count A. A. Arakcheyev, a singularly unpleasant man, who from Military Secretary had become Alexander's closest confidant and adviser. Arakcheyev had few friends. 'No one except the vilest toadies could ever tolerate him,' writes a contemporary. 'The Vampire' was the name given him by the Russians, while Joseph de Maistre calls him 'The Hyena'. A brutal and not very efficient administrator, Arakcheyev was responsible, amongst other things, for the establishment in different parts of Russia of what were known as Military Colonies, where several hundred thousand conscripted peasants, living with their families under the most deplorable conditions, were employed on combined military and agricultural duties, their womenfolk being automatically registered and their children put into uniform at an early age. None of which contributed in any way to the popularity either of the Tsar or of his former Military Secretary.

In September 1825, Alexander travelled south to Taganrog on the Sea of Azov to join his beautiful but much neglected wife Elizabeth, who was convalescing there. But, on reaching his destination, he himself fell ill, his condition worsened and on 1 December he died. Elizabeth herself died not many weeks later.

It was perhaps characteristic of so enigmatic a figure that even his death was surrounded by mystery. In due course a story was to spring up that Alexander had not in fact died at Taganrog but had lived on for another forty years or so as a hermit in a monastery in western Siberia under the name of Fyodor Kusmich. A story which found fresh credence when his coffin in the Cathedral of St Peter and St Paul was discovered on examination to be empty.

Someone who may possibly have played a part in the mystery is Major General Lord Cathcart, who, like his father before him, was for many years British Ambassador to Russia. Being a general as well as an ambassador, Lord Cathcart had accompanied Alexander on his campaigns against Napoleon and in the course of them had become a close personal friend of the Emperor.

In November 1825, as it happened, Lord Cathcart was cruising in his yacht in the Black Sea. Nothing more natural, therefore, than that the story should have got about that Alexander had not in fact died, but that his old friend Cathcart had taken him on board in the middle of the night at Taganrog and smuggled him to an Orthodox Monastery in the Holy Land where, as plain Fyodor Kusmich, he could study to be a hermit. What lends special interest to the story, however, is the fact that any account of the yacht's movements during the period in question happens to be missing from its log (just as Alexander's body is missing from its coffin in the Cathedral of St Peter and St Paul). Nor is it unamusing in the circumstances that a few weeks later the Duke of Wellington, who attended Alexander's state funeral in St Petersburg on behalf of King George IV, should have taken with him as his ADC Lord Cathcart's third son George, who, for his part, was to be killed thirty years later fighting the Russians as a divisional commander in the Crimea.

Though Alexander I never fulfilled the early hope that he might prove a liberal ruler and showed himself latterly as repressive as most of his predecessors, his reign was nevertheless notable for the first stirrings of what can best be described as a rudimentary public opinion, indeed of a new national feeling.

On the Russian people the effect of their country's participation in the Napoleonic wars had been profoundly unsettling. Western ideas, Thomas Masaryk was to write, were of a necessity bound to have an explosive, a revolutionary impact in Russia. And now, for the first time in history, numbers of Russians of all classes had left their country and had come into direct contact with the people and the way of life of Western Europe. Don Cossacks had bivouacked in the Champs Elysées and serfs from Saratov had seen with their own eyes the prosperous peasantry of Germany and central France. Their officers, meanwhile, subject to rank and social status, had mingled by the thousand in French society at one level or another and had fraternized freely with their allied comrades in arms. An intoxicating experience for men hitherto so carefully restricted in outlook and habit and one which came at a moment in history when the Russian people were for the first time experiencing a novel feeling of national awareness and identity.

The new ideas found expression in the writings of Alexander Pushkin, greatest of all Russian poets, and of other young writers who flourished at this time, as well as in the thoughts and conversation of many of the more liberally and romantically inclined young officers and noblemen. Both the ideas and their proponents were, needless to say, profoundly suspect to those in authority. In Russia to hold an unorthodox idea is to be part of a conspiracy. 'A word of truth dropped into Russia,' wrote the Marquis de Custine early in the new reign, 'is like a spark landing in a keg of gunpowder.' The heritage which Alexander left to his successor was not to prove an easy one.

Nor, as it happened, was the transition from one reign to another as smooth as might have been hoped, being marred as so often before by doubts about the succession. Alexander left no children and, under a law passed in 1797, his successor should have been his brother Constantine, the second of Paul's four sons. Constantine, having made a morganatic marriage, had, in fact, with Alexander's approval, secretly renounced the succession two years earlier in favour of their next brother, Nicholas. But neither Nicholas himself nor, for that matter, the high officials most immediately concerned had been clearly informed of this. With the result that on Alexander's death at Taganrog utter confusion supervened. While Constantine, who was Commander-in-Chief in Warsaw, swore allegiance to Nicholas, Nicholas, in St Petersburg, swore allegiance to Constantine. 'The Russian Empire,' wrote the London *Times*, 'is in the strange position of having two self-denying Emperors and no active ruler.' Nor, owing to innumerable failures of communication and endless prevarication on the part of all concerned, were matters in the end settled until Nicholas, aware of his own unpopularity with the army, especially with the Imperial Guards, and realizing the danger of further delay, finally on 14 December issued a manifesto ordering both the army and the civilian population to take the oath of allegiance to him as Tsar.

But by now the harm had been done. For some years now groups of liberal-minded young officers and others had been meeting privately to discuss literary topics and, incidentally, the prospects of reform. But, as is the way in Russia, what had begun as discussion groups developed into secret societies; their members became conspirators who, from discussing the prospects of reform, came to discuss the means, as often as not revolutionary, by which it might be effected.

For no very good reason people attributed to Constantine liberal tendencies and aspirations. Nicholas, on the other hand, was well known to be a thorough-going reactionary. The apparent elimination of Constantine and substitution of Nicholas, following three weeks of uncertainty, sufficed to bring the somewhat half-hearted conspirators to a decision. On the bitterly cold morning of 14 December, an hour or two after the members of the Senate had taken the oath to Nicholas and while a number of military units were doing the same nearby, some three thousand soldiers from various regiments, egged on by their officers, assembled with their muskets in the Senate Square near the statue of Peter the Great, refusing to take the oath and cheering, when invited to, for the Grand Duke Constantine and for *Konstitutsia*, a Constitution, many of them, apparently, under the impression that *Konstitutsia* was the Grand Duke's wife. In this they were joined by some sailors and some onlookers.

For a long time nothing very much happened. Owing to a misunderstanding, the leaders of the conspiracy were nowhere to be found; the soldiers stamped their feet to keep warm and gave another cheer or two for Constantine and *Konstitutsia*: no one knew what to do next. The Tsar, reluctant to use force, tried sending intermediaries to reason with the mutineers. But these could find no one to listen to them and in the confusion one of them, Count Miloradovich, the Governor-General of St Petersburg, was shot and killed.

Finally, with night coming on, Nicholas decided to take more drastic action. The insurgents were surrounded on all sides by loyal troops. First cavalry and then artillery were employed against them. Soon the square was littered with corpses. By nightfall the surviving insurgents had fled and it only remained to remove the bodies of the dead and clear up the mess. To his brother Constantine the new Tsar wrote ruefully that he had won the throne 'at the price of his subjects' blood'.

St Peter and St Paul Fortress, Leningrad

Palace Square, Leningrad

The Admiralty, Leningrad

Palace Square, Leningrad

The inevitable investigation was now opened and numerous arrests followed. The Tsar made it his business personally to examine the conspirators, using his considerable natural charm to gain their confidence and extract from them endlessly revealing and endlessly compromising confessions. 'My friends of the Fourteenth of December', he would call them afterwards, referring to this strangely ambivalent relationship.

All this took a long time. In the end 120 of those arrested were brought to trial. Of these no more than five were ultimately executed, their original sentence of death by quartering being graciously commuted to hanging. Even so those responsible made a messy job of it. 'They can't even hang a man properly in Russia,' said one of the five irritably after both his legs had been broken in a first attempt by some clumsy hangman. The rest of the Decembrists were sent to Siberia, some to remain there until finally amnestied thirty years later by Nicholas's successor. 'The late conspiracy,' the British Minister in St Petersburg wrote to Canning, 'failed for want of management and want of a head to direct it and was too premature to answer any good purpose. But,' he added, with remarkable foresight, 'I think the seeds are sown which one day will produce important consequences.'

The December Conspiracy, half-hearted and ineffectual though it was, left its mark on Russia. First and foremost on the new Tsar, who derived from it the profound conviction that his mission in life was to save Russia from revolution. 'Revolution,' he said to his younger brother Michael on the day after the insurrection, 'stands on the threshold of Russia. But I swear it will never enter Russia while my breath lasts.' It also convinced him of the uselessness and unreliability of the nobles on whom he laid the chief responsibility for what had happened and whom he resolved henceforth to do without. At heart a bureaucrat, he would govern through bureaucrats. 'By the middle of the century,' wrote Professor Klyuchevski, 'Russia was governed neither by aristocracy nor democracy, but by bureaucracy.'

Not for the first (or the last) time in Russian history a shock to the body politic led to an increase in centralization and bureaucratic control. But it led to something else as well. 'Theories,' said Alexander Herzen, who belonged to the next generation of revolutionaries, 'inspire convictions; example shapes conduct.' The five Decembrists who died on the gallows and their comrades who endured exile became the first martyrs and also the precursors of a revolutionary movement which was to gather ever greater momentum for the next ninety years. 'Out of the spark,' wrote a Decembrist poet, 'will come a conflagration.' *Iskra* ('The Spark') was the title Lenin was to choose for his first illegal newspaper.

It would be a mistake to suppose that Nicholas was satisfied with the state of affairs he had inherited from his brother or that he was in principle totally opposed to reform. From his 'friends of the Fourteenth of December' he had learned something of the discontent prevailing in Russia. But, like his predecessors, he was to become ever more aware of the limitations which the need to preserve the autocracy imposed on any actual programme of reform. Serfdom he called 'the unmistakable evil of Russian life'. 'But to touch it,' he quickly added, 'would prove a still greater evil.' He recognized, too, the need for a better educational system, but never lost sight of the danger that it might serve as a carrier of revolutionary ideas. And so, to consider these and other possible reforms, a profusion of secret committees were set up which sat for years on end without ever coming to any firm conclusion. And the Tsar, with all the conscientiousness and attention to detail of his bureaucratic nature, concentrated, for his part, on building up and extending the gigantic, all-pervading bureaucracy, tellingly described by Gogol, which, under his own personal supervision, came gradually to envelop the entire life of the country. It put out fresh tentacles everywhere, involving all concerned in its meshes and, through the infamous Third Section, ably presided over by his personal friend General Count Alexander Benckendorff, keeping an eye on anyone, foreigner or Russian, who might need watching. 'The leaden eyes of the Tsar,' wrote Alexander Herzen, 'looked at a boy from everywhere.'

For all this, the intellectual ferment of the early years continued unabated. In Russia a new phenomenon had come into being for which the Russians coined a new Russian name: *intelligentsia*. It was to act as a hotbed for subversive and indeed revolutionary ideas. 'Almost from its inception,' wrote the liberal historian Paul Milyukov, 'the Russian intelligentsia has been hostile to the governmental system.' Rootless, it became an internal emigration, hostile to the bourgeoisie from which it sprang, detached from the working class of which it knew nothing, out of touch above all with reality and real life. Worst of all, its efforts took a form which Edmund Burke had said no revolutionary movement should ever take – a striving after abstract ideals rather than actual human wants.

Among the intelligentsia, two main groups reflected the eternal dichotomy of Russian thought: Westerners and Slavophiles. While the former, blaming Russia's backwardness on its Byzantine and Eastern connections, looked to the West for enlightenment, to France, Britain or America, the latter, abhorrent of Western materialism, sought salvation and spiritual and national unity in pure Slav orthodoxy, uncontaminated by contact with the West, rooted in Russian history and in the mediaeval Russian peasant commune or *mir*, and destined, they hoped, to supersede the West as the universal civilization of the future. Both, though for different reasons, were equally critical of the regime and equally suspect to it. In 1836 the controversy gained fresh impetus and notoriety from the publication of an essay by Peter Chadayev, a former hussar officer and friend of the Decembrists, who bluntly declared that Russia's past was irrelevant, that the supposed influence of Byzantium was disastrous, and that Russia, having failed to assimilate the cultural traditions of either East or West, had in the end developed none of its own. 'We have never,' he wrote, 'walked hand in hand with other nations. We do not belong to any of the great families of mankind, neither to the West nor to the East. Nor do we have the traditions of either.' And again: 'To look at us, one would say that the general law governing humanity had been revoked on our account. Alone among all the peoples of the world, we have learned nothing from the world. We have contributed nothing to the progress of the human mind; we have only disfigured it.' That the Censor should ever have allowed the publication of such blasphemy is amazing. In the event, however, his oversight was quickly redeemed, Chadayev being shortly after declared insane and placed under immediate restraint (a precedent which in more recent times has again been found useful).

While seriously concerned at the danger of revolution from within, Nicholas, like other rulers of Russia before and since, was no less seriously concerned at the danger of contagion from without. He saw himself as the saviour, not only of Russia, but of Europe from the horrors of revolution. 'The infamous July Revolution' of 1830 in France came as a first shock to him; the armed rising which took place under his own nose in Poland in November of that year as a worse one. For what the Poles, whom he had never liked, were demanding, indeed looked like taking for themselves, was independence from Russia and a republic of their own. Clearly drastic action was called for.

Nicholas's brother Constantine and the troops under his command had been chased out of Warsaw at the start of the rebellion. In the spring Nicholas despatched a Russian army of 150,000 men to invade Poland. They met with fierce resistance. But in the end sheer weight of numbers prevailed and in the late summer Warsaw surrendered, to Field-Marshal Paskevich, who was duly rewarded with the title of Prince of Warsaw. The relatively liberal constitution bestowed on Poland by Alexander was now abolished and Poland became an integral part of Russia under Prince Paskevich as Viceroy. Even the use by the Poles of the Polish language was henceforth restricted. Once again the Polish problem, now a purely internal one, had been successfully disposed of.

Having secured its northern and western frontiers, Russia had now begun to look increasingly southwards and eastwards. Like his predecessors, Nicholas had his eye on the Balkans and Constantinople and, or so the British believed, on Central Asia and beyond. In 1774 Catherine the Great, in addition to considerable territorial gains, had, by the treaty of Kutchuk Kainardji, won for Russia not only the freedom of the Black Sea, but access through the Dardanelles to the Mediterranean. Nine years later, in 1783, she had taken under her protection the ancient kingdom of Georgia and less than twenty years after that Georgia had been formally incorporated in the Russian Empire. War with Persia had followed, giving Russia a foothold at Derbend and Baku on the western coast of the Caspian Sea. Further Russian expansion in either direction could only be at the expense of the Sultan of Turkey or the Shah of Persia and this both rulers were determined to resist. In 1825 a further war with Persia had, after a successful campaign by Count Paskevich, ended in the surrender by Persia in 1828 of Erivan and the adjacent parts of Armenia, thus neatly rounding off Russia's possessions in the Caucasus (see my book *To Caucasus*, chapter 4). Meanwhile, Russian intervention in the Greek war of independence (jointly with France and Great Britain and, in this instance, on the side of the insurgents) had led to the Russo-Turkish war of 1828, which brought Russia minor territorial gains in the Caucasus and at both ends of the Black Sea as well as an informal protectorate over the Danubian principalities.

But the Russians were still not satisfied. What they were now looking for was a fresh pretext for intervention in Turkey. The opportunity arose in 1833. Taking advantage of an attack on the Sultan by Mohammed Ali, the Pasha of Egypt, the Russians landed troops on the Asiatic side of the Dardanelles to help the Sultan, so they said, defend Constantinople and the Bosphorus. Under the Russo-Turkish 'Alliance for Peace' which was now concluded, Russia, from an enemy, became the self-appointed protector of the 'Sick Man of Europe', as Nicholas liked to call Turkey.

By this time, Great Britain was thoroughly alarmed by Russia's evident determination to make the Black Sea a Russian lake and by the threat, however remote, which her eastward advance seemed to present to British India. France and Austria were also uneasy. Constantinople now became the scene of much high-powered diplomacy, with Great Britain in particular energetically represented by Lord Stratford de Redcliffe and doing everything in her power to counteract Russian influence. In 1841 the signature of the Straits Convention, forbidding the passage of the Dardanelles to all foreign warships in peacetime, to some extent relieved the anxieties of Great Britain and the other powers concerned and at least averted war, which at one time had seemed a possibility. The Tsar's state visit to England in 1844 did not, however, prove as reassuring as had been hoped. 'His profile is *beautiful*,' wrote Queen Victoria, 'but the expression of the *eyes* is formidable and unlike anything I ever saw before.' 'His mind,' she added, neatly clinching the matter, 'is an uncivilized one.'

In 1848 the revolutions which broke out in France, Germany and Hungary roused Nicholas to a frenzy. He was only with difficulty dissuaded from despatching an army of 400,000 men to put things right in France and would gladly have done the same for Prussia had his offer of help been accepted. The Emperor Franz Josef, for his part, was glad of any help he could get against an insurrection which threatened his very throne and, side by side with the Austrians, a Russian army from Poland under Prince Paskevich ruthlessly put down Kossuth's rebellious Magyars. 'The Gendarme of Europe' was the name now given to Nicholas.

In Russia, meanwhile, there was a general tightening up. Political repression, which in previous reigns had been more or less haphazard, now became highly organized. An important step had been taken in the direction of a police state. Any idea of reform was forgotten. Police rule became more oppressive, the Third Section more active, the censorship stricter. More and more people were sent to Siberia, more and more people were flogged, often to death. 'Orthodoxy, Autocracy and Nationalism' was the slogan coined by Nicholas's Minister of Education, Count Uvarov. None of which, needless to say, improved Russia's image in Great Britain or inspired any affection there for its deeply reactionary Tsar.

Such was the background to the major international conflict which, for the first time since Waterloo, now came to disturb the peace of Europe. The basic causes of the Crimean War lay in the Western powers' dislike of Russia and its system and in their deep-seated distrust of its expansionist tendencies and, in particular, of its designs on Turkey. Using as a pretext a dispute with Turkey over the Holy Places in Palestine and invoking Catherine the Great's treaty of Kutchuk Kainardji, the Russians in July 1853 marched into the Turkish Danubian provinces of Moldavia and Wallachia. War with Turkey followed. While Prussia and Austria, alarmed by the Russian threat to the Balkans, assumed a threatening attitude, the French and British fleets now appeared in the Bosphorus, and in March 1854 Great Britain and France entered the war on Turkey's side.

Though operations ranged from the Baltic to Kamchatka and from the Danube to the Caucasus, the main theatre of war was the Crimea. Here the allies, using Constantinople and Scutari as bases, landed an expeditionary force of 60,000 men in September 1854, their chief objective being to destroy Russia's naval power in the Black Sea. First defeating a smaller Russian force on the River Alma, in September the French and British laid siege to Sebastopol, the principal base of the Black Sea Fleet. The Russian garrison held out with great courage and tenacity; the conduct of the campaign by the allies was outstandingly inept and their administrative arrangements as chaotic as those of their opponents. The siege, with heavy casualties and much suffering on both sides, dragged miserably on for month after month, a constant drain on Russian resources. Meanwhile across the Black Sea in the Caucasus the hardy tribesmen of the Imam Shamyl were after twenty years still carrying on their relentless fight against the Russians, calling from time to time for help from a British government which, failing to grasp their potential as allies, studiously ignored their appeals.

For Tsar Nicholas, whose expansionist tendencies and jealous regard for the rights of the Orthodox Church had sparked off the quarrel with Turkey in the first place, who had persuaded himself that he had nothing to fear from the British and regarded Napoleon III of France as a dangerous revolutionary, who had hoped for help rather than hostility from his fellow emperor Franz Josef of Austria, and whose elaborate war machine, for all the heroism of his troops, had, when put to the test, been proved a sham, the Crimean War was profoundly disillusioning. Conscientious and dedicated as ever, he worked on, never sparing himself, issuing endless orders and counter-orders, appointing and dismissing functionaries, interfering where there was no need for him to interfere, writing away till the early hours in his bare little room high up in the Winter Palace and sleeping, when he did sleep, on a camp bed with a straw-stuffed mattress. It was there, in the Winter Palace, that on 2 March 1855 he died, a saddened, disappointed man, of an affliction of the lungs, it was announced, but some believed of poison, self-administered.

# 7 Gathering Storm

'I HAND OVER to you my command,' said Nicholas I on his death-bed to his son Alexander. The military turn of phrase was not mis-placed. From earliest childhood Alexander II had been brought up to be Tsar and on his father's death he succeeded to the throne without question. He had much the same military tastes and view of life as his father. The son of a Prussian princess and, like his father, uncle and grandfather, fascinated by the minutiae of the parade-ground, he was certainly no liberal. On the contrary, at thirty-six he had the reputation of being as rigid a disciplinarian as his father. But the facts he faced on his accession quickly con-vinced him that, if disaster was to be averted, drastic reforms were necessary. Clearly a great country whose creaking commissariat could not support a campaign in one corner of its vast territories against a no less incompetent enemy with far longer lines of com-munication and relatively weak forces had something radically wrong with it. Russia's shortcomings were more than purely mili-tary. They were social, economic and political as well.

First the war had to be brought to an end. After a siege lasting almost a year Sebastopol had finally fallen to the British and French in the autumn of 1855. A Russian victory against the Turks at Kars in Transcaucasia somewhat redressed the balance. The fighting now died down and any enthusiasm there had ever been for the war began to disappear. Early in 1856 peace negotiations were opened and on 31 March a treaty of peace was signed in Paris. Russia withdrew from Moldavia and Wallachia (shortly to become Romania) and also from Kars and Batum; the assembled powers guaranteed the integrity of Turkey; the Black Sea was neutralized and the Straits Convention of 1841 reaffirmed.

The war over, the Tsar could turn his attention to domestic problems. The crux of the matter, now, as it had been for the last century or more, was the question of the serfs. For years it had been becoming increasingly clear that Russia's essential backwardness, the shortcomings of its economic system and its inability to move with the times were rooted above all in the institution of serfdom. So long as this barbarous anachronism survived, Russia could never hope to compete on equal terms with the other great powers.

Alexander's predecessors had paid lip-service to the idea of freeing the serfs. He took the bull by the horns. 'The existing system of owning souls,' he said in a speech to the gentry of Moscow in the spring of 1856, 'cannot remain unchanged. It is better to abolish serfdom from above than to wait for it to abolish itself from below.' But it was not enough to free the serfs. To a peasant, freedom without land was useless. Late in 1857 Alexander stated his second, equally important principle, that the serfs, when freed, must be enabled to acquire land of their own.

Nor was it enough to enunciate principles. The necessary land must be found and made available on conditions acceptable to all concerned, to the landowners in particular. Bargains would have to be struck with a quarter of a million individual landlords, who for their part were already preparing to fight a long rearguard action in defence of their rights. Clearly the problem bristled with difficulties. But the Emperor refused to be put off. A main committee and numerous local committees were set up in whose work he himself took an active part and early in 1861, just five years after his original announcement, he was able to sign the Emancipation Statute, an Imperial Edict, followed by sixteen more decrees, abolishing serfdom for ever and enabling some forty million freed peasants to buy their holdings from their landlords on credit with the help of long-term loans from the state.

This settlement was, needless to say, as unpopular with the peasants as it was with the landlords. The latter resented the government's action in taking their land (not to mention their serfs) away from them, even in return for reasonable compensation. The former complained that the amount of land they had been given was inadequate for their needs and that they were having to pay more for it than they could afford. But at least it had given freedom of a kind to millions of men, women and children, who before this could be bought or sold at auction. What the end result of it would be, only time could show.

The emancipation of the serfs was by no means Alexander's only measure of reform. Though a conservative at heart, he nevertheless recognized the need for change, always provided that it could be kept within limits, and, being by nature stubborn, was prepared to use his position as Autocrat to push through the necessary reforms, whatever opposition they might encounter. There was, it is true, as yet no question of the constitution for which some liberals still hoped. But in January 1864 a law was introduced providing for the election of local councils, known as *zemstvos*, with limited powers at district and provincial levels. In these some of the more optimistically inclined of their members discerned a first step in the direction of constitutional government. The provincial councils were later followed by town councils, the suffrage for both being, as was only to be expected, heavily weighted in favour of the property-owning classes. At the same time a reform of the Russian legal system was undertaken with the object of bringing it more into line with Western legal practice and establishing as a principle the independence of the courts. In the field of education the secondary schools were reorganized and an attempt was made to introduce some kind of primary instruction. Finally a whole series of badly needed army reforms were introduced, leading up to the Conscription Law of 1874, under which the former life-sentence of twenty-five years service was reduced to six years with the Colours and nine years with the reserve.

As part of his more liberal policy, Alexander II had on his accession amnestied many of the Polish patriots who had taken part in the insurrection of 1831, had allowed them to return to Poland and had in 1861 even granted Poland a limited degree of self-government. These conciliatory measures led, not unnaturally, to an immediate demand from the Poles for complete independence and, when this was refused, to an attempt on the life of the Russian Viceroy, followed in January 1863 by a fresh nation-wide uprising. This took the Russian army eighteen months to put down and it was not until the summer of 1864 that order was finally restored. It was followed by a period of more than usually vigorous repression and Russianization. An attempt by Great Britain, France and Austria to intervene diplomatically was firmly rejected as unwarranted interference in Russia's domestic affairs.

When halted in the West, Russia has traditionally always turned eastwards; and vice versa. Though for the time being the Peace of Paris had placed a check on Russia's ambitions in south-eastern

Europe, there was no equivalent obstacle to its expansion in Central Asia and the Far East. Reaching out across Siberia into the territories of a much debilitated Chinese Empire, the Russians between 1858 and 1860 relieved the Chinese, then at a low ebb, of the whole of what are now the Soviet Far Eastern provinces and in the latter year established the port of Vladivostok (or 'Lord of the East') on the Pacific seaboard, five thousand miles from Moscow. With the help of ice-breakers, this could be kept open all the year round. Russia was now firmly established as a Far Eastern power.

Nearer home, having finally crushed the rebellious tribesmen of the Caucasus, the Russians set about extending their dominion beyond the Caspian and the Kara Kum to the independent khanates and emirates of Turkmenia and Turkestan and to the Kazakh and Kirghiz nomads of the desert, appropriating in the space of a few years an area the size of the whole of Western Europe. Such resistance as there was was quickly overcome; one after another the native potentates capitulated; soothing circulars were addressed to the great powers; and in 1867 a Russian Governor-General with authority over the whole of Turkestan set up his headquarters in a great yellow brick mansion in Tashkent (for a fuller account, see *To the Back of Beyond*, chapter 6).

By this time what Professor Platonov calls 'Russia's civilizing mission' had carried its armies uncomfortably close to Afghanistan and the borders of British India, thereby causing considerable concern to the British government of the day. But now suddenly there was a fresh change of course and all at once attention was again focussed on the Balkans and Constantinople. Over the past hundred years, the Russians, recalling their ancient links with Byzantium, had, as we have seen, come to regard themselves as the natural protectors of the Christians in the Balkans. At the same time, as a natural development of the earlier Slavophile movement, a strong Pan-Slav movement had come into being, aimed at the eventual reunion of all the Slav races under Russian suzerainty.

It was thus only natural that, when in 1875 and 1876 rebellion against Turkish rule broke out in Bosnia-Herzegovina and Bulgaria, and when the little semi-independent Slav principalities of Serbia and Montenegro lent it their support, Russian public opinion should have become thoroughly aroused and that thousands of Russian volunteers, with or without government backing, should have flocked to fight for their fellow-Slavs. The Turks, sturdy realists where their Christian subjects were concerned, reacted predictably and despite the sympathy it aroused abroad the insurrection did not prosper, the Serbs being heavily defeated by the Turks while the atrocities committed by the latter in Bulgaria and elsewhere made headline news. Egged on by an excited public opinion and an increasingly powerful Pan-Slav movement throughout the country, the Russian government now called sternly upon the Turks to desist; their ultimatum was rejected, and in April 1877 Russia declared war on Turkey, attacking simulta-neously through Romania and Bulgaria and the Caucasus. The Turks fought back stubbornly and much bitter fighting ensued on both fronts. But in the winter of 1877 the Russians finally managed to break through the Balkans; Turkish resistance collapsed and by February 1878 a Russian army stood before Constantinople, before Tsargrad, for close on a thousand years the symbol of Russian aims and aspirations. Only to find, however, that the British Mediter-ranean Fleet was already lying at anchor off Ismid in the Sea of Marmara, ready to sail at a moment's notice up the Bosphorus to the defence of the Sultan and his capital.

The situation was a dangerous one. Twenty years after the Cri-mea, the British were as determined as ever not to let the Russians control the Straits. Nor did they like their simultaneous advance in Central Asia. Queen Victoria, for her part, wanted Disraeli to 'have it out' with the Russians. 'Oh, if the Queen were a man,' she wrote, 'she would like to go and give those Russians, whose word one cannot believe, *such a beating.*' And these sentiments were wholeheartedly echoed by her loyal subjects. 'We don't want to fight,' they sang in the music-halls, 'but, by Jingo, if we do ...'. In Russia, meanwhile, feeling was running equally high. The two powers were closer to war than at any time since the Crimea.

Though resented by Russia, the overall settlement reached in June 1878 at the Congress of Berlin, with the help of the German Chancellor Bismarck in the role of 'honest broker', was at least a peaceful one. But it left a host of problems unresolved. In return for some limited territorial gains at the expense of Turkey, Russia withdrew her troops and for the time being abandoned her designs on Constantinople and the Straits. Subject to certain safeguards and limitations, the Turks retained a hold on the Balkans. Austria was given control of Bosnia and Herzegovina. But the Bulgars, the Serbs and the Montenegrins felt cheated and betrayed. And so, on the whole, did the Russian people, who were inclined to blame the Tsar and his government for the disappointment they felt.

During the 1880s the Russian government rounded off their possessions in Central Asia with the conquest of Turkmenia and the capture of Kushk and Merv, thereby winning a measure of popularity and causing the British administration of the day a momentary attack of what the Duke of Argyll wittily called 'Mervousness'. For a time relations between the two countries were once more strained. But, with the rapid rise of imperial Germany the tension between Russia and Great Britain was already lessening and soon there was to be a regrouping and realignment of alliances between the great powers.

Despite, or perhaps because of, thirty years of unrelieved censorship and repression under Nicholas I, despite or, again, perhaps because of a temporary relaxation of the censorship and a varied mixture of reform and repression under Alexander II, despite all the alarms and excursions of Russian foreign policy, the underground radical and revolutionary movement, which had first come to the surface in December 1825, was still very much in existence fifty or sixty years later and growing steadily. In its early stages the movement had been largely intellectual and had found a convenient means of expression in literary criticism, providing, as this did, a useful but not immediately obvious vehicle for radical ideas. Now it began to take on a more active and extreme character.

Of the new revolutionary movements the first were the *Narodniki* or Populists, to be followed in due course by the Socialists. Meanwhile the debate between Westerners and Slavophiles continued with unabated vigour. The Socialists, curiously enough, were from the start fundamentally hostile to the materialist bourgeois standards of the West, preferring the old Slavophile concept of Russia as the repository of the true faith, a concept later described by Trotski in a characteristically virulent phrase as 'the messianism of backwardness' and by a more recent commentator as 'anarcho-conservatism'. The Populists, for their part, vaguely discerned in the ancient, if largely imaginary, tradition of the *mir* or village commune a truly Russian form of socialism, based on the peasantry and providing protection at once from the threat of an all-powerful state and from the perils of excessive individualism. Their well-meaning attempts to share their ideas with the actual peasantry met, as can be imagined, with a somewhat mixed response.

Under Nicholas the debates of radicals and reformers, even of revolutionaries, had been restricted to theoretical discussion. But, in the atmosphere of restlessness engendered by Alexander's programme of reforms and the fresh problems they provoked, the revolutionaries became bolder. Secret societies emerged of which the avowed purpose was terrorism and political assassination. 'Nihilists,' Turgenyev called them, using the term for the first time in his novel *Fathers and Sons* and going on to define a Nihilist as 'a man who does not bow before any authorities, who does not accept any single principle on trust'.

Much has been written about the role of the Russian intelligentsia and of Russian literature in the revolutionary movement of the nineteenth and early twentieth centuries and to Nicholas I's Minister of Education, Count Uvarov, is attributed the remark that, only when literature ceased to be written, would he be able to sleep peacefully, an observation which echoed, albeit unconsciously, the mediaeval Russian saying that all evil comes from opinions. Undoubtedly the great Russian novelists of the nineteenth century made a powerful contribution to the intellectual ferment of the period. But, in so far as their writings were subversive, it was mainly in the sense that, through their characters, they questioned existing values. As Maxim Gorki was to put it many years later, 'the basic theme of pre-revolutionary literature was the tragedy of the individual to whom life seemed cramped, who felt superfluous in society, who, seeking a congenial niche in it, failed to find it, and either suffered, died or reconciled himself to society that was horrible to him or else took refuge in drunkenness or suicide.' Rarely, however, did the great Russian novelists of the day offer any concrete alternative solution, revolutionary or otherwise, beyond vaguely extolling, as did Tolstoi, the virtues of rural life and of a return to the land. Thus Pushkin's Onegin and Lermontov's Pechorin, like a whole succession of not very different characters in the stories of Turgenyev and Chekhov, are both essentially negative, self-destructive, anti-heroes, denied by society (or by their own temperament) the opportunity to make use of such talents as they had. Nor does Turgenyev in any way align himself with the Nihilists he depicts, dwelling rather on the ultimate futility of their efforts and in his later works even satirizing their activities, while Dostoyevski, having started as a radical, ended up as a downright reactionary.

But, for all that, with the rejection of accepted values went hand in hand an underlying feeling of foreboding, or rather perhaps of expectancy. 'An economic revolution,' noted Tolstoi in his diary in 1881, 'not only may, but must come. It is extraordinary that it has not come already.' And a score of years later, in Chekhov's *Three Sisters*, Baron Tuzenbach is made to say, 'The time has come. An avalanche is moving down on us. A mighty, health-giving storm is brewing, is approaching, is already near and will soon sweep away from our society its idleness, its indifference, its prejudice against work, its foul *ennui*. I shall work and in twenty-five or thirty years everyone else will work too.'

Of the new secret societies, the most effective in the long run was *Narodnaya Volya*, the People's Will, openly pledged to assassinate the Tsar and led by a beautiful and unusually resourceful young woman, Sophia Lvovna Perovskaya, daughter of a former Governor-General of St Petersburg. Plots to assassinate public figures are notoriously liable to go wrong, especially in Russia. Despite careful preparations, an attempt to blow up the imperial train led only to the destruction of the train immediately preceding it. A powerful charge of high explosive placed under the Tsar's dining-room in the Winter Palace was successfully detonated with considerable loss of life, but some minutes, as it turned out, before the Tsar himself went in to dinner.

The conspirators, however, were not so easily put off. On the morning of 13 March 1881 Alexander had agreed to sign a proclamation granting not a constitution, but something which might have led to one. That same afternoon, in accordance with a plot personally directed by Sophia Perovskaya, a bomb was thrown at him on his way back from a military parade. It killed several people, but missed the Tsar. Disturbed by yet another attempt on his life, Alexander got out of his carriage to talk to his would-be assassin. He had, however, reckoned without the beautiful Sophia, who this time had been far-sighted enough to have another conspirator ready with a second bomb which, more accurately aimed than the first, fatally injured the Tsar.

The assassination of Alexander II was not unnaturally the signal for a new period of repression. This had the wholehearted support of his burly, bearded son Alexander III, who had never approved of his father's reforming tendencies and whose first action on coming to the throne was to tear up the newly drafted proclamation which he found on his desk. Count Loris-Melikov, an intelligent and relatively liberal Armenian general, who, as Minister of the Interior, had presided over the late Tsar's programme of reform, now resigned and was replaced as the power behind the throne by Constantine Pobedonostsev, the new Tsar's former tutor and Chief Procurator of the Holy Synod, a convinced and bigoted reactionary. Henceforward Poles, Finns and Balts were increasingly Russianized and the large Jewish population of the Empire methodically persecuted. Alexander II's reforms were as far as possible watered down or nullified and the power of the nobles and gentry to some extent restored. The *Okhrana* or security police, which had superseded the Third Section, became more powerful than ever and an intensive security drive was undertaken against terrorists and revolutionaries. Even so, plots continued. For his part in one of them young Alexander Ilich Ulyanov, the son of an Inspector of Schools from Simbirsk, was in 1887 sentenced to death and executed. His execution made a lasting impression on his seventeen-year-old brother Vladimir, later to be known as Lenin.

Alexander III died on 1 November 1894 in his bed. He had successfully avoided assassination or serious civil disturbances and for a dozen years had kept his country out of war. His son Nicholas II, a small, mild-looking man with a beard, bearing a strong physical resemblance to his cousin, the future King George V of England, was to be less fortunate in both respects. Worthy, ineffectual and of limited intelligence, Nicholas managed to be both vacillating and obstinate, a particularly unhappy combination under the circumstances prevailing in his country at the time. Influenced, like his father, by the theories of Constantine Pobedonostsev, he regarded the principle of autocracy as a sacred trust which it was his personal duty to preserve. But from the start the dice were heavily loaded against him. Contrary to more superficial appearances, the situation both at home and abroad possessed beneath the surface a deep-seated imbalance and instability, which would have been sufficient to daunt a much wiser and stronger man.

The population of the Russian Empire had by now grown to 128 millions, three and a half times what it had been a century before. Owing to the inadequacy of the holdings made available to them, the peasants, serfs no longer and still accounting for the vastly greater proportion of the population, suffered, in general, from acute land hunger which in the long run could only be satisfied at somebody else's expense. Nor were things made any easier by the glaring disparity which already existed between the poorer peasants and those who, from an equally unpromising start, had in the space of a few years somehow managed to acquire more land and to prosper. It was a disparity which in years of crop failure and famine meant for many the difference between an adequate standard of living and actual want and served further to sharpen the conflict latent in the countryside. The opening-up of Siberia at about this time to peasant settlers alleviated, but came nowhere near to solving, the problem.

Meanwhile Russia was no longer as exclusively rural as it had been even a hundred years before. Since the beginning of the century industrialization and urbanization had been making rapid progress. By 1900 some three million workers, for the most part uprooted peasants, were employed in industry, as against 200,000 a century earlier. As many as thirteen per cent of the total population now lived in towns, compared with only four per cent in 1800. Iron works and coal-mines were being developed in southern Russia, textiles manufactured in St Petersburg and Moscow, oil was being produced in the Caucasus. The railway system was also being expanded. In 1891 began the building of the Trans-Siberian line.

A leading part in promoting Russia's industrialization and economic development at the end of the nineteenth and beginning of the twentieth centuries was played by Sergei Yulyevich Witte, who held the post of Minister of Finance from 1893 to 1903. A man of outstanding ability, it was he who helped stabilize the country's finances, attracted capital from abroad, greatly expanded the railway system (he had started life as a station-master) and by vigorous state intervention brought about the rapid expansion of Russia's heavy industry. If she was to hold her own in the modern world, if she was to be a great power in the true sense of the phrase and not a mere dependency of the West, Russia, he realized, must at all costs be industrialized.

As was to be expected, Russia's industrial revolution was attended by many of the same problems as Great Britain's a hundred years earlier, notably by bad working conditions. Nor was the solution to these immediately at hand. To Russia's other problems, and they were many, was added that of a rootless and restless industrial proletariat.

To finance industrialization, the banking and financial system was expanded and a new class of industrialists and entrepreneurs emerged. Large sums were raised at home and abroad. Even some members of the Imperial Family became involved in more or less profitable, more or less reputable speculation. From having been patriarchal or feudal, Russia was at long last beginning to fall within the scope of Marxist theory by becoming, to a limited extent, industrialized and capitalist.

In February 1898, just in time to take advantage of this, the first Russian Marxist party came into being. Known as the Russian Social Democratic Labour Party, its message was directed in the main to the still relatively small urban proletariat. Five years later it split into two factions: *Menshevik* and *Bolshevik*, the latter, led by Lenin, a man of thirty-three, burning with revolutionary ardour, being rather more radical in their approach. In the years that followed the leading members of the new party spent most of their time in exile abroad, bickering amongst themselves on points of doctrine.

More obviously dangerous to the regime were the Social Revolutionaries. Founded in 1900 in the *Narodnik* or Populist tradition, these put their faith in terrorism as an instrument of policy. They also declared that they stood for the common ownership and fair distribution of land, thus making an immediate appeal to scores of millions of land-hungry peasants. As terrorists, the Socialist Revolutionaries were by no means unsuccessful, accounting in a relatively short time for a Grand Duke, the Minister of Education and two successive Ministers of the Interior.

Needless to say, this upsurge of revolutionary activity provoked an immediate response from the police, who resorted to every strategem they could devise in order to distract public attention and further confuse the issue. One of these was deliberately to encourage anti-semitism by planting anti-Jewish rumours and sponsoring pogroms in areas with a big Jewish population in the hope, as Plehve, the new Minister of the Interior, put it, of 'drowning the revolution in Jewish blood'. In order to penetrate the recently formed labour movement and revolutionary parties, the police made lavish use of *agents provocateurs*, while the revolutionaries, for their part, were busy penetrating the police. With the result that, on both sides of the hill, large numbers of double or even treble agents were working to achieve their diverse ends, there-

137

by greatly adding to the confusion and bewilderment of all concerned.

It was thus, for example, that the highly paid police spy and in-
former Yevno Azev was also for years head of the Social Revolutionary Party's Combat Section or murder squad and author of
some of its most successful outrages. Where his true sympathies
can have lain, as his well-planted bombs went off and he simultaneously betrayed his accomplices to the police, is an interesting
subject for speculation (see my book *Take Nine Spies*). But, whatever the answer, industrial unrest, strikes, acts of terrorism and
attempts at assassination continued until Plehve gave it as his view
that what was needed to restore order and distract the attention
of the public, was 'a successful little war'.

The Russo-Japanese War, which started in February 1904 must,
however improbably, have seemed like an answer to his prayer.
China was at this time in a state of advanced decomposition and
the principal cause of the war was Japanese concern at increasing
Russian encroachment there and at the Russian occupation of Port
Arthur and other parts of Manchuria and Korea, acts of policy
directly inspired by the Tsar, who in his own somewhat restricted
way was stubbornly obsessed with the idea of expansion in the Far
East.

From the first the war went badly for the Russians. The
Japanese, they found to their cost, were no longer backward orien-
tals, but first-class fighters employing modern equipment and
modern methods of warfare. An early Russian defeat on the Yalu
River in Korea was followed by the forced surrender of Port
Arthur, by a Russian withdrawal from Mukden and finally, after
an epic round-the-world voyage, involving a spirited engagement
with some British fishing-boats off the Dogger Bank, by the total
annihilation of the Russian Baltic Fleet at the battle of Tsushima
in May 1905. Only Japanese exhaustion followed by American
mediation saved the Russians from further disasters and in August
1905, thanks to the skilful diplomacy of S. Y. Witte, who led the
Russian delegation, a treaty of peace was signed at Portsmouth,
New Hampshire, under which Russia abandoned all claim to Port
Arthur, Korea, South Manchuria and the southern half of Sakhalin
Island. The war, with its humiliating outcome, dealt a severe blow
to Russia's military prestige and caused Germany and Austria to
take less account of it than ever in their calculations for the future.

Plehve's 'successful little war' had boomeranged. The Far Eastern campaign had from the first only served to aggravate popular discontent. In particular it had done nothing whatsoever to enhance the popularity of the Emperor, already at a low ebb. Plehve himself was killed by a bomb in July 1904. Amid catastrophic news from the front, his successor found himself swamped by demands from all quarters for freedom of speech and assembly, agrarian reform, industrial legislation and above all an elected national assembly. The outlook was anything but reassuring. 'This country,' wrote the British Chargé d'Affaires, 'has no real Government ... each Minister acts on his own, doing as much damage as possible to the other Ministers. ... It is a curious state of things. There is an Emperor, a religious madman almost, without a statesman or even a council, surrounded by a legion of Grand Dukes ... with a few priests and priestly women behind them. No middle class, an aristocracy ruined and absolutely without influence, an underpaid bureaucracy living, of necessity, on corruption.'

Things finally came to a head on Sunday, 22 January 1905, when vast crowds of workers, carrying holy icons and singing the national anthem and various Orthodox hymns, converged on the Winter Palace to petition the Tsar in person. They were led by an Orthodox priest, a certain Father Gapon, an equivocal, histrionic figure associated alike with the revolutionaries and with the security police. The authorities had taken such precautions as they thought necessary to control the procession. In the event, however, panic set in. Or possibly someone, for reasons of his own, was determined to precipitate a crisis. The troops on duty were given the order to fire on the entirely peaceable and orderly crowd; the Cossacks charged; several hundred people were killed in cold blood; by nightfall Tsar and government were facing a truly revolutionary situation.

Bloody Sunday, as it was to be called, was followed by a succession of strikes, riots, demonstrations and mutinies which continued throughout the year 1905, culminating in October in a general strike and the formation in St Petersburg of a Workers' Council or *Soviet*, quickly dominated by a dynamic young revolutionary known as Trotski. (*Soviet*, it may be observed, is simply the Russian word for a council of any kind and had hitherto possessed no ideological connotation.) Nor was the unrest confined to the towns or to the still relatively small industrial proletariat. Throughout the country the peasants rose in their millions, evicting the landlords and taking possession of the land. At the same time widespread mutinies broke out in the armed forces, the most famous being that on board the battleship *Potyomkin*.

By mid-October more peasant riots, more mutinies in the army and navy and the widespread stoppage of labour had led to a general collapse of authority, while the newly formed St Petersburg Soviet was, for its part, already distributing arms to its followers and fast assuming the guise of a revolutionary government. Something had to be done. On 30 October, the Tsar, yielding to the advice of his ministers, unwillingly issued an Imperial Manifesto, which, while maintaining the principle of autocracy, provided for the election by popular franchise of a National Assembly or Duma with strictly limited powers and for a Council of Ministers presided over by someone who was in effect a Prime Minister, a post held for a few months by Count Witte, the former Minister of Finance, at whose instance the Tsar had reluctantly issued his manifesto in October.

Though the Tsar's grudging concessions fell far short of what the liberals had hoped for, they successfully drove a wedge between them and the out-and-out revolutionaries with whom they had hitherto made common cause. The weeks that followed were uneasy ones, but by mid-December the Government felt strong enough to arrest the majority of members of the St Petersburg Soviet. In Moscow, where another Soviet had been formed and where Lenin, returning hastily from abroad, had managed to provoke something approaching an insurrection, serious fighting now broke out and lasted for a week, at the end of which the government, using regular troops and artillery, finally managed to crush the insurgents at a total cost of more than a thousand lives. There followed a period of savage repression in town and country alike. By the new year the revolution had been defeated. To Lenin, looking back years later, it had been above all a 'dress rehearsal' for what was yet to come. '*La Révolution est morte, vive la Révolution*,' was Trotski's characteristic comment.

Though the Tsar now did his best to water down and whittle away his forced concessions and at the first opportunity readily accepted Count Witte's resignation, he could not prevent the election of an Assembly and a first Duma, with powers still further restricted, was duly opened by him in the spring of 1906 in the Winter Palace, whence it moved in due course to the Tauride

Palace, the handsome residence originally built by Catherine the
Great for her lover Prince Potyomkin. The first Duma was, however, dissolved a couple of months later after an early difference
of opinion with the government. The same fate overtook the next
Duma, which was elected the following year. The third Duma,
which, thanks to a radical revision of electoral procedure, inclined
further to the right than its two predecessors, was more fortunate,
running for its full term of five years from 1907 to 1912.

Meanwhile power had passed to Peter Stolypin, a former
Minister of the Interior, who now became Prime Minister. A strong
character, who had shown himself ruthless in stamping out the
revolution, he at once set about pushing through a policy of
agrarian reform, designed to reduce the powers of the village commune or *mir* and create a class of prosperous independent peasant
proprietors, drawn from what he called 'the sober and the
strong', who, he hoped, would act as a stabilizing element in
society. He also did much to increase the scope and extent of public
education in what was still an appallingly backward country. Inevitably Stolypin, bitterly detested by the revolutionaries, had also
made enemies at Court and in the Duma. In September 1911 he
was killed at the Kiev opera by a Socialist Revolutionary who, it
later emerged, was also a police agent, though from whom he had
received his instructions on this particular occasion was never made
clear. Stolypin's death was not, however, followed by any marked
change of policy. A fourth Duma, elected in 1912 and also right-
wing in complexion, continued along lines similar to those he had
laid down.

In spite of everything Russia now had the beginnings of a system
of constitutional government. A number of tentative social reforms
had been introduced. The benefits of education were more widespread. Thanks to agrarian reform, the peasants now owned three-
quarters of all the arable land in European Russia. Industry was
developing at a satisfactory rate. Despite initial restrictions, trade
unions were becoming a reality. The lot of the industrial worker
had improved. The living standards of both peasants and workers
were better than ever before. General prosperity was increasing.
A middle class was at last emerging. The tide of revolution was
at a lower ebb than for many years. A gradual evolution to democracy seemed at least a possibility. Though clearly fruitless, it is
tempting to consider for a moment how things in Russia might

have turned out if all these relatively hopeful trends had been given the opportunity to develop.

But already in Europe the storm clouds were gathering. 'A war between Austria and Russia would be a very helpful thing for the revolution,' said Lenin in 1913. 'But it is not likely,' he continued, 'that Franz Josef and Nikolasha will give us that pleasure.' In fact, he had misread the situation. In the last twenty-five years there had been a gradual realignment of the great powers. In Central Europe, Germany, under its brash young Kaiser, and Austria, under its tired old Emperor, remained allies, with Italy as a junior and far from reliable partner. As a counterbalance to this con-glomeration of power, republican France, the defeat of 1870 still rankling, had over the years come together with autocratic Russia. Finally in 1904 Great Britain, emerging from almost a century of isolation, was, after some hesitation, moving closer to these two seemingly disparate allies. Meanwhile Turkey, traditionally the friend of Great Britain, was from nervousness of Russia now mov-ing closer to Germany. During the ten years that preceded 1914 almost everything that happened in the world, whether in the Near East or in Africa or still further afield, was inevitably seen in terms of this grouping and counter-grouping of powers. In the Balkans, in particular, Austria and Russia jealously watched each other's every move. Inexorably, Austria's annexation of Bosnia and the subsequent assassination at Sarajevo of the Archduke Franz Fer-dinand led to the catastrophe of August 1914 and all that was to follow thereafter.

The Russians entered the First World War with enthusiasm, but with an army that, though strong in manpower, was from the start badly equipped, badly led and badly supplied. The utter defeat of the Russian Second Army by Hindenburg and Ludendorff at Tannenberg in East Prussia in August 1914 with heavy casualties and a loss of 125,000 prisoners and 500 guns was a bad start. It was followed by disaster after disaster on other fronts, a sequence of misfortune only relieved by the short-lived success of General Brusilov's Galician offensive.

In three years the Russians, who had mobilized thirteen million men, lost a couple of million dead. As always, the Russian soldier at the front showed immense courage and endurance, but was almost invariably let down by confusion, incompetence and, as became more and more evident, corruption at the rear. By the spring of 1915 men were being sent to the front without rifles to fight against a well-trained, well-equipped enemy. That summer the Germans and Austrians assumed the offensive along the entire front, taking possession of the whole of Poland, most of the Baltic provinces and vast areas of the Ukraine and White Russia. The casualties suffered by the Russians were astronomic; their supply system was grossly inefficient. In August the Tsar himself assumed supreme command of his armies. This in itself was disastrous enough. More disastrous still was the opportunity it gave his wife Alexandra to interfere in government.

German, unpopular and stubborn, the Tsaritsa had some years earlier fallen under the influence of Grigori Rasputin, a self-proclaimed holy man from Siberia, whose alleged hypnotic powers could, she was convinced, alone cure her son the Tsarevich of the haemophilia from which he suffered. 'Our Friend', she and the Tsar called him. Drunken and dissolute, but endowed with peasant shrewdness and apparently with some kind of hypnotic powers, Rasputin used his position to the full, making and breaking generals and ministers as the mood took him and freely enjoying the favours of various ladies of the Court. His orgies became famous and his influence paramount. 'His gaze,' wrote the French Ambassador, 'was at once piercing and caressing, naive and cunning, far off and concentrated. When he is in earnest conversation, his pupils seem to radiate magnetism. He carries with him a strong animal smell, like that of a goat.'

For those in authority this was scarcely a reassuring background against which to wage war. General Brusilov's campaign had by now collapsed. The casualty rate was worse than ever. Desertion was becoming more frequent. Food was short at the front and in the capital. There were more and more strikes. In the prevailing confusion, revolutionary and, in particular, anti-war propaganda fell on fertile ground.

On 30 December 1916 Prince Felix Yusupov and the Grand Duke Dmitri decided on drastic action. Acting from what they regarded as patriotic motives, they invited Rasputin to visit them; plied him with poisoned food and drink; and, when, to their dismay, the poison seemed to have no effect on him, shot him again and again, finally throwing his bullet-riddled body, still alive, through a hole in the ice of a neighbouring canal, where it was found later, by then frozen stiff, clutching the supports of the nearest bridge. But it was already too late. Nicholas and Alexandra, saddened by the loss of their friend, seemed unaware of the danger that threatened them and brushed aside all warnings of impending doom.

The revolution, when it came, started spontaneously, almost fortuitously. Early in March the continuing shortage of bread led to rioting in St Petersburg or Petrograd, as it had now been renamed to make it sound more Russian. Organized demonstrations followed. Tens of thousands of workers came out on strike and thronged the streets, stoning the police when they tried to disperse them. The Cossacks, called out in support of the police, did nothing. In a letter to the Tsar, who was at his headquarters, Alexandra wrote on 19 March that there was nothing to worry about. Next day the Tsar dissolved the Duma. On 10 March two regiments of the Imperial Guard went over to the rioters; the arsenal was seized and weapons were distributed to the crowd. There were now 200,000 workers on strike. While in one wing of the Tauride Palace a provisional committee of the Duma debated the consequences of the Tsar's decree dissolving that body, a hastily elected Soviet of Workers' and Soldiers' Deputies took possession of the other. On 14 March a provisional government was formed under Prince Lvov, a leading figure in local government. Events now succeeded one another with bewildering rapidity. Not for the first time in the history of Russia, the military intervened decisively in the affairs of their country. On 15 March, under pressure from the members of his own high command, the Tsar abdicated in favour of his brother Michael, who, however, hurriedly declined the offer. As far as anyone could judge, the Revolution of March 1917, unplanned and haphazard as it had been, had achieved success at the cost of no more than a few hundred casualties.

# 8 *Who? Whom?*

*Who, whom?*
LENIN

THE MARCH or rather the February Revolution, as it has come to be called, found many of the Russian revolutionary leaders in exile. After visiting Russia briefly in 1905, Vladimir Ilich Ulyanov or Lenin, leader of the Bolshevik section of the Social-Democratic Party had, for his part, spent the last few years in Switzerland. It now became of the utmost consequence for him to return to Russia immediately. As things turned out, he was enabled to do this by courtesy of the German General Staff, who, in the hope that they were thereby improving their own chances of ultimate victory, deliberately arranged for him to cross Germany in a sealed train – 'like a plague bacillus', wrote Winston Churchill.

Lenin, who was now forty-seven years old, arrived on 16 April 1917 at the Finland Station in Petrograd. He was received there with enthusiasm by his followers and by a delegation from the Petrograd Soviet. While a band played the 'Marseillaise', he was presented with a large bouquet of flowers by a lady of noble birth and radical views known for her firm belief in free love. He was then conducted amid much chatter to what until recently had been the Imperial Waiting Room.

Lenin lost no time in stating his position. In the speech which he delivered on arrival at the station and in subsequent pronouncements elsewhere, he made it absolutely clear that what he stood for was not co-operation with a bourgeois provisional government in defence of a bourgeois revolution. What he stood for was immediate, uncompromising, socialist, proletarian revolution in Russia and everywhere else, with, as a first step, all power for the Workers' Soviets and peace, bread and freedom for the people. 'Long live,' he concluded, 'the world-wide Socialist Revolution!'

This forthright statement of policy came as a shock even to some members of the Bolshevik Party. But for Lenin it won immediate popular support in the country. Food and an end to the war was what most people wanted. By at the same time promising the con-fiscation and redistribution of agricultural land and workers' con-trol in the factories, he made the strongest possible appeal to both peasants and industrial workers. During the weeks that followed Bolshevik influence increased by leaps and bounds.

'The freest of all the belligerent countries of the world,' Lenin called Russia at the time of the February Revolution. During the next six months the Bolshevik agitators took full advantage of this freedom. Soon, with their help, most of Russia had been reduced to a state of near anarchy. At the front, discipline had broken down; more and more soldiers deserted; and early in July a last attempt at a Russian offensive in the south-west came to nothing. In the countryside, the peasants simply took possession of the landlords' estates, looting and burning their houses. In the towns and indus-trial areas, more and more factories were taken over by the workers.

Power, meanwhile, as Lenin had predicted, was passing to the Soviets, now springing up all over the country. In the newly formed All-Russian Congress of Soviets, the Bolsheviks, with 105 dele-gates, were still heavily outnumbered by the Social Revolutionaries with 285 and the Mensheviks with 248. But Lenin's leadership and singleness of purpose more than made up for any lack of numbers. In July the Bolsheviks led an attempt at armed insurrection (the July Rising) against the Provisional Government. This was put down by force and an order was issued for the arrest of the Bol-shevik leaders. But Lenin escaped across the border to Finland, thence to make his dispositions for the eventual seizure of power.

The leadership of the Provisional Government now passed to Alexander Kerenski, a Socialist lawyer whose talents as an orator greatly exceeded his gifts as a statesman or administrator. By this time the Provisional Government had in practice abandoned any idea of continuing the war. In September an attempted counter-revolutionary coup by their own newly appointed Commander-in-Chief, General Kornilov, was put down by Kerenski. This was done with the help of the Petrograd Soviet, whose position was thereby further strengthened.

By now the Bolshevik faction within the Petrograd Soviet had achieved almost complete ascendancy. As in 1905, the Soviet was

largely dominated by Trotski, who in July had formally joined
the Bolsheviks and who, through the Soviet's newly established
Military Revolutionary Committee, soon controlled the entire
Petrograd garrison. At the beginning of October Lenin returned
clandestinely to Petrograd and established himself at Smolni,
the famous school for the daughters of the nobility which the
Bolsheviks had made their headquarters. He had by now definitely
decided to resort to armed insurrection.

The proposed elections to a Constituent Assembly were to be
preceded by a meeting of the All-Russian Congress of Soviets. This
was scheduled to take place on 7 November. It afforded Lenin the
opportunity he required to administer his coup de grâce to the Provisional Government. Early that day detachments of garrison
troops and armed factory guards, all under Bolshevik control,
seized the principal buildings in Petrograd. To the accompaniment
of a salvo of blanks from the six-inch guns of the cruiser *Aurora*,
lying at anchor in the Neva, the Winter Palace, which served as
Kerenski's headquarters and was garrisoned by a force of army
cadets, was seized by Red Guards and most members of the Provisional Government were put under arrest. Kerenski himself
managed to escape in a car provided by the American Embassy
and, after lying up for some months, was eventually smuggled out
of the country.

The Bolshevik October Revolution, for this is what it was, had
passed off with a minimum of disturbance. To the British Ambassador, Sir George Buchanan, taking a stroll that afternoon along
Palace Quay towards the Winter Palace, everything seemed much
as usual. 'The aspect of the Quay,' he wrote, 'was more or less
normal, except for the groups of armed soldiers stationed near the
bridges.' The schools and government offices remained open and,
at the theatre, the opera and ballet performances continued as
advertised.

On the evening of 8 November a new government was formed,
the *Soviet Narodnikh Kommisarov* or Council of People's Commissars, known for short as *Sovnarkom*. Of this Lenin was Chairman
and Trotski Commissar for Foreign Affairs, with J. V. Djugashvili
or Stalin, a cobbler's son from Georgia with a long record as an
active revolutionary, as Commissar for Nationalities. Once formed,
the new government, which included representatives of the Social
Revolutionaries, lost no time in issuing two decrees. The first of

these called on the peoples and governments of the combatant nations to open negotiations for an early and just peace. The second announced the abolition of the private ownership of land and its provisional transfer to the control of the Peasants' Soviets.

In the capital, as in many other large towns and some country areas, the Bolsheviks won a quick and easy victory. In Moscow, where some three thousand cadets put up a determined resistance and the Kremlin twice changed hands, it took them several days to establish their authority. In the rest of Russia, over much of the countryside, in the Cossack lands, the Ukraine and in Transcaucasia, counter-revolutionary forces proved stronger. Here a confused, uncertain situation still prevailed, to be resolved in due course by bloody civil war.

On the evening of 7 November 1917 the All-Russian Congress of Soviets of Workers' and Soldiers' Deputies gave its formal approval to what had happened earlier that day. It did this by 390 votes out of 650, with the support of a number of non-Bolsheviks. Lenin and his supporters, still heavily outnumbered by both Mensheviks and Social Revolutionaries, represented a minority of extremists in what was itself a minority group of Socialists. But, as Lenin himself put it at the time, 'for the Bolsheviks to wait for a formal majority is naive.' Not for the first time in Russian history, a revolution had been imposed 'from above', in this case by a determined and well-organized elite taking full advantage of an inherited revolutionary tradition and of a promising revolutionary situation.

In Petrograd there was little expectation that the Bolsheviks would remain in power for any length of time. But Lenin knew what he was doing. In December 1917, within six weeks of coming to power, he set up, in the old Russian tradition, the *Chrezvychainaya Kommissiya* or *Cheka*, an efficient, ubiquitous and utterly ruthless secret police force, expressly created for the smelling out and suppression of counter-revolution and counter-revolutionaries – a task to which it immediately turned its attention with devastating effect. To this body were recruited as a matter of course many experienced old hands who had formerly worked for the Tsarist *Okhrana*. It is even said that this is something that goes from father to son and that there are men in the KGB today who claim descent from the *Oprichniki* of Ivan the Terrible.

In November genuinely free elections had produced the long-awaited Constituent Assembly. This finally met in the Tauride

Palace on 18 January 1918. Out of a total of 707 seats, the Social Revolutionaries had gained 410 as against 175 won by the Bolsheviks. Next day the members were dispersed and the Assembly was dissolved by the Bolshevik guards on duty, who thereby ensured that their leaders, who had achieved power by force of arms, should not be deprived of it by an adverse vote. In Lenin's scheme of things there was, as he put it, no place for 'parliamentary illusions'. His attitude towards parliamentary democracy was on a par with that of his Imperial predecessors: Russia, he maintained, was not ready for it. If control were to be relaxed, a misguided majority might take over and chaos ensue. It is an attitude which, by and large, has been maintained ever since. Once secured, the authority of the Congress of Soviets was all that was needed. In July 1918 it was formally announced that sovereign power would henceforth be vested in the Congress of Soviets.

The Bolsheviks were by this time in complete control of the machinery of government and the first thing the Congress of Soviets did was to ratify the carefully prepared constitution of a Russian Socialist Federative Soviet Republic, now presented for their approval. Under the new system the primary source of authority was the local Soviet or Council, either village or urban, election to it being by show of hands. The members of the local Soviet elected – again by show of hands – the members of the cantonal Soviet, and so on, right up through district, provincial and regional Soviets to the Congress of Soviets itself.

In the latter stages, in particular, representation was strongly weighted in favour of the urban areas, an equal number of representatives being accorded to every 25,000 town- and every 125,000 country-dwellers. When the Congress of Soviets was not sitting, full legislative authority was delegated to its Central Executive Committee, a body of some three hundred members, which in turn was directed by a small Inner Praesidium. Nor, conveniently enough, was there any clear distinction between its legislative functions and the legislative functions which the Soviet Government or *Sovnarkom* somehow combined with their normal executive powers.

Of the Russian Communist Party (Bolsheviks) the constitution made no mention. In practice, however, it had become the universal instrument of policy, the framework or cement which held together the whole structure of the state. At the apex of the pyramid the members both of the Soviet Government and of the Praesidium of the Central Executive Committee of the Congress of Soviets were almost exclusively drawn from the inner circles of the Party, while lower down, at every level, a built-in Party cell guided the decisions of every government department.

Such was the machinery set up to build socialism in Russia, to socialize agriculture and industry, capital and commerce, in short to bring the whole economy and eventually everything else as well under the absolute control of the state.

These aims of the Bolshevik Revolution were now well on their way to fulfilment. But were they in fact quite as revolutionary as they sounded? Did they not rather accord with long-established Russian tradition? For years, after all, under the Tsars, the state had been the biggest landowner, the biggest industrialist, the biggest trader, the biggest capitalist and the biggest employer of labour in the country. It had also boasted the biggest and most cumbrous bureaucracy in the world – another imperial tradition religiously continued by the Bolsheviks. But all this still lay in the future.

The immediate problem confronting the new rulers of Russia was how to end the war with Germany and Austria. Already in December 1917 peace negotiations with the Central Powers had been opened at Brest Litovsk, while the Soviet Government of their own accord had granted the right of self-determination to the subject peoples of Poland, the Ukraine, the Baltic States, Finland and Transcaucasia. But the problem was not an entirely simple one. In the event the peace terms proposed by the Germans were so unfavourable to Russia that even the Bolsheviks hesitated to accept them.

It was now that Lenin's influence proved decisive. Convinced that revolution was imminent in Germany and fearing for the future of his own revolution if hostilities were resumed, he threw all his weight on the side of peace. Trotski, the Soviet negotiator on the spot, was in full agreement with him. 'There are,' he declared, 'only two alternatives: either the Russian Revolution will bring about a revolution in Europe or the European powers will destroy the Russian Revolution.' The German terms were accepted and on 3 March 1918 a treaty of peace was signed at Brest Litovsk. Under this Russia, in addition to ceding Kars and Batum to Turkey, handed over Finland, eastern Poland, the Baltic States and the Ukraine to what was in effect German control. In other words it was at a stroke surrendering no less than a quarter of its population and of its arable land, three-quarters of its iron and coal and half its industrial plant.

The news of this humiliating settlement deeply shocked a great many patriotic Russians of all shades of opinion. It also alarmed the Western Allies, now left to face the common enemy without Russian support. Soon it was being whispered that Lenin was in fact a German agent. Disillusionment with the Bolshevik regime increased. The government's large-scale requisitioning of grain, its expropriation of the more prosperous peasants and its encouragement of class conflict in the villages did much to make it even more unpopular in the countryside, especially with the peasant-orientated Social Revolutionaries, who now withdrew from the government. Reinforced from a variety of quarters, the forces of counter-revolution gained strength and the threat of civil war and Allied intervention became increasingly serious.

The small Volunteer Army, raised in southern Russia by a number of generals all determined to resist the Bolshevik take-over, had originally found its main support in the Cossack country of the Kuban and Don. Now, under General Denikin, the movement spread further afield. To add to their other troubles, the Bolsheviks also found themselves confronted with an army of some forty thousand Czech volunteers, who had originally been recruited from Austro-Hungarian prisoners and deserters and who were now on their way via Vladivostok, supposedly to fight on the western front. Resisting all attempts to intern or disarm them, these Czechs had managed in the disturbed state of the country to get possession of most of the towns along the Trans-Siberian Railway from the Urals to the Pacific.

Meanwhile, on the political front, the breach between the Bolsheviks and Social Revolutionaries was now complete. In July 1918 the latter, true to their terrorist traditions, had taken the drastic step of murdering the German Ambassador, Count von Mirbach, in the hope of thus provoking German intervention against the Bolsheviks. In August they followed this up by assassinating the chief of the Petrograd Cheka and attempting to assassinate Lenin. This led, not unnaturally, to savage reprisals by the Bolsheviks, with the result that most dissident socialist elements now allied themselves with the forces of counter-revolution. On the Volga, meanwhile, and in western Siberia, where the Bolsheviks had not yet consolidated their hold, the Social Revolutionaries had staged a 'democratic counter-revolution' which, in turn, prepared the way for the 'White' counter-revolutionary government later set up by Admiral Kolchak in western Siberia.

In the spring of 1918 the Allies, worried by Russia's withdrawal from the war and by its repudiation of foreign debts and anxious to ensure that the large quantities of arms and supplies which they had sent to Russia did not now fall into enemy hands, had despatched small expeditionary forces to Murmansk, Archangel and Vladivostok (to be followed later by others sent to Transcaucasia, Central Asia and the Crimea). The general, though not very carefully thought-out, objective of these moves was somehow to get rid of the Bolsheviks and bring Russia back into the war on the side of the Allies.

Hard-pressed on every side, the Bolsheviks now took a step which did nothing to improve their image in the West. Though there had been no attempt to restore the monarchy and few Russians had in fact given much thought to the Imperial Family for more than a year, on 16 July 1918 Nicholas, his wife, young son and daughters were together taken down to the cellar of the house in the dreary Siberian town of Ekaterinburg, where they were being kept, and there shot in cold blood.

Relatively little blood had been shed during the October Revolution. By contrast, the Civil War which followed it and raged over most of Russia for the next couple of years was to be marked by appalling atrocities, freely perpetrated by all concerned. Perhaps the worst excesses of all were committed in the Ukraine, where, following the withdrawal of the German forces of occupation, Reds, Whites, Ukrainian Nationalists and peasant guerrillas vied with each other in an orgy of competitive savagery, and the Jewish population, in particular, were yet again the victims of repeated pogroms.

The Civil War began badly for the Bolsheviks. General Denikin had first set up his headquarters in the northern Caucasus in June 1918. By September his army had increased from 9,000 to 40,000 men and by February 1919 he had driven a Bolshevik army, 150,000 men strong, out of the northern Caucasus. During the summer and autumn of 1918, while the newly formed Red Militia was still in training, the brunt of the fighting, on the Bolsheviks' side, had been borne by the Red Guards and Workers' Detachments. Winter brought a measure of relief to the Bolsheviks. But by the early summer of 1919 their situation had again deteriorated and Admiral Kolchak's army in western Siberia was now all set to advance into central Russia. Heavy fighting ensued and by October General Denikin, advancing from the south, had reached Orel, within two hundred miles of Moscow, whither the Bolsheviks had by now transferred the seat of government. In the north-west, meanwhile, the troops of General Yudenich, another White commander, were fighting in the suburbs of Petrograd.

Victory now seemed within Denikin's grasp. His forces, numbering 150,000 men, held Kharkov, Odessa, Kiev and Orel. He had won back 400,000 square miles from the Bolsheviks, had established contact with Admiral Kolchak's left wing in western Siberia and set up a provisional government in south Russia.

By this time, however, the Red Army, thanks largely to the resolute and brilliant leadership and organizing ability of Trotski, now People's Commissar for War, had become a much more formidable fighting force. As the weeks went by Bolshevik resistance stiffened. In November 1919 the Red cavalry under the future Marshal Semyon M. Budyonny, a former cavalry non-commissioned officer with a gigantic moustache, broke through the enemy's lines and forced them to retreat. Divided amongst themselves and incapable for one reason or another of enlisting and exploiting the potential support of a thoroughly disgruntled peasantry, the Whites had somehow managed to throw away their initial advantage. Early in 1920 the Bolsheviks reoccupied Rostov and Krasnodar, and Denikin withdrew his remaining troops from Novorossisk to the Crimea, whence, with Allied help, they later escaped to Constantinople.

But the Bolsheviks' troubles were not yet at an end. On coming to power, they had, it will be recalled, granted the Poles, together with most of the other border nationalities, the right of self-determination, at the same time handing over much of Poland to the Germans under the treaty of Brest Litovsk. Following the German defeat, the Western Allies, meeting at Versailles, had established the Curzon Line as the new Poland's frontier with Russia. But the Poles, intoxicated by their new-found freedom and remembering their past glories, wanted more and in the spring of 1920 set out to take it by force of arms.

The ensuing war was short but full of incident. Advancing boldly into the Ukraine, then still in the throes of civil war, the Poles seized Kiev, only to be quickly forced back on Warsaw by a sweeping advance of the Red Army, who, disappointed in their hopes of setting off a revolution in Poland, were in their turn driven headlong back into Russia. An armistice in October was followed in March by a treaty of peace which fixed the Russo-Polish frontier well to the east of the Curzon Line. Neither side, needless to say, was completely satisfied, nor had the Polish question been finally solved. But the Poles had successfully defended their independence and the Russians were now better able to concentrate on restoring peace and order in their own country.

By the end of 1920, though here and there pockets of resistance still held out and small foreign expeditionary forces, including a Japanese contingent in the Far East, still remained on Russian soil, the Civil War was in practice at an end and the Bolshevik Government in effective control of a battered and considerably diminished Russian Empire, now adequately guarded against further foreign interference by a relatively efficient military machine. By this time Poland, Finland, Latvia, Estonia and Lithuania were fully fledged sovereign states, while in the Caucasus Georgia and Armenia and in Central Asia Khiva and Bokhara were enjoying their last few months or weeks of precarious independence.

Six years of war, revolution and civil war had brought Russia to the verge of collapse. Communications had broken down. The economy no longer worked. Money had lost its value. Industry was in ruins. Agricultural production had dwindled to starvation level. The Revolution had left some twenty-five million small-holders working minute plots of land by the most inefficient methods conceivable. Famine stalked the land. Nor had the so-called War Communism of the Bolsheviks, based on wholesale confiscation, expropriation, rationing and the forcible direction of labour, done much to redress the balance or reassure public opinion.

It would have been hard to conceive of a less promising background than this for the great experiment in social, economic and political engineering to which the Bolsheviks were committed. But in Lenin they had a leader who combined utter dedication to their cause with complete realism. His high hopes of revolution beyond the frontiers of Russia had, it is true, been momentarily dashed by the negative turn of events in Germany and Hungary and elsewhere. But he did not abandon them. In March 1919 he had formed, in Moscow, the *Comintern* or Communist International for the express purpose of undermining capitalism and promoting and encouraging revolution throughout the world and this cumbrous machine was even now embarking on its equivocal and as often as not unrewarding task. Meanwhile, at home he faced a situation which demanded all his determination and skill.

With the Civil War barely at an end and outbreaks of peasant unrest still disturbing the countryside, the first months of 1921 brought a sharp reminder that the Bolshevik regime was not universally popular even with those who had once been the most fervent revolutionaries. In March a mutiny broke out in the naval barracks at Kronstadt, for two hundred years Russia's chief naval base in the Baltic and three years earlier a focal point of the October Revolution. Seizing the fortress and two ironclads, the insurgents defied all comers. Their demands were simple and direct: a fair deal for the peasants and real power for the Soviets. In other words, they felt that the Revolution, which they had helped to bring about, had been betrayed. To such heresy there could only be one answer. After a bombardment lasting several days the Red Army, on Trotski's orders and led by the future Marshal Tukachevski, attacked in strength at night across the ice; the mutiny was ruthlessly suppressed and an example made of the surviving mutineers. From now onwards, in European Russia at any rate, there were to be few further signs of overt opposition to the regime.

But on Lenin, realistic as ever, the lesson had not been wasted. The Kronstadt mutiny had only underlined what the state of the economy, aggravated by a bad harvest, by now showed all too clearly. 'The flash which lit up reality better than anything else,' he called it. Something had to be done to gain the co-operation of the peasants (who, after all, still accounted for eighty-five per cent of the population) and in general to prevent the economy from grinding to a standstill. And so it was announced that grain requisitioning would be abandoned and replaced by a system of taxation in kind and that peasants would in future be free to dispose of their surplus produce on the open market.

The attendant complications of what might, at first sight, have seemed a minor concession to one section of the community were enormous. It involved, inevitably, a limited return to private trade and industry as well as a number of not inconsiderable concessions to private capital and capitalists. The New Economic Policy, as it came to be known, amounted, in short, to a sudden reversion to a kind of capitalism and to all that that implied. What is more, it worked. Production and exports quickly increased. Soon a new class of profiteers, the NEP men, as they were called, were living it up in fine style and, in company with the foreign capitalists now once more admitted to Russia, flaunting their new-won riches in the restaurants and night-spots of the capital with a nonchalance worthy of grand dukes.

But although no doubt as disturbing to doctrinaire socialists as encouraging to wishful thinkers abroad, Lenin's temporary retreat from socialism was no more than tactical. His ultimate aim remained the same. The state had retained control of what he called 'the commanding heights' of the economy. Once he had taken full advantage of the respite he had gained, he would once more devote all his energies to the creation of a socialist and ultimately a communist state. In the meantime, despite appearances and despite the emergence of a measure of private enterprise in trade, the state retained its control of large-scale industry and its monopoly of foreign trade.

Lenin's immediate purpose had been to increase production. In this and in much else he succeeded. By 1924 the currency had been stabilized and production in some sectors of the economy had reached the level of 1913. Industry was decentralized and further concessions were made to the peasants. But already collective planning was heralding the advent of the first Five Year Plan.

In every other field the Bolsheviks were busy establishing and consolidating their power. In the schools religious instruction had been abolished and replaced by anti-God propaganda and the study of dialectical materialism. In place of Christianity, Marxist dogma and doctrine were drummed into the rising generation. Before many decades had passed, the one had effectively replaced the other. Or very nearly. There was a new hagiography, a new hierarchy, a new liturgy, and there were new faces on the icons. The Russians are a deeply religious people. A new, but equally pervasive Orthodoxy had been substituted for the old. For Russians Russia remained Holy Russia, a country with a cause, a country set apart, a country not as óthers were.

Meanwhile, in the long line of succession to the *Oprichniki* Lenin's original Cheka had in 1923 been succeeded by the no less ubiquitous or formidable GPU or State Political Directorate (*Gosudarstvennoye Politicheskoye Upravlenye*). Thousands of political prisoners or potential opponents of the regime swelled the labour force, while throughout the country the principle of equality between the sexes provided a convenient pretext for the use of male and female labour under what were often equally painful conditions.

During the years that followed, the independent republics of Georgia and Armenia in Transcaucasia and in Turkestan the Emirates of Khiva and Bokhara were by one means or another brought back into the fold, while at the same time the centralized power and authority of Moscow were, through the Communist Party, consolidated and extended to every corner of Russian territory. By 1924 the stage was thus set for the most important step of all, the formation, on a federal basis, of the Union of Soviet Socialist Republics, consisting of the original Russian Socialist Federative Soviet Republic (which now included Siberia), the Ukraine, White Russia and the Soviet republics of Transcaucasia and Central Asia. In theory, the constituent republics possessed the right to secede at will from the union. In practice, as some early separatists found to their cost, any such suggestion was unthinkable.

By now most of the great powers had grudgingly reconciled themselves to the substitution of a communist state for the empire of the Tsars, granting first *de facto* and in due course *de jure* recognition. A Soviet–British trade agreement was signed in March 1921 and in April 1922, much to the dismay of France and Great Britain, a Soviet–German treaty for mutual aid and technical co-operation was concluded at Rapallo – a treaty, incidentally, which was to be of the greatest benefit to both powers and which effectively deprived the Western powers of their capacity to control events in eastern Europe. In 1924 Great Britain led the way in according Soviet Russia *de jure* recognition, being followed in this by most other European countries, though the government of the United States, for their part, held aloof for another ten years. From its Moscow headquarters, meanwhile, the Comintern was, through the world communist movement, making such trouble as it could for governments of all political complexions, with which its *alter ego*, the People's Commissariat for Foreign Affairs, was at the same time maintaining more or less correct diplomatic relations.

It was at this moment, barely six years after the Revolution, that

Soviet Russia suffered an incalculable loss. In May 1922 Lenin had been stricken by a first seizure, followed in March 1923 by a second which almost completely incapacitated him. In January 1924 at the age of fifty-three he died, leaving the shortly to be constituted Soviet Union to face an uncertain future without the benefit of his inspired and resolute leadership.

After Lenin the outstanding figure among those who had made the Russian Revolution was Trotski. Or so it must have appeared to most people in January 1924. In fact, however, things in those bleak winter months were not entirely as they seemed. During the past couple of years, while Lenin lay stricken in the elegant classical mansion at Gorki outside Moscow, where he had gone to die, changes had taken place in the power structure of the Party and in its balance which in the long run were to be of far greater significance than anyone at the time could possibly have realized, though in fact Lenin on his sick bed came nearer to realizing it than most.

In May 1922, Josip Vissarionovich Stalin, the cobbler's son from Georgia, since 1917 Peoples Commissar for Nationalities, had been appointed Secretary General of the Central Committee of the Party, an important though hitherto not predominantly important post. Stalin was quick to realize and exploit the potentialities of his new position. Within six months he had used it to such good effect that Lenin, partially recovered from his first stroke, felt disturbed. In December the sick man expressed his fears in a letter, which has been called his political testament. The new Secretary General, he wrote, was too rude and crude and was concentrating too much power in his own hands. He was afraid that this would cause trouble in the Party and suggested that Stalin should be removed from his job. But a couple of months later, before anything could be done, came Lenin's second stroke. Stalin did not waste a moment. Less than a year later Lenin's death found him more firmly established than ever and able to enter the struggle for the succession from a position of considerable strength.

The new Secretary General's technique was to ally himself temporarily with two or three of his Party colleagues in order to strike down any dangerous rivals, and then, with the help of fresh allies, to strike down his former associates in their turn. In this political in-fighting he displayed unparalleled ruthlessness, resilience and skill. Any organized opposition was quickly confounded.

The doctrine to which Stalin now officially lent his support was that of Socialism in One Country. As far as he was concerned, world revolution could wait; he had always disliked and distrusted foreigners. This brought him into direct opposition to Trotski, who, following Lenin, still clung to the wider concept of world revolution. The debate, in a new form, was that of a century before, between Westerners and Slavophiles: should Russia look outwards or inwards? At a Party Congress held in December 1925 Stalin won a majority for his theory and at the same time an endorsement of his own authority. Suggestions that he had abused his position or was betraying the Revolution were summarily brushed aside.

Stalin next proceeded to deal, stage by stage, with his most formidable rival. In 1926 Trotski was removed from the all-powerful *Politburo* or Political Bureau of the Party. A year later he was expelled from the Party itself. In January 1928 he was exiled to Alma Ata in Kazakhstan. And early in 1929 he was expelled from the Soviet Union, to become, for Stalin's propaganda machine, the ultimate scapegoat, the embodiment and source of all evil, the arch-traitor and spy-master, ultimately responsible for every disaster and for every act of treachery or sabotage, real or imagined, committed in the Soviet Union during the next ten years. Dismayed by his fate, Stalin's lesser opponents quickly came to heel and recanted, only, in the long run, to be dragged from the obscurity in which they had taken refuge, publicly defamed and humiliated in a series of nightmarish state trials and, after serving as a salutary warning to others, finally shot.

For the next quarter of a century power was concentrated in Stalin's hands, greater power than that exercised by Lenin or by any of his Imperial predecessors, power unquestioned and absolute, power ruthlessly used, power that reached out into the remote valleys of the Caucasus and Pamirs and across the frozen Siberian tundra, power supported by an active and ubiquitous secret police. 'Imagine Jenghiz Khan with a telephone,' Tolstoi had said towards the end of his life. His prophecy had been more than fulfilled.

Once again Russia had fallen under autocratic rule, this time more autocratic than ever before. 'I do not know,' Baron von Herberstein, the envoy of the Holy Roman Emperor, had written four hundred years earlier, 'whether it is the character of the Russian nation which has formed such autocrats or whether the autocrats

159

themselves have given this character to the nation.' The answer to this question has yet to be found.

Having thus secured his own position, Stalin now turned his attention to the task of building socialism (his kind of socialism) in one country. To this he brought the same concentrated energy and ruthlessness that he had displayed in other contexts. His immediate purpose was to transform a backward agricultural country into a modern industrial state, self-sufficient and capable of holding its own against a hostile world, and to do this in the shortest possible time. It was, in a sense, the same task that Sergei Yulyevich Witte had set himself at the turn of the century.

Stalin's programme took the form of a series of Five Year Plans, formally launched in October 1928 and pushed through, against all probability, well ahead of the appointed time. To the attainment of this end everything else was consciously sacrificed, the well-being and standard of living of the Russian people first and foremost. Hand in hand with the Five Year Plans for industrialization went a programme for the massive collectivization of agriculture, designed at one and the same time to cure the peasant of the bourgeois concept of private property, to increase agricultural output by widespread mechanization and finally to release peasant labour for work in the factories.

The implementation of this policy involved a struggle with the peasants (who still amounted, after all, to over eighty per cent of the population) more formidable that any phase of the Revolution or Civil War, more formidable even, he told Winston Churchill ten years later, than the worst moments of World War Two. 'It was,' he went on, 'all very bad and difficult – but necessary.'

Faced with collectivization, the Russian peasant showed a deep-seated stubbornness which surprised even Stalin. By the end of 1929 it had become necessary to use force. In theory the ensuing campaign was directed against the *kulaks* or richer peasants; but in fact the term was used to cover any one of the millions of peasants who owned a horse or two and a couple of cows. Houses were burned, grain and cattle were forcibly requisitioned and, when serious resistance was encountered, the peasants concerned were simply killed out of hand or carted off to forced labour camps. In the fertile Ukraine and the northern Caucasus, where peasant resistance was strongest, the fields were left untilled and people died by the million in a man-made famine. Soviet agriculture suffered appalling losses. Several million peasants lost their lives.

But in the end Stalin won. By 1933 collectivization was a fact, the first Five Year Plan successfully completed and the second already begun. Stalin was well on the way to doing what he had set out to do, namely to industrialize, however ruthlessly, a relatively backward country. Meanwhile, politically his personal position was now completely secure. Though still contenting himself with the post of Party Secretary, he had in ten years become the *Vozhd*, the Leader, of the Soviet Union.

But the year 1933 brought something else: Adolf Hitler's accession to power in Germany. Germany now also had a Leader and one with a bee in his bonnet about communists and communism. Within months Hitler had brought to an end the mutually beneficial Soviet–German co-operation of the past ten years. Soon it had become clear to all save the most incurable optimists that a second world war was inevitable, a war in which, of a necessity, the Soviet Union would be involved.

Though no one could have wanted war less, Stalin felt bound to prepare for one. In his latest Five Year Plan greater emphasis than ever was placed on defence, while to the current hunt for native Trotskists and deviationists was added a no less intensive search for foreign spies, agents and saboteurs, accompanied by a tidal wave of xenophobia and paranoiac suspicion, combined with deliberately drummed up Great-Russian patriotism. No one was safe. No one could trust anyone else. Fear and suspicion were universal, hanging over everything, seeping in everywhere, like a poisonous mist.

These trends culminated in the notorious purges and treason trials of the late 1930s, a reign of terror unparalleled in the whole bloodstained history of Russia. The signal for them was given by the assassination in December 1934 of Sergei Kirov, the Leningrad Party Secretary and a close associate of Stalin's, though whether he was murdered by 'an enemy of the people', as was alleged at the time, or by Stalin's own secret police, and whether in that case the latter were acting independently or on orders from Stalin, has never to this day been finally cleared up. Certainly Kirov's death, besides removing a potential rival, provided a convenient pretext for what followed. During the next four years millions of innocent people met their deaths and millions more were sent into exile, while the Secret Police, which from the GPU had in 1934 become the People's Commissariat of Internal Affairs or NKVD (*Narodni Kommissariat Vnutrennikh Del*) dominated the scene more completely than ever before.

In the space of two or three years the great purge wiped out the flower of the Old Bolsheviks, the élite of industry, science, the academic world, the civil service and the army, navy and air force. From the confessions of the accused and from the so-called evidence produced at their trials it was possible to draw the conclusion that the whole Soviet government machine, from Lenin's closest collaborators right down to the newest joined ensign in the army, was rotten with corruption and treachery and filled to bursting-point with British, German and Japanese spies. If you could not accept this preposterous conclusion, then the whole thing could only be a gigantic fabrication. To the innocent observer, watching it all from the welcome shelter of a foreign embassy, the choice was, to say the least of it, a bewildering one.

In 1934 the Soviet Union, suddenly converted by the threat of German aggression to the doctrine of collective security, had joined the League of Nations. But what passed as collective security seemed unlikely to stop Hitler, who chose this moment to withdraw from Geneva. Convinced, understandably, that the Western powers did not mean business, the *Vozhd* decided early in 1939 to do a deal with the *Führer*, who for reasons of his own was also ready to buy time. Overnight the Soviet propaganda machine was put into reverse, while Stalin for his part publicly toasted his fellow-dictator.

The Nazi–Soviet Pact of 23 August 1939 made war a certainty. It broke out a week or two later. To his own way of thinking, Stalin no doubt felt that he could congratulate himself on what had happened. By his deal with Hitler, Russia could hope to regain half of Poland, Finland, the Baltic states and part of Romania, thereby greatly strengthening its line of defence against 'the capitalist encirclement'. More important still, he had managed, or so he thought, to keep out of a war which with any luck would weaken both sides, greatly to Moscow's advantage. His was the classical role of *tertius gaudens*. In the event, Finland's sturdy resistance to Soviet aggression and Hitler's triumphant *Blitzkrieg*, followed by the rapid collapse of France, to some extent threw out his calculations. By occupying the Baltic states and parts of Romania, in July 1940 he reinsured his position as far as he could. The German occupation of the Balkans came as another shock. But even so, despite the clearest warnings from a number of sources, he remained convinced that his new-found ally would not attack him.

For all these reasons Germany's invasion of Russia with 175 divisions in June 1941 must have come as a serious shock to him. The speed of the enemy's advance was terrific. As the Red Army retreated headlong before them, town after town fell to the Germans. By September they had reached the outskirts of Leningrad. By October the battle for Moscow had begun. For a couple of months the outcome of the campaign hung in the balance. Then more trained Soviet divisions were brought up from further east and in the course of the winter – the worst in living memory – the Germans were somehow pushed back and the capital was saved.

By now the Soviet propaganda machine had again made the necessary adjustments. With Russia's involvement, the war, from being the Second Imperialist War, had become a Patriotic War, a War of National Liberation, a War against Fascist Aggression, and all the resources of the nation, even including those of the Orthodox Church, were harnessed behind the war effort. In addition to Party Secretary and *Vozhd*, Stalin, rising to the occasion, became in turn Chairman of the Council of People's Commissars, Commissar for Defence, Marshal and ultimately Generalissimo.

Meanwhile, for month upon month Leningrad remained beleaguered and further south the Red Army continued to retreat, until at last in the late summer of 1942 a stand was made at Stalingrad on the Volga, the German advance checked, the threat to the Caucasus and its oil-fields averted, and, after a siege lasting six months, a German army of 100,000 men encircled and forced to surrender. It was a turning-point in the war. There followed on other fronts the battle of El Alamein and the successful Allied landings in North Africa and in Italy. By the early summer of 1944 the Germans had started to withdraw from Russia. In June came the opening of the second front in the West and the simultaneous advance of the Red Army through Eastern Europe. In the spring of 1945 the armies of the Soviet Union and the Western Allies met in Germany. Their meeting was quickly followed by the unconditional surrender of Germany and victory in Europe. In the Far East a well-timed declaration of war, six days before the Japanese surrender in

August 1945, brought the Soviet Union the fruits of victory without, in this case, the inconvenience of prolonged hostilities.

In the course of four years of war the Soviet Union had suffered appalling losses, far greater than those of any of the Western Allies: some ten million dead; millions more crippled or blinded or maimed for life; many thousands of towns and villages utterly destroyed; twenty-five million people rendered homeless; innumerable factories, power plants and collective farms put out of action; the communications system disrupted; the achievements of twenty years of sacrifice and effort very largely wiped out. But the Russian people were, as always, courageous, disciplined and infinitely long-suffering. The war had brought no real change in the character of the regime. As soon as hostilities had ended, under Stalin's relentless leadership, the Russians turned once more to a fresh series of Five Year Plans and to the strenuous task of building socialism.

Of building socialism in one country or world-wide? The issue this time was no longer as clear-cut as it had been twenty years before. 'War,' Trotski had once said, 'is the locomotive of history.' Twice in his lifetime, in 1905 and 1917, events had proved him right. Now it looked very much as though, posthumously, events were to prove him right yet again. And in another context as well. For, despite its losses, Russia had emerged from the Second World War infinitely stronger than when it entered it and better able from a position of strength to impose its will and with it its ideology on large areas of the world. Trotski was dead, murdered in Mexico in 1940 by a hired assassin with an ice-axe, but now, under Trotski's old rival, Josip Stalin, the prospects for his doctrine of world revolution seemed better than ever before. 'He is,' said the Patriarch Aleksei at the solemn *Te Deum* held by the Orthodox Church to celebrate Stalin's seventieth birthday, 'the acknowledged Leader of all the peoples of the world.'

The hard-fought victories of the Red Army and the heroic conduct of the Russian people had won the admiration of Western opinion. Russian prestige had never stood higher. After the war most people in Western Europe and America looked forward to a future of friendship and continued co-operation between East and West. Had not the Comintern, that bogey of the Bolshevik-baiters, been formally dissolved? Were not the members of the Soviet government now called Ministers instead of Commissars?

Was not Lenin's threat to support the British Labour Party 'as the rope supports the hanged man' a thing of the remote past? 'Left will talk to left in comradeship and confidence,' said Ernest Bevin hopefully in 1945. But this was not to be. Under Stalin's guidance the Russians again withdrew into surly isolation, while what Winston Churchill in a memorable phrase called an Iron Curtain cut them and their empire off from all but the most superficial contacts with the outside world. No sooner was the war against Germany at an end than a Cold War began between her former adversaries.

As usual, Stalin left nothing to chance. While the Western Allies demobilized their armed forces and greatly reduced their armaments, the Russians maintained theirs at crisis level. To powerful conventional forces was added in due course the nuclear weapon and with it the prospect of eventual parity with the United States. But by now the Western powers had come to realize the danger that threatened them. Stalin's attempt in 1948 to blockade West Berlin into submission was frustrated by timely Allied action. In Korea in 1950 the Soviet-prompted aggression of the North against the South was in the end beaten back with the active support of a United Nations expeditionary force, while, as an answer to the threat of Soviet aggression, came the North Atlantic Alliance, to be countered six years later by the Warsaw Pact. Soon a desperate armaments race was in progress, at astronomic cost to all concerned.

In Eastern Europe, meanwhile, the Russians, apart from their own considerable territorial gains, had sought to protect themselves against any threat of capitalist encroachment by creating a cordon of communist satellite states, stretching from the Baltic to the Balkans and constituting an extended Russian empire greatly exceeding the wildest dreams of the Romanovs. Having arrived as liberators, they had remained as protectors. Or so the story went.

Nor was this all. Thousands of miles away, on the eastern frontiers of Russia's far-flung empire, an even more significant change had taken place in the world's ideological balance. After more than twenty years spent, literally, in the wilderness, China's Communist Party had, with very little help from anyone, come to power and China, with more than twice the population of the Soviet Union, had joined the communist *bloc*. Surely, from Moscow's point of view, from the point of view of the Comintern (recently defunct, but somehow surviving under another guise), this must be the ultimate, the crowning glory?

There was only one little fly in the ointment. It had soon become clear that one satellite ruler at any rate was not entirely content with the part allocated to him. President Tito of Jugoslavia, having by his own efforts liberated his country from the Germans, saw himself in a different role. He saw himself, quite simply, as ruler of an independent state and, after a few acrimonious exchanges with Moscow, said so loud and clear. And continued to say so despite all Stalin's fulminations and machinations.

Tito's rebellion and subsequent survival were a direct challenge to the absolute authority and infallibility of the Kremlin, the principle upon which the whole communist system rested, both inside and outside the Soviet Union. And, obviously, where one satellite had found the way to abstract itself from Kremlin control, others might follow.

The problem posed was a decidedly awkward one. Clearly an example must be made of Tito. Clearly he must be liquidated. 'I will lift my little finger,' said Stalin confidently, 'and there will be no more Tito.' But how was this desirable object to be achieved? With his own people Tito was now more popular than ever. The answer to the problem had still not been found when, on 3 March 1953, death, as it must come to all of us, came to Josip Vissarionovich Djugashvili, alias Stalin.

One day not long before his death, Stalin, no doubt sensing its approach, looked sourly at the assembled members of the Politburo and addressed them as follows. 'You are blind,' he said, 'like little kittens. You cannot recognize an enemy when you see one. What will become of Russia when I am gone?'

After a quarter of a century of unchallenged dictatorship, of total control by one able, ruthless, relentlessly determined and pathologically distrustful individual, the vacuum created by his departure was immense. The man who, after some initial manoeuvring and shuffling, eventually stepped into his shoes, possessed an entirely different character and disposition from his formidable predecessor. Where Stalin had been preternaturally cautious and totally inhuman in his approach, Nikita Sergeyevich Khrushchov was by nature a gambler with a human side to his character, a man who, in the exceptional circumstances in which he now found himself, was prepared in the ultimate analysis to take a chance, prepared, up to a point, to make allowances for human nature. The chance Khrushchov took was a very considerable one. There can in politics be no more difficult or dangerous task than to try to relax or liberalize a dictatorship, especially a dictatorship that has several hundred years of history and tradition behind it. Yet this in effect is what Khrushchov now set out to do.

As a first step, Stalin's successors had, at a meeting of the Politburo, summarily disposed of Beriya, the Georgian who, under Stalin, had for the past fifteen years controlled the all-powerful Secret Police, but who now, curiously enough, was belatedly discovered to have been for more than thirty years a British spy. By liquidating him, his colleagues had not only removed a dangerous rival but had at the same time shifted the emphasis away from terror as an instrument of government. From 1953 onwards, as part of a programme of deliberate de-Stalinization, more and more prisoners were released from concentration camps and allowed to return to their astonished families.

By the Twentieth Party Congress, held in February 1956, Khrushchov felt strong enough to denounce Stalin by name and to catalogue in detail his innumerable misdeeds. It was thus that the people of the Soviet Union, who for a large part of their lives had been encouraged to regard their former leader as the embodiment of perfection, now suddenly heard him described as a homicidal maniac. Quite clearly there was a risk that, after so violent a psychological shock, they would never believe anything again. But, once more, this was a risk that Khrushchov was prepared to take. For Khrushchov was shrewd enough to realize that you cannot run a modern technological society with a horde of brain-washed helots. 'Under Stalin,' he said to a friend of the author, 'the whole machine was fast seizing up.' In the field of science and technology people, he realized, must be taught to think for themselves, must even be allowed access to new ideas and to the trends of thought current in the outside world. Simultaneously he shifted the balance of the Soviet economy, hitherto relentlessly geared to heavy industry, slightly more in the direction of the long-suffering Soviet consumer. Soon people were a good deal better fed, better dressed and better housed than they had ever been before. In all this Krushchov was again taking a risk, was setting foot on a slippery slope. Because clearly, if people were taught to think for themselves on technological subjects, they would soon start thinking for themselves and expressing themselves on other subjects too. Nor could there be any doubt that, given a slightly better standard of living and rather more freedom of speech, they would soon be demanding a much better standard of living and much more freedom of speech.

In the field of foreign affairs Khrushchov also took a more flexible line. Once again, it reflected an increase in Soviet self-confidence. Proceeding to Jugoslavia in 1955 he publicly apologized for Stalin's attitude towards that country and in the end arrived, though not without difficulty, at a *modus vivendi* with President Tito. On the other hand, when this departure from precedent was followed by signs of unrest on the part of the other satellites, he suppressed it unhesitatingly, notably in Hungary in 1956. Again, in his relations with the West he was a good deal more forthcoming than Stalin had ever been, meeting the President of the United States, visiting the United Kingdom and making a spectacular appearance at the United Nations, when, to emphasize a point he was making, he removed his shoe and hammered with it on the rostrum.

But unfortunately for him none of this, coupled with his extrovert nature and bonhomous approach to life, endeared him to his own people or to his own colleagues, who seem to have felt that, like the first pseudo-Dmitri, he somehow lacked dignity. His apparent mishandling of Soviet relations with China and his Cuban adventure, when, after rashly seeking to establish a Soviet missile base in Cuba, he was in 1962 forced by what amounted to an ultimatum from President Kennedy to remove it, further diminished him in their eyes.

'*C'est la déstalinisation,*' said Jean-Paul Sartre perceptively, '*qui déstalinisera les déstalinisateurs.*' At first show-down with the Party hierarchy in 1957 had brought victory for Khrushchov and curtains for his opponents. A second confrontation in October 1964 ended differently. Having once again confronted his adversaries, he found that this time they were ready for him. A clear majority came out against him; his resignation was accepted; and without further ado he was removed from office and retired into private life. Seven years later the death of Pensioner N. S. Khrushchov passed almost unnoticed by the Soviet Press.

It was, by Russian standards, a novel but nonetheless effective method of getting rid of a ruler who for one reason or another was

considered to have outlasted his usefulness and become an embar-
rassment. But when the history of the period comes to be written,
there can be little doubt that, seen in its proper perspective, the
figure of Nikita Sergeyevich Khrushchov will loom larger than it
does at present. In his ten years of power Khrushchov radically
changed the character of the Soviet regime and steered the Soviet
Union safely through what could have proved a very difficult and
dangerous period. He also, in a sense, set Russia's course for the
future, a course from which his successors, as we shall see in a later
chapter, have not to any marked extent departed.

# 9 *Moscow*

WHERE should one begin to describe the present face of Russia? Russia, in the widest sense of the word, is an enormous country. I have written elsewhere of the Russian plain, stretching away end-lessly into Asia, into a remote, always slightly menacing distance. It was in the midst of this Russian plain that eventually little groups of hardy men and women, abandoning their nomad existence, founded the first settlements, scarcely more than encampments protected by wooden stockades, choosing for them in that vast expanse of forest and marshland sites marked out by a convenient river or perhaps by some slight rise in the ground. Of these early settlements, some were swept away almost as soon as they were built; others have survived in one form or another until our own times, perhaps as a few crumbling ruins in the open fields, perhaps as some forgotten village or small town. But one, neither the oldest nor for many years the most significant, has, from a remote citadel standing on a bluff above a river, become a great city and the capital of what today is inelegantly known as a super-power.

For me Moscow will always symbolize Russia, first mediaeval Russia with the Tartar threat never very far removed; then modern Russia, the doom-laden Russia of the thirties and now the more cheerful, more prosperous, more outward-looking, space-age Russia of today. It was to Moscow that I first travelled forty years ago by train across the snowy expanse of the Russian plain and it is to Moscow that I still return whenever I can, drawn there by an unfailing and never completely satisfied curiosity.

Moscow is unlike any other city in the world, at once a great metropolis and an overgrown village. The countryside, from which the great majority of Russians are only a generation removed, is always encroaching on it, and vice versa. On its outskirts peasants' huts and miniature allotments still mingle with high-rise buildings;

onion-domed churches are dwarfed by mighty and equally ornate skyscrapers; and magnificently laid out avenues tail off into muddy lanes. For Moscow is expanding at a tremendous rate and each time you go back there you notice the fantastic scale of the latest urban developments which have already gone a long way to solve what until recently was an appalling housing problem.

A very Russian institution, as important to Muscovites now as before the Revolution, is the *dacha*, the country cottage. However far out Moscow spreads, the *dachas* will always start on its out-skirts. You see them from the air as you fly in to Sheremetievo airport, each set in its individual patch of green. Already the *dachas* of twenty or thirty years ago have long since been swallowed up in the city itself. Looking at the new ones which have taken their place, five or ten miles farther out, but still barely ahead of Moscow's urban sprawl, you are constantly reminded that a couple of generations back eighty-five per cent of the population of Russia were peasants. The pull of the village and the countryside is still enormously strong. Anyone who can possibly buy or build himself a *dacha* within reach of Moscow, or share one with a friend or even hire himself a room in one, will get out there whenever he can.

In size and style *dachas* vary enormously, from the palatial villas of the ruling class to what are virtually wooden shacks, sub-divided to fit in as many friends and relations as possible. Muscovites go to their *dachas* not only in summer but in midwinter through deep snow by whatever means of transport comes handy, to sit and talk and eat and drink endless glasses of weak, sweet tea, on the porch or round the stove, and snacks and little glasses of vodka. Here, in suburb or country, in the warm, cosy, intimate atmosphere of the *dacha*, one realizes, better perhaps than anywhere else, the true Russian genius for intimacy, for hospitality, for rural life. However small, every *dacha* has some little patch of ground on which the proprietor can grow some flowers or a few vegetables.

Half-way to Asia, far out on the great Eurasian plain, on the direct route through the centuries of successive invasions and movements of peoples, Moscow is in more ways than one an Eastern city. Of the faces you see on the street many have an oriental look, while the older buildings, designed as often as not to keep out the Tartars, themselves have an indefinable Eastern flavour. And what remains of the original trading quarter across the Red Square from the Kremlin still bears the name of Kitai Gorod, literally 'China

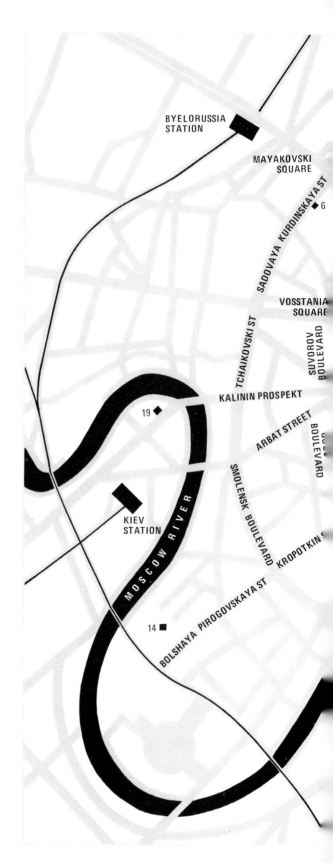

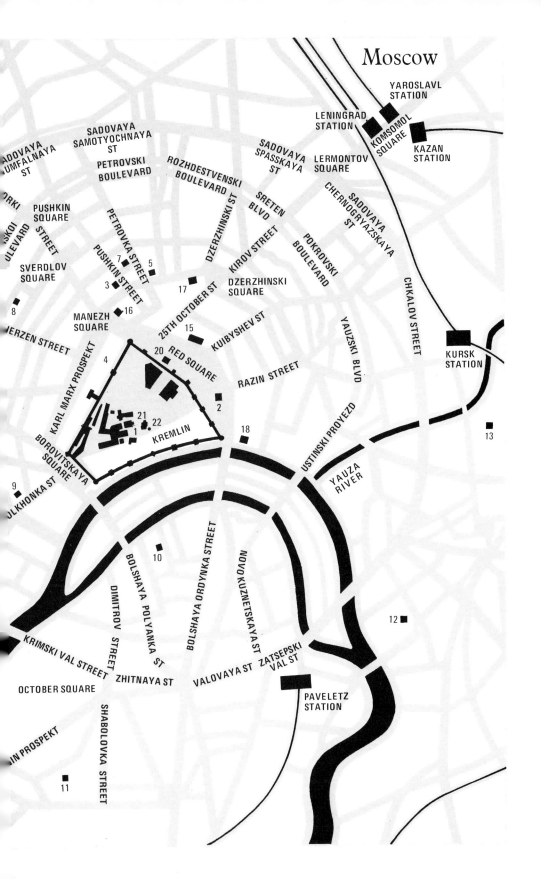

# Moscow

YAROSLAVL
STATION

LENINGRAD
STATION

KOMSOMOL
SQUARE

KAZAN
STATION

SADOVAYA
SAMOTYOCHNAYA
ST

SADOVAYA
SPASSKAYA
ST

LERMONTOV
SQUARE

PETROVSKI
BOULEVARD

ROZHDESTVENSKI
BOULEVARD

SADOVAYA
CHERNOGRYAZSKAYA
ST

ADOVAYA
UMFALNAYA
ST

SRETEN
BLVD

PUSHKIN
SQUARE

ORKI

POKROVSKI
BOULEVARD

CHKALOV STREET

ULEVARD

STREET

PETROVKA STREET

DZERZHINSKI ST

KIROV STREET

USKOI

7

SVERDLOV
SQUARE

PUSHKIN STREET

5

DZERZHINSKI
SQUARE

3

17

KURSK
STATION

8

MANEZH
SQUARE

16

25TH OCTOBER ST

YAUZSKI BLVD

HERZEN STREET

15

KUIBYSHEV ST

4

20   RED SQUARE

RAZIN STREET

KARL MARX PROSPEKT

21

22

2

13

1

KREMLIN

18

BOROVITSKAYA
SQUARE

USTINSKI PROYEZD

9

YAUZA
RIVER

ULKHONKA ST

10

BOLSHAYA ORDYNKA STREET

NOVO KUZNETSKAYA ST

BOLSHAYA POLYANKA ST

DIMITROV STREET

12

KRIMSKI VAL STREET

ZHITNAYA ST

VALOVAYA ST

ZATSEPSKI
VAL ST

OCTOBER SQUARE

PAVELETZ
STATION

IN PROSPEKT

SHABOLOVKA STREET

11

Town', though this is said not to be its correct derivation. If you are looking for something to compare with the Kremlin, it is not so much to western Europe that you turn, though there are walled and fortified towns there too, but rather to Peking with its Forbidden City or to the Old Fort in Delhi or to the walled cities of Khiva and Bokhara. Even the ubiquitous onion dome recalls a mosque as much as it does a Christian church.

Just as Moscow is the heart of Russia, so the Kremlin is the heart of Moscow. In the end it is always to this that you return: to the original inner city, to the great walled fortress rising above the Moscow River, remote and fantastic with its spires and towers, its golden domes, its palaces and belfries and fortifications glittering in the sunlight or emerging like phantoms from the mist and snow. A city within a city, standing where it has stood for eight or nine hundred years, since the time when, in place of the massive red-brick walls that now surround it, there was no more than a wooden palisade protecting a lonely frontier post from the attacks of a variety of enemies.

For two years in the 1930s I lived directly across the river from the Kremlin, looking out at it throughout the day and again every night when a floodlit flag flapped blood-red above it and the luminous red stars, which had lately replaced the old imperial double eagles on its gates and towers, shone out like beacons on an unregenerate world. Each night at the stroke of twelve the chimes of the great clock above the Spasski Gate would play the old *Internationale*, that sad and yet somehow triumphant melody which in those days still doubled as Soviet National Anthem and call to world revolution, summoning the poor and oppressed of all nations to arise and cast off the chains.

The Kremlin was then still closely guarded and relentlessly closed to all comers. In it lived Stalin, cocooned in mystery and paranoia. Sometimes, as you were passing the Spasski Gate, suddenly red lights would flash, a bell would ring menacingly and insistently and a convoy of three or four long black limousines with windows of semi-opaque green bullet-proof glass would shoot out across the Red Square at high speed and disappear down hastily emptied streets to some mysterious destination in the country. Through the thick green glass, you could, if you were sufficiently quick or endowed with a lively enough imagination, sometimes catch a glimpse of an eagle nose and drooping, Asiatic moustache.

But that was the closest view most people ever got of the Kremlin or its inmates. And so it remained, remote and mysterious, a treasure-house full of marvels which one could never hope to see.

Returning to Moscow twenty years later, I found it almost impossible to believe that under a new dispensation and with Stalin safely out of the way, you could simple stroll into the Kremlin and survey it all at your leisure, as a previous generation had done under the Tsars. Now, as you walked amongst the churches and palaces, an official car would likely as not drive past with Mr Khrushchov in it, jaunty, plebeian and looking anything but sinister. It was a surprising contrast and to me symbolized better than anything the changes there had been in Russia since Stalin's death.

For centuries the Kremlin has stood at the heart of Russian history. *Kreml*, the Russian word for it, signifies fortress or stronghold. There was a kremlin at the centre of most mediaeval Russian towns. More than eight hundred years ago, at the beginning of the twelfth century, a local boyar, called apparently Kuchko or Kuchka, dwelt in one such stronghold, situated among some pine-trees on a little hill 120 feet high at the junction of the Moscow River and of a stream known as the Neglinnaya, which then ran down the middle of what are now the Alexandrovski Gardens, but has long since disappeared underground. The Moscow River was a tributary of the Oka, by which it was linked in turn with the mighty Volga.

Grasping the strategic and commercial advantages of such a site, which straddled the main inland waterways of Kievan Rus and was situated near the head-waters of four major rivers, the Oka, the Volga, the Don and the Dnieper, Prince Yuri Dolgoruki of Rostov and Suzdal called on Kuchko and then, claiming that he had not been received with sufficient respect, killed his host and seized his stronghold for himself. He also seized Kuchko's dazzlingly beautiful daughter, Ulita, and sent her to Vladimir as a wife for his son Andrei. But Ulita, evidently not appreciating the honour which had been done her, and irked by the unresponsiveness of her pious, ascetic husband, later contrived to have him assassinated, thereby bringing down upon herself the most appalling retribution and earning from the Chronicler the epithet of treacherous.

From the Chronicler we also learn that in 1147 Prince Yuri invited to his new stronghold his friend and ally Prince Svyatoslav of Chernigov and there entertained him royally. On the strength

of this the year in question has been taken to mark the city's foundation and an imposing equestrian statue of its founder Prince Yuri,
erected in 1947, now occupies a commanding position in the centre
of the city.

Having thus taken possession of it, Prince Yuri and his successors proceeded to strengthen and enlarge Kuchko's little fortress. By the end of the twelfth century, it was further protected
against attack by a wooden stockade which afforded shelter to an
ever-increasing population of artisans and merchants. From a fortress, Moscow had become a small fortified town, though a town
which only occupied one-third of the area covered by the Kremlin
today. Some forty years later, in 1238, the need for yet more effective
fortifications was to be dramatically demonstrated when the Mongol invaders under Batu Khan successfully stormed the Kremlin
and burned it to the ground.

But Moscow, in a sense, benefited from the Mongol invasions. The city now grew in importance. By the beginning of
the fourteenth century its Princes were well on the way to achieving
the supremacy over their neighbours at which they aimed. Their
capital became the seat of the Metropolitan of All Rus and, one
after another, four fine stone cathedrals made their appearance
within the wooden walls of the Kremlin, emphasizing the essential
'holiness' of Russia and the continuing association of temporal and
spiritual, or to use a more contemporary term, ideological power.

The first of these was the Metropolitan's own Cathedral of the
Assumption (Uspenski Sobor), built in 1326. The second, built in
1329, took the form of a belfry dedicated to St Ivan. The third,
which followed in 1330, was the Cathedral of the Saviour (Spasski
Sobor). The fourth, dedicated in 1333 to the Archangel Michael,
was to serve as burial-place for the Grand Princes and Tsars right
down to the time of Peter the Great. Built on four sides of a square
and richly adorned with icons and frescoes, they stood on the same
site as the churches of the same name which stand there today and
effectively symbolized Moscow's spiritual and political supremacy.

The original rough stockade which ran round the Kremlin was
now replaced by a solidly built wall of oak almost a mile long. A
moat dug on its eastern side, separating it from what later became
the Red Square, rendered it more easily defensible. Twenty-five
years later, in the reign of Prince Dmitri Donskoi, the victor of
Kulikovo, these wooden fortifications were in turn replaced by a

Tsar Cannon, Moscow

Guards Officer in Moscow

Cathedral of the Assumption, Kremlin

Tsar Bell, Moscow

new and considerably longer wall of white stone, triangular in form, on an alignment roughly corresponding to that of the present walls of the Kremlin and reinforced by nine stone watch-towers. This, as we have seen, did not prevent the Kremlin from being again stormed in 1382, two years after Kulikovo, by the Tartars under Toktamish, who, gaining entry by a *ruse de guerre*, burned everything they could and massacred 24,000 men, women and children. But what had been destroyed was quickly rebuilt and in 1393, to celebrate her late husband's victory at Kulikovo, Dmitri Donskoi's widow, Evdokia, added yet another cathedral to the Kremlin churches : the Cathedral of the Nativity of the Virgin, parts of which still survive though now incorporated in other buildings.

A century later, under Ivan the Great, came a further military and political advance, marked once again by a wholesale refurbishing of the Kremlin and its cathedrals. The Tartar threat had now receded. Rus was unified under Moscow, and Ivan as ruler of the largest country in Europe and nephew by marriage of the last Emperor of Byzantium, saw himself as successor to the Caesars. It was time, clearly, to replace the dilapidated walls, the plain white stone churches and modest wooden palaces of Ivan Kalita and Dmitri Donskoi with something more worthy of the Third Rome. Encouraged by his wife, Ivan imported a galaxy of foreign talent from abroad and set about this congenial task with a will. One of the first things he did, as part of his scheme of improvements, but also no doubt as a political gesture, was to tear down the former palace of the Khans, from which in the days of the Tartar yoke their emissaries had issued their instructions and collected the tribute due to them.

Work began in 1475 with the building of a new Cathedral of the Assumption, the original church of 1329 having fallen down in an earthquake some years earlier. To build it, Ivan employed Ridolfo Fioravanti, a sixty-year-old architect brought back to Moscow from Bologna in Italy in 1475 by the boyar Simeon Tolbuzin, a special emissary of Ivan III, and renamed Aristotle by the Russians on account of his exceptional intelligence and skill. But, before starting work, Fioravanti was first despatched to Vladimir to study the ancient churches built there three or four hundred years earlier in the improved Byzantine tradition of Vladimir-Suzdal, and to study in particular Vladimir's splendid Cathedral of the Assumption. Fioravanti's new cathedral took five years to build. When it was finished, with its five great golden domes and its walls of white limestone, those who saw it marvelled. 'A church,' wrote the Chronicler, 'marvellous in size and height, in brightness and resonance and wonderfully spacious.'

It can have changed very little in the last five centuries, except, of course, that since the Revolution it has ceased to be a church. With the years, some of the original icons and frescoes have disappeared, but many more have since been added. Inside the cathedral all four walls and the great columns that support the vaulted roof are covered from top to bottom with a multitude of splendid icons, frescoes and painting of saints, martyrs and angels, and so is the great golden iconostasis or icon-covered screen, which, in accordance with Orthodox practice, hid the officiating priest from the congregation during much of the service.

Here, through the centuries, right down to Nicholas II, successive Tsars were crowned on the splendidly carved throne of Ivan the Terrible (or, according to some accounts, of Vladimir Monomakh) and here successive Mertopolitans were laid to rest. Not much daylight filters in through the narrow windows. The cathedral is lit by a number of gilded chandeliers hanging from the roof, which lend a warm glow to the golden haloes and richly coloured robes of the saints and angels on the pillars and walls. The effect is at once magnificent and mysterious. 'We see Heaven!' cried Ivan, his courtiers and clergy when they first entered the completed building. None of which prevented Napoleon, practical as only a Frenchman can be, from using it as a stable for his cavalry and removing from it, when he left, five tons of silver and five hundred pounds of gold.

Fioravanti next turned to the Kremlin's walls and fortifications. The work that he began was to continue for more than a quarter of a century. The old white walls of a hundred years earlier were torn down and the present battlements and watch-towers of red brick erected in their place. Today, if you look carefully, you can still see what could be the remains of the old white stone masonry emerging here and there at the foot of some of the red-brick towers and walls. Simultaneously the moat on the east side was deepened and extended, so that the Kremlin now had water on all three sides of it, and drawbridges, portcullises and barbicans installed. For water the garrison depended on a supply pumped up from the Moscow River and the round tower standing at the point where

the Neglinnaya flowed into it was given the name Vodovzvodnaya
(or 'Water-pumping-tower').

While Fioravanti himself is thought to have determined the
overall layout and design of the fortifications, other architects and
craftsmen, some Russian and some Italian, put his plans into execution and worked on individual stretches of the wall, the whole being
carefully planned from a strategic and tactical point of view and
each tower designed to serve as a self-contained fortress. Of the
five great gate-towers of the Kremlin each has its own name and
is built in its own individual style: Spasskaya, the Gate of the
Redeemer, Troitskaya, the Gate of the Trinity, Borovitskaya, the
Gate of the Pine Wood, Nikolskaya, the elegantly neo-Gothic Gate
of St Nicholas, and Tainitskaya, the Secret Gate.

Between 1480 and 1490, while work was going ahead on the fortifications, Russian architects from Pskov were celebrating the Tartar
withdrawal by building the little Church of Rizopolozheniye
(the Laying by of the Virgin's Vestments), modelling this too on
the Cathedral of the Assumption at Vladimir. On the same side
of the square the same architects built the Cathedral of the
Annunciation (Blagoveshchenski Sobor) with its nine cupolas,
which served the Grand Princes and their Imperial successors as
a kind of Chapel Royal. Originally quite small, it was later increased
in size by the addition of a covered gallery on three sides. Its floor
is paved with agate and jasper. It contains some remarkable early
fifteenth-century frescoes, rediscovered as recently as 1947, and a
large number of magnificent icons, including some of the finest
work of the great mediaeval Russian painter Andrei Rublyov
(1370–1430) and of Theophanes the Greek and their respective
schools. The cathedral's iconostasis is said to be the oldest in
Russia.

Opposite the Cathedral of the Annunciation, on the south side
of Cathedral Square, stands the five-domed, faintly Italianate Arkhangelski Sobor, the Cathedral of the Archangel Michael, built by
Alevisio Novi from Milan between 1505 and 1509 on the site of
the older cathedral of the same name. This served as the burial
place of the Grand Princes and Tsars right down to the time of
Peter the Great. Next to the altar, in the holiest place of all, is the
brass-bound coffin of Ivan the Terrible. Only Boris Godunov is
buried elsewhere, in the Troitsko-Sergiyevskaya Lavra at Zagorsk.

To the north of the Cathedral of the Assumption stand the Palace of the Patriarch and the Church of the Twelve Apostles, both built in the middle of the seventeenth century. After Peter the Great had abolished the Patriarchate in 1700, the palace, built less than fifty years earlier, fell gradually into disuse but has nevertheless remained in a good state of preservation.

High above all the other buildings of the Kremlin rises the bell-tower of St Ivan, popularly known as Ivan Veliki or Ivan the Great, with its shining golden dome. Built early in the sixteenth century by Bono Friazin, another Italian architect, on the site of an earlier, fourteenth-century structure, it was raised a century later to its present height of 250 feet by Boris Godunov, as though to symbolize his own soaring ambition and self-assertiveness. In times of trouble it was used as a watch-tower and its great bell served as a tocsin to summon the inhabitants of the surrounding countryside to take refuge within the Kremlin walls. To Ivan Veliki was added in the mid-seventeenth century a further, auxiliary belfry carrying a whole new peal of bells, dedicated to the memory of the Patriarch Philaret.

At the foot of Ivan Veliki is the Tsar Bell (Tsar Kolokol), a gigantic bell weighing, or so it is said, two hundred tons and intended to be the biggest bell in the world. Originally cast for Boris Godunov for the bell-tower of Ivan Veliki, it had no sooner been hoisted in position than it fell to the ground and broke to bits. Recast a century later on instructions from the Empress Anna, whose virtues and attributes are commemorated in a suitable inscription, disaster once again overtook it. Before it could be hoisted into position, a fire broke out in the shed in which it was being kept. In the ensuing confusion water was thrown on to the red-hot bell and it cracked in two places. Since then it has remained silent on the ground, at first half-buried, but later raised on to a solid base especially provided for it in 1835 by Tsar Nicholas I.

Nearby stands the product of another imperial whim: the Tsar Cannon (Tsar Pushka), a gigantic sixteenth-century cannon seventeen feet long and weighing forty tons, which, if it had ever been used, would have fired two-ton cannon-balls. A pile of these lie ready to hand, made for show in the nineteenth century. But it, too, was doomed to idleness and silence and today serves mainly as a background for holiday snapshots.

Apart from some chapels now incorporated in larger buildings, these are the main churches of the Kremlin. Before the Revolution there were even more. In Stalin's day the ancient Chudov (Miracles) and Voznesenye (Ascension) Monasteries near the Spasski Gate were cleared away to make room for some new administrative buildings. The little Church of the Redeemer in the Wood (Spas na Boru), first built in the twelfth or thirteenth century, when a dense pinewood grew on the Kremlin Hill, and in the nineteenth century enclosed on all sides by the massive masonry of the Great Kremlin Palace, was also torn down at about the same time because it 'took up too much room' in the courtyard in which it stood. Now, fortunately, the destruction of old buildings in the Soviet Union seems to have been halted and those that remain are being carefully restored and preserved.

The oldest surviving secular building in the Kremlin is the Granovitaya Palata or Palace of the Facets, built for Ivan III towards the end of the fifteenth century by two of the Italian architects who had helped Fioravanti build the fortifications, Marco Ruffo and Pietro Solario, and so called because of the faceted pattern of its walls, reminiscent of the Palazzo Pitti in Florence and of other palaces of the Italian Renaissance. The effective if somewhat ornate windows were added in the seventeenth century. Its lower floor was used for administrative purposes while the upper floor contained a vaulted throne-room or audience chamber, supported by a massive central pillar. Adjoining the Granovitaya Palata was the Krasnoye Kriltso or Red Staircase, the scene of so many historic events and once the main entrance to the palace.

From Richard Chancellor, the first of the English merchant-adventurers to visit Russia, we learn of a great feast which Ivan the Terrible gave in the Granovitaya Palata on Christmas Day 1553. Chancellor, who himself attended the dinner, gives a vivid first-hand account of the scene: 'The Emperor, sitting upon a high and stately seat, apparelled with a robe of silver and with another diadem on his head; our men being placed over against him, sit down .... There dined that day in the Emperor's presence,' he continues, 'above 500 strangers and 200 Russians, and all they were served in vessels of gold.'

Ivan III also built for himself the Teremnoi Palace, a name that comes from the Greek *teremnon*, meaning 'women's quarters'. This was to serve as the official residence of the Tsars until the capital was moved to St Petersburg by Peter the Great. First built in about 1500, it was enlarged and reconstructed in the seventeenth century and later damaged by fire and again rebuilt. Its five-storied façade, with its rows of ornate windows, elaborate cornices and string-courses of brightly coloured tiles, offers a good example of fine seventeenth-century plaster-work, while the interior presents a picture of barbaric magnificence, with its low corridors, vaulted ceilings, arched doorways and richly patterned walls (though the rich patterns are clearly of considerably later date). From the largest and most lavishly ornamented of its many windows, the Petition Window, a basket was occasionally lowered into which petitioners would place their requests to the Tsar.

Within the precincts of the Teremnoi Palace are a number of small chapels or churches, of various periods and styles of construction, the eleven golden domes of which, emerging above the roof, all add to the gaiety and confusion of the skyline. They include the Church of the Redemption behind the Golden Railing (Spas na Zolotoi Reshetkoi), also known as the Upper Cathedral of the Redemption (Vrhospasski Sobor), the Church of St Catherine (Tserkov Ekaterini) and the Church of the Crucifixion (Tserkov Raspiatia). Adjoining the Teremnoi Palace is the Poteshni or Pleasure Palace, a tall, green-painted building dating from the mid-seventeenth century and containing yet another chapel. This was originally the house of the boyar Miloslavski (Maria Miloslavskaya married Alexis the Gentle), but was later turned into a theatre and as such was the scene of the first theatrical performances ever to be given in Russia.

Early in the seventeenth century a spire and various other fanci-ful Gothic adornments were added to the Gate of the Redeemer (Spasski) and later similar additions were made to the other eigh-teen towers, further enhancing the Kremlin's fairy-tale appear-ance. In 1625 the Spasski Gate was also provided with a great chim-ing clock, made by Christopher Galloway or Halloway. A watch-maker who had arrived from England four years earlier, Galloway also designed its spire and later installed the pumping equipment in the Vodovzvodnaya. While in Moscow he received from the Tsar a salary of sixty roubles a year in addition to his food and a waggon-load of wood every week.

Another happy addition to the Kremlin was the Tsarskaya Bashnia, a little baroque belvedere or look-out, with columns like twists of barley-sugar, especially built near the Spasski Gate in 1680 to enable the Tsar, when he felt so inclined, to watch what was happening on the Red Square. During the war with Sweden the Kremlin's fortifications were further strengthened and a great Arsenal was built in its north-western corner, a solid-looking yellow building in front of which now stand a fine collection of ancient cannons.

The eighteenth century was, in the words of one authority, 'a difficult period for the Kremlin'. Not many years after her accession Catherine the Great, on a sudden impulse, gave orders for a vast new pillared palace more than two thousand feet long to be built within its precincts, indeed practically in substitution for it. The plans for this mammoth building, which was to cost even in those days no less than thirty million roubles, were drawn up by one Vasili Ivanovitch Bazhenov, an enterprising young architect with a passion for columns. Stretching the full length of the Kremlin's river frontage between the Spasski and Troitski Gates, it would effectively have hidden from view the Kremlin's Cathedrals and other ancient buildings and given it, from the south at any rate, a uniformly classical appearance. A model at present in the Moscow Academy of Architecture shows clearly enough the use Bazhenov proposed to make of colonnades and columns. The completed building, he claimed ecstatically, would be nothing so much as 'a hymn to the column'.

In 1769 work was begun and part of the Kremlin's south wall torn down to make way for the new colossus. On 1 June 1773 the corner-stone was laid with due ceremony. But then, fortunately I feel, something distracted the Empress's attention; the idea was forgotten; instructions were eventually issued for work to be stopped and the Kremlin remained much as it had been before. Catherine's contribution, when it did come, was smaller and less obtrusive. Not long after, she proclaimed the need for a suitable building to house a Duma or Senate. Part of the Kremlin's appeal lies in its diversity and the elegant, domed, triangular building, devised for her by the great Kazakov, fits well enough into its surroundings. Not being needed for a Senate, the new building was used under the Tsars to accommodate the Law Courts and is now occupied by the offices of the Praesidium of the Supreme Soviet. Above its low green copper dome flies a large Red Flag which at night is most effectively floodlit.

By the time Napoleon and his troops had done with them, a number of the buildings in the Kremlin had suffered serious damage.

In particular the departing French soldiers amused themselves as they withdrew by bombarding the great bell tower of Ivan the Great. In the years that followed some of the buildings, including Ivan Veliki, were restored and others simply demolished. In place of a palace built by Rastrelli for the Empress Elizabeth a century earlier and of several other much older buildings, Nicholas I erected the Great Kremlin Palace. Four hundred feet long and ninety feet high (the flat central dome is even higher) and built between 1839 and 1849 by Academician A. K. Ton in a style more or less happily combining Byzantine with classical and ancient Russian elements, this resplendent building, painted a cheerful shade of yellow neatly picked out in white, stretches boldly along the river frontage of the Kremlin. Today it is fashionable to decry these massive products of nineteenth-century architecture, but, while regretting the older churches and palaces that once stood in their place, I feel bound to admit that, once the eye gets used to them (which it very quickly does), they seem to fall quite happily into place amid the prevailing and to me enjoyable jumble of periods and styles.

Inside the Great Palace, the accent, not unnaturally, is heavily on magnificence, the endless succession of vast saloons being lavishly provided with painted ceilings, giant bronze candelabras, and massive columns and pilasters of polished marble and granite, of white and gold. Under the Tsars four of the biggest rooms were dedicated to the four great Russian orders of chivalry, the St George, St Vladimir, St Alexander and St Andrew, the fourth of these serving also as a throne room. In Stalin's day the St Andrew and St Alexander rooms were thrown together to make an even bigger room which houses the Supreme Soviet of the USSR, while the other rooms are used for banquets and other state occasions. Incorporated in the Great Palace are parts of various older buildings, including the Sacred Vestibule, a long, vaulted passage which led through to the Palace of Facets and the Red Stairway, as well as a part-fourteenth-, part-sixteenth-century church dedicated to St Lazarus and the Nativity of the Virgin. To the north, the Hall of St Vladimir serves as a link with the Teremnoi Palace.

Adjoining the Great Kremlin Palace is the Arsenal, which since the sixteenth century had housed workshops for the manufacture of arms and armour and with the passage of time became a centre for yet other arts and crafts. This was now rebuilt by the same architect and in the same style as the Great Kremlin Palace and is painted the same cheerful yellow. Today it contains a truly remarkable collection of treasures, every one of which has the power to evoke some period or incident or character in Russian history. Here, amongst a wealth of other objects of one kind or another, all possessing scarcely less fascinating associations, one comes in the space of a single hour on Yuri Dologoruki's golden chalice; on Vladimir Monomakh's jewel-studded fur-fringed cap, inherited from his imperial grandfather, Constantine Monomakh; and on a whole collection of princely or imperial jewelled crowns, orbs, sceptres and robes; on Ivan the Terrible's ivory throne; on the jewel-studded throne presented to Boris Godunov by Shah Abbas of Persia; and on the great metal double throne used jointly by Peter the Great and his feeble-minded half-brother Ivan, with a window in the back of it for their fat sister Sophia to look through. Here are Peter the Great's immense boots, made by himself for himself; the vast state coach given, one is told, to Boris Godunov by Queen Elizabeth I of England; Catherine the Great's elegant open summer carriage, also made in England, together with numerous other state coaches, carriages and sledges and a mass of jewelled saddlery and harness. Here are displayed a profusion of ambassadorial presents from all over the world, all vying with each other in lavishness and richness and any number of magnificent sixteenth- and seventeenth-century Bibles in jewelled and enamelled bindings. Here, finally, you may see the little gold and platinum clockwork model of the Trans-Siberian Express made in 1900 for Tsar Nicholas II, with its tiny golden travelling chapel at the rear; a musical-box made by Fabergé in 1904 in the shape of a highly stylized model of the Kremlin and a number of Fabergé's other products, right down to the supremely elaborate egg created in 1913 to mark the third and, as it turned out, last centenary of the Romanov dynasty.

Nor, if your taste for treasure is not by now blunted, need this be all. Leaving the building by one door and re-entering it by another, you can, if you like diamonds, visit one of the most fantastic collections of these stones in the world, diamonds of all sizes, in old settings and new and in no settings at all, displayed in a series of underground glass cases and effectively guarded by a number of smart, well-armed and extremely alert-looking sentries in the uniform of the special troops of the KGB. To steal the

Crown Jewels from the Tower of London would, I suspect, be child's play compared with a break-in here.

The Great Kremlin Palace and the Arsenal were not Academician Ton's only major achievements as an architect. He also built, once again in the Russo-Byzantine manner and at no great distance from the Kremlin, the equally massive Church of Christ Saviour. After nearly a century of existence, however, this was dynamited in the 1930s to make way for a great new Palace of the Soviets.

Surmounted by a gigantic statue of Lenin, this latter-day Tower of Babel was to be the tallest and biggest building in the world, dwarfing the Empire State Building and the Eiffel Tower. So many accounts of it were circulated and so many models of it displayed that in the end, though living in Moscow at the time, I (and I dare say many others) almost came to believe that it actually existed and had to peer through a crack in the tall wooden fence that surrounded the site to convince myself that there was nothing really there but an enormous hole in the ground. Then one day, perhaps because the site was found to be too boggy or perhaps because Stalin, like Catherine the Great 160 years earlier, had simply changed his mind, the idea of a great tower was suddenly abandoned; it became, in company with Tsar Pushka and Tsar Kolokol, one of the great non-events of history. In the end, the decision was taken to dig down rather than build up; and much to the delight of the many inhabitants of Moscow who enjoy a swim winter or summer, what may well be the biggest and deepest and best-heated swimming-pool in the world was much more appropriately put in its place.

In 1961, partly perhaps as a substitute for the Palace That Never Was, a completely modern building was boldly inserted among the ancient churches and palaces of the Kremlin: the Palace of Congresses. Its architect, M. V. Posokhin, has made clever use of glass, bronze and white marble to produce a structure which, for a modern building, has unusual lightness and spaciousness and accords well enough with the spires and towers and golden cupolas that surround it. The interior is equally successful. A lofty foyer, abundantly lit by tall windows, or rather glass panels rising to the roof, leads through to a generously laid out and proportioned auditorium with sloped and graded seats looking on to an enormous stage, where, when it is not being used for congresses and conferences, the best companies from the Bolshoi Theatre regularly perform.

Between the acts a moving staircase conveys you painlessly and expeditiously to an upper floor where you are confronted with an altogether fantastic phenomenon: a gigantic multiple snack-bar capable of feeding three thousand people in the space of ten minutes with excellent snacks, both hot and cold, and wine, beer, tea and coffee, all at individual counters marked accordingly. From the windows and balconies, you enjoy, as you eat, an unrivalled close up view of the great golden domes of the neighbouring churches. The last time I went there, there were, of all things, caviar sandwiches and a hot *julienne* of game, and I returned to my seat, as the curtain went up, much refreshed and in the best possible frame of mind for the next act. Catering in the Soviet Union can be haphazard. But this, by any standards, is a *tour de force*.

In the years that followed the great fire of 1812 Moscow, as the map shows, was rebuilt in a series of concentric circles spreading outwards from the Kremlin and marked by broad, tree-lined boulevards. These correspond to the line of the former fortifications, of which no other trace now remains: an inner line, with nine gates and twenty-eight towers, built in the sixteenth century at a distance of some two kilometres from the Kremlin, and an outer ring, now marked by another ring of tree-lined boulevards, the Sadovaya.

The containing wall of the Kremlin, which thus forms, as it were, the core of the city, is roughly triangular in shape. One side faces the Moscow River, a turgid, fast-flowing, brownish stream, offering a remarkable spectacle in the spring time when the ice breaks up and comes crashing downstream on its way to the sea. From across the river you get by far the best view of the Kremlin, a fantastic panorama of towers and spires and golden domes stretching away on either side. To the west, the Kremlin looks out on the Alexandrovski Gardens, much frequented by pigeons, dogs, small children and courting couples and marking the line of the former Neglinnaya River. At one end of the gardens, with its eternal flame, stands the monument to the Soviet Unknown Soldier, upon which newly married brides in their wedding dresses traditionally and devoutly deposit their wedding bouquets. The third wall of the Kremlin, once protected by a moat, forms one side of the Red Square, the vast cobbled expanse which has witnessed so many decisive

Lenin's Tomb, Moscow

Changing the guard

episodes in Russian history and has seen many of its more significant figures come and go, not a few as dismembered corpses. Its
name, which it has borne for centuries, has no revolutionary or
ideological connotation, but derives from the age-old Russian predilection for the colour red, the Russian word for this, *krasni*,
being in Old Russian synonymous with 'beautiful'.

On the Red Square, immediately beneath the Kremlin wall,
stands the low, dark-red basalt mausoleum in which Lenin's
embalmed body has lain under glass for more than half a century,
to the edification of an endless line of visitors from all over the
Soviet Union and beyond, who, shepherded by security guards,
file devoutly and docilely in at one end of the tomb and out at the
other. After 1953 Lenin was joined in his transparent sarcophagus
by Stalin and for some years the two lay side by side, a 'gruesome
twosome', as some irreverent diplomat once called them. Only after
the Generalissimo's eventual fall from favour was he taken out and
relegated to a modest little grave round at the back, now rather
belatedly embellished by a bust.

Outside the door of the Mausoleum two sentries with fixed
bayonets stand guard night and day, the guard being changed at
regular intervals with admirable smartness and precision. The Russians have always loved parades. On the occasion of the May Day
and 7 November Parades, when an impressive flood of marching
troops and military hardware rolls past it for hours on end, the
Mausoleum is used as a saluting base and grandstand by the more
exalted members of the Soviet hierarchy. It was here, on May Day
1937, that I first saw Stalin, a squat, rather menacing figure, with
hawk-like nose and downward turned moustache, watching inscrut-
ably as infantry, cavalry, armour and artillery swept swiftly past
him.

Across the Red Square from the Kremlin stands GUM, the
gigantic state department store, formerly known as *Torgovliye
Ryadi* or 'Trading Rows', a nineteenth-century Russian equivalent
of Burlington Arcade, but forty times the size and built in the Early
Russian style, with shops and booths on three separate levels,
linked by ornamental iron bridges and passageways, and golden
fountains down the middle. The whole is under a glass roof the
height of the Crystal Palace and permanently crowded at all levels
with myriads of jostling, excited shoppers and children with ice-
cream cones, who pass through it, one is told, at the rate of several

hundred thousand a day. Here, once you have got the hang of the place, you can buy cameras and cooking pots, food, fur hats and gramophones, canned goods, caviar and jewellery, champagne, evening dresses, dinner-jackets, grand pianos and household linen. As elsewhere, it is simply a question of having enough money and getting into the right queue. Here, for those who care to see it, is the epicentre of the consumer revolution, a veritable Marxist Marks & Spencers. It is a sight of which I never tire.

The northern end of the Red Square is partly filled by the Historical Museum, a massive red-brick structure also built in the Early Russian manner, apparently by a late nineteenth-century English architect in a brave attempt to beat his Russian colleagues at their own game. Though neither GUM nor the Historical Museum have any great architectural merit, they fortunately possess a sufficiently strong element of the fantastic to make them a not altogether unworthy foil for the mediaeval fantasies of the Kremlin across the way.

But for sheer improbability nothing can beat the Cathedral of St Basil, which stands in all its crazy magnificence at the southern end of the square. 'A masterpiece of caprice,' the Marquis de Custine calls it. 'Certainly,' he continues, disparaging as only a Frenchman can be, 'the land where such a monument is called a place of worship is not Europe; it is India, Persia, China, and the men who pray to God in this box of crystallized fruits are not Christians!' St Basil's was built by Russian architects between 1556 and 1560 in the reign of Ivan the Terrible and dedicated to Basil the Blessed, a mendicant miracle worker or Holy Fool, to whom Ivan rightly or wrongly attributed his victory of 1552 over the Kazan Tartars. It is an extreme example of the exuberant native Russian style of the sixteenth century, recalling the wooden-built churches of the countryside and marking, like them, a complete departure from the earlier Byzantine tradition. Totally asymmetrical (no two of the nine onion domes, which sprout like pineapples round its central dome and each contains a separate chapel, bear any resemblance to each other), it was originally white all over, but was repainted a hundred years later in all the colours of the rainbow. According to a possibly apocryphal legend, Ivan was so delighted with it that on its completion he had its two architects blinded so that they could never build another church to rival it. Immediately in front of St Basil's stands a handsome early nineteenth-century monument to the two strangely assorted leaders of the national rising of 1611, Kuzma Minin, the butcher, and Dmitri Pozharski, the prince, both looking equally heroic in their severely classical way.

In the sixteenth century Christ's entry into Jerusalem was regularly celebrated each Palm Sunday by a procession which made its way from the Kremlin to St Basil's with, at its head, a tree, drawn on a cart and hung with apples and raisins and followed by acolytes bearing icons and incense. After this came the nobility and clergy and last of all the Patriarch, mounted on an ass, or rather a horse draped to resemble an ass and led by the Tsar in person. 'Meanwhile,' wrote a contemporary visitor, 'the bells rang violently, so that the earth trembled and shook.'

A hundred yards or so from St Basil's and not much further away from the well-stocked shop-windows of GUM stands what seems at first sight to be a circular, stone-rimmed well-head or cistern. When one peers over the edge, however, it proves to be a large raised and enclosed stone platform. But a platform with a horrendous history. For this is Lobnoye Mesto, the Place of the Skull. Here, in less civilized times, stood the gibbet. And here convicted traitors and others who had incurred the Tsar's disfavour were publicly drawn and quartered, burnt, boiled alive or otherwise disposed of. Rather significantly, it was also used for theological debates, the proclamation of Imperial ukazes and, on occasion, for the proclamation of a new Tsar, Thus the False Dmitri was proclaimed Tsar here in 1605 and his mutilated body dragged here the year after. Here it was that Prince Shuiski was proclaimed Tsar in 1606 and Michael Fyodorovich Romanov in 1613. Here Stenka Razin was barbarously executed in 1671, while today a nearby street is named after him. Here, in 1699, took place Peter the Great's mass execution of the *Streltsi*. Of more recent years it has, of course, become customary to carry out the liquidation of criminals and other offenders a good deal more discreetly.

While on the subject of the Russian penal system, it is perhaps worth recalling that the famous Lubyanka, which over the last fifty or sixty years has achieved almost equal notoriety, is situated on Dzerzhinski Square, at no great distance from the Red Square, in capacious, solid-looking, rather ornate nineteenth-century premises, which before the Revolution housed a well-known insurance company. In front of it, in the middle of the square most appropriately named after him, stands a handsome monument to

Felix Dzerzhinski, the original founder of the Cheka and, by extension, of its various successor organizations. Across the square from the Lubyanka is Detski Mir, the Children's World, the main toyshop of Moscow, filled with smartly dressed Soviet children accompanied by their clearly adoring parents, for the Russians are utterly devoted to their children.

The only time I was ever inside the Lubyanka, my surroundings struck me as somehow less horrific than might have been expected. But then I went there merely as a visitor on business that was quickly discharged. Of late, or so one is told, the Lubyanka has ceased to be used as a jail and simply accommodates some of the many different administrative departments of the KGB.

A far more disturbing experience than my brief visit to the Lubyanka was to attend, as I did in March 1938, for ten hours a day for ten days on end, the last (one hopes) of the great State Trials, that of Nikolai Ivanovich Bukharin and those who were tried with him. This was held in the Dom Soyuzov or House of the Trade Unions, a handsome late eighteenth-century building by Kazakov which stands on the corner of Pushkin Street and Karl Marx Prospekt and was once the Nobles' Club. ('Good balls, concerts and fêtes,' says my 1914 *Baedeker* encouragingly; but these entertainments, we know, were by then soon to come to an end.) Through the Club's great white pillared ballroom, where the *jeunesse dorée* of Moscow had once disported themselves, passed in the space of three or four years the flower of the Old Bolsheviks, the heroes of the Revolution, who, after confessing at great length to any number of highly improbable crimes, were duly sentenced to be shot and then led away to execution.

Even for a detached young diplomat, with not a care in the world and no particular reason to be concerned at the vagaries of the Soviet legal system, to see this actually happening was a horrifying experience, the nightmarish memory of which has remained with me for more than forty years, being suddenly revived when not long ago I found myself in the self-same ballroom listening to a concert given by a celebrated American pianist with a mop of fair hair and the clear pink-and-white complexion of a college boy.

If you leave the Kremlin, the Red Square, GUM and the Cathedral of St Basil behind you and walk downhill in the direction of the Moscow River, you will suddenly catch sight, on your left, of an enormous modern building. This is the Rossiya or Russia, the biggest hotel in Europe, or so one is told, built a dozen years ago as a kind of Soviet answer to Hilton. Massively square and a dozen storeys high, built round an inner courtyard with an additional twenty-three-storey tower providing even more exclusive and luxurious accommodation, it covers over thirty acres and contains more than three thousand rooms, each with air-conditioning, bath, telephone and *confort moderne* of every description and capable of accommodating over five thousand guests. The Rossiya is for the most part tastefully decorated in impeccable pastel shades, possesses innumerable lifts and, when first built, represented a definite break-through on the Soviet hotel front. In addition to a dozen smaller 'eateries', it also boasts two gigantic, gold-spangled restaurants, each capable of seating a thousand people at a time and echoing to the strains of two of the most resonant jazz-bands in the world.

But even the Rossiya, that haven of the high-class tourist, has its off-beat moments. My happiest recollection is of a scene I witnessed there one morning at about nine. The lobby, packed with groups of blue-rinsed, brightly chattering American matrons about to set out on a tour of the Kremlin, looked surprisingly like a hotel lobby any place. I was just reflecting on this, when all at once two magnificent commissionaires in royal-blue uniforms liberally laced with gold made their appearance at the head of the fine marble staircase leading down from the mezzanine floor. Each had hold of one leg of what appeared to be a dead middle-aged man in a crumpled brown suit. Slowly descending the stairs, they pulled him after them, his skull knocking woodenly on each marble step in turn. Then, elbowing their way through the Daughters of the American Revolution (whose twittering, for once, was momentarily hushed), they dragged him across the lobby to the great double swing-doors, opened them and then quite silently tossed him out into the snow. Who he was, where he had come from, where he was going to, remained a mystery, though I couldn't help feeling that a bottle or two of vodka probably came into it somewhere.

The Rossiya definitely repays a visit, especially to its giant restaurants, but I would not for my own part necessarily choose to stay there (though whenever I have done so I have been extremely comfortable). My favourite hotels in Moscow are the Metropol, built some eighty years ago in much the same spirit as the Rossiya, namely one of emulation and lavish luxury, and the National, built in a new upsurge of the same spirit five or ten years later. This spirit and the décor that went with it have somehow survived a Revolution and two World Wars. The main dining-room of the Metropol is a masterpiece of late Victorian magnificence, with its high gilded ceiling, its great gilt candelabras twelve feet tall, its alcoves and plush-upholstered love-seats, and, best of all, its great fountains, with flowers and greenery rising from their waters, into which at some stage of the evening, when the dancing becomes fast and furious, somebody is almost bound to fall. ('I can so well remember your climbing up those candelabras back in 1912, Your Excellency!' I heard an aged Russian waiter whisper forty years ago to an equally aged foreign diplomat.)

The bedrooms and private sitting-rooms of both these older hotels are also magnificent in their way, with oil paintings and grand pianos and china cabinets and giant vases and marble ink-stands and yards of crushed plush. But nothing in either hotel or indeed anywhere else can equal for sheer splendour the looking-glass in the best suite (Room 101) at the National, an Edwardian *chef d'oeuvre* which leaves one flabbergasted. It was at the National that Lenin usually stayed during the Revolution and one cannot help applauding his choice. Meanwhile, each night from the roof of the Metropol (which in its own way is as expensive and exclusive as any hotel anywhere) flickering lights blazon forth, to my enduring satisfaction, the stirring slogan: RAISE HIGH THE BANNER OF PROLETARIAN INTERNATIONALISM.

Another hotel of which I have uniformly happy memories is the Sovietskaya, built by Stalin soon after the last war, regardless of cost, for official delegations. This, too, is truly magnificent in a rather restrained classical manner. To gain admission to it one needs to be an official guest of the government, which is itself a rewarding and interesting experience. Adjoining the Sovietskaya, and now linked with it by a communicating door, is, surprisingly enough, the Yar, a famous restaurant of pre-revolutionary days, full of minstrels' galleries and *cabinets particuliers*, to which one went to look at (and not only look at) the gypsies. Today it is a most popular place for wedding breakfasts and at frequent intervals shiny limousines deposit a succession of simpering, white-clad brides and elegantly decked-out bridgegrooms on its doorstep.

Both the Metropol and the National, and for that matter the Rossiya, are near the centre of the city, a great advantage for anyone who, like myself, enjoys walking about Moscow in a leisurely way, looking at things for himself. As E. M. Forster said of Alexandria, the best way to get to know Moscow is to walk about it aimlessly. For this reason amongst others, I avoid the Ukraina, a vast thirty-storey skyscraper like a wedding cake on the edge of the city, where you are apt to spend far too much time waiting for lifts that never come and most of the remainder getting back and forth into Moscow.

But, whichever hotel you choose, even if it is the ultra-modern Rossiya, the success or otherwise of your stay will largely depend on the relations you are able to establish, not so much with the management, as with the *dezhurnaya* or housekeeper-receptionist on your floor. She is likely to be a solid, middle-aged woman with hennaed hair of the sensible, hard-working type fortunately very prevalent in Russia. Sitting on each landing, these ladies watch everything that goes on, as they gossip with their colleagues and hand their bedroom keys to the hotel guests. If you are foolish enough to get across your *dezhurnaya*, it will be the worse for you. But if you get on the right side of her, she will provide you with tea in the middle of the night or an extra blanket or a new bulb for your bedside lamp or even, if you insist, a better room. Her title – *dezhurnaya* – comes incidentally from the French *de jour* and means, literally, officer (or whatever it may be) of the day. Which is exactly what she is.

Apart from hotels, Soviet restaurants and food are a subject on which there is room for more than one opinion. I personally enjoy my visits to Russian restaurants enormously. But, in order to do this, one needs a good deal of resilience and also a certain amount of experience and background knowledge.

The first rule is never to allow oneself to become exasperated by the slowness of the service. Russians (and this was even truer before the Revolution) regard a restaurant as a place to which you go for an evening out and quite certainly not as somewhere to snatch a quick snack before rushing on to another engagement. Under the Tsars it was, I believe, customary for the maître d'hôtel to enquire whether you wished to wait an hour or only half an hour between courses. This gave you plenty of time to talk and also to absorb a certain amount of drink. Russians, to my mind very sensibly, drink with their meals rather than between them. In Russia only alcoholics take, as we do in the West, gulps of raw spirits hap-hazardly throughout the day. When one goes to a Russian restaurant one should therefore enter into the spirit of the thing and set out quite frankly to enjoy oneself and make the most of a meal which may last for several hours.

On the assumption that you are not a teetotaller, you begin in principle with vodka, never by itself, but always accompanied by some kind of *zakuski* or hors d'oeuvre. Ideally, these should include caviar, fresh, pressed or red. (For my taste pressed caviar can be almost as good as any but the finest fresh caviar. The red, though also acceptable, is something completely different.) *Blini* or pancakes with sour cream and melted butter are a welcome (and extremely filling) accompaniment to any caviar you can find. But in practice caviar is now hard to come by and very dear when you find it. Failing caviar, however, you can usually get cold smoked salmon or sturgeon, crab, herring or other fish; various forms of mixed 'Russian salad', with fish or meat or eggs mayonnaise, known in Russia as Capital Salad, and, best of all, *julienne*, a delicious hot mixture of chopped ham and game cooked in a hot cream sauce and served in little individual copper pots. You also eat, at this stage of the meal and right through it, any amount of excellent Russian bread (preferably black) and butter. Russian black rye bread is unique. It has a taste and consistency unlike anything else in the world and, once you have acquired a taste for it, you will never rest until you have discovered a source of supply.

But perhaps the most satisfactory course of all in Russia is the soup. This is infinitely varied: clear *bouillon*, served with *pirozhki*, delicious miniature sausage rolls; *bortsch*, with a large spoonful of sour cream; *shchi* or cabbage soup, also with sour cream; *solyanka*, a meal in itself, with meat, cabbage, lots of sour cream, but a sausage or two thrown in as well, and finally *okroshka*, a delicious cold cucumber and sour cream soup made with *kvas*, a strange, beerlike drink, brewed from fermented bread and perfect in hot weather. *Kvas* you can also often buy from street vendors who sell it from barrels on wheels. Many people find it a most refreshing drink in summer. It is something, as far as I know, that is only found in Russia.

Unless you happen to be on the coast or near a lake or trout-stream (for instance in the Caucasus), the supply of fish is apt to be limited, but sturgeon, hot or cold, is often available and, when you can find it, nearly always good. For my taste it is best of all eaten *na vertelye* or grilled on a spit.

As regards red meat, until quite recently steaks were better avoided in the Soviet Union, for the simple reason that they were very, very, tough. Of late there has been an enormous improvement and I have eaten some excellent ones, but they are still apt to be a gamble and one is often safer with something like *Boeuf Stroganov* (chopped beef cooked with onions and sour cream), which is to be found almost everywhere and which the Russians excel at making. (The Russian use of sour cream in cooking is something we should study.) There is also quite a good kind of *escalope* of beef or veal called a *langet*. Another classical Russian dish, *Poulet à la Kiev* or *Kievski Kotlyet*, breadcrumbed breasts of fried chicken coiled expertly and explosively round a core of melted butter, is also on most menus. Then, in restaurants which go in for more exotic specialities, there are such Central Asian or Caucasian dishes as *Kebab* or *Shashlik* and *Pilaff* or *Plov*.

To round off your meal, you cannot do better than order ice-cream. All Soviet ice-cream is excellent and the variety known mysteriously as *Plombières*, presumably after *Plombières-les-Bains*, a favourite resort of the Empress Eugénie, is particularly good. (It is interesting to me that the people of the two super-powers, the Russians and the Americans, also happen to be the best makers of ice-cream.) *Smetana* or thick sour cream, eaten by the glass, is equally delicious. There are also quite often some perfectly eatable cakes and pastries.

Sometimes, though no longer very often, you strike a restaurant that is out of almost everything or a *bufyet* or snack-bar with only a limited repertory. This is when I fall back on an omelette or ham and eggs, and a lot of black bread and butter. On such occasions Soviet sausages, in other words Frankfurters, are another useful standby, as is *Kolbasa* or cold sausage.

Meals are served in Soviet restaurants for a large part of the twenty-four hours with sudden arbitrary intervals. Having started with a snack and a glass or two of tea for breakfast, most Russians eat a hearty dinner (with soup), known as *obyed*, at sometime between ten in the morning and six in the evening and another, rather lighter, meal, called *uzhen* or supper, between six in the evening and two in the morning.

With these often somewhat strangely timed and strangely assorted meals, you can drink Soviet beer (Riga beer is the best) or a bottle of Georgian or Armenian wine (both red and white can be excellent) or, if all else fails, more vodka. For the teetotaller there are various kinds of mineral water and several kinds of fruit juice. Fizzy Soviet lemonade I quite frankly do not like and will not drink if I can possibly avoid it. Tea – Russian tea – is the drink to end up with. It is taken hot and sweet and the Russians drink it from first thing in the morning till last thing at night. If you want coffee, Turkish coffee is preferable.

As in capitalist countries, the respective reputations of the various restaurants in Moscow or any other Soviet city are liable to fluctuate. Which is why I am careful to make enquiries before setting out for one. In my experience, however, a very safe bet is the Praga, on the Arbat, a restaurant famous from pre-Revolutionary days, which suffered bomb damage during the war but has since been splendidly restored to its original Edwardian magnificence. Several of the private rooms are worth a visit for aesthetic reasons alone. In general, surroundings, food and company all fulfil one's highest expectations and one should allow several hours to make the most of them. Other restaurants where I have enjoyed myself include the Sofia and the Berlin. There is also, ironically enough, the Pekin, where you are said to be able to get Chinese cooking. The Aragvi and an Armenian restaurant, the Ararat, provide Caucasian cooking, while an excellent Uzbek restaurant, the Uzbekistan, specializes in Central Asian dishes. For the historian, the Aragvi has the added attraction that it was here, in this building, then the Hotel Duseaux and later the Saxonia, in a private room upstairs, that the famous General Skobelyov, one of the great heroes of the Balkan and Central Asian campaigns, was struck down at the early age of thirty-eight, while evidently over-exerting himself with two young ladies of easy virtue.

Of late, in deference to foreign impatience, and to meet the criticism that you cannot get a meal in Moscow in under three hours, a special new restaurant had been opened in the Hotel Intourist, known as the Starlit Sky. Here, in return for a cover charge of some two pounds a head, you can get a table immediately, plus quick service and service with a smile. The cooking is good; everything on the menu is available; and the floor-show, with its blondes in see-through pyjamas unerringly exploding multi-coloured balloons with steel bows and arrows, is quite something. Those on the look-out for something really Russian, however, and with plenty of time to spare should try the Slavyanski Bazar. This was a famous res-

taurant in Tsarist days. Opening in 1870, when the Pan-Slav movement was already gathering momentum, it quickly became a
favourite meeting-place for writers, intellectuals and people connected with the theatre. One of the smaller rooms bore the name
Beseda (or *Causerie*), as though set aside for intimate conversation,
whether literary or romantic. It was at the Slavyanski Bazar that
in 1898, after sitting over their dinner for a great many hours, Stanislavski and Nemirovich-Danchenko took the historic decision to
found the Moscow Arts Theatre. This, too, was the meeting-place
of Gurov and Anna Sergeyevna in Chekhov's 'Lady with a Little
Dog'. After the Revolution the restaurant was closed and the
premises put to other uses, to reopen a dozen years or so ago,
restored to its former splendour or at any rate something roughly
resembling it. In addition to the main restaurant, there are a
number of ingeniously contrived *cabinets particuliers* on the first
floor, decorated in every kind of Old Russian style and kept for
private parties. The food, like the decor, is deliberately Russian,
but none the worse for that. I found the roast duck, cooked with
sour cream and apples, quite excellent. Russian *blini*, or pancakes
of various kinds, are another speciality and in hot weather the big
jugs of iced *kvas* are exactly what you need. Some of the waiters
are already dressed in embroidered Russian shirts and on my next
visit I confidently expect to see the waitresses also decked out in
some form of national dress.

But, as in most other countries, food in people's houses in Russia
is apt to be better than restaurant food. Russians are by nature immensely hospitable. They also enjoy their food and drink and are
proud of their national specialities. The whole family clusters
round and helps to cook. All this makes them wonderful hosts and
their parties great social and gastronomic occasions.

A serious problem for the hearty eater in Moscow is how to get
enough exercise, especially in winter, when the days are short and
everything is covered in snow. I solve the problem myself by quite
firmly going everywhere I can on foot. This has the added advantage that you see things – shop windows, people, places, situations
– for yourself at close quarters instead of remotely from the splendid isolation of an Intourist limousine, and return to wherever you
are staying refreshed and ready for the next round of *vodka* and
*zakuski*.

But you do not need to walk. If you cannot find a taxi (of which

Stalin spectacular, Moscow

there are now far more than formerly) you can always take the Metro. In the 1930s the new Metro was the pride of Moscow. 'Have you been on our Metro?' Uzbek peasants would ask me on my travels through Central Asia. The first time I was asked this question in Samarkand by a Central Asian who had himself evidently made the golden journey to Moscow, I was obliged to admit shamefacedly that I had not. 'I can see,' he replied pityingly, 'that it could be a terrifying experience for anyone not accustomed to such things.'

In due course I rectified my omission and was duly impressed by the magnificence of what I saw. The Metro, not only in Moscow but in such remote places as Tbilisi, has become my favourite means of transport. Not only is it clean, speedy and efficient, but the stations, built of polished basalt, marble and bronze and usually adorned with gilded bronze *torchères* or crystal chandeliers, are of unparalleled splendour. And now, with new branch-lines shooting off in every direction, it will take you almost anywhere you want to go and do so at a modest and uniform price.

During the forty years since I first went there, Moscow has, of course changed enormously. Returning in 1958 after an absence of twenty years, I was immediately struck on my way in from the airport by the vast new residential suburbs – block upon block of high-rise apartment houses and shopping centres – which have all sprung up since the war and which seem to spread deeper and deeper into the surrounding country every time I go back. Housing accommodation may still be short, but at least a determined attempt is being made to tackle the problem and some of the new buildings possess considerable architectural merit.

Personally I do not share the now almost universal detestation of the wedding-cake style skyscrapers of Stalin's day. Whatever anyone may say about them they have a fantastic quality all of their own, reproducing, as they do on a gigantic scale, and in ferro-concrete, the earlier fantasies of the Middle Ages and Renaissance so brilliantly exemplified by the towers and spires of the Kremlin. Though I would sooner not stay there, the Ukraina Hotel, with its massive pillared entrance, is well worth looking at. So are some of the new Ministries and apartment houses of twenty-five years ago. And so is the new Moscow University on the Lenin Hills (not to be confused with the beautiful eighteenth-century University building across the road from the equally fine early nineteenth-

century *Manège* (or Riding School) of about the same period near
the Kremlin). But for a classical building of the Stalin era, you
cannot beat the stately administrative palace he built at the
entrance to the race-course, with a splendidly prancing quadriga
on top of it. It is by any standards magnificent.

Nearer to the centre of the city, there has also been much new
building and tearing down and the Moscow skyline, like that of
most cities, has been dramatically altered by startling new skyscrapers. But much of the old Moscow fortunately still survives
and you can still find whole streets of characteristically Russian
early nineteenth-century low, stucco-fronted houses dating back to
the years that followed the great fire of 1812. One or two storeys
high, comfortable, practical and warm, usually with a yard or little
garden behind, some are in a good and some in a less good state
of preservation. Quite often in these quiet back streets, you will also
find an old church, sometimes, in the Russian phrase, still working,
sometimes derelict or turned into a movie-house, with giant
pictures of filmstars' faces posted round the porch.

An entirely new street, driven through the centre of the city,
is the Kalinin Prospekt, which, with its vista of modern department stores and towering high-rise buildings, is at first sight indistinguishable from the main street of almost any American town in
the Middle West, except that when you look closely you will find
a small, brightly coloured, very Russian, onion-domed church,
which has fortunately been spared by the planners and nestles at
the foot of one of the tallest skyscrapers. It has, I discovered on
investigation, been converted into an aquarium. Following the
Prospekt Kalinina, you come to the Arbat, so called from a Tartar
word signifying market and today a swirling mass of traffic con-
verging from all directions.

Among the shops on Kalinina is a spacious and splendidly
equipped bookshop filling two whole floors and divided into clearly
designated sections for different types of books: sport, music,
travel, science, technology, art, literature, political science and so
on. Here at last, I thought triumphantly, is a bookshop where I
shall be able to buy some of the classics, and made for the department labelled literature. But no. Pushkin, Gogol, Dostoyevski,
Tolstoi, Chekhov – not a single volume by any one of them was
to be found. Returning there three or four times, I always had the
same experience until finally persistence was rewarded and, joining

a queue, I was able to snap up a paperback edition of two of Turgenyev's stories for the modest sum of forty-nine kopeks before the limited stock was exhausted. The books, it appears, really do exist, though in restricted quantities, and sometimes even reach the stores. But they are then immediately snapped up by the customers who happen to be there when they first arrive or else have a friend among the sales-ladies. Meanwhile the works of Marx and Lenin, like the poor, are always with us. However, hope springs eternal and, encouraged by occasional successes over the last forty years, I still persist in my search.

Further down the Kalinina, on the other hand, we found a ladies' dress-shop, where, chaperoned by my wife, I witnessed, on payment of a rouble, a display of the latest Soviet fashions: day dresses, trouser-suits, sports-wear, cocktail-dresses, ball-dresses and so on. Both the dresses and the young women who modelled them, swaying along a cat-walk and turning at the end with a highly professional twist of shapely hips, I found appealing, though not quite as appealing as those I saw at the House of Fashion, which, I am told, is frequented by the really fashion-conscious. Here both dresses and models display an altogether higher degree of sophistication – the difference, I suppose, between Christian Dior and a department store.

Something that most people instinctively connect with Russia is the ballet – the Russian ballet. And rightly so. For the last couple of hundred years the ballet has played a very important part in Russian life. Like many other things in Russia (communism and the Orthodox Church included), it was originallly imported from abroad but has with the years become deeply and intensely Russian. This Russian affinity for the ballet is no doubt due partly to a traditional Slav love of dancing and partly to the emergence in Russia in the nineteenth and early twentieth centuries of an exceptional galaxy of native talent: such great composers as Tchaikovski, Borodin, Glinka, Stravinski and Rimski-Korsakov; a great impresario, Diaghilev; several great choreographers, Benois, Petipa and Fokin; Bakst, a great designer of costumes and scenery; and a succession of such great dancers as Pavlova, Nijinski, Karsavina, Semyonova, Ulanova and, more recently, Lepeshinskaya and Plisetskaya.

As a form of artistic expression, the ballet appeals to something deep down in most Russians: to their feeling for colour, for the

High Fashion

dramatic and the romantic, to their love of music and movement, to their explosive sense of rhythm. It also provides something not unnecessary in the world of today, in Russia no less than anywhere else: an escape from reality. 'Your equivalent of our Bolshoi Ballet,' a Russian said to me recently after listening avidly to my description of a British Royal wedding.

Under both Tsars and Commissars the ballet and those involved in it have occupied a special, privileged position in Russian society. The tradition is unbroken. Indeed, it is said that performances were not interrupted for more than a few days at the height of the October Revolution. But, even so, for the ballerinas of the Bolshoi Ballet life has never been all orchids and champagne in the company of grand dukes or high party officials. They have always needed to work phenomenally hard just to keep pace. And their every move, both on the stage and off it, is closely watched, both by those whose duty this is as well as by any number of keen rivals and competitors.

From the age of seven onwards, a prospective ballerina leads a dedicated, isolated existence, away from all disturbing influences, in a school where, though other subjects are included in the curriculum, dancing is what counts: the School of the Bolshoi Ballet. This, as a great privilege, I was once taken to see by the late Elena Nikolayevna Furtseva, a remarkable and at the same time very feminine woman and, in her own highly personal way, a considerable Minister of Culture.

The ballet school is still housed where for all I know it was housed under the Tsars, in a tall, rather shabby nineteenth-century building, which you approach through a courtyard. It possesses a floor for every year from seven to eighteen. Starting at the ground floor, you follow the *cursus honorum* of these dedicated moppets from childhood, through puberty and adolescence to the ultimate flowering of the fully-fledged ballerina ten floors up. On each floor, you find the same large, low room, the same practice *barre* and the same, or almost the same, ballet-teacher, middle-aged, austere and extremely authoritative, taking her class through increasingly intricate exercises with ever greater precision and perfection. To have witnessed this process and to realize that it is something that has continued uninterrupted for a hundred years or more helps one to understand why, in so many respects, the Russian ballet remains unsurpassed. I have never seen the training of the male ballet-

Bolshoi Ballet

dancers, but from their proficiency I imagine that it is no less arduous.

In the Soviet Union enthusiasm for the ballet is not limited to any one class or group. A ticket for the Bolshoi is as much prized in Moscow as a ticket for a big soccer match would be in Glasgow or London. Not that the Muscovites do not share in the by now universal passion for football. On the contrary, the fortunes of Spartak or Dynamo are followed locally with scarcely less enthusiasm than those of Celtic and Rangers.

For the aspiring ballerina (as indeed for most Soviet ballet enthusiasts) the Bolshoi Theatre is the ultimate target. It possesses unrivalled glamour and prestige, though the Kirov (formerly Mariinski) Theatre in Leningrad runs it close in popularity. The original Bolshoi Theatre was destroyed by fire and rebuilt in the 1850s. Classical in style, with a great pillared portico fronting on Sverdlov Square (or Theatre Square, as it used to be called), in many ways it resembles Covent Garden. Inside the auditorium, with room for three thousand people, is decorated in the grand manner of the period: with plenty of gold and red plush everywhere and tiers of boxes and galleries rising one above the other.

In the intervals, the audience, smart and a trifle self-conscious in their best clothes (blue suits or uniforms and party dresses), parade up and down in the foyer and corridors, looking at each other and greeting their friends. For here, in the best seats, are the élite, the cream of Soviet society. Or, if they have not yet got that far, they hope to get there soon. And often, in the old Imperial box you will see the leaders of the government and Party, entertaining visiting notabilities. But, whatever the social overtones and whether they are seated in the Tsar's box or the topmost gallery, this is an audience of enthusiasts, of *aficionados*, who follow expertly every note and every movement.

Some critics maintain that in Russia the ballet has not moved with the times, that it has scarcely evolved since the days of Diaghilev, indeed that in some respects it has lost ground since Diaghilev's departure. But this is at best a half-truth. When I first went there in 1937, Russia was the only country in the world where you could see the great classical ballets such as *Swan Lake*, *Giselle* and *The Sleeping Beauty* regularly performed in their entirety. Elsewhere companies danced for the most part brief excerpts from the classics or short, incomplete, modern compositions often amounting to little more than choreographic sketches. Since then there has been a great resurgence of ballet in the West. For the past thirty years, the Royal Ballet and the New York City Ballet have been competing with the Russians on their own ground, as well as producing a quantity of new ballets, and during this period the West has naturally made great progress and produced a number of outstanding ballerinas, *premiers danseurs* and choreographers. The Russian ballet, meanwhile, especially in its more modern productions, has not entirely escaped the rather old-fashioned rigidity which the Soviet system manages to impose on most of its art forms. There is also, as elsewhere, a sizeable gap between its best performances and its worst. For me, nevertheless, partly perhaps for nostalgic reasons, an evening at the Bolshoi still offers an experience I can find nowhere else.

Adjoining the Bolshoi (or Great) Theatre on Theatre Square and, like it, only a few hundred yards from the Metropol Hotel, is the early nineteenth-century Mali (or Little) Theatre with, outside it, a statue of the playwright Ostrovski, pensive in his chair. And not far away are the Moscow Arts Theatre (MKHAT), the Stanislavski Theatre and others. Like the ballet, the theatre plays a very important part in Russian life, due partly to a tremendous nineteenth-century flowering of talent in this field and partly to an innate Russian love of drama and theatre. How indeed could it be otherwise in a country which in a century and a half produced such authors as Pushkin, Ostrovski, Gogol and Chekhov; such producers as Stanislavski and Nemirovich Danchenko; an abundance of good actors; plenty of critics intelligent and sensitive enough to appreciate them and the plays they act in; and above all an enormous and infinitely enthusiastic public?

Something that no visitor to Moscow should miss is Obraztsov's famous puppet theatre. I would not have believed that puppets could be made to live or used to such effect or that I myself could have derived quite such pleasure from them. At Obraztsov's magic touch the puppets simply come to life, displaying every human characteristic and expressing every human emotion in the comic or dramatic situations which he so ingeniously contrives for them. As a performance, it is like nothing else I have ever seen and the effect is further enhanced by the attractive design of Obraztsov's new theatre.

Few visitors leave Moscow without being taken to the theatre

or ballet, but it would not be impossible for an uninitiated and un-
informed visitor to miss the Soviet capital's two best collections of
pictures: the Pushkin and Tretyakov Galleries, which somehow
often seem to get left off the ordinary tourist schedule. In fact
both collections are quite exceptional. At the end of the nineteenth
and beginning of the twentieth century three or four rich Russians
had the good taste (and good sense) to spend their money on buying
a number of the very finest works of the French Impressionists,
a great many of which (having passed into the custody of the state)
are now assembled in the Pushkin Gallery, just across the road from
the Kremlin. They are most certainly worth visiting.

With one or two exceptions, the Tretyakov Gallery, also originally a private collection, only contains pictures by Russian artists.
Apart from a few agreeable eighteenth-century portraits and some
highly dramatic scenes from Russian history, a great part of the
collection consists of nineteenth-century conversation-pieces and
other pictures illustrating different aspects of everyday life in
Russia. Thus, in addition to their artistic merit, which is often considerable, they constitute a fascinating historical document, all the
more interesting because so much of the life and traditions they
depict has necessarily vanished for ever. What could be more
charming, for instance, or more evocative than Brullov's early nineteenth-century painting of a pretty young girl starting off from an
elegant country house for a ride through the woods on a spirited
horse, with her pet dog barking and her little sister in a frilly dress
waving her goodbye.

The Tretyakov Gallery also contains a magnificent collection of
icons, brought together from a number of different sources. In
addition to some of the finest works of the great sixteenth-century
painter, Andrei Rublyov, it includes the famous *Virgin of Vladimir*, the most beloved of all icons, venerated for centuries as the
guardian and protector of Holy Russia, which after the Revolution
was moved here from the Cathedral of the Assumption in the Kremlin (where it has been replaced by a fifteenth-century copy). This
great masterpiece depicts the Virgin and Child with exceptional
reverence and depth of feeling but also with infinite warmth and
compassion, thus reflecting a different kind of religious experience
from that symbolized by the wooden austerity and severity of some
earlier representations. It is in short the first true 'Virgin of Ten-
derness', as icons painted in this manner came to be called. In the

centuries that followed, the cult of Mary in Russia was to emphasize the concept of maternity rather than virginity, with the result that the Mother of God became, as one authority has said, the mother-image of All Russia.

Painted, some say, by St Luke, but a good deal more probably by an unknown Byzantine artist in the twelfth century, the *Virgin of Vladimir* was originally brought to Kiev from Constantinople and is not therefore, strictly speaking, of Russian origin. It was later removed from Kiev as a prize of war by Prince Andrei Bogolyubski and taken by him to Vladimir. Here, from the miracles it worked, it became known as the miraculous *Virgin of Vladimir*. In 1395, when Moscow was threatened by the hordes of Tamerlane, the icon was brought to the beleagured city to help defend it against the infidel. Whereupon Tamerlane himself experienced a vision of a lady clad in purple robes leading a mighty army to block his advance on Moscow. This, it is said, rather than any purely military or political considerations, was what induced him to return so rapidly whence he had come. To this same icon was also attributed Ivan the Terrible's victory over the Tartars at Kazan, whence it is sometimes known as the Virgin of Kazan. In 1612 the icon again saved Moscow, this time from the Catholic Poles, when its presence caused the Russians, appalled at the thought that it might fall into enemy hands, to redouble their efforts and ultimately throw back the invaders. 'It is better,' they said, 'for us to die rather than let the image of the Immaculate Mother of God be desecrated by falling into the hands of Polish heretics.' Thereafter it was kept in the Cathedral of the Assumption in the Kremlin until moved to the Tretyakov Gallery after the Revolution. Another famous icon now in the Tretyakov Gallery is Rublyov's *Trinity*, moved there from the Monastery of the Trinity and St Sergius at Zagorsk. This shows three seated angels and alludes to the three heavenly beings who appeared to Abraham as well as to the Trinity, thus linking the Old Testament with the New.

Walking or driving round Moscow, one comes on a number of other old monasteries, put to a variety of uses and in varying states of preservation. Two which I have always enjoyed visiting for the escape which they provide from the turmoil of the metropolis are the Monastery of the Don (Donskoi Monastir) and the Monastery of the New Redeemer (Novospasski Monastir).

The Monastery of the Don, situated on the southern fringes of the city, in a loop of the Moscow River, was built on the site of an older fortress of which the massive outer wall and twelve fortified towers still survive. Founded in 1591 by Tsar Fyodor Ivanovich to commemorate the defeat of the Golden Horde under Khan Kazi-Ghirei, it is dedicated to the Virgin of the Don, whose gem-studded icon was kept until the Revolution in the largest of the seven churches enclosed by its walls. This, a five-domed baroque cathedral, built towards the end of the seventeenth century, was founded by Peter the Great's sister, Catherine. More interesting in some ways is the smaller church with a single dome, built a hundred years earlier, when the monastery itself was first founded. On the gravestones and memorials which stand all round it under the trees you may read the names of many of once great Russian families: Tolstoi, Golitsin and so. Latterly the church has been turned into an architectural museum.

On the left bank of the Moscow River, a couple of miles south-east of the Kremlin and surrounded by a high white wall, stands the Novospasski Monastir or Convent of the New Redeemer, its towers, domes and ramparts mirrored in a fish-pond. Founded by Ivan Kalita in the fourteenth century and said to be the oldest convent in Moscow, it moved to its present site rather more than a hundred years later in the reign of Ivan III. Individually, none of its five churches, repeatedly destroyed and rebuilt, are of very great interest, but, taken together, with the belfry which rises above the entrance gate, they are impressive enough. In the graveyard of the convent are buried Marfa, the mother of Tsar Michael Fyodorevich, together with various other members of the Romanov family.

Two more monasteries which can quite easily be reached on foot from the centre of the city are the Upper Petrovski Monastery (Visoko-Petrovski Monastir) and the Spaso-Andronikov Monastery. To reach the former, you walk from Theatre (or Sverdlov) Square straight along the Petrovka, once one of Moscow's most famous shopping streets, leaving behind you on your left the Bolshoi Theatre and on your right what before the Revolution was the emporium of Messrs Muir and Merrilees and is now TSUM (Tsentralni Universalni Magasin), a rather smaller rival of GUM. Founded in the fourteenth century, the Visoko-Petrovski Monastery contains the tombs of the Narishkin family. Most of the buildings, including the tall, onion-domed campanile, date from the end of the sixteenth century. The Spaso-Andronikov Monastery, also founded in the fourteenth century, stands in a commanding position above the River Yauza in the south-eastern quarter of the city. It contains a fine fifteenth-century cathedral which was largely destroyed in 1812 but subsequently rebuilt. It now houses a fine collection of icons.

Originally far beyond the limits of old Moscow, but since increasingly encompassed by the city's urban sprawl, is perhaps the most interesting of Moscow's many convents or monasteries: Novodevichi, the Convent of the New Virgin, now a branch of the Historical Museum. Primarily a nunnery, founded by Vasili III in 1525, Novodevichi was also an important strong-point, strategically sited at a bend in the Moscow River and forming a vital link in the chain of Moscow's outer defences. In 1591 the cannon of Novodevichi, firing from the battlements, turned back an attack by the Khan of the Crimea and again in 1612 the convent played an important part in the defence of Moscow against the Poles. The great walls, built in the sixteenth century with a battlemented tower at each of the four corners and lesser fortifications in between, still stand. It was here, as we have seen, that Peter the Great imprisoned his turbulent half-sister Sophia in 1689, causing the corpses of her fellow conspirators to be strung up outside the window of her cell as a reminder of the price exacted for treachery and insubordination. Confined in the monastery for fourteen years, Sophia sensibly turned her attention from politics to architecture, building within its walls a church, several chapels, a bell tower, refectory and hospital, as well as various useful outbuildings, most of which are still standing. She lies buried under the southern wall of the convent.

The principal church of Novodevichi is the great five-domed Smolensk Cathedral, built at the time of the convent's original foundation in 1525 to celebrate the re-capture of Smolensk and standing at the centre of the space enclosed by its walls. It possesses a particularly fine seventeenth-century iconostasis. Novodevichi was always a rich foundation, being generously endowed by the numerous great ladies who were admitted to it as nuns. With time it lost its strategic significance and thereafter its incumbents concentrated more on its beautification than on its defence. In 1812, however, Novodevichi narrowly escaped demolition by the French, being only saved at the last moment by some nuns who with great presence of mind managed to extinguish the fast-burning fuses.

Paul of Aleppo, an Orthodox Byzantine priest from Syria who visited Novodevichi in the seventeenth century, was filled with admiration by the convent and by the Smolensk Cathedral in particular. 'This church,' he wrote, 'is of vast dimensions ... the cupola above the table is admirable, being all covered with gold, with arch upon arch supported by angels .... We found no likeness, not even among the Emperor's churches, to the beauties of this church. The Patriarch,' he continues, 'told our master from his own mouth: we possess no convent equal to this in riches; and this is because all the nuns who reside in it are widows or daughters of the great men of the Empire and come with all their property and possessions and their plate, gold and jewels, which they then settle upon the convent.'

Over each of the main entrances of the convent is built a typical late seventeenth-century gate-church, the Church of the Intercession (Pokrovskaya) above the southern gate and the Church of the Transfiguration (Preobrazhenskaya) above the northern. A tall bell-tower adjoining the Church of the Assumption and the Refectory belong to the same period. All these are built of red brick with white stone ornamentation in a style vaguely recalling Dutch baroque. Many of them date from the time when the Tsarevna Sophia was living in the convent, others from the period of her regency.

Outside the immediate precincts of the convent lies an equally well known burial ground, in which are buried many famous Russians. Walking along its paths one can pick out the graves of Gogol and Chekhov, of the heroes of the wars against Napoleon and Hitler and of the Bolshevik Revolution and its aftermath, all lying in close proximity one to another, some with elaborate monuments, some with plain headstones, some with crosses over them and some with more secular symbols. A much visited grave is that of Stalin's wife Nadezhda Alliluyeva who shot herself in 1932, a tragedy which her husband attributed to the unhappy influence of *The Green Hat* by Michael Arlen – 'that filthy book,' as he called it. Others felt she might have had other reasons for taking her life. On feast days and particularly on All Souls Day the cemetery is crowded with Russians who come with flowers to put on the graves and often bring picnics, which they eat sitting among the tombstones on little seats provided for the purpose. The last time I was there, someone, a relative or perhaps just a sympathizer, had left a pathetic little bunch of three or four flowers on Nadezhda's simple grave.

For anyone who ever met him it is positively startling, on rounding a corner, to come face to face with the late Mr Khrushchov
in white marble. The likeness is an excellent one from the chisel
of Ernst Neizvestni, a brilliant young sculptor who at one time incurred Khrushchov's displeasure by his insufficiently conventional
approach to sculpture. After Khrushchov's departure from office,
however, the two became friends and after Khrushchov's death it
was Neizvestni whom his family entrusted with the creation of his
memorial.

'Religion,' said Karl Marx, 'is the opium of the people.' With
the partial (but by no means total) eclipse of religion in the Soviet
Union, other means have had to be found of keeping people happy.
There can, I suppose, be few more characteristically Soviet institutions than the Park of Rest and Culture or rather, for that is the
order of priority indicated by its Russian title, of Culture and Rest.
You will find one in every Soviet town, large or small, varying from
something approximately the size of Coney Island or Battersea Fun
Fair to a more modest version comprising a couple of flower beds,
a bench or two, six trees, a see-saw, some swings and a sand-pit.
Whatever its extent, however, it will inevitably be adorned with
one or more larger than life portraits of Lenin, usually flanked by
Marx and Engels, and with numerous inspiring exhortations on
posters and banners to work harder and do better. It will also contain a number of plaster statues, usually silvered or gilded and
representing allegorical figures, rugged-looking workers and
peasants or, as often as not, magnificent semi-nude sports girls,
diving, slamming tennis balls or otherwise exerting themselves.
(Before de-Stalinization there would also, invariably, be some
statues of the late *Vozhd*, usually in uniform, beaming benev-
olently on the passer-by. But these have long since disappeared.)
From loud-speakers, meanwhile, come political harangues or the
strains of martial music.

The biggest and best of all these far-flung pleasure gardens,
covering three hundred acres, is situated on the banks of the
Moscow River. My own first memories of it go back more than
forty years, to the winter of 1936–7. With the first frosts the authorities flooded it to its full extent, thus converting it into a gigantic
skating-rink. At night it was brilliantly illuminated and loud-
speakers dispensed the waltzes of Strauss, Lehar and Tchaikovski.
Along the frozen alley-ways the plaster workers and sports girls were

capped with snow. Having dined well with a group of congenial friends, one would drive to the entrance gates, strap on one's skates and launch oneself boldly into the whirling, spinning crowd, keeping a wary eye on agile little Soviet boys who shot past one like rockets at sixty miles an hour. Some of the alley-ways are quite sharply inclined and, once launched, one would often suddenly find that one was skating downhill, an unusual and exhilarating experience. Above us all loomed the great floodlit portraits: Marx, Engels, Lenin and, in those days, of course, larger and more significant than all the rest: Stalin. It is a cheerful memory from an otherwise grim period.

In summer the park provides rest and culture in a number of ways. In addition to the portraits and the posters and the loudspeakers and the statues, there are any number of side-shows: open-air theatres, jazz concerts, shooting-galleries, bowling alleys, dispensers of ice-cream and fizzy lemonade, hot-dog stands and stands where you can buy cigarettes and magazines and tiny models of the Kremlin and postcards of film stars and of Lenin as a Victorian child with blue eyes and golden curls. There are also a variety of swings and roundabouts and a giant wheel offering a panoramic view of the city and, when you reach the top, uncomfortably reminiscent of *The Third Man*. Finally, for those who feel so inclined, there is (or was) a tower from which you could leap down on a captive parachute (for me, in 1938, an uncanny foretaste of things to come).

But of all these attractions none for my taste can equal the pleasure of simply strolling about watching one's fellow seekers after rest and culture: senior citizens taking the air; young men and girls dressed to kill and on the look out for a link-up; soldiers and sailors on leave; giggling teenagers; harassed parents of large and uncontrollable families. But all out to enjoy themselves and, in the main, succeeding in their object.

A similar crowd, supplemented by even more visitors from the outlying republics of the Union, Uzbeks, Kazakhs, Georgians, Armenians and so on, is to be found wandering round the Exhibition of Economic Achievements of the USSR which in a single year is visited by some 6,900,000 Soviet citizens, not to mention a hundred thousand foreigners, amounting to a grand total of seven million people. This remarkable and also typically Soviet institution is a permanent exhibition which lies on the outskirts of Moscow

Small Fry

and can be reached by Metro from the centre of the city. It bears a marked resemblance to the famous British Empire Exhibition held more than fifty years ago at Wembley at a time when 'Empire' had not yet become a dirty word. Just as at Wembley each British colony and dominion had its own pavilion proudly displaying its own produce and achievements, so today each Soviet Socialist Republic has a splendid palace of its own, flying its own flag and built in its own individual style.

You approach the exhibition through a great triumphal arch in the grand classical manner. It is surmounted by giant twin statues of a man and a woman with their hair streaming out behind them, one holding a hammer and the other a sickle and both rushing frantically forward into the future. These were originally made for the Soviet Pavilion at the Paris Exhibition of 1937, which also boasted a map of the Soviet Union entirely made of precious stones and a vast picture depicting Stalin surrounded by his Marshals. By the time I reached it on leave from Moscow in the summer of 1937, Marshal Tukachevski, the Deputy Commissar for Defence, had already been shot. To the Soviet officials in charge of the pavilion, this presented a problem. But not an insuperable one. The group, I found on arrival, was still there, Tukachevski's place in the picture having been taken by an anonymous marshal with a great black beard painted in posthumously.

Once inside the Uzbek Pavilion you can, beneath domes recalling Samarkand, and under the guidance of Uzbeks in national costume, admire bales of cotton and bottles of champagne from Uzbekistan. And so on. There are also, as there were at Wembley, restaurants producing national dishes, as well as enough swings and roundabouts to provide light relief for juvenile visitors. Strategically placed at the centre of the exhibition is a great round fountain surmounted by a truly magnificent circular group of monumental statuary made from what appears at first sight to be highly polished eighteen-carat gold. Facing resolutely outwards, in what would otherwise resemble a ladies' sixteensome reel, four times four well built and scantily clothed golden goddesses, each bearing her own national attributes and all glittering brilliantly in the sunshine, superlatively symbolize the sixteen Soviet republics. It is, if ever there was one, a sight for sore eyes.

In addition to the national pavilions of the various republics, the exhibition can also boast a number of impressive technical exhibits, space satellites, giant pieces of industrial and agricultural machinery, computers and the like, and also, more readily comprehensible to the non-specialist, aircraft you can climb into, model hydrofoils that whizz round a pond, and, finally, in the farming section, real live pigs that grunt and bees that buzz. It was here, oddly enough, in the bee-keeping section of this essentially orthodox exhibition, that there was held early in 1975, after several false starts and various public displays of vandalism and intolerance, the first semi-officially sanctioned exhibition of non-orthodox, non-representational art to take place in the Soviet Union for more than ten years. Though the seventy-odd exhibits displayed were, by Western standards, neither very daring nor of very high artistic quality, the fact that they were exhibited at all, let alone in the official headquarters of the Soviet Bee Club, marked, in this most orthodox of all countries, a mild victory for unorthodoxy.

The Economic Exhibition also has a few farm horses that occasionally trot round a track. But, if you enjoy watching horses trotting or indeed galloping round a track, the place to go to is Konni Zavod I, or Horse Factory No. I, the biggest and best of all the State Stud Farms, a couple of hours' drive from Moscow. There, if you have a friend in the Ministry of Agriculture, or, better still, if you are a potential purchaser of bloodstock, you will see any number of magnificent thoroughbred mares and stallions as well as horses of various native breeds. The stud farm is pleasantly situated in a secluded spot amongst woods and fields. On my first visit there I was lavishly entertained to lunch by Colonel Rogalevich, an agreeable former artillery officer whom I had met when he was buying bloodstock in England and who, after a distinguished war career had, on retirement from the army, been put in charge of bloodstock breeding at the Ministry of Agriculture. After lunch, which was in the best Newmarket tradition, one magnificent horse after another was trotted out for our inspection and, after we had seen some of the horses at exercise, the afternoon ended with a most exhilarating drive in a troika at breakneck speed round and round a circular track a couple of miles long. On that fine summer's day it was an exciting and enjoyable experience and I formed a firm resolve (not yet put into execution) to repeat it in mid-winter with snow on the ground and runners in the place of wheels.

On the outskirts of Moscow, not far from the Exhibition of Economic Achievements and situated on what was originally part of the same estate, is Ostankino, once a country house belonging to the Sheremetyev family and now, in part at any rate, a museum devoted to the subject of serfdom. Built at the very end of the eighteenth century for Count N. P. Sheremetyev to the designs of the famous Italian architect Quarenghi, with dome, pediment and pillared portico, it is in the purest and most elegant classical style. Though this is not apparent, it is also entirely built of wood. All the work on it, which is of the very highest quality, was done, one is told, by serfs from Count Sheremetyev's estate. In those days this included not only the area today occupied by the Exhibition of Economic Achievements, but some fine formal eighteenth-century pleasure-gardens now re-named in honour of Felix Dzerzhinski, the founder of the notorious Cheka. Near the house is an ornate late seventeenth-century Russian baroque church with five onion domes, canopied belfries and a typical free-standing campanile.

The mansion house at Ostankino is as it were built round a great pillared ballroom, which could by the ingenious use of pulleys be transformed into a private theatre and was especially designed by Count Sheremetyev for Parasha, the beautiful young actress with whom he fell in love and who in the end became his wife. A contemporary portrait shows a lively, expressive and yet wistful face, the face of a girl doomed, as in fact she was, to die young. Like the skilled architects, surveyors, and craftsmen who helped to build the house, Parasha was born a serf. For anyone who is interested, Ostankino throws a curious and often revealing light on the whole institution of serfdom as it had developed by the late eighteenth century.

Another fine eighteenth-century manor on the fringes of Moscow, which also once belonged to the Sheremetyev family, is Kuskovo. This, too, was entirely built of wood by serf craftsmen and artisans working for two famous serf architects, Argunov and Mironov. A vast, well-proportioned building, it stands beside an artificial lake in the middle of an extensive and elaborately laid out park, in which, besides a number of statues, some grottoes and an open-air theatre, are various fanciful orangeries and pavilions in the Dutch or Italian manner on which the serf architects clearly let their imagination run riot. A mile or two away is the village of Kosino, with a couple of old churches and a miracle-working lake, which until the Revolution was visited by many thousands of pilgrims in search of health and holiness.

The Sheremetyevs were naturally not the only noble family who owned estates and houses in the vicinity of Moscow. Standing in a fine park of pines and beeches, falling away in a series of balustraded terraces to the banks of the Moscow River, fifteen miles or so due east of the city and not far beyond Tushino Airport is Arkhangelskoye, another great country house, built in the eighteenth century by the Golitsin family and later sold by them to Prince Yusupov. This, too, is built of wood covered with stucco and possesses an imposing pillared façade. Like Ostankino, it has its own private theatre, as well as a fine library much used, it is said, by Pushkin, who celebrated it in verse, and also by Alexander Herzen, the great nineteenth-century revolutionary who, it appears, was a frequent guest of its noble proprietors. Designed in the first place by Quarenghi or one of his contemporaries, Arkhangelskoye was later altered by Rastrelli and also by various Russian architects. It is dominated by a tall central tower or belvedere. Not far from Arkhangelskoye is the village of Peredelkino, famous as a writers' colony. Here Pasternak had his *dacha* and here he lies buried under the pine-trees. Partly as a tribute to his greatness as a writer, but partly also as a result of the persecution he endured during his lifetime, his grave has now become a regular object of pilgrimage for dissident Soviet intellectuals and enterprising foreign tourists.

Due south of Moscow on the road to Tula and also agreeably situated on a bend of the Moscow River is Kolomenskoye, an ancient village founded in the thirteenth century by the inhabitants of the not very far distant town of Kolomna, from which it derives its name and which is also well worth a visit. Adjoining it, at the end of the village street, is a former royal estate, originally laid out in the fourteenth century by Dmitri Donskoi. It was also a favourite resort of Ivan the Terrible and it was here that Peter the Great came as a child to escape the revolt of the *Streltsi*. The great wooden palace built here by Tsar Alexis Mikhailovich in place of the older palace of Ivan the Terrible has now disappeared, though a scale model in the museum gives some idea of its appearance. To make up for its loss, an early eighteenth-century wooden house, once inhabited by Peter the Great, has been brought here from Archangel on the shores of the White Sea as has a fortified wooden tower, also from northern Russia.

But of the various buildings to be seen at Kolomenskoye by far the most remarkable is the Church of the Ascension, built in 1533, with its extraordinary sugar-loaf spire 230 feet high and its decoration of *kokoshniki*, so called after the head-dresses of the same shape once worn by Russian peasant women. In a moment of enthusiasm Hector Berlioz, who visited Kolomenskoye in the 1840s, compared it most favourably with the Cathedrals of Strasbourg and Milan. How far one can safely accept the great composer's judgement in matters of architecture is another matter. Personally, while admitting the undoubted energy and picturesqueness of all three buildings, when it comes to purity of style, I have serious reservations about them all, as indeed one might about Berlioz's own music.

At Kolomenskoye a terrace overlooking the Moscow River gives you a good view of the neighbouring country as far as the south-eastern suburbs of Moscow. Near the Church of the Ascension is a tall, brick-built tower, known as the Falcon Tower, where Tsar Alexis kept his hawks and falcons, with, next to it, a sixteenth-century campanile dedicated to St George. Some distance away, on the other side of a rather handsome gate, is the Church of Our Lady of Kazan, with its bright-blue onion domes. This was built towards the middle of the seventeenth century. It is still in use and last time I went there was filled to capacity by a large, well dressed and devout throng of worshippers. Near me in one of the aisles lay two open coffins. Their occupants, also wearing their Sunday best and surrounded by their friends and relations, seemed simply a part of the congregation. Further up the valley on the river bank above the village cemetery stands the Church of St John the Baptist in Djakovo, built in 1529. Both this and the Church of the Ascension are said to have influenced the design of St Basil's Cathedral in Moscow.

Five or six miles beyond Kolomenskoye is the village of Tsaritsino, formerly known as Black Mud. Here in the year 1775 Catherine the Great set out to build herself a summer residence in a mixture of the Gothic and Moorish styles. After work had begun, she somewhat characteristically had second thoughts and countermanded it, only to change her mind once again and give orders for it to be finished. But in the end it never was completed and stands today as it stood at the time of her death, a gaunt skeleton with its Gothic arches and tall white stone pilasters rising from the surrounding trees. All around it in the park are scattered little classical temples and pavilions – the Temple of Love and the

Temple of Ceres – as well as a selection of picturesque Gothick ruins. Little wonder that for generations it has been a favourite haunt of poets and writers. Indeed Turgenyev chose it as the scene for parts of his short novel *Nakanune (On the Eve)*.

Some twenty miles beyond Kolomenskoye is Gorki, now Leninskye Gorki, a charming early nineteenth-century nobleman's residence in the classical manner pleasantly situated in a well laid out park which once belonged to the Morozov family. It was here that Lenin, by now a dying man, chose to spend the last year or two of his life and here that he died in January 1924. The house, now a museum, is kept exactly as it was at the time of Lenin's death. Part of the estate that went with it has been turned into an extremely up-to-date and efficient collective farm, designed, amongst other things, to provide the city of Moscow with fresh fruit, vegetables and dairy produce. Linked as it is with Lenin and bearing his name, no pains are spared to make it an unqualified success and its magnificent hot-houses, milking-parlours and mountains of manure filled me with envy.

Venturing rather further afield, about an hour's drive in a north-north-easterly direction from Moscow brings you to the Monastery of the Trinity and St Sergius at Zagorsk, the former Sergievo, a famous place of pilgrimage, which, like so many other monastic foundations, possessed considerable strategic as well as spiritual significance and for many years constituted yet another important link in Moscow's defences. Indeed it is its proud boast that it never fell to a foreign invader.

Founded in the fourteenth century by St Sergius of Radonezh, it was from him that the little town took its earlier name of Sergievo. Its present name derives, one is told, from a certain V. M. Zagorski, a successful and possibly estimable Party Secretary, though scarcely of the same calibre as the town's original founder.

St Sergius, the Builder of Russia, who blessed the assembled Russian armies before their victory over Mamai Khan and his Mongols in 1380 and became a great national leader and one of Russia's favourite saints, believed in poverty and humility and built much of the original structure with his own hands from timber he cut in the surrounding forest. With time, however, the monastery, from a group of log cabins, became a walled city of magnificent buildings, full, according to Paul of Aleppo (whom we last encountered at Novodevichi), of 'objects surprising to the mind and dazzling to the sight', of panelling studded with emeralds and rubies, and vestments 'loaded with gold, gems and pearls'. Sergius was the first abbot of the monastery he founded and is buried under the golden cupolas of the Cathedral of the Trinity. Despite his frequently expressed wish to be buried 'among the poor', he lies, says Paul of Aleppo, enshrined 'in a silver chest, covered with huge plates of solid silver and veiled with a portrait of the Saint in gold tissue set with pearls and precious stones'. The ceremonial pall bearing his portrait is still preserved at Zagorsk and shows him as a lean, bearded ascetic with piercing eyes and hollow cheeks. One of the early monks of the Monastery of the Trinity was the painter Andrei Rublyov. For the Cathedral of the Trinity he painted a large number of murals and icons, including what is probably his masterpiece, the serenely beautiful fresco of the Trinity now in the Tretyakov Gallery.

Though Paul of Aleppo complains, *en passant*, of being worried by fleas and of being obliged to attend a six-hour service in the cathedral that began at two in the morning, his general conclusion was that the monastery was 'perfect in all respects' and he also writes with evident approval of feasts of 'princely meats and an infinite variety of royal liquors'. This happy tradition has, I am glad to say, continued at Zagorsk. On a visit there some years back, I had the honour and pleasure of being lavishly entertained by the Rector to a feast of caviar and broiled sturgeon. It was, he explained, a Wednesday and he could therefore not offer me meat. But, he added, there was nothing in Orthodox dogma or doctrine to prevent us from drinking with our fish, and this we accordingly did. On us, as we sat at luncheon in the Refectory, there looked down from among the icons a large portrait of Lenin. When I observed to a distinguished foreign theologian who happened to be with me that to some this might seem incongruous, he replied aptly enough, I thought, 'To none more than to Lenin.'

As no doubt in the days of Paul of Aleppo, the monastery, viewed from the south, surrounded on three sides by water and with its glittering domes and spires emerging from the surrounding fortifications, is a breath-taking spectacle, one, indeed, that comes near to equalling the Moscow Kremlin itself. The oldest of its churches, the white limestone Cathedral of the Trinity with its single golden dome, was built in 1422, the year when St Sergius was canonized and formally proclaimed Protector of the Land of Russia. The cathedral's magnificent iconostasis is largely the work of Andrei Rublyov and his school. The nearby Church of the Holy Ghost, with a peal of bells ingeniously fitted in under the drum of its single dome, was built fifty years or so later, in 1476, by craftsmen from Pskov.

The splendid five-domed Church of the Assumption, now the Monastery's main cathedral, was begun in 1559 in the reign of Ivan the Terrible and completed twenty-five years later under Tsar Fyodor. What might otherwise have been the severity of its lines is relieved by its magnificent proportions and by the generous curves of its star-spangled onion domes. The frescoes within date from the late seventeenth century. Near the north-western corner of the cathedral is the family burial vault of the Godunov family and just outside the main entrance is the tomb of Tsar Boris Godunov himself. Other, earlier Godunovs are buried at Kostroma on the Volga, where the family first settled in the fourteenth century. At the other end of the cathedral's west front is the elaborately decorated and cheerfully coloured Nakladezhnaya or Chapel-over-the-Well, typical of the so-called Narishkin style of the late seventeenth century, when that family were in a position to set the tone in architecture and in much else besides. Inside rises a spring of cold clear water with a strong taste of iron. A good gulp of this, I was told, is guaranteed to wash away your sins. Hopefully, I took my place in the line.

The monastery's Refectory, remodelled in about 1690 from a much older building, the Hospital, with church attached, and the Chertogi Palace, in which the Tsar used to stay when visiting the monastery, are all good examples of Russian late seventeenth-century architecture. The Palace of the Metropolitan, on the other hand, took almost three centuries to build, the ground floor being built in the sixteenth century, the first in the seventeenth and the top storey in the eighteenth, when the whole building was stylistically brought more or less into line. The little Church of St Micah, near the Refectory, was also built in the eighteenth century.

The main entrance to the monastery was through the Pilgrims' Tower in the northern wall. Towards the middle of the eighteenth century the tower was rebuilt and a number of old buildings inside the walls were cleared away to open up the approaches to the two cathedrals. It was at about this time that a very considerable Russian eighteenth-century architect, Dmitri Ukhtomski, was commissioned to build the elegant, purely classical church of the Virgin of Smolensk and the splendidly baroque five-tiered, pale-blue and white campanile which towers above it. Together they strike a different, but by no means discordant note among the mixture of earlier styles. The campanile was formerly attributed to the Italian architect Rastrelli, whose work it strongly resembles.

Another entrance to the monastery was through the handsome red and white Gate-Church of St John the Baptist, built at the very end of the seventeenth century by the Stroganov family of merchant-adventurers with the help, no doubt, of the very considerable revenues coming in from their numerous and extremely lucrative enterprises in Siberia.

Though of no very great height, the monastery's walls, first built in about 1550, successfully withstood a sixteen-month siege at the hands of Jan Sapieha and his Poles sixty years later. After this they were very sensibly heightened and those of the eleven towers that had suffered damage rebuilt. All eleven are still standing today, including the great round towers at the four corners. Outside the walls are two more churches, both built in the mid-sixteenth century, another little chapel with a well in it, and a late eighteenth-century *manège*.

From Zagorsk a detour of thirty-odd miles brings you to Alexandrova Sloboda, or, as it is now called, Alexandrov, a town abounding in interesting historical associations. It was to Alexandrova Sloboda, for a time the principal residence of the Russian Tsars, that Ivan the Terrible withdrew in 1564, thence to issue his amazing proclamation denouncing the boyars and the clergy and threatening to abdicate. It was from here that he subsequently announced the formation of the Oprichnina and directed its ensuing reign of terror. It was here, finally, that Ivan used to play the part of abbot and presided over the semi-obscene, semi-religious orgies which were such an important part of his life.

Ivan was not the only ruler of Russia to use Alexandrov for his own purposes. Here, after a preliminary stint at Novodevichi, Peter the Great kept his half-sister Sophia confined from 1698 to 1707, sending her back in due course to be buried at Novodevichi. Here, too, Peter's daughter, the future Empress Elizabeth, spent nine years as an exile. The little town also has revolutionary associations, for it was here that in 1905 was declared the short-lived Workers' Republic of Alexandrov.

Today Alexandrov is a pleasant enough place. The white-walled churches and buildings of the monastery stand among groves of silver birches with the wooden houses of the little town scattered among them. The oldest building is the single-domed, square, white Cathedral of the Trinity, built early in the sixteenth century, but in the simpler style of an earlier age. Its doors, of copper engraved with gold, are two hundred years older, having been brought here by Ivan the Terrible in 1570 as loot from the Church of St Sophia in Novgorod. The nearby Church of the Intercession (Pokrovskaya), reconstructed in the seventeenth century, was Ivan's personal chapel. The Church of the Assumption (Uspenskaya) is said to have been built by his father Vasili III, but has been rebuilt so many times in the intervening centuries that it has lost any character it ever had. The Church of the Purification (Stetenskaya) was also built in the second half of the seventeenth century on the foundations of an older church. The monastery's tall sugar-loaf belfry, with its three rows of curved *kokoshniks* and a faceted spire, was, it appears, superimposed in the seventeenth century on an existing sixteenth-century bell-tower. Near it is the modest building where for nine years, 1698–1707, Peter the Great's half-sister Marfa lived in exile after he had forced her, too, to become a nun.

These are only a very few of the great number of ancient churches, monasteries, great country-houses and idyllic villages that are to be found within an hour or two's drive from Moscow. For the purposes of this book I have confined myself to those I have myself visited and which I know to be open to the general public. As communications improve, however, and the widespread work of restoration and rehabilitation at present being undertaken progresses, there will soon be no end to the number of excursions open to the enterprising visitor.

# 10 *Leningrad*

LENINGRAD is different from Moscow in any number of ways. Moscow has 800 years of history behind it; Leningrad barely 250. Leningrad was deliberately planned and laid out as a great city; Moscow, from a fortified village on a wooded hilltop, has, with the years gradually become one. Leningrad is Western; Moscow, Eastern. Leningrad is elegantly classical; Moscow, extravagantly exotic. Leningrad, on the shores of the Baltic and banks of the Neva, is maritime and aquatic in outlook and climate; Moscow, half-way to Asia, is deeply continental.

The difference, however, though very real, is not as simple as that. It represents, rather, a certain dichotomy in the Russian make-up. Moscow, as we have seen, is profoundly and essentially Russian. But Leningrad, in a sense, is no less Russian, embodying those other, westward- and outward-looking aspects of the Russian character. Nor has Leningrad in the 250 years of its existence played an any less decisive part than Moscow in determining the course of Russian history.

From the time of its first foundation as Peter the Great's northern stronghold and window on Europe, it has symbolized a deep-seated wish on Russia's part to look westwards. While pursuing, like Peter himself, their eastern ambitions, his Imperial successors necessarily felt in their northern capital the continuing influence and attraction of Europe and the West. No less were the thoughts of successive generations of St Petersburg intellectuals focussed, as far as this was possible, on things Western. To take one, all-important example, the liberal and radical ideas, which in less than a century took Russia from the Decembrists' revolt to the Bolshevik Revolution, reached St Petersburg from the West. Indeed, it could, rather perversely, be argued that, by shifting its headquarters from Petrograd back to Moscow, the Dictatorship of the Proletariat was

deliberately turning its back on the West and assuming the resolutely Eastern and Byzantine character it has possessed ever since.

But this was not all. For Leningrad, the scene, first of Peter's
and then, two hundred years later, of Lenin's revolution, another
turning-point, another moment of destiny was still to come. For
if in 1941 the former capital, with its elegant prospects and palaces,
had not abruptly reverted to its original role of northern stronghold
and for two and a half terrible years fought off, at appalling cost
in lives and suffering, the onslaught of Hitler's armies, the course
of history not only for Russia, but for the world at large, could
well have taken a different turn.

As with Moscow, so with Leningrad, it is perhaps best to begin
at the beginning, with the city's foundation by Peter the Great.
Near the mouth of the River Neva, where it flows out into the Gulf
of Finland, are a number of islands. One of these, a little islet close
to the north bank of the river, Peter picked as a base, a strong-
point for the defence against the Swedes of his newly won access
to the Baltic. Hare Island, the local Finnish fishermen called it.
Landing on it on 16 May 1703, the Tsar cut two strips of turf with
a bayonet and laid them one across the other. 'Here,' he said, 'there
shall be a town.' A foundation-stone was then laid and a blessing
bestowed and Peter gave the town its name, a Dutch name: Sankt
Piterburkh.

From the first, Peter took the keenest personal interest in his
new fortress-town. To supervise the work, he built himself a
wooden hut on a neighbouring island, while his mistress and future
wife, Catherine, was installed in a miniature palace at a convenient
distance downstream. It was not long before he decided to make
St Petersburg his capital in place of Moscow. A Swiss-Italian architect from Lugano, Domenico Trezzini, was called in and soon vast
resources of man-power and money were being lavished on building and embellishing the town. In 1710, after Peter's victory at Poltava had finally eliminated any serious threat from Sweden, the
Court and the royal family were moved there from Moscow and
all the great nobles were required to build themselves palaces there.
In place of his wooden hut, piously preserved to this day as a monument to his memory, the Tsar now built himself a little Summer
Palace set in a pleasant formal garden on the south bank of the
Neva at its junction with the Fontanka. Designed for him by Trezzini, it resembles in size and style a medium-sized Dutch or English

# Leningrad

APTEKARSKI
ISLAND

BOLSHAYA

NEVA

KARL MARX BOULEVARD

KIROV PROSPEKT

GORKI
PROSPEKT

PIROGOVSKAYA QUAY

FINLAND
STATION

ARSENAL QUAY

6

PETROGRAD Q.

22

ROBESPIERRE QUAY

KUTUSOV QUAY

11

1

20

25

10

KHALTURIN ST

SALTIKOV–ZHCHEDRIN ST

LITEINI PROSPEKT

13 23

ALACE
UARE

27

28

NEKRASOVA STREET

MOISENKO STREET

GRIBOYEDOV CANAL

MAYAKOVSKI ST

VOSSTANIA ST

SUVOROVSKI PROSPEKT

EET

5

4

ER

19

2

LOMONOSOV ST

3

18 17

31

NEVSKI PROSPEKT

EKHANOV ST

DZERZHINSKI ST

STREET

32

MOSCOW
STATION

14

SADOVAYA

MIRA
SQ.

FONTANKA
CANAL

ZAGORODNI PROSPEKT

VITEBSK
STATION

LIGOVSKI PROSPEKT

MOSKOVSKI PROSPEKT

OBVODNI CANAL

manor-house of the period and is furnished to match. Here you may see his bedroom, with its four-poster bed and painted ceiling representing Morpheus, the poppy-scattering God of Sleep; his sitting-room and the great oak Admiralty Chair from which he presided over the meetings of his Board of Admiralty; his workshop, with the travelling lathe he took with him on his journeys and the dials which showed him the direction and velocity of the wind; his dining-room, with the mahogany table at which he and half a dozen friends would take their meals, and the well planned Dutch-tiled kitchen, with its stove and the iron and copper pots in which his food was prepared.

In 1712 St Petersburg was officially proclaimed capital of the Empire. Though Peter's original plan had been to build on the north bank only, the city had by now begun to extend along both sides of the Neva as well as to Vasilievski Island, the triangular wedge of land blocking the mouth of the river and dividing the Greater from the Lesser Neva. But the original fortress on Hare Island, the Fortress of St Peter and St Paul, hexagonal in shape and built to the designs of Lambert, a pupil of the great Vauban, remained in a sense the focal point of the city. Within the fortress walls stands Trezzini's Cathedral of St Peter and St Paul, its slim golden spire thrusting upwards to the sky. A rather austere, classical building from without, its interior is exuberantly baroque. Here Peter and, with two exceptions, his successors lie buried. Alexander I's tomb was, as we have seen, found on inspection to be empty, leaving yet another question-mark to hover over that enigmatic personality. As for the remains of the last of the Romanovs, Nicholas II, these are believed to lie at the bottom of a disused Siberian mine-shaft.

Across the river from the fortress, on the south bank, were the shipyards, soon to be known as the Admiralty. Between these and the Summer Palace Peter built his Winter Palace, a relatively modest dwelling, to be superseded over the years by several larger and ever more splendid edifices. Diagonally from the Neva in an easterly direction he laid out one of the most famous streets in the world, the Nevski Prospect, where two hundred years later elegant ladies were to shop for Faberge's famous Easter eggs, but where in 1705, during the building of the city and before the marshes through which it ran had been effectively drained, Peter himself was almost drowned by a sudden flood, while across the river on

buildings of the same blue, forms a singularly effective architectural group.

No less successful in its way than Rastrelli's cathedral at Smolni is the slightly smaller Sailor's Church or Cathedral of St Nicholas (Nikolski Sobor), built a few years later by his pupil Chevakinski in much the same style at the other end of the city. Also painted blue and white, it possesses an elegant, free-standing campanile which makes one wish that Rastrelli had been able to complete his original plan for one at Smolni. Like Rastrelli's cathedral at Smolni, the Cathedral of St Nicholas also has five golden domes. But these are spaced out, with one in the middle and one at each corner, an arrangement which I personally prefer to Rastrelli's closer grouping round a larger central dome. Nor do I dislike Chevakinski's wider and more generous façade, with its well-spaced groups of three columns and two. The Nikolski Sobor is still in use as a church. Indeed it is one of the busiest in Leningrad.

Adjoining Elizabeth's convent at Smolni is the equally famous Smolni Institute, a school for the daughters of the nobility, built twenty years later for Catherine the Great by another Italian archi- tect, Giacomo Quarenghi. In contrast to the baroque exuberance of Rastrelli's cathedral, Quarenghi's institute, with its plain pediment and pillared portico, is austerely classical. It was here that, up to the Revolution, the great families of the capital sent their daughters to be educated, away from the disturbing influence of home, and in accordance with a number of high-sounding principles originally laid down, though certainly not practised, by Catherine herself. It was here, too, in a room still proudly shown to the public that, in October 1917, the last of the noble young ladies having been summarily evicted, Lenin set up his headquarters, moving in two iron bedsteads for himself and Krupskaya. Trotski, of course, also had a room at Smolni, but this, needless to say, is not on the tourist schedule. Since then the square in front of the Institute has been appropriately renamed Dictatorship Square and further embellished by the addition of two neo-classical Soviet propylaea, one of which bears an inscription calling upon the workers of the world to unite, while the other carries another no less edifying message. Smolni later became the Leningrad Party Headquarters and it was here that Kirov, then Party Secretary, was assassinated in 1934.

A particularly interesting building in the Smolni district is Kikina Palace, the house of A. V. Kikin, a prominent associate of Peter the Great, who built it in 1714 but later became involved with Peter's son Aleksei and, after a brief but meteoric career, was executed for high treason in 1718. A magnificent early eighteenth-century palace, it was, after its owner's downfall, put to various uses, underwent extensive alterations and fell into disrepair. But now, after suffering further damage in the Second World War, it has been admirably restored to its original form. Still painted dark-red and white, the fashionable colour in Peter's day, it now serves as the headquarters of the local Pioneers, or communist youth movement, who can be seen streaming in and out of it in their neat white shirts and red neckties.

Rastrelli is perhaps best remembered for his last work, his final version of the Winter Palace. His earlier building, together with what was left of its predecessors, was demolished in 1754 and work was begun on the new palace. This took eight years to complete. It possesses, one is told, fifteen hundred rooms and a hundred or more staircases. Green and white in colour and baroque in style, it looks northwards across the Neva to the Fortress of St Peter and St Paul. Its proportions are magnificent. The façade is decorated by two ranges of white columns, divided by a string-course and reaching from ground to roof, while along the front runs an ornamental white balustrade topped by a variety of characteristically baroque statues and urns. The varied surrounds of the three rows of windows, two above the string-course and one below, are also picked out in white. The southern façade, similar in design, looks on to Palace Square, which, with the addition seventy years later of Rossi's War Ministry on the far side, was to become one of the finest architectural ensembles in the world. The western front of the palace, with two short wings enclosing a garden, faces the Admiralty, while to the east it adjoins the neighbouring Hermitage, with which it forms a combined frontage extending along the Neva for perhaps five or six hundred yards.

Of Rastrelli's original interior, part was remodelled under Catherine the Great and much destroyed by a fire in 1837 in the reign of Nicholas I. Fortunately, owing to the good taste and good judgement of Stasov, the architect employed to restore the palace after the fire, one magnificent example of Rastrelli's Russian baroque style has survived much as he designed it. This is the famous grand

New Holland, Leningrad

Chesme Church

Kikina Palace, Leningrad

staircase, known as the Jordan Staircase or Staircase of the Ambassadors, leading down to the main entrance of the palace on the Neva.

It was by this door that on 6 January each year the Tsar, his court and his clergy would leave the palace to descend, bareheaded, to the frozen river for the traditional Blessing of the Waters, the opportunity being taken by the pious to scoop up as much of the freshly blessed river-water as they could through a hole in the ice for use as medicine, for driving away evil spirits and for future baptisms. Some would even bring their babies to be dipped in the icy water right away. 'A very extraordinary ceremony and certainly very unseasonable ... without hats, fifteen degrees below freezing point, *imaginez*, in the open air upon the river,' writes Mrs Disbrowe, the wife of the British Minister Plenipotentiary. 'It has happened,' she continues censoriously (and other accounts confirm this) 'that the shivering priests let the unfortunate little creatures slip through their icy fingers under the ice. "Mais quel bonheur l'enfant alloit tout droit au paradis", was the consoling reflection for the superstitious.' Clearly there was much about the scene that was characteristic, both of the country and of the age, not least the British diplomat's lady and her consciously superior attitude to these most un-English goings-on.

Apart from the Ambassador's Staircase, the rest of the interior, with its great gilded and pillared galleries and ballrooms and saloons, is for the most part in the style of a later period, but a style which, as so often in Russia, itself reflects or continues an earlier tradition. 'In Russia,' writes the Marquis de Custine, who attended the great court ball given to celebrate the palace's reconstruction after the fire of 1837, 'everything is copied, even time. . . .' But for once even he was impressed by the Winter Palace. 'What I admired even more than the ballroom, all golden as it is, was the gallery where supper was served. Everything was colossal, innumerable, and I did not know which to admire more, the ensemble or the separate objects. A thousand people were seated at table in this one room.'

The Empress Elizabeth died in 1762 and with her death the period of Rastrelli's greatest achievements came to an end. He himself left Russia soon after and, though he later returned, the completion of the Winter Palace was to be his last major assignment.

Catherine the Great, who, having quickly discarded her insignificant husband, now ascended the throne, made as powerful and as immediate an impact on the architecture of the capital as on every other aspect of Russian life. A woman of spirit and imagination, she saw herself as being in every way the successor of Peter the Great, to whose memory she erected the famous equestrian statue by Falconet, which stands opposite St Isaac's Cathedral on its massive block of granite in the middle of Senate Square. She was utterly determined to leave her own mark on the city he had founded. Another of her purposes, and a very feminine one, was to give her surroundings a new look, entirely distinct from anything her immediate predecessor had left behind her. 'The truth of the matter is that my worthy aunt was imposed on,' she remarked to the famous Giacomo Casanova, while strolling with him in the Summer Garden after he had let drop a hint that the statues there were in the most deplorable taste. In any case, like most of her immediate contemporaries, she preferred a plainer, more formal, more strictly classical style to the baroque exuberance of twenty or thirty years earlier. She knew what she wanted and she saw that she got it. The neo-classical architectural and stylistic trend which she now set was to endure, as things turned out, far into the next century. Indeed, thanks to Stalin, who liked it too, into our own times.

One of Catherine's earlier projects was the construction of the Little Hermitage, as a private, unofficial residence for herself, adjoining and directly linked with the Winter Palace. Built in 1764 to the designs of a French architect, Vallin de la Mothe, this elegant little palace possesses a sizeable hanging garden laid out at first-floor level. Another of its purposes was to house Catherine's collection of pictures. But this grew so rapidly that in ten years it became necessary to build yet another palace, now known as the Old Hermitage. To this a small private theatre, connected with the main building by a bridge, was added in 1784 by Quarenghi and a further palace, the New Hermitage, in the first half of the nineteenth century, harmoniously rounding off the long line of imperial palaces which stretch along the banks of the Neva.

Leaving these behind you and following Palace Quay, you come to the famous Marble Palace (almost the only stone building in St Petersburg), presented by Catherine the Great to her lover Grigori Orlov and now occupied by the Lenin Museum. This stands between the Quay and the Bolshaya Millionnaya or Millionaires'

Row, now known as Khalturin Street, and once the smartest or at any rate the richest street in St Petersburg. Its severely classical façade, designed for Catherine by Antonio Rinaldi not long after her accession, clearly marks the departure from the more florid style of Rastrelli. A little further along Palace Quay, by the Kirov Bridge, is the pleasant, green-painted classical building which before the Revolution housed the British Embassy. Further on still, you come to the Summer Gardens with their graceful eighteenth-century statues, so despised by Casanova, and to Peter the Great's charming little Summer Palace.

Though Peter assembled a number of curiosities in his Kunstka-mera on Vasilievski Island, offering a glass of vodka to anyone who could be bothered to come and look at them, and also bought some pictures for his various residences ('Do not buy any bad pictures' was his beautifully simple directive to his agents), Catherine the Great was the first real collector of the dynasty. Her magnificent collection of pictures, begun for her own personal pleasure ('Only the mice and I can admire it all') and added to by her successors, now fills not only the Hermitage, but the great gilded saloons of the Winter Palace as well. It contains some of the greatest pictures in the world, ranging from Raphaels, Leonardos and Rembrandts to the pick of the French Impressionists. It also contains an astounding collection of other works of art of every kind, coming from every part of the world, including a unique collection of early Scythian gold artifacts from south Russia and the Ukraine.

Towards the end of the nineteenth century the purely Russian portion of the collection, particularly rich in icons and early Christian painting, was transferred to the Mihailov Palace, a handsome building originally put up by Alexander I in about 1820 for his brother Michael to the strictly classical designs of Carlo Rossi and now known as the Russian Museum. The square of which the Mihailov Palace forms one side was also built to Rossi's designs and includes the famous Mali or Little Theatre. A few hundred yards away, on Brodski Street, which links it to the Nevski, is the Hotel Europe, externally at any rate as classical as its neighbours, but done over internally around 1910 in spectacular *art nouveau*.

Among the first visitors to the new palace was Mrs Disbrowe. 'Very handsome,' she wrote of the Grand Duke's new gold and silver plate, 'but nothing extraordinary, a great many naked ladies as handles and pedestals. The good things in the dishes,' she added wittily, 'are to keep them warm, I suppose.'

Alexander's Mihailov Palace, it may be observed, is not to be confused with his father Paul's moated Mihailov Castle, now known as Engineer's Castle and built by the latter on the nearby Champ de Mars some twenty years earlier in a variety of styles and at a cost of nearly twenty million roubles, in the vain hope that its massive walls would somehow save him from assassination.

Carlo Rossi, the architect of Alexander's Mihailov Palace, was the son of an Italian ballerina by a Russian father (possibly the Emperor Paul). Another of his more notable achievements was the Alexandrinski (now Pushkin) Theatre, built to his superbly classical design in 1832 in a little garden off the Nevski. Behind it, the former Teatralnaya, or Theatre Street, also designed by Rossi, now bears his name. A long, unbroken classical façade occupies each side of the street (that on the left being built to house the Imperial School of Drama). At the far end it opens into a fine classical crescent, also designed by Rossi to accommodate a couple of government departments.

But perhaps Rossi's greatest achievement of all was his completion of Palace Square (immediately behind the Winter Palace) by the addition on the north side, facing the Winter Palace, of a splendid semi-circle, housing the Ministries of War, Finance and Foreign Affairs, with, at its centre, the great double triumphal arch, surmounted by a chariot and winged victory, which leads through to the Nevski Prospect. In the centre of the square itself stands a tall pink granite column to the memory of Alexander I, surmounted by the statue of a winged angel or archangel holding a cross. It was here on Palace Square that at ceremonial parades the Emperor, escorted by the *Chevaliers Gardes* in white on their chestnut horses and the *Gardes à Cheval* in scarlet on their blacks, both with glittering breastplates and helmets, would take the salute from the hundreds of thousands of troops marching past him. It was here too that on 9 January 1905 the troops and police fired volley after volley into the crowd of demonstrators led by Father Gapon, thereby precipitating the revolution of 1905 and all that followed. It was from Palace Square, finally, that in October 1917 the crowd burst into the Winter Palace.

Not far away, on the Moika, looking out over it, is the little house where Pushkin lived during the last years of his life in an apartment put at his disposal by Prince Volkonski. It was from here that he set out on that fatal morning in January 1837 to meet his second at the pastrycook's round the corner on the Nevski Prospect and it was here that he was brought back fatally wounded after the duel. Today the house is a Pushkin museum, where you may see the double-breasted jacket he was wearing when he was killed, the new English books, by Crabbe and Wordsworth and Southey, which he ordered from Belizard's bookshop on the Nevski and the clock with the hands stopped at the time of his death. Lermontov, too, lived at one time on the Moika, while Gogol had a house in the neighbouring street which now bears his name.

To the west of Palace Square, at one end of the Nevski Prospect, facing a garden full of fountains and statues, stands the solid bulk of the Admiralty. This was built at the beginning of the nineteenth century by A. D. Zakharov on the site of an earlier building and shipyard dating from the time of Peter the Great and until 1844 still possessed its own wharves on the Neva. Its slender golden spire, matching the golden spire of St Peter and St Paul across the river, rises from a massive yellow and white entrance-gate which, while strictly classical in style, somehow recalls the ancient gates of Vladimir and Novgorod. 'The mast of a golden ship set on the roof of a Greek temple,' wrote Théophile Gautier rather aptly in 1866. Opposite the two wings of the Admiralty stands the Old Senate, built in about 1830 by Rossi in the classical manner and linked by a bridge across the street to the former Synod building.

Above the Admiralty and above pretty well everything else in Leningrad looms the vast golden dome of St Isaac's Cathedral, of which the construction was begun under Alexander I in 1818 and continued on and off for the next forty years. It is a stupendous building, designed to hold a congregation of thirteen thousand. The central dome rests on a drum encircled by twenty-four gigantic columns of polished granite. To make up the statutory five, four smaller golden domes, supported by pediments and more columns, surround the central dome. On the northern and southern sides of the cathedral are two porticos, each composed of sixteen polished granite columns with bronze bases and capitals fifty feet high. These form the chief entrance to the cathedral. The interior, entered by colossal bronze doors, is no less lavishly decorated with lapis lazuli and malachite, mosaics and polished polychrome marble, not to mention a number of immense chandeliers and candelabras, of which under the Empire the candles were at midnight on Easter Sunday suddenly all set alight simultaneously (or very nearly) by means of a guncotton fuse. After which, amid clouds of incense and to the thunder of 101 guns, the great doors were flung open and a procession of golden-clad clergy poured into the body of the church chanting the Easter hymn.

After the Revolution the cathedral was converted into an anti-God museum. From the centre of the dome, from which once hung a six-foot dove representing the Holy Ghost, a giant pendulum was suspended, busily demonstrating, for those who cared to watch it, the perpetual rotation of the terrestrial globe and all that that implies.

As if one such cathedral were not enough, you have only to walk a few hundred yards along the Nevski Prospect to find another, the Cathedral of Our Lady of Kazan, built fifteen or twenty years earlier than St Isaac's on a scarcely less imposing scale and now, like it, an anti-God museum. With its Italianate metal dome resting on a pilastered drum and its semi-circular colonnade of 136 Corinthian columns, it was clearly designed to rival St Peter's in Rome. Just to the right of the entrance is the tomb of General Kutuzov on the spot where, suddenly recalled from exile, he is said to have stood and prayed before leaving to take command at Smolensk in 1812. Outside it stands his statue, matching that of his one-time comrade at arms, General Barclay de Tolly.

A little further along the Nevski, at the corner of the Sadovaya, is the Gostini Dvor, a sprawling two-storeyed eighteenth-century shopping arcade, originally built by Vallin de la Mothe in the reign of Catherine the Great and rebuilt (rather unsuccessfully) a hundred years later. Originally containing two hundred or more individual shops, it has now been turned (again rather unsuccessfully) into a giant department store on the lines of Moscow's more famous GUM. It was here, on the corner of the Nevski Prospect and the Sadovaya, that in the July Rising of 1917 the troops of the Provisional Government first fired on a crowd of Bolshevik supporters as they marched down the Nevski on their way to demonstrate outside the Duma.

Two other celebrated shops nearby are the enormously ornate premises once occupied by Yeliseyev, the famous pastrycook, at 56 Nevski, and now known as Gastronom No. 1, and, at 24 Morskaya, those of the even more famous jeweller Fabergé, later converted into a State Commission Shop or pawnbroker's establishment, and now partly occupied by an airline.

Across the Nevski from the Gostini Dvor is the elegant little blue and white Armenian Church of St Catherine, built in strictly classical Western style by that excellent architect Yuri Veldten and originally endowed, it appears, by an Armenian merchant called Lazarev, who, coming by chance on an enormous diamond, which had been stolen and smuggled out of India by a sepoy, sold it, at a suitable profit, to Count Orlov, who, in turn, presented it to Catherine the Great to be set in her sceptre. For which, in due course, Lazarev was ennobled.

Of the older Leningrad hotels, the Astoria, built across the square from St Isaac's Cathedral in the Ritz-like style of 1912, with delightful mock-Louis XV bedrooms, has enormous charm and a continuing tradition of good food and good service. Outside it, a florid equestrian statue of Nicholas I in the full-dress uniform of the Imperial Horseguards, also carries you back, visually at any rate, to Tsarist days. Another nearby reminder of the past is the ponderously super-colossal Embassy which the Imperial German Government built for itself on the far side of the square in 1912, just two years before the outbreak of what, rightly or wrongly, was to become known as the Kaiser's War. They were not, as things turned out, to get much use from it.

Situated, as already indicated, just off the Nevski, on Brodski Street, the Europe, built in 1854 and refurbished in 1910, also carries on the old, pre-revolutionary tradition. Apart from the excellent food, the *art nouveau* and stained glass of its dining-room alone repay a visit. Next door to the Europe, on the corner of the Nevski, is Sadko, one of the better of the city's restaurants. Of the modern, Hilton-style hotels, the largest is the Leningrad, situated somewhat remotely on the far side of the river.

None of the once-famous restaurants of St Petersburg, Cubat, Donon, Old Donon or the Myedvyed or Bear, have survived as restaurants, though it is still possible to identify Donon's original premises in a crumbling courtyard off the Moika ('Entrance by *porte cochère*,' says my 1914 Baedeker helpfully, adding encouragingly that it is much 'frequented by the *demi-monde* at night after the theatre'.)

Two of Leningrad's most famous theatres are the Kirov (formerly Mariinski), with its elegant light-blue and silver auditorium, and the Mali or Little Theatre, the former on Theatre Square and the latter on Mihailov or Arts Square. The Kirov Ballet rivals and sometimes surpasses the Moscow Bolshoi Ballet. Indeed it was here in the nineteenth and early twentieth centuries that Russian ballet attained the peak of perfection and that Diaghilev and Fokin, Pavlova and Nijinski first came to fame.

Not far from the Anichkov Palace, Carlo Rossi's Alexandrinski Theatre looks out on to its pleasant little park off the Nevski, dominated by a majestic representation of Catherine the Great, sweeping irresistibly forward, sceptre in hand, with the pick of her marshals, statesmen and lovers gracefully grouped at her feet. Above the theatre's yellow and white portico prance the four horses of a quadriga, while across the pediment beneath them reclining Graces reach lovingly out towards a central lyre, no doubt substituting for the former Imperial arms. It was from this so reassuringly classical theatre that in October 1896 Chekhov fled in despair after the disastrous first night of *The Seagull*, to wander disconsolately until two in the morning among the indifferent crowds on the Nevski.

Of the palaces on the Nevski, perhaps the finest is that built by Rastrelli in about 1760 for Prince Stroganov, the head of the great family of merchant-adventurers who opened up Siberia. It stands at the point where the Nevski meets the Moika. The handsome pillared front of the palace, originally painted orange and white, but now green and white, is mirrored in the canal. Further along, at the corner where the Nevski crosses the Fontanka, stands the Anichkov Palace, its façade also turned towards the canal. This, as we have seen, was the work of more than one architect, but it was Giacomo Quarenghi who gave it its present, strictly classical character and endowed it with the splendid colonnade that is reflected in the waters of the Fontanka. Adjoining the Anichkov Palace is the Vorontsov Palace by Rastrelli, while not far away on the Moika is the palace Quarenghi built for the Yusupovs, in the basement of which Prince Felix Yusupov and his friends murdered the abominable Rasputin in December 1916.

Two other imposing palaces on the Fontanka are those of the Sheremetyevs and Shuvalovs. It was Count Boris Sheremetyev who in 1702 led the force which captured Nöteborg or, as Peter the Great renamed it, Schlüsselburg, the Key Fortress, commanding the junction of Lake Ladoga and the Neva. Ten years later, in

1712, he obediently settled in the Tsar's new capital, building himself a one-storeyed wooden house on the Fontanka. Thirty years after this his son, who had married a rich wife, commissioned Rastrelli's talented pupil, Chevakinski, to design for him the fine yellow baroque palace ornamented with white stucco which, after various vicissitudes, today houses the Office of Arctic Exploration.

Opposite it, on the other side of the Fontanka, is the Shuvalov Palace, now used as a House of Friendship or official place of entertainment for foreign delegations. Originally built for the Narish-kins, the family of Peter the Great's mother, possibly by Quarenghi, it passed by marriage to Count Shuvalov, whose family owed their prominence to an ancestor's happy association with the pleasure-seeking Empress Elizabeth. By him it was, towards the middle of the nineteenth century, endowed with its present Renaissance façade, and the interior was at the same time redecorated, not unsuccessfully, in a variety of styles, Gothic, baroque, Renaissance and neo-classical, which one must hope are now a source of wonderment and joy to workers' delegations from Cuba and Peru, from the Congo and Gabon. Immediately across the Nevski from Anichkov Palace, also looking out on the Fontanka, is the Belo-selski-Belozerski Palace, a mid-nineteenth-century structure in a rather painful mixture of styles.

Leningrad takes a lot of knowing. On my last visit I came by chance, while wandering along the banks of the Moika, on a group of large and handsome classical buildings, evidently built for some special purpose, which I had never before noticed. These, I discovered, formed part of the shipyards known as Nova Hollandia or New Holland. From the Moika a splendid gate, designed in Catherine the Great's day by Vallin de la Mothe, leads through to an inner harbour shaped like an axe-head. Though no distance from the centre of the town, they are quite easily missed amid the profusion of better known and better documented buildings.

'The streets,' wrote Dr Edward Clarke, who visited St Petersburg at the end of the eighteenth century, 'seem to consist entirely of palaces.' Though it is hard to pass over so many architectural masterpieces, it is clearly impossible to give an account of them all. But one more, at least, requires our attention. Situated at some distance from the centre of the town, on a bend in the river not far from Smolni, where open fields once sloped down to the Neva, is the Tavricheski or Tauride Palace, still standing in its own ornamental gardens, now a Children's Park. A remarkably handsome building, it is also of considerable interest historically, having originally been built by Catherine the Great for the most famous of all her favourites, Grigori Potyomkin, created in 1787 Prince of Tauris to celebrate his victories against the Turks in the Crimea, then still known by its ancient name of Tauris. Built to the designs of I. E. Starov in the purest neo-classical style, the palace was completed in 1789. In the middle of its golden-yellow façade, one storey high, but with two rows of windows, stands a portico of six white Doric columns supporting a plain pediment. Above this rises a flattened green cupola in the manner of the Roman Pantheon. From a vestibule you enter the Cupola Hall, a vast octagonal room rising to the full height of the dome, from the centre of which hangs a great chandelier of gilded bronze. Thence you pass between open columns into the great Colonnade Hall or Ballroom, more than 120 feet long and over 50 feet wide, supported on each side by eighteen tall Ionic columns and lit by a series of three-tiered chandeliers, lavishly ornamented with gilded double eagles.

It was here, in the Colonnade Hall and in the adjoining Winter Garden, with its palm-tree columns and frescoed foliage, that on New Year's Day 1791 the fifty-year-old Prince Potyomkin, his uniform so laden with diamonds and decorations that he could hardly stand, entertained his royal mistress at a reception that was to become famous. 'The Empress,' we are told by C. Masson in his secret memoirs,

entered the vestibule to the sound of lively music, executed by upwards of three hundred performers ... the Grand Dukes Alexander and Constantine leading the flower of all the young persons about the Court, performed a ballet. The dancers, male and female, were forty-eight in number, all dressed in white, with magnificent scarves and covered with jewels, estimated to be worth about ten millions of roubles. ... A magnificent stage now appeared. On it were performed two ballets of a new kind and a lively comedy ... there followed an Asiatic procession, remarkable for its diversity of dresses, all the peoples subject to the sceptre of the Empress being represented.

'A table spread in a manner corresponding to the splendour of the festivity next awaited the company,' writes another contemporary, H. von Storch. 'Six hundred people sat down to it, the rest being served at side tables and among the pillars of the hall. All the vessels and implements used were of gold or silver.'

Within a year of his house-warming, Prince Potyomkin was dead, having enjoyed his great mansion for barely twelve months. After his death, Catherine took it for herself and until her own death in 1796 went back there each spring and autumn to mourn her dead favourite, who, even after their passion had cooled, remained her closest friend and adviser, helping to pick fresh lovers for her as and when this became necessary.

On Catherine's own death, her son Paul wreaked posthumous vengeance on his greatly detested mother and her lover by turning their palace into a barracks for a regiment of his Horse Guards, at the same time removing her statue from the Winter Garden and carrying off the furniture to his own new Mihailovski Castle, the strange, four-square fortress-palace on the Fontanka, which he had built especially to satisfy his mania for security and where a year or two later he met his dreadful end.

For just over a hundred years, the Tauride Palace was to remain without the main current of affairs, being used on and off for one purpose or another by various members of the Imperial Family and at least once, in 1904, by the young Sergei Diaghilev, to hold an art exhibition. Then, in April 1906, it was suddenly dragged back into the limelight by the decision to make it the seat of the hastily constituted and assembled Imperial Duma, with a refurbished Winter Garden as the Hall of Session and the great pillared Ballroom as a Salle des Pas Perdus or Lobby. A dozen years later the February and October Revolutions brought still greater animation to its elegant salons. After the dissolution of the Duma, the Petrograd Soviet met in one wing, while the Revolutionary War Council met in another. It was here, too, that in January 1918 the short-lived Constituent Assembly held its one and only meeting. Today it serves as a regional school for the Leningrad branch of the Communist Party.

On the opposite side of the Neva, to the north of Smolni and the Tauride Palace, lies Viborg, the main industrial quarter of the city, which already in Tsarist days possessed a strong revolutionary tradition. 'Those who wish to visit the unattractive Viborg District,' wrote Baedeker discouragingly in 1914, 'should use the tramway.' Whatever your means of transport, however, the Liteini (formerly Alexandrovski) Bridge, which incidentally commands a fine view of the river, takes you straight into the middle of it. Here you will find the Finland Station, where Lenin arrived in April

1917 in his sealed carriage from Switzerland. The old station has since been torn down and rebuilt, but the ancient locomotive that pulled Lenin's train has been religiously preserved and is displayed for all to see on its own short length of track in the forecourt. Here, too, on Karl Marx Boulevard, stands the vast new Leningrad Hotel for foreign tourists and businessmen, while tied up to the quayside across the narrow stream of the Little Neva is the famous cruiser *Aurora* from which were fired the blank rounds which heralded the outbreak of the October Revolution, blanks surely more far-reaching in their ultimate impact than live rounds from any gun in the world.

Directly across the Bolshaya Neva or main stream of the Neva from the Admiralty is Vasilievski Ostrov (Vasilievski Island or the Island of Basil), linked at this point to the southern bank of the river by Palace Bridge. This takes you to the narrow easternmost point of the island, known as the Strelka or Arrow and dominated by the former Bourse or Stock Exchange, now a naval museum. A fine green and white classical building of the early nineteenth century, the Bourse was modelled by its architect, Thomas de Thomon, on the Temple of Paestum. In front of it stand two tall rostral columns adorned with the prows of ships and bearing colossal statues of Neptune and Amphitrite, which were traditionally used as landmarks by shipping. (It was the practice of the ancient Romans after a naval victory to cut off the prows (*rostra*) of captured enemy ships and incorporate them in a victory column.) Near the Bourse is the former Tamozhnaya or Customs House, another handsome classical building of rather later date, decorated with statues of Mercury and Fortune and now containing a Museum of Russian Literary History.

The Neva is at this point almost a mile wide and, looking out from the Strelka, you enjoy a magnificent view of the river and both its banks: northwards to the Fortress of St Peter and St Paul and southwards to the Admiralty and Winter Palace. As you continue northwards, another bridge carries you across the fast-flowing stream of the Little Neva to St Peter and St Paul and to the Petrograd Quarter on the north bank of the river.

It was Peter the Great's intention, when planning St Petersburg, that Vasilievski Ostrov should be the academic centre of the new city. The tradition was continued by his successors and University Quay, on its southern shore, can boast some of the finest eighteenth-century buildings in Leningrad. In addition to Trezzini's Twelve Colleges and the University Library, there is the city's first museum, Peter's blue and white Kunstkamera, with its lantern dome, built for him by Zemtsov; Giacomo Quarenghi's austerely splendid Academy of Science; and Vallin de la Mothe's neo-classical Academy of Arts, founded by Catherine the Great in 1757. All these buildings are still used for approximately the same purposes as those for which they were originally designed, though with the years many of them have overflowed into neighbouring buildings.

In a way, perhaps the most fascinating of the buildings on Vasilievski Island is the splendid Palace of Prince Menshikov. First built for Peter the Great's favourite by the Italian architect Giovanni Maria Fontana in 1710, it was later extensively altered by Gottfried Schädel and other architects, but even so retains a number of its original features. Still painted the deep red, picked out with white, that found favour in Peter's day, it stands on the embankment, facing the Admiralty across the river. Originally it possessed its own quay and landing stage on the Neva, so that quite large ships could berth opposite its front-door. Two pedimented wings flank a pilastered central block with rounded tops to the windows on the first floor, a line of circular windows above them and a curved central pediment above a pillared entrance porch. From an old engraving it appears that in the course of the eighteenth century these relatively restrained features replaced the more ornate design of the original building, but, despite this and despite the change in its proportions brought about by the subsequent construction of the embankment on the Neva, it still keeps much of its original character.

The story is told that Menshikov built his great palace after Peter the Great had left for the wars, having instructed his favourite to go ahead with the building of a university on Vasilievski Ostrov and told him that, if he felt inclined, he could keep a small plot of land there for a house for himself. When he found what Menshikov had done in his absence, Peter is said to have boxed his favourite's ears in public. Which did not, however, prevent Menshikov from building himself, a few years later, an even bigger palace at Oranienbaum on the Gulf of Finland.

After Menshikov's fall from favour during the brief reign of Peter II, his palace was made into a military academy, housing six or seven hundred officer-cadets. Two French tourists who visited it in 1790 found a plaque at the foot of one of the trees in the garden with an inscription on it to say that, before leaving for exile in Siberia in 1727, Prince Menshikov drank a last cup of coffee under the tree in question. The palace later fell into disuse and decay. Visiting it in 1917, Lenin was fortunately interested by what he saw and decreed that it should be preserved as a historic building. This was remembered through the busy years that followed; some fifty years later work was begun on its restoration and at the time of writing is still in progress.

In Tsarist days the islands in the Neva Delta, of which there were at least a hundred, were famous for their restaurants and other places of entertainment. 'In spring,' wrote Baedeker, 'some are inundated, but by the beginning of summer all have assumed the appearance of verdant parks.' It was here, amid the greenery, that people had their *dachas* or country retreats; it was here that one went to sail or play golf; and it was here, in the summer nights of June and July, that after the more formal parties of the capital were over, one went between dusk and dawn, under the pale midnight sky, to take supper with the gipsies.

Today, in a sterner age, not much of this survives, though there are still those who are fortunate enough to own *dachas* on some of the islands and suitable accommodation is no doubt provided for many others in well equipped sanatoria and rest-houses. Two of the islands, however, are well worth a visit: Kamenni Ostrov, the Isle of Stones (now Workers' Island), once the favourite retreat of what Baedeker calls 'the rich citizens of St Petersburg', and Yelagin Island, now the Kirov Central Park of Culture and Rest. On Kamenni Island, which is reached by a bridge from the Petrograd Quarter, Catherine the Great built in about 1780 a fine neo-classical palace for the heir to the throne, which for a time was occupied by the unfortunate Paul and is now a sanatorium. A long, low two-storeyed building, it has a handsome apricot-coloured façade on the River Nevka with a plain classical portico of eight white Doric columns. On the other side, a second portico of six Tuscan columns looks out on the garden. Nearby is a charming little eighteenth-century Gothick chapel.

From Kamenni Island another bridge takes you to Yelagin Island. This was bought in 1817 by Alexander I, who commissioned the young Carlo Rossi, said by some to be his half-brother, to build a palace there for his mother, the Dowager Empress Maria. The resulting palace, which was Rossi's first independent commission and did much to establish his reputation, was on an ambitious scale. Set on a wide stone terrace, the principal façade has a central portico of six Corinthian columns with further columned porticos on each side. On the garden side, which looks out across the Nevka to Kamenni Island, a central bay, topped by a flattened dome and two pedimented porticos, matches the corresponding feature on the front. The kitchens, also designed by Rossi, after due consultation with the Emperor's Confectioner, Signor Belardelli, and his maître d'hôtel, Signor Riquetti, occupy a separate one-storeyed semi-circular building of equal elegance, without windows but decorated with handsome classical statues and with its own pillared and pedimented portico. To complete the royal residence, Rossi landscaped the whole island, converting it into a park in the English manner. Here, we learn from a contemporary, people 'from all classes of society' came to take the air and listen to the band, a tradition which, with interruptions dictated by circumstances, has continued ever since.

No less splendid than the palaces of Leningrad itself are the former Imperial country residences which lie within easy reach of the capital. Of these, perhaps the most famous is Tsarskoye Selo or, as it is now called, Pushkin. Tsarskoye Selo, which in Russian signifies Imperial Village (though the name is in fact derived from two Finnish words meaning 'a high place'), is situated some fifteen miles due south of Leningrad. In 1836, under Nicholas I, these fifteen miles were triumphantly spanned by the first railway to be built in Russia. A print of the period shows the arrival at Tsarskoye of an early locomotive, puffing busily along the slightly elevated track to the obvious delight of the local population and followed by six open coaches, with another locomotive at the other end ready to pull them back to St Petersburg. Before the Revolution the nearby railway restaurant at Pavlovsk ('popular concerts with a good band every evening in the summer') was called Voksal or Vauxhall, after the well known pleasure gardens outside London, and this, in turn, has, by some strange process of popular etymology become the regular Russian word for a railway station.

Tsarskoye began, like Versailles and other no less magnificent royal residences, as a hunting lodge, a small stone house with a formal Dutch garden, built as a surprise for Peter the Great by his wife Catherine in 1718 during one of his absences abroad. On Catherine's death, ten years later, it was left to her daughter, the future Empress Elizabeth, then a girl of nineteen.

It was only in 1741, after the coup that made her Empress, that Elizabeth could start to transform the modest stone house she had inherited into the splendid palace which she had long been contemplating and which she named Yekaterinski after her mother Catherine. Building was one of her great enthusiasms. Once started, work went ahead fast, both on the main palace and on a variety of pavilions in the park. An army of builders and craftsmen and a number of different architects were kept busy: Zemtsov, A. V. Kvasov, Stasov, Chevakinski, and finally Rastrelli. Building and rebuilding (for the Empress constantly changed her mind) continued merrily throughout the 1740s. 'It was,' wrote her daughter-in-law, Catherine, 'like the task of Penelope. The work of today was all destroyed on the morrow.'

Then, after ten years, in 1752, Elizabeth saw what was needed. In Bartolomeo Rastrelli she had found a chief architect whose exuberant and enthusiastic temperament was well attuned to her own. Money was no object. She would make a fresh start. She would give Rastrelli his head.

After the vicissitudes of two centuries, the palace he built her still takes your breath away. You are confronted on arrival with its tremendous pillared blue and white baroque façade, a thousand feet long, with a pavilion at one end and a great golden-domed church by Chevakinski at the other. Eighty tall French windows with wrought-iron balconies are separated from each other by gigantic male caryatids, once gilded with pure gold leaf, but now of a duskier hue. The main entrance to the palace is through a splendid wrought-iron gate set in an arc of one-storeyed out-buildings built by Rastrelli in collaboration with Chevakinski round a semi-circular courtyard. On the far side, the palace looks out on to a formal garden with trees and ornamental water and a baroque Hermitage for intimate banquets, at which the tables came up, ready laid, through the floor. In the centre of the garden façade Rastrelli set a pillared portico with columns set in pairs.

Within the palace, as without, Empress and architect worked in close sympathy, devising a succession of saloons and galleries of surprising splendour. Near the centre of the building Rastrelli's

Great Hall, 260 feet long with two rows of windows looking out on the park and, between them, tall gilded mirrors specially ordered 'from abroad', made a perfect setting for the balls and receptions in which the Empress took such delight. She was rarely in bed before dawn. 'Few people,' wrote the British Minister of the day, 'know where she sleeps.' For security and no doubt for other reasons she seems to have changed rooms almost nightly. Leading out of the Great Hall is the charming Knights' Dining Room, with more mirrors and tiered gilt sconces for candles on the walls and a great porcelain stove reaching to the ceiling and decorated with Dutch tiles.

In the Picture Gallery, paintings, some of them of reasonably good quality, entirely cover every inch of the walls from top to bottom, while one vast painting reaches across the whole of the ceiling.

Much of all this was damaged or destroyed during the last war, when the Germans occupied Tsarskoye, and has since been lovingly restored or replaced. One interior, clearly remembered from a first visit some forty years ago, it proved impossible to restore: the Amber Room, panelled by Rastrelli with looking-glasses and golden yellow Persian amber. The amber, given to Peter the Great, who happened to admire it, by the King of Prussia, in return, it is said, for 'fifty-five guardsmen of exceptional stature', was, it appears, taken back to Germany by Hitler's forces of occupation in 1944 and never seen again.

Catherine the Great's tastes in architecture were, as we have already seen, different from those of her predecessor. 'There is going to be a terrible upheaval at Tsarskoye Selo,' she wrote with evident glee not long after her accession to the throne. For the baroque exuberance of Rastrelli she substituted whenever possible restrained, neo-classical elegance. The Italian's gilded plasterwork was repainted in bronze and his statues and urns swept from the roof of the Great Palace. She, too, was an enthusiastic builder. '*Je mehr man bauet*,' she wrote, '*je mehr man will bauen; das ist eine Krankheit, so wie das Saufen*,' ('The more you build, the more you want to build; it's a disease, like drinking.') In Charles Cameron, an expatriate Scot, she found, though not until seventeen or eighteen years after her accession, the ideal architect for what she had in mind at Tsarskoye. Cameron came from London. The elaborate Highland and Jacobite background which he invented for himself seems to have been largely a fabrication. But Catherine was delighted with him: '*A présent je me suis emparée de Mister Cameron, Ecossais de nation, Jacobite de profession, grand dessinateur nourri d'antiquités, connu par un livre sur les bains anciens; nous façonnons avec lui ici un jardin en terrasse avec bains en dessous, galerie en dessus; cela sera du beau, beau, comme dit maître Blaise.*'

By the time he reached the age of thirty-eight, Cameron had studied in Rome and written a book on ancient baths, but had so far built nothing. Catherine, who believed in trying out her architects on something of minor importance (just as her prospective lovers were first tried out on her ladies-in-waiting) first commissioned him to construct, decorate and furnish a suite of eight not very large rooms at the northern end of the Great Palace, leading to Chevakinski's church, in place of an entrance-hall by Rastrelli which she now demolished. Catherine was well satisfied with the result. 'These apartments', she wrote in 1781, 'will be superlatively good. So far only two rooms are finished, and people rush to see them because they have never seen anything like them before. I admit that I have not grown tired of looking at them for the last nine weeks. They are pleasing to the eye.'

The first suite was followed by two more, also on the first floor. Almost completely destroyed during the war, most of the rooms have now been restored with immense care and skill to their original condition. They show the full extent of Cameron's talents, not only as an architect, but as a decorator, a colourist and a designer of furniture. All in the purest classical style, they and their contents have a lightness and elegance and show an inventiveness in the use of materials for which it is hard to find a parallel even in the finest French work of the period.

For the present, visitors can see the Green Dining Room, in a style reminiscent of Adam; the Blue Drawing Room; the Chinese Drawing Room; the Ante-Room to the Church; and a bedroom of which the ceiling is supported by fifty columns of fluted faience in pistachio green and white. I missed, on my last visit, Catherine's private rooms, like other parts of the palace not yet fully restored. These I remember from before the war as an improbable but exquisite fantasy of violet glass columns against a background of walls panelled with clouded white glass, decorated with a delicate design in bronze and specially made Wedgwood medallions. Clearly, like the other foreign architects who worked in Russia, Charles

Cameron found in the exotic, lavish atmosphere and in the irrepressible enthusiasm of his Imperial patron something that brought out and encouraged his native Scottish genius, giving it, as it were, an entirely new dimension.

Having successfully completed Catherine's three suites, Cameron turned his attention to other work: the building of a Palladian church for the neighbouring village of Sophia; designs for a palace for Catherine's son Paul; and a variety of pavilions and follies for the park at Tsarskoye. It was not until 1784 that he set to work on 'the terrace garden with baths below and a gallery above', mentioned by Catherine in her letter.

The site chosen for this project was at the far end of the Great Palace, behind the south-east corner. This would make it possible for Catherine to walk out of her new apartments on the first floor and straight into the Hanging Garden, which in turn led to the Agate Pavilion or bath-house and to Cameron's new Colonnade or Gallery. On the level of the Hanging Garden, the Agate Pavilion consists of a low, single-storeyed rotunda of Ionic pillars under a flattened green cupola, with wings on either side fronted by more Ionic pillars set in pairs. Within are the elegant Great Hall and Jasper Hall, supported by whole columns of jasper, porphyry and other semi-precious stones with bronze Corinthian bases and capitals and decorated with medallions and bas-reliefs. Lavish and ingenious use is also made of malachite, lapis-lazuli and alabaster, the floor being inlaid with intricate designs in different coloured stones. From the garden level, stairs of red agate with a bronze balustrade lead down to the baths and dressing rooms below.

Also adjoining the Hanging Garden is the Colonnade or Cameron Gallery, jutting out at right angles to the Great Palace and thought by some to be Cameron's supreme achievement. It consists of a central area, glazed in to afford protection on either side and lined with the bronze busts of fifty-four philosophers and statesmen. These originally included, curiously enough, the British statesman Charles James Fox, who had momentarily attracted Catherine's favourable attention by a speech he had made in the House of Commons against war with Russia, but was later removed for showing himself unduly favourable to revolutionary France.

From the Great Palace the ground slopes away abruptly to a large ornamental lake. This allowed Cameron to provide the Gallery (and also the Agate Pavilion) with a lower floor and at the same time to end his colonnade with a pedimented portico like a Greek temple, supported by four Ionic columns, and with a splendid double staircase leading steeply down from it to a further flight of steps which in turn lead down to the lake. With the years, however, Catherine, who enjoyed strolling by the lake, found this arrangement, though supremely successful architecturally, increasingly hard on the leg-muscles and in due course Cameron was commissioned to build for her a *pandus* or *pente douce* leading from the other end of the gallery by gentle degrees down to the ground.

Thanks to the whims and fancies of successive sovereigns, the park at Tsarskoye is filled with any number of agreeable monuments, pavilions and follies, built at different times during the eighteenth and nineteenth centuries. Around the lake are a baroque grotto by Rastrelli; a Gothick boat-house or Admiralty, built for Catherine in 1773; a delightful little Turkish Bath with a dome and a minaret, like a small pink mosque, built by an Italian architect in the middle of the nineteenth century; and a Palladian Bridge of grey Siberian marble on a base of red granite, copied from the well known bridge at Wilton. From the middle of the lake rises a Rostral Column erected to celebrate Aleksei Orlov's naval victory off Chesme, also celebrated by the palace and church of that name on the outskirts of Leningrad. Also to be found scattered about the park are a monument to Catherine's young lover Lanskoi and another to her dogs, Zemir, Duchesse and Sir Tom Anderson; a charming little eighteenth-century Chinese Pavilion with floors made specially to creak; a Chinese Arch of the same period with a summer-house on top of it; and (all part of the same fit of *chinoiserie*) the remains of a Chinese Village, once used to house lesser courtiers but now crumbling into disrepair.

Finally, on a much larger scale, there is the splendidly proportioned yellow and white Alexandrovski Palace built by Catherine the Great in 1761 towards the end of her reign for her much-loved nineteen-year-old grandson, the future Tsar Alexander I, who spent much of his childhood there, away from his father and under the aegis of his formidable grandparent, and retained a great liking for it all his life. It stands, in its own grounds and with its own lake, only a few hundred yards from the Great Palace. Thought by many to be the masterpiece of the great Quarenghi, it is in the Palladian manner, elegantly neo-classical with an austerely plain central block and a magnificent double row of

Corinthian columns linking two independent pavilions and so forming a courtyard.

The Alexandrovski Palace was also a favourite residence of Tsar Nicholas II. It was here that he and his family usually spent the spring and summer and here that they came to live after his abdication in 1917, before being sent to Siberia. Before the war the palace (now closed, presumably for restoration) was open to the public, who, if they chose, could visit the last Tsar's study, with its windows overlooking the park, inspect his desk, with the photographs of his family still on it, and spell out, word by pathetic word, the last entries in his diary.

Half-way between Leningrad and Tsarskoye Selo, at a staging point on the old coaching road from St Petersburg, are two buildings which no enthusiast for the exotic should fail to visit, either on the way there or on the way back: the Church and Palace of Chesme. So named, or rather renamed by Catherine the Great to celebrate Aleksei Orlov's naval victory over the Turks off Chesme on the coast of Anatolia in 1780, they are built *à la Turque*, in the 'Turkish' manner, in a splendid mixture of eighteenth-century Gothick and Eastern styles, apparently designed by the architect, Yuri Veldten, to recall the kiosks and pavilions of the Bosphorus. The palace is triangular in shape, with a round tower at each of the three corners and a central keep in the middle, supporting a flattened cupola, at the moment under restoration. The three towers are crowned with three more domes. Between the towers, the walls were provided with battlements and the windows given a Gothic lancet form.

Chesme Church is completely fantastic. Painted a cheerful pink and shaped like a quatrefoil, it has an apse for each point of the compass. Each apse is surmounted in turn by a turret with a cupola, the four of them clustering round a large central dome, making a total of five, in accordance with Orthodox practice. The pink walls of the church are lavishly encrusted with Gothick designs in white stucco, like icing on a wedding-cake, which in fact is what this curious structure resembles most. A more whimsical place of worship it is hard to conceive.

Built primarily as a staging post on the route to the capital, Chesme seems in fact to have been little used by the Imperial family. Indeed the only recorded instance of an Emperor or Empress spending a night there was when the mortal remains of both Alexander I and his consort rested there on their way back from their fateful expedition to Taganrog in 1825. (Though whether it really was the Tsar that the coffin contained, or a substitute, or no one at all remains a matter for speculation.) Today church and palace stand rather incongruously in the middle of a modern housing-scheme.

To show her pleasure at the birth of her grandson Alexander in 1777, Catherine the Great had presented her otherwise unsatisfactory son Paul and his wife Maria (the former Sophie of Würtemberg) with an estate of some fifteen hundred acres two or three miles south-east of Tsarskoye Selo. To this was given the name of Pavlovsk. At about the same time, Charles Cameron was starting work at Tsarskoye nearby and at Catherine's suggestion (she was, after all, footing the bill) he drew up the plans for a pair of relatively modest wooden mansions (Paullust and Marienthal) to be built there. This was an age of lavish construction. Catherine, as we know, was a compulsive builder and, whether at her instance, or of their own initiative, it was not long before the young couple called upon Cameron, though they did not in fact greatly admire him, to design for them a residence rather more appropriate to their exalted station. In 1781, taking time off from his work at Tsarskoye, he drew up plans for a great stone Palladian palace and (for no park could be complete without something of the kind) a Temple of Friendship and an Apollo Colonnade.

Having given their orders (or had them given for them) Paul and his consort now left on a prolonged tour of Western Europe, whence they continued to bombard the unfortunate Cameron (who liked to design everything himself) with irritating instructions on points of detail, usually sent through a third party. 'My husband consents, though regretfully,' wrote the Grand Duchess, 'to having a vaulted ceiling in the bedroom, but on condition that it takes the least disagreeable form possible ... so beg Cameron, in God's name, to try to do something good, above all that he takes care not to add any arabesque ornament.' And again: 'The medallions, being part of the ornaments, ought all to be in white; to do the contrary is to ignore the rules of architecture.'

Towards the end of 1782, they returned from their travels to find that not much progress had been made and two years after this, in 1784, the palace was still not finished, greatly to the indignation of the Grand Duchess. Catherine now presented Paul with the immensely solid, 700-roomed palace by Rinaldi, which she had built almost twenty years earlier at Gachina for Grigori Orlov, one of her earliest lovers and the murderer, it will be recalled, of her husband and Paul's putative father, Peter. Even so, Paul seems to have been delighted with Gachina and gradually to have lost interest in Pavlovsk, leaving it more and more to the care of his wife. Of this the latter took advantage to play one architect off against another, calling in Quarenghi (who, to do him justice, demurred) and Vincenzo Brenna in competition with Cameron.

In the end, Brenna, who had started as Cameron's assistant, seems to have supplanted him as chief architect. As work progressed (and it was to continue for years) other architects were brought in, including Quarenghi and the young Carlo Rossi, all of whom made contributions of varying value. But in the main Cameron's original plan prevailed, at any rate as far as the exterior design of the palace was concerned, and it is this, despite a serious fire in 1803, modifications which continued for another twenty years and the war damage of 1944, which still predominates today.

The palace, which is painted a warm golden yellow, has a square central block of three storeys, a ground floor, serving, as it were, as a base for the two upper floors, a *piano nobile* and a more modest upper floor, the two latter being spanned, both at the front and at the back of the palace, by the tall white Corinthian columns of the central projection. At the front, these support an ornamented architrave and, on the façade overlooking the park, an architrave and pediment, the ornamentation of the architrave being continued in a frieze which runs round the rest of the building. But what gives Pavlovsk its essential character is the low green dome, supported by a colonnaded drum, encircled with slender white columns, masking scarcely-seen windows, which rises from the roof of the central block.

From the central block sprang, in Cameron's original design, low, semi-circular open galleries on the entrance side, ending in two pavilions. To these Brenna added two curved wings, two storeys high, almost enclosing the resulting courtyard, a dubious improvement on the elegant simplicity of the original plan, and, to the south, a further protuberance, embodying a church.

On first entering the palace from the courtyard, the State Staircase takes you from the Egyptian Vestibule on the ground floor

Pavlovsk

to the State Vestibule on the first floor, lavishly decorated by Brenna in bas-relief with trophies, banners and breastplates, all very much to the mad military taste of the Emperor Paul, who, a contemporary reports, used from the terrace to watch the sentries in the park through a spy-glass, sometimes then walking half a mile to slip a rouble into the pocket of a soldier whose uniform and bearing he liked or to cane one who for some reason happened to displease him.

From the State Vestibule you enter Cameron's splendid Italian Hall. This is situated at the exact centre of the building. Directly under the cupola and lit by the windows in its colonnaded drum, it occupies two floors, its full height being broken by a gallery at the base of the cupola.

From the Italian Hall an arch leads directly to the even more magnificent Grecian Hall, also by Cameron and bearing a strong resemblance to the Great Hall built by Robert Adam some twenty years earlier at Kedleston. Supported by massive columns of fluted green marble with white marble bases and white Corinthian capitals, it is lit by two great bronze hexagonal lanterns and by a number of smaller lamps of classical design. In its white marble walls are a series of niches containing classical statues. At either end is a splendid white marble chimney-piece, surmounted by a looking-glass and decorated with bronze and an inlay of lapis lazuli.

Turning left or right from the Grecian Hall, you come on the one side to the apartments of the Grand Duchess Maria Fyodorovna (beginning with the Hall of Peace) and on the other (beginning with the Hall of War) to those of her husband Paul. All white and gold, in the grandest possible manner, with a wealth of trophies, plaster garlands, cornucopias, fasces, helmets, breastplates and musical instruments, both halls and the apartments that follow are more than worthy of Versailles, where the whole concept clearly had its origins.

To Cameron's original low, semi-circular galleries on either side of the central block a second storey was, as we have seen, later added. In the southernmost of these, in 1797, the year after Paul's accession to the throne, Brenna built a curving Picture Gallery, leading in turn to the Throne Room or State Dining Room, which he had added to the southern of Cameron's two pavilions. In the corresponding curved space on the other side, a fine library, with a barrel-vaulted ceiling and five great windows looking out on the park, was added some twenty-five years later by Carlo Rossi, who thus successfully restored the symmetry of the whole.

Had Charles Cameron been left to complete his own designs in his own way, Pavlovsk might well have been a building of greater architectural purity and of even greater beauty than it is. But such a hypothesis makes no allowance for the vagaries of human nature or the vicissitudes of history. And looking back after an interval of almost two hundred years, one can be thankful that Cameron received the commission in the first place, that the architects who followed him were as capable as they were, and, finally, that the whole building was not simply wiped from the scene by war or revolution.

For Pavlovsk some of the credit must surely go to Paul's wife, Maria Fyodorovna, who, however infuriating to Charles Cameron, as a character clearly had much to recommend her. Snatched as a young girl from the relative calm of a minor German kingdom, abruptly converted to Orthodoxy, rechristened, married to a half-mad husband and exposed at close quarters to a mother-in-law like Catherine the Great, she seems somehow to have retained her sanity, remaining calm, affectionate and industrious throughout – qualities clearly reflected in a rather pleasing portrait of her which I found still hanging in the palace she once occupied. After her husband had been brutally murdered and their son placed on the throne by his assassins under the most shocking circumstances, she quietly spent the next twenty-seven years (which were also far from uneventful) doing good works and continuing to embellish her palace and park, though towards the end of her life passing much of her time in her new palace on Yelagin Island.

The park at Pavlovsk, to which Maria Fyodorovna devoted so much care and attention, has fortunately survived unspoilt, with its ornamental water, its trees and flowers and its innumerable classical temples and monuments and pavilions. With the advent in 1836 of the railway and the opening of the famous outdoor restaurant or Vauxhall, it became, a contemporary writes, 'the principal place of recreation of the middle classes of St Petersburg, who resort there daily in such numbers to enjoy the country, to dine and to drink punch and champagne, that they are, in fact, almost the exclusive supporters of the railway'. Today there is, in theory, no such thing as a middle class in the Soviet Union. But the railway still runs to Pavlovsk and, whatever the precise social status of the passengers, this pleasant tradition has continued unabated, to the great satisfaction of all concerned.

Of all the palaces round Leningrad perhaps the most spectacular, more spectacular even than Tsarskoye Selo, is Peterhof or, in its Russian form, Petrodvorets. Its position, on the Gulf of Finland a dozen miles due west of the new capital, was Peter the Great's own choice. In about the year 1707, while his great new bastion against the Swedes was being built on the island of Kronstadt, he had two wooden houses put up on the mainland immediately opposite, in one of which he took up his quarters while superintending the building operations. The site, right on the shore, appealed to him and four or five years later he decided to build something more permanent there.

The result of this decision was a small seven-roomed, one-storeyed house, originally known as the Dutch House and later renamed Mon Plaisir. This consists of a large central living-room with a beautifully painted and decorated ceiling, probably by Carlo Rastrelli, the father of Bartolommeo, panelled walls and a marble floor; a Dutch-tiled kitchen and pantry; three more panelled rooms – a bedroom, a sea cabinet, where Peter worked, and a room for his secretary; and a tiny lacquer cabinet, panelled with Chinese red lacquer. Low galleries link it on either side with two pavilions. 'The house and furniture,' wrote Archdeacon Coxe, an English clergyman who visited it in 1784, 'have been preserved with a kind of religious veneration exactly in their original state.' The same, despite all that has happened in the interval, is true today. Peter's memory is still revered in Russia; there are always fresh flowers on his tomb; and both the Summer Palace and Mon Plaisir, like Lenin's various places of residence, are meticulously preserved in the state in which their original occupant left them.

But, though Peter's private and personal tastes were modest, he was fully conscious of the need to keep up appearances. While he was building Mon Plaisir, with its seven rooms, his friend and Prime Minister, Prince Menshikov, not content with his splendid residence on Vasilievski Island, had hired the Italian architect Giovanni-Maria Fontana to build him a great palace five miles further along the coast at Oranienbaum. Peter, when in France, had seen Versailles. Now he wanted something comparable, within easy reach of his own capital. Something with fountains.

The planning of Peterhof began with the search for a suitable site for a Grand Cascade. One day, on a walk with his nobles in the nearby hills, the Emperor struck water; a reservoir and pipes were installed; and the Palace of Peterhof was built above the cascade which now gushed from the side of the hill.

Its construction had been entrusted to Jean-Baptiste Leblond, who designed a relatively simple two-storeyed building with a wing on either side. Immediately below this, and exactly corresponding to it in width, the Grand Cascade, springing from the hillside, flowed down a series of high stone steps marked by a line of fountains, interspersed with lead statues, later to be gilded, and then into a canal, which in turn emptied itself into the sea, a quarter of a mile away.

But the palace, it soon appeared, was too small and plans were made to enlarge it. In 1725, however, just as work was beginning, Peter died and the whole project was abandoned, not to be revived until after the accession of Peter's daughter Elizabeth in 1741. Rastrelli, whom Elizabeth entrusted with the work, did not demolish Leblond's original building, but simply added another storey to it and doubled it in length, making it now twice the width of the Grand Cascade. But this was not all. At each end he prolonged the wings with single-storeyed galleries, one ending in a church and the other in a Heraldic Pavilion. Each of these he characteristically finished with a single gilt baroque onion dome, topping the one with a cross and the other with a heraldic weather-vane of three double-headed eagles. This, as was to be expected, got him into trouble with the Orthodox hierarchy, who demanded the removal of the single dome from the church and its replacement by the five required by ecclesiastical tradition. These changes destroyed the all-important symmetry of his building. But the hierarchy insisted and the five offending domes remained there for the next two centuries, until ultimately demolished by Hitler's hordes. In the end, however, it was Rastrelli who won, for, when the Soviet authorities came to restore the palace after the war, they rebuilt it with a single dome at each end, at the same time converting the church into a post-office. But a post-office with a cross above it.

Looking up at Peterhof from the foot of the Grand Cascade, you see today a long, beautifully proportioned, three-storeyed, yellow and white building, with the four flat pilasters of the central block twice repeated on each of the extended wings, while the classical triangular central pediment of the façade is varied with rounded pediments on the wings. Linked to these by Rastrelli's low galleries are his two domed pavilions, one with its cross, the other with its triple double-headed eagle. Against this majestic background the terraces of the Grand Cascade, with their spurting fountains and rows of glittering gold statues, form a truly fantastic foreground.

Of Rastrelli's characteristically exuberant interiors, many were destroyed during the war. (Some had already been modified by Veldten at the behest of Catherine the Great.) But a number, with their profusion of scrolls and garlands and white and gold plaster-work, either still survive or have been so admirably restored as to be indistinguishable from the originals. There is, for example, the Cabinet of Modes and Graces, or Rotari Room, with its magnifi-cent gold and white rococo doors and rows of hundreds of portraits by the Italian painter Pietro Rotari, allegedly of girls from every part of the Empire, but in fact of the same eight sweetly smiling girls painted over and over again in different attitudes and cos-tumes. Two rooms, originally designed by Rastrelli but later altered by Veldten, are the Partridge Room and the White Dining Room. Another is the spacious Throne Room, with its highly effec-tive double row of rounded windows (a feature much favoured by Rastrelli) lighting it from both sides. At one end of it is the famous equestrian portrait of Catherine the Great, carrying a drawn sword and wearing the uniform of the Semyonovski Guards in which she made her triumphant entry into St Petersburg after the successful coup of 1762 which put her on the throne in place of her husband.

The grounds at Peterhof are divided by the palace itself into an Upper Park, consisting of a relatively small formal garden laid out round a central fountain and situated immediately behind the palace, and the much larger Lower Park. This lies between the palace and the Gulf of Finland in front of the Grand Cascade and on either side of the ornamental canal into which its waters flow and is lavishly provided with statuary and fountains, including a number of trick fountains designed to spray unwary visitors with water. In addition to Mon Plaisir, the Lower Park contains Marly, another little house built by Peter the Great and called after Marly-le-Roi, which he had visited when in France, and the Hermitage. The latter is an elegant, pleasantly proportioned stucco pavilion, built in the last years of Peter's reign in the style which we connect with

William and Mary and situated, like Mon Plaisir, right at the water's edge.

Every summer under the Tsars, Peterhof was the scene of a *fête champêtre* on a gigantic scale, the palace and grounds being thrown open to anyone who cared to come and the Tsar's generous invitation being taken up enthusiastically by well over a hundred thousand people of all sorts and conditions, many of whom would camp out in the park for the night. Clearly, it was a very Russian occasion. Mrs Disbrowe, the British diplomat's lady, who with her husband was lucky enough to be asked to dinner with the Emperor on one such occasion, was considerably impressed by what she saw later in the evening. 'People of every class,' she writes, 'were admitted to the palace; and it was a striking spectacle to see courtly dames in gold and jewels, Emperor, Grand Dukes and Duchesses, Princes and Counts, whirling through crowds of rustics, men with long beards, women with russet gowns, who gazed with respectful astonishment, and, though in close contact with the grandees, showed no symptoms of rudeness and were as quiet and unpresuming as if they had been bred to palaces and balls.' And she goes on to speculate about how badly the English or French lower orders would have behaved themselves, if admitted in this way to St James's Palace or the Tuileries.

From another British visitor a few years later we have a somewhat unexpected picture of the normally austere and aloof Nicholas I who 'at the great summer fête at Peterhof, where thousands of people are assembled ... dances and capers among them, as merry and free as any goat of them all'. Monsieur de Custine, who was there the same year, was for his part more cynical and possibly more discerning. 'It seems to me,' he writes, pursuing a favourite idea, 'that the Emperor, by this false display of popularity, abases the great without exalting the humble. All men are equal before God and for the Russians God is the Emperor ... When he opens his palaces, he does not say to the workman or the merchant: "You are a man like myself," but rather he says to the great Lord: "You are a slave like them and I, your God, am exalted above you all." As a spectator,' he concludes, 'I observed that all this was more pleasing to the Sovereign and to the serfs than to the professional courtiers.'

Five miles further along the coast from Peterhof is Oranienbaum, the great palace built for himself between 1710 and 1725 by Prince Menshikov. Its name, literally 'orange tree', seems to derive from the heated orangeries which for the great nobles of Peter the Great's Russia were the ultimate status symbol. Like Peterhof, Oranienbaum stands on a slight eminence overlooking the sea. To it Gottfried Schädel, Menshikov's Prussian architect, gave the not unusual form of a massive central block linked to large domed pavilions by sweeping semi-circular galleries. In front of the palace, a terrace and formal garden lead down to a quay or landing-stage, approached by a much wider canal than that at Peterhof, and enabling a man-of-war to tie up at its steps. The cost of building it must have been scandalously large and no doubt contributed, amongst other things, to Prince Menshikov's downfall in 1727, when, with neither Peter the Great nor Catherine I, his former mistress, there to protect him, he was, at the behest of his many enemies, simply sent off to Siberia by the young Tsar Peter II.

Together with Menshikov's other house on Vasilievski Island, Oranienbaum was taken over by the state in 1737 and turned into a naval hospital. But not for long. Six years later, in 1743, Elizabeth I presented it as a summer residence to her fifteen-year-old nephew and heir, the future Tsar Peter III and future husband of Catherine the Great. It was not, however, until 1756 that work was begun at Oranienbaum by Antonio Rinaldi. His first task was to build a new small, square, rather box-like, two-storeyed pink and white palace for Peter, while at the same time extensively redecorating the interior of Menshikov's great palace.

Apart from drinking, poor Peter's only pleasure was playing at soldiers. At Oranienbaum he had himself built a special fortress (of which only one gateway remains) and some barracks for the troops he amused himself by drilling. But these military proclivities were to be of no avail when in 1762, barely a year after his accession to the throne, his wife and her lover Grigori Orlov and the latter's brother Aleksei decided that the moment had arrived to get rid of him. Brought from Oranienbaum to Peterhof on Catherine's orders, Peter meekly signed the act of abdication in favour of his wife. After which he was allowed to depart to Ropsha in the hills near Peterhof with Mopsy, his poodle, and Narcissus, his negro servant, and there done away with by the Orlov brothers a week later.

While not hesitating to rid herself of her husband, Catherine wisely kept his architect. That same year she commissioned Rinaldi to build her a small Chinese Palace in the park at Oranienbaum. The result, a pink baroque single-storeyed pavilion of seventeen rooms, on a stone terrace overlooking an artificial lake, is charming, inside and out. Only the mixed rococo and *chinoiserie* of three or four of the rooms (with rococo predominating) justifies the name by which it is known. But that, if you consider the superlative quality of its decoration and contents, is scarcely important. In addition to a number of magnificent state rooms, the Chinese Palace possessed a suite of private apartments for the Empress and another for the Grand Duke Paul. But although during the remaining thirty-odd years of her reign she occasionally used it for entertaining, Catherine never, as far as is known, spent a night there.

Another remarkable pleasure pavilion in the park at Oranienbaum is Katalnaya Gorka or the Switchback Pavilion. The Russians (hence the phrase, *montagnes russes*) have always enjoyed tobogganing, on ice-runs in winter and in roller-coasters during the rest of the year. At first sight, Katalnaya Gorka, built in three tiers with columns, pilasters and balustrades at all levels, with a bell-shaped dome on top to round it off and painted sky-blue and white, resembles a magnificent wedding cake. It is only when one studies contemporary prints of it that one grasps how, launching themselves from its upper terraces, the bolder members of the Imperial Court could hurtle merrily down specially prepared chutes and slides at break-neck speed to the immense delight of the onlookers. These assembled in large numbers on the balconies and terraces of the pavilion, while others took refreshments inside in an exquisitely decorated Circular Hall and a scarcely less exquisite Porcelain Room, of which the walls were adorned with brackets supporting pieces of the finest Meissen.

There was nothing unusual about a switchback pavilion in eighteenth-century Russia. Another such pavilion was installed by Rastrelli at Tsarskoye and in the reign of the Empress Anne a similar contraption was rigged up in the courtyard of the Winter Palace. From a Mrs Ward, the wife, once again, of a British diplomat, comes an account* of the 'new diversion we have had at court this winter'. 'There is,' she writes,

a machine made of boards that goes from the upper storey down to the yard ... this had water flung upon it, which soon froze, and then

* *Letter from a Lady* (London, 1775).

more was flung, till it was covered with ice of a considerable thickness. The ladies and gentlemen of the court sit on sledges, and they are set going at the top, and fly down to the bottom; for the motion is so swift, that nothing but flying is a proper term. Sometimes, if these sledges meet with any resistance, the person in them tumbles head over heels; that, I suppose, is the joke.... I was terrified out of my wits for fear of being obliged to go down this shocking place, for I had not only the dread of breaking my neck, but of being exposed to indecency too frightful to think on without horror.

# 11 *Journey Into History*

FROM a strictly historical and chronological point of view, there would have been a strong case for starting any description of European Russia, not with Moscow or Leningrad, but with Novgorod or Pskov, or Kiev, or with those other early predecessors of Moscow, Suzdal, Rostov and Vladimir. In fact, other considerations prevailed. But, having reached this point in my book, I decided to repair the omission and restore the balance by visiting or revisiting as many of these towns as I could. I accordingly set out, as and when the opportunity offered, to tramp round them with notebook and camera, returning in due course with a rather better picture of the remote mediaeval world in which Russia's history has its roots and a clearer idea of the brightly coloured background against which many of its stranger scenes took place. It was a rewarding and, as usual, an entertaining experience.

The Vikings started in the north-west with Novgorod. And, all things considered, there is much to be said for following their example. Novgorod, after all, was where it all began. It was the people of Novgorod who in the year 862 invited Rurik to come and sort out their affairs. Novgorod, the New Town or New Market on the banks of the Volkhov – or Holmgard, as Rurik himself no doubt called it – was the first and one of the most important of the trading posts on the route which led 'from the Varangians to the Greeks', a base from which Russian culture and influence could spread in the north-west. It was from Novgorod that Alexander Nevski sallied forth to do battle with the Swedes and the Teutonic Knights. At the height of its power, Lord Novgorod the Great could more than hold its own with any other city in Russia. It was in Novgorod, finally, that the rulers of Muscovy saw the main obstacle to their ambitions, an obstacle which they set out to eliminate by all and every means.

Novgorod lies some three hundred miles from Moscow and 120 miles from Leningrad. It can be reached quite easily from either by road or train and the Sadko, to which one is conducted on arrival, is a perfectly adequate modern Soviet hotel, within walking distance of the centre of the town. Novgorod lies on both sides of the River Volkhov, which thus divides it into two halves linked by a bridge: the Sophiskaya Storona, or Sophia Side, on the west bank and the Torgovaya Storona, or Market Side, on the east bank. The Sophia Side, indeed the whole town, is dominated by the Kremlin or Detinets, as it is called locally, built on a slight eminence above the river, and by the golden-domed Cathedral of St Sophia, which stands within its walls. The Market Side centres round the Yaroslavovo Dvorishche or Court of Yaroslav (so called after Yaroslav the Wise), which lies immediately across the river from the Kremlin and consists of a group of ancient churches, of which the oldest and most important is the Cathedral of St Nicholas. Right round both halves of the old town, for a distance of some six miles, runs what is left of a line of massive earthworks dating back to the twelfth century and once strengthened and embellished by as many as fifty towers of wood or stone, which have now long since disappeared with the exception of a single massive, circular tower, known as the White Tower and situated at their southernmost point.

Whether the area enclosed by these ramparts represents the site of the original town or whether there was a still earlier Varangian settlement on a different site, has proved a fruitful subject for debate among the experts, one school maintaining that, because Novgorod means New Town, there is bound to have been an earlier town somewhere else. This in spite of the Chronicler, who, writing of Rurik, declares with the utmost clarity, 'He came to Lake Ilmen and built a town above the Volkhov and called it Novgorod and settled there.'

What we know for certain is that a first Church of St Sophia, built of oak with thirteen cupolas, was put up in 989 on the site of the present church by a certain Joachim, sent by St Vladimir from Kiev to be the first Bishop or Archbishop of Novgorod. As in other mediaeval Russian towns practically all the houses in Novgorod were built of wood. In 1044, however, the Kremlin walls were rebuilt in stone and a year later work was begun, apparently by Greek architects, on the present Cathedral of St Sophia which took the place of Bishop Joachim's wooden church. This was done at the behest of Prince Vladimir, the son of Yaroslav the Wise, whom his father had made Prince of Novgorod in 1036 and whose aim it now was to make his city at least as beautiful as Kiev, where the new cathedral of the same name was already becoming world-famous.

The church he built is a magnificent example of early Russian architecture. Like its counterpart in Kiev, it has five aisles separated by rows of piers and is dominated by open galleries on its north, south and west walls, designed to accommodate the Prince and his entourage, while the rest of the congregation were packed into the body of the church below. On the outside are stone pilasters corresponding to the five aisles inside. The church has, however, only five domes and is rather more austere in style than its Kievan prototype. Perched on its principal golden dome is the figure of a dove. It is said that when the dove flies away, this will mean the end of Novgorod. Of particular interest are a pair of splendid bronze doors on the west side of the cathedral, decorated with a variety of Biblical scenes and said to have been captured from the Swedes in 1187. There is reason to suppose that they originally came from the German town of Magdeburg.

Since the beginning of the eleventh century Novgorod had to all intents and purposes been a separate principality, in practice independent of Kiev. The power of the reigning Prince was undisputed and St Sophia served as a glorified Chapel Royal. In the first half of the twelfth century, however, power passed to a *Veche* or Assembly of boyars and leading citizens to whom the Prince was henceforth responsible and whose servant in practice he became. There was a corresponding increase in the power of the Archbishop and of the *Posadnik* or Mayor. This political change was to have a marked effect on Novgorod's future development as a city.

The Princes now moved out of the Kremlin, which had hitherto been their place of residence. At the same time St Sophia ceased to be their personal place of worship. Having established themselves in the *Gorodishche* or Fort, a mile or so south of the town on the east bank of the river, at the point where it flows out of Lake Ilmen, they set about building themselves a number of other handsome churches in the hope of thus saving face and to some extent reasserting their authority. Thus in 1113 Prince Mstislav of Novgorod built as his personal church the five-domed Cathedral

273

of St Nicholas in Yaroslav's Court on the Market Side of the town, immediately across the river from the Kremlin. Clearly intended to rival St Sophia, it is built in the same austere, somewhat monolithic style and gives the same impression of simplicity and strength. Its clergy were responsible to the Prince and not to the Archbishop and when, some years later, the Archbishop refused to marry the reigning Prince to what he evidently considered an unsuitable local girl, we are told by the Chronicler that the Prince simply 'bade his own priest marry him at St Nicholas's'.

In 1119 Prince Vsevolod in his turn built the Monastery and Cathedral of St George at Yurievo a mile or two to the south of the town on the west bank of the Volkhov where it flows out of Lake Ilmen. The Chronicler tells us that the architect was a certain Master Peter. St George is another worthy rival of St Sophia. Prince Vsevolod followed it with two more churches, the Church of St Ivan in Opoki, built in 1127, and the Church of the Assumption in the Market Place, built in 1135, both close to St Nicholas's Cathedral in Yaroslav's Court on the Market Side.

In 1136 Prince Vsevolod was driven out of Novgorod, which now became to all intents and purposes a republic, while even more authority devolved on the *Posadnik* and the Archbishop. The position of subsequent Princes was still further diminished. '*Koli khud Knyaz*,' yelled the populace, '*tak v gryaz*' ('If the Prince is no good, into the mud with him'). And into the mud he would go.

From now onwards such churches as the Princes built were on a more modest scale. During the twelfth and thirteenth centuries most of the building was done by boyars or rich merchants, such as the Stroganov family of merchant adventurers, who were natives of Novgorod, or by groups of citizens. Thus, in 1207 a group of merchants engaged in foreign trade built the Church of St Paraskeva on the Market Place, which, though later considerably rebuilt, reveals a thoroughly individual architectural approach and stands out on its own from the surrounding churches in Yaroslav's Court. Experts attribute this to the influence of the Smolensk school of architecture. The method used in its construction of alternating courses of stone and brick, set in a mixture of crushed brick and lime, is an interesting one.

Though Novgorod suffered less from the depredations of the Mongols than Moscow and the towns of the north-east and was never in fact captured by them, it naturally did not altogether escape the effects of the Mongol invasion and the blight it cast on Russia. For the next fifty years few churches were built.

By the beginning of the fourteenth century things had changed. The Swedes and the Livonian Knights had been defeated by Alexander Nevski and Novgorod, having built up extensive trading connections with Western Europe as a member of the Hanseatic League, entered on a period of great prosperity. In architecture and the arts as well as politically, the people of Novgorod maintained their independence and went their own way. For the city the fourteenth century was a period of considerable architectural achievement and a number of beautiful churches, many of which still survive, were commissioned by rich boyars and successive Archbishops and *Posadniks*, as well as by trading corporations and groups of ordinary citizens. Two of the finest of these were the Church of St Fyodor Stratilates, built in 1360 by the *Posadnik* Semyon Andreyevich, and the Church of Our Saviour on Ilyina Street, built in 1374 and apparently commissioned by the inhabitants of Ilyina Street. Both are near the Cathedral of St Nicholas on the Market Side. This architectural revival continued during the fifteenth century and the people of Novgorod continued to have the highest possible opinion of themselves and their city. 'Who,' they would enquire, 'can resist God and Novgorod the Great?'

The answer was not far to seek. Already Novgorod's independence was seriously threatened by Moscow. A staunch upholder of his city's independence was Archbishop Euphymius, who, during his tenure of the Archbishopric from 1429 to 1458, added the handsome Granovitaya Palata or Palace of Facets and various other stone buildings to the Vladichni Dvor or Residence within the walls of the Kremlin and also built the Watch-tower or Clock-tower which still bears his name.

But despite his efforts Novgorod's days as an independent state were numbered. In 1478 the city was annexed by Ivan III; its independence was, as we have seen, officially abolished and it became in practice no more than a dependency of Moscow. During the next ten years or so thousands of its leading citizens and their families were deported and their place taken by reliable Muscovites. In 1499 the confiscation of all church and monastery lands in the Novgorod diocese and their transfer to Muscovite incomers completed the process.

Henceforward much of the building in Novgorod was done at the behest of Moscow or of Muscovite settlers. Thus in 1484 Ivan III gave orders for the Kremlin walls to be rebuilt (approximately in their present form), and ten years later the city's outer defences were also reconstructed. Most of the churches built during the sixteenth century were commissioned by Muscovite merchants and built as often as not in the Muscovite manner, one of the first being the strangely named Church of the Myrrh-Bearing Women in Yaroslav's Court, built in 1510 for a certain Ivan Syrkov.

The Muscovites left nothing to chance as far as Novgorod was concerned. The slightest sign of independence was followed by immediate retribution. Ivan the Terrible, it will be remembered, took a particularly savage vengeance on the city, causing the Archbishop and many of his clergy to be strangled and letting loose his *Oprichniki* on the unfortunate population, sixty thousand of whom were massacred by them. It was in Archbishop Euphymius's Palace of Facets that in 1570 the Tsar gave his famous banquet for the boyars and clergy, in the course of which, at a prearranged signal from the host, his henchmen set upon the assembled company and murdered them all. By the seventeenth century there was no longer anything to distinguish the art or architecture of Novgorod from that of the rest of Russia, and the population, which had once stood at 400,000, fell to little more than two thousand.

In the eighteenth century, under Catherine the Great, plans were made for the replanning and rebuilding of the city. These fortunately do not seem to have got very far, though Novgorod possesses a number of solid-looking public buildings (including several in the Kremlin), which date from this period. One is the Putyevoi Dvorets or Travelling Palace, a rather squat classical building dating from 1771 and at present painted a particularly brilliant shade of shocking pink. It appears that a number of these were erected all over the country, so that Catherine, when travelling, could, if she chose, always stay in one of her own palaces. It stands near the river on the Market Side, not far from the bridge, and is now used, it appears, as a House of Culture.

In August 1941 Novgorod was taken by the Germans and remained in enemy hands until its recapture by Soviet troops in January 1944. For much of the time it was near the front line and suffered severely in the course of the heavy fighting which raged all round it. By now, however, thanks to the dedicated efforts of those responsible, most of the damaged buildings have been restored to something very like their original appearance.

The first thing to make for on arriving in Novgorod is the Kremlin or Detinets. Its massive late fifteenth-century towers and ramparts (roughly contemporary with those of the Moscow Kremlin) provide an impressive setting for the Cathedral of St Sophia, itself a masterpiece of mediaeval Russian church architecture. On a marble plaque in one of its walls is an inscription recalling that it was from here that Alexander Nevski set out to do battle with the enemies of Russia in 1240 and 1242. It was here, too, that Novgorod's famous *Veche* assembled when summoned by its bell and here that state business was carried on.

Near the cathedral, at the southern end of the Kremlin enclosure, are the Vladichni Dvor or Archbishop's Residence (which includes the Palace of Facets, where Ivan the Terrible gave his dinner-party of unhappy memory) and the Tower of Archbishop Euphymius, built in 1436, as well as various other buildings dating from the same period including the little Church of St Sergei, built in 1463. There is also the Sofiskaya Zvonitsa or St Sophia's Belfry, a rather clumsy-looking structure, apparently built at different periods from the fifteenth to the seventeenth century. Its bells, one of which crashed disastrously to the ground in 1659, have, as a measure of precaution, since been placed in a row at its foot.

Facing St Sophia's Cathedral, at approximately the centre of the Kremlin enclosure, is the Millenary Monument, an astonishing bronze memorial erected in 1863 to commemorate the thousandth anniversary of Russia's existence as a state. It consists of a winged angelic figure bearing a cross and balancing on an orb or globe which in turn is surrounded by a number of the leading figures in Russian history, such as St Vladimir and Peter the Great, and supported by an ornamental circular pedestal, decorated with a frieze depicting in serial form all the main events in Russian history from Rurik right down to Alexander II, who thus end up next to each other with nothing but a neatly draped curtain between them to mark the passage of a thousand years. This remarkable work of art is visited daily from dawn to dusk by a constant flow of Soviet school-children and other sight-seers, who listen open-mouthed while guides regale them with the tale of Russia's past glories, so vividly illustrated for them in this fashion.

Near the Millennary Monument, which is surrounded by neatly

planted flower-beds, are several large late eighteenth- or early nine-teenth-century public buildings, of no particular architectural merit or interest.

As I was wandering round the Kremlin on my most recent visit a clap of thunder and a sudden downpour of rain caused me to take shelter in the nearest building, the little white Church of the Intercession, nestling against one of the great towers of the Kremlin wall. This I found on closer inspection had been converted into an Olde Russian Restaurant specializing in Olde Russian Cooking, and, being, as I now realized, extremely hungry, I decided to try my luck.

Apart from the slight feeling of uneasiness which came from eat-ing in a deconsecrated place of worship (but worse things, I reminded myself, had been done in and with churches, and not only in Russia) I thoroughly enjoyed my lunch. The Detinets, as it is called, is furnished with massive mediaeval tables and benches and lit by guttering candles in wrought-iron candelabras. Though the neat waitresses had not as yet been decked out as serving wenches *à la Williamsburg*, the food was served on rough earthen-ware dishes and plates and the knives and forks were to match. The spoons were of wood, lacquered with traditional Russian de-signs. As a first course, *Borshch Tsarski* or *Borshch à la Tsar* is strongly to be recommended. (I could not help wondering whether this is what Ivan the Terrible served at his famous banquet.) Hav-ing been told that, as a main course, *Pokrovski Kotlyeti* (Cutlets Intercession) were off, Comrade, I made do with *Srazi*, a regular old Russian dish, rather like beef olives. These, in the dim religious light, I inadvertently transformed into a curry by emptying an earthenware dish of olde Russian red pepper over them. The end result, however, was excellent, especially when washed down with a jug of olde Russian mead, which, coming on top of a good solid tot of contemporary Soviet vodka, I found most invigorating and re-emerged into the now prevailing sunshine feeling a good deal better than when I went in. Though the Detinets is presumably mainly designed for tourists, it seemed on that particular day to be full of local Novgorodians enjoying a good meal and pouring down pots of mead.

From the Kremlin, a short walk across the bridge over the river, past Catherine's Travelling Palace and along the Alexander Nevski Embankment on the Market Side, brings you to Yaroslav's Court and the Cathedral of St Nicholas. Clustered round this are several other churches: the twelfth-century Churches of the Assumption and of St Ivan na Opokakh and the thirteenth-century Church of St Paraskeva-Piatnitsa as well as the fourteenth-century Churches of St Fyodor Stratilates and Our Saviour on Ilyina Street and the sixteenth-century Church of the Myrrh-Bearing Women. Nearby, too, is the seventeenth-century gate-house of the Gostini Dvor or Market.

For anyone who has the time and inclination this need only be a beginning. Both sides of Novgorod abound with ancient churches which, for the enthusiast, all deserve a visit. Not to be missed on any account are Prince Vsevolod's Church and Monastery of St George at Yurievo, a ten-minute taxi-drive southwards from the centre of the town near the point where the Volkhov rises in Lake Ilmen. Situated on the water's edge, with the lake stretching away into the distance, they give you, better even than St Sophia and the Kremlin, the feel of mediaeval Russia and of the north-west in particular.

Pskov is a bare 120 miles due west from Novgorod, but, when I suggested that I might go directly from one to the other, I was told that this was impossible. I must go back to square one, in other words back to Moscow, and start again. I knew it was useless to argue. Clearly something unutterably secret must lie between the two towns which I could not be allowed to see. In the end, however, it was agreed after a tussle that, in this never-ending game of snakes and ladders, I need only go as far as Leningrad and start again from there. Always glad of a pretext to spend a few hours in Leningrad, I cheerfully agreed and at eleven the following night, after an excellent dinner at the Astoria, featuring some really superb cold sturgeon mayonnaise and a bottle of *Tsolikauri*, an excellent dry Georgian white wine I had never before tasted, I caught the bright-blue Baltika Express, bound for Riga.

The unusually engaging young woman in a pale blue nightdress with whom I shared my sleeper was sleeping peacefully when we arrived at Pskov at three the next morning. Doing my best not to disturb her, I slipped out of the carriage and on to the platform of Pskov railway station, an agreeable nineteenth-century classical building painted a soothing shade of green. It was here, I recalled, in the Imperial train, that on the afternoon of 15 March 1917

Nicholas II, Tsar of All the Russias, reluctantly abdicated in favour of his brother Michael, who sensibly refused the assignment. Apart from the Hammer and Sickle which had replaced the Imperial Eagle on the station-master's cap, little seemed to have changed during the past sixty years. Day was about to break. The train gave a long-drawn-out wail and moved off in the direction of Riga, while I made my way to the Hotel October, where I was to spend the rest of a rather disturbed night.

The Hotel October is one of those solid-looking Soviet hotels, built in the late 1930s to satisfy Stalin's urge for the monumental. Its staff, I soon found, made up for any slight shortage of bathrooms by the warmth of their welcome, which, as every hotelier knows, is what matters most. Few foreign tourists seem to reach Pskov and those who do are received with open arms, not least in the Aurora Restaurant downstairs, a large room, rather sketchily decorated in the Archaic Greek manner, with Aurora's chariot careering wildly across the ceiling. Its great speciality, *Bifstek Avrora*, a surprisingly good steak with an egg, sunnyside-up, perched on top of it, ingeniously resumes the Aurora theme. The Aurora also boasts what I think must be the noisiest jazz-band in the Soviet Union, indeed in the world, which, whenever I went there, was belting out 'Hello Dolly' to the unrestrained delight of a series of large and extremely lively wedding parties. It is the sort of place I rather enjoy.

I was prepared to like Pskov and did. A good deal smaller than Novgorod (as befits that city's 'Younger Brother') it has managed to keep rather more of its original character, though a good deal less than Saki found when, to the amazement of his Russian friends, he insisted on visiting Pskov in 1905. Like Novgorod, it centres round its Kremlin (or Krom), robustly fortified and magnificently poised in a commanding position at the junction of two rivers, the Velikaya and the much smaller Pskova. Towering above the massive battlements of the Kremlin is the great square white Cathedral of the Trinity, first built on this site in the twelfth century in place of an earlier wooden church, but completely rebuilt in 1699. It is still very much in use as a church and was crowded with worshippers when I visited it.

Where the Pskova flows into the Velikaya, twin towers on either bank guard the mouth of the former river which was formerly blocked by a water-gate or boom. Near the tower on the further bank of the Pskova from the Kremlin are the fifteenth-century Church of St Varlaam and the sixteenth-century Church of the Resurrection as well as two seventeenth-century merchants' houses.

In the Middle Ages, Pskov, like Novgorod, was, as we have seen, an independent republic of which the Kremlin was the military, religious and administrative centre. It was within the walls of the Kremlin that the *Veche* assembled when summoned by its famous bell and here, too, that the victorious Alexander Nevski was acclaimed in 1242, for Pskov was an important bastion against Russia's northern enemies, the Swedes and the Teutonic Knights. It was here also, in the Prikaznaya Palata (an interesting example of seventeenth-century civic architecture) that the city's government was carried on. Indeed it is said that in this building twenty buckets of ink were consumed every week by the busy bureaucrats employed there. Adjoining the Kremlin is Dovmontov Gorod (Dovmont's Town), so called after Prince Dovmont, a thirteenth-century Prince who beat off the attacks of the Teutonic Knights and was subsequently canonized. Before the Revolution Prince Dovmont's sword was still displayed in the cathedral; now a symbolic representation of it hangs on the Kremlin wall and the original sword is in the museum. Guarded by Basil's Tower, Vasilievskaya Bashnia, this little settlement contained in the Middle Ages no less than nineteen churches, of which now only the foundations remain.

In 1510, as we have seen, Pskov finally lost its independence to Moscow. In 1570 Ivan the Terrible, suspecting its inhabitants of treachery, advanced on the city with the intention of destroying it, but was, it appears, restrained from putting his project into execution by the timely intervention of a monk named Nicholas of Salos, who won the Tsar over by feigning madness, a phenomenon for which, as we know, Ivan possessed a healthy respect. Like Prince Dovmont, Nicholas of Salos was subsequently canonized and buried next to him in the cathedral.

Pskov was to remain an essential link in Russia's northern defences, withstanding the attacks of Stephen Batory the Pole in 1581 and of Gustavus Adolphus of Sweden in 1615 and playing a no less important part in the northern campaigns of Peter the Great.

The Torg or Market Place of Pskov, now renamed Lenin Square, is not far from the Kremlin. Here stands the fourteenth-century Church of the Archangel Michael, while a little further on, on

October Street, in the direction of my hotel, I found several more interesting old churches: the Church of St Basil on the Mound and the Church of St Nicholas, both built in 1371, and two fifteenth-century churches, those of St Anastasia and the Ascension.

The fortifications of the Kremlin were given their present form in the fifteenth century, though the first stone wall had been built round it in the thirteenth century and it had existed as a fortress for two hundred years before that. In addition to these, Pskov, like Novgorod, possesses a ring of outer fortifications built of the local limestone, six miles in length and also dating from the thirteenth century. A good part of these still survive, including several of the old towers, notably the Pokrovskaya Bashnya or Tower of the Intercession, built in the fifteenth century and strengthened and rebuilt by Peter the Great in 1701. This stands on the bank of the Velikaya at the far end of the town from the Kremlin. Immediately inside its gate is the little double Church of the Nativity and Intercession with its twin domes and belfry. Not far away is the Pskov Rowing Club, whose members, athletic-looking young men and women, skim rapidly up and down the Velikaya in a variety of light craft.

From the Pokrovskaya Bashnia you look across the river to the Mirozhski Monastery, beautifully situated on the far bank by the water's edge. This was founded in the eleventh century and its Cathedral of the Redeemer built in 1156. Also on the left bank of the Velikaya, nearly a mile away and roughly opposite the Kremlin, is the Church of St John the Baptist, originally part of the Ivanovski Monastery and dating from the thirteenth century or earlier. Rebuilt a number of times in the intervening centuries, the church was restored to something more like its original appearance after being partly destroyed in the Second World War.

For anyone who wants to examine either of these monastic establishments more closely (and they are well worth looking at), it is an easy walk across the bridge near the Kremlin. As you cross the river, you see immediately on your right the Church of the Assumption by the Ferry. The present church was built in 1521, but there are references to an earlier church on this site. Evidently a ferry preceded the bridge. I like to think (though without, I must say, any special justification) that it was at this ferry that the beautiful and ruthless St Olga was employed as a ferry-girl. For it seems that Olga, who is believed to have been of Slav rather than Norse origin, started life operating a ferry at Pskov. One of her passengers, the Varangian Prince Igor, gave her a ring in return for her services. After which (knowing what we do of her character) the story could only have one ending. She married him and became Grand Princess and, in the fullness of time, a saint.

These are only a few of the churches which adorn Pskov. You come on a fresh one every few hundred yards and, as in Novgorod, anyone with sufficient enthusiasm for early Russian architecture can happily spend a week examining them. Also of considerable interest are the houses of the rich merchants of Pskov, dating mostly from the seventeenth century. This, as we have seen, was a period of no little turbulence, being marked not only by foreign wars, but by constant internal strife and dissensions. To guard against such emergencies, the merchants seem to have built themselves massive stone mansions, like fortresses, with small windows high up so as to be able if necessary to withstand a siege by envious townspeople, angry customers, Teutonic knights, or anyone else who might come along. Perhaps the best example is the house of the Pogankin family, situated in the southern part of the town, on Nekrasov Street, not very far from the Churches of St Anastasia and the Ascension. This comprises what are really three buildings, dwelling-house, warehouse and shop, and is now a museum. The walls are six feet thick, the small windows barred and shuttered, and the entrance is provided with double iron gates. The style, which shows signs of Baltic or Scandinavian influence, is austere in the extreme. Nearby are the three houses of the Menshikov family and several other similar mansions.

On the banks of the Pskova, near the fifteenth-century Church of St Peter and St Paul, in the Okolni Quarter, is another group of merchants' houses, also dating from the seventeenth century, the most interesting being the house of the merchant Yamski on Yedinstvo Street, where Peter the Great stayed in 1710. Nearby are the house of the Rusinovs, the Guryev house and, a little further on, the Solodezhnaya or Malt House, with its two vaulted rooms, the Pechenko House and the two seventeenth-century Churches of St Nicholas and the Intercession on the Market Place.

Pskov and its surroundings were, like Novgorod, the scene of much heavy fighting in the last war and the town itself was held by the Germans from the summer of 1941 until the summer of 1944, suffering severely in the process. Here, too, a great amount of successful restoration has been carried out. Indeed in Pskov, as in Novgorod, it is difficult to tell how much has been patched up or restored and how much completely rebuilt. But at least the general impression is convincingly mediaeval and will doubtless become more so, as the years go by.

Lenin spent some time in Pskov in about the year 1900 and some seventy miles to the south of the town is the sixteenth-century Monastery of Sviatogorsk, where Pushkin and his parents, who came from these parts, lie buried. The neighbouring village, near the family's estate of Mikhailovskoye, has now been renamed Pushkinskiye Gori in the poet's honour.

But to my mind a more worthwhile excursion is due west from Pskov to Izborsk and Pechori on the border with Estonia. Here you are quickly in country which before the war was part of independent Estonia. Now Estonia itself is part of the Soviet Union, but the frontier between Russia and the Soviet Socialist Republic of Estonia has been adjusted to give Russia this additional territory on the grounds, apparently, that, while part of the population speak Estonian, almost all of them are Orthodox by religion rather than Protestant or Catholic and that it can thus be regarded as being historically part of Russia—a sufficient reason, presumably, to satisfy the Soviet Estonian government.

Between Pskov and Izborsk the countryside is green and flat, with tidy, prosperous-looking villages and well cultivated fields and orchards. My chief memory of the drive is of an abundance of apple blossom and of neat, stone-built peasant houses, with the stones laid flat one on top of the other as in a dry-stone wall.

Both Izborsk and Pechori are fortified monasteries or monastic fortresses, according to how you like to look at it, but in any case outposts of Slavdom and Orthodoxy in the low-lying marshlands of the north-west. Leaving the road just short of Izborsk, you come first to a village cemetery, in a little birch-wood on the edge of a great sweep of plough-land. It is still in use and the graves under the birch-trees, with their stone or wooden crosses, are carefully tended. Almost every grave has the traditional bench and table beside it, so that on certain days, or just when the spirit moves them, the relatives of the dead can come and picnic there in their company. Emerging from the wood I suddenly found myself, owing to the lie of the land, looking out from the top of a high hill. Above me a little church was perched, dedicated, I found, to

St Nicholas, but closed and still bearing the marks of war damage. It was a grey day; a light rain was falling; no one was in sight; but, looking over a wide prospect of green fields and woods, I had a feeling not of desolation, but of peace and quiet.

From the top of the escarpment on which I was standing, I looked across the valley to Izborsk itself, founded, so it is said, by Rurik's brother Truvor or Trevor and strategically sited on a neighbouring hilltop. Within the massive fortress walls, which date from 1303, was another church dedicated to St Nicholas, who seems to have been the patron saint of the district. As Saki says of this part of Russia, 'the Powers of Darkness were as carefully guarded against in those old days as more tangible human enemies.'

On my way into the church, I met, coming out, the funeral procession of a very small old lady whose waxen face gazed serenely up at the grey sky from her open coffin, while her heavily bearded husband shambled dazedly along behind her in a cloud of incense amid much vigorous chanting by two burly, golden-robed and no less heavily bearded Orthodox priests. After these followed the whole village, men, women and children of all ages under the pouring rain. She must have had many friends.

Another nearby church has been turned into a museum and, after glancing briefly at this, I pushed on through the rain to Pechori. Here, the weather cleared and, as I approached the fortress, I saw the golden domes of the monastery shining in the sunlight among the surrounding greenery, for the monastery precincts are well planted with trees. Exactly when the monastery was first founded I failed to find out. The story is that in 1470 a hunter, wandering through the woods, suddenly heard singing, proceeding apparently from underground and, on investigating further, found some holy men chanting in a cave. (The name Pechori comes from the Russian *pech*, meaning 'cave'. Indeed the cave in question was incorporated in the monastery and is sometimes shown to the public.) But when this was no one could tell me. The fortress itself, with its tremendous stone walls and towers, was built or rebuilt in about 1560, on orders from Ivan the Terrible, and the towers and walls were further strengthened by Peter the Great, in support, presumably, of his northern campaign. Today, thanks to careful maintenance, they are in excellent order and look as if they could still withstand a siege. The monastery, housed in buildings varying in period from the fifteenth to the nineteenth century, is, in the Soviet phrase, 'still working', indeed has never stopped working since it was first founded, its inclusion in independent Estonia having no doubt saved it from the wave of extreme anti-religious zeal which followed the Russian Revolution. To this day there are still monks living underground in the caves. Though probably built in the fifteenth century, or earlier, the main church of the monastery, which stands above the original cave in the woods, was rebuilt and refurbished two or three hundred years later in the style of the Russian Baroque. This gives it a cheerful if somewhat unexpected appearance which it shares with the underground Cathedral of the Assumption, which was also done over in the mid-eighteenth century.

Standing in a row in front of it are three bells presented by Ivan the Terrible, Boris Godunov and Peter the Great respectively, an interesting selection of donors. The fine forest trees with which the precincts of the monastery are planted provide a perfect background for the churches and other monastery buildings, which are painted different colours and are in a wide variety of styles. Several of them date from the eighteenth and nineteenth centuries, while the great white Church of the Archangel Michael, built in 1820 by a well known architect from St Petersburg to celebrate the defeat of Napoleon, takes the form of a classical temple, with a central dome, a portico with columns on each of three sides and a semi-circular apse on the fourth. Altogether, the monastery, within its massive walls, with its robed and bearded monks striding busily from one extraordinary building to another and its crowds of sight-seers and worshippers, gives a lively enough impression.

Mysteriously, my journey overnight from Pskov to Moscow took nearly fourteen hours. On finding myself in a 'hard', as opposed to a 'soft', carriage, with a young married couple, an eleven-month-old baby and a man whose only luggage was a bicycle tyre carefully wrapped in newspaper, I must admit that I felt momentary misgivings. But they were without foundation. 'Hard' carriages are very different from what they were forty years ago, when they were inclined to be rather like cattle-trucks. Indeed apart from perhaps slightly firmer bunks, this one was indistinguishable from a 'soft' carriage. The young couple, who, after a few days' holiday in Pskov, were on their way to Outer Mongolia (where the husband was employed and which we discussed at length), were charming, plying me endlessly with delicious food and drink, including great heaps of whitebait, apparently a speciality of Pskov. The baby was beautifully behaved. And the man with the bicycle tyre slept soundly on his upper bunk all the way from Pskov to Moscow.

If you still choose to follow in the footsteps of the Varangians, your next stop after Novgorod and Pskov will be Kiev, the Mother of Russian cities, as Oleg proclaimed it in 882. I flew there from Moscow, putting up at one of the large, impersonal, but quite comfortable new hotels which are now beginning to make their appearance in all the larger Soviet cities.

Driving into Kiev from the airport on a fine summer's day, the first things you catch sight of, as you come to the bridge over the Dnieper, are the glittering golden cupolas of what I later discovered to be the Pecherski Monastery or Monastery of the Caves, standing out against a background of bright-green trees on the high ground across the river – a sight that at once fixed Kiev in my mind as a city of green trees and golden domes.

Since 1934 capital of the Ukrainian Soviet Socialist Republic, a country the size of France, Kiev stands, like Moscow, and for the same reasons, on a hill above a river, in this case the Dnieper. From the ninth century onwards the Dnieper was a vital link in the trade route between north and south, 'from the Varangians', as the saying was, 'to the Greeks'. To Kiev came traders from the Baltic and the great fur-producing areas of the north, but also from Arabia and Byzantium, so that by the second half of the ninth century it was already an important economic and administrative centre.

Though Kiev's origins stretch far back into pre-history, it was in 882 that the Varangian Prince Oleg of Novgorod (or Holmgard, as he probably called it) sailed down the Dnieper with his *druzhina* of warriors and, entering the city by a strategem, killed Askold and Dir, its princes, and seized it for himself, proclaiming it forthwith the Mother of Russian Cities and making it the capital of a newly unified Russian state which soon stretched from the Black Sea to Lake Ladoga and from the Volga to the western Bug.

Kiev reached the height of its splendour under St Vladimir at the end of the tenth and the beginning of the eleventh centuries. By converting his country to Christianity, Vladimir linked it more closely to Byzantium and to the rest of Europe. Soon Kiev was one of the most resplendent of European cities and an outstanding centre of European culture and civilization.

The site of the original city, built on the high ground above the Dnieper, is not far from where the great Cathedral of St Sophia now stands. Here the Grand Prince had his palace and here were the mansions of the nobles and other notables. Here too, near where the Church of St Andrew is today, stood the first stone church in Russia, Desyatinaya Tserkov, the Tithe Church or Church of one Tenth, dedicated to the Virgin Mary and built by Prince Vladimir at the end of the tenth century. Of this only the foundations now remain. Near here, almost a thousand years later, in 1853, was erected on the steep, wooded hillside above the Dnieper a massive bronze statue of St Vladimir, holding his cross on high and looking confidently out across the river, as though in search of fresh fields to conquer.

On the lower ground to the north of old Kiev, in the area now known as Podol, were situated in those early days the dwellings, the warehouses and the workshops of the merchants, the craftsmen and the artisans. As time passed, Lower Kiev became an important trading centre, doing business with foreign merchants from all over the known world, numbers of whom settled there in parts of the town specially allotted to them.

In the first half of the eleventh century, under Vladimir and his son Yaroslav, Kiev became one of the most beautiful and prosperous cities in Europe. Fresh dynastic connections linked it with a number of European ruling houses. Massive fortifications protected it against attack. Under Vladimir the immensely strong Golden Gates, parts of which still survive, served as the principal entrance to the city and were adorned by him with a pair of doors of solid gold which he had contrived to carry off as booty from the Chersonese. Above the gates, Prince Yaroslav built in 1037 a small, golden-domed Church of the Annunciation, now long since disappeared, which also served as a watch-tower. So strongly were the Golden Gates fortified that even the Mongols, when they stormed Kiev in 1240, were unable to force an entrance by them and were obliged to effect their breakthrough elsewhere. Four hundred years later, it was through the Golden Gates that Bodgan Khelmnitski entered Kiev in triumph after his great victory over the Poles. With the years they became buried under successive layers of earth and were only rediscovered and literally unearthed as lately as 1832.

In 1037, after his victory over the Pechenegs, Yaroslav built on the very battlefield the Cathedral of St Sophia, which to this day remains one of the world's great masterpieces of ecclesiastical architecture. In it he himself lies buried in a magnificent carved marble sarcophagus.

Built with the characteristically Russian cross-dome formation, St Sophia was originally divided by twelve carrying piers into a nave and four aisles ending to the east in five corresponding apses. In all it had thirteen cupolas, the largest being above the nave, while the four aisles each supported three more. On three sides the cathedral was surrounded by an open arcade, to which a second storey was later added. A series of alterations and additions were made to the cathedral from 1054 onwards and a tower was added towards the end of the eleventh century.

The pleasing tale is told that, originally, somewhere high up in the great church was fixed up a kind of periscope or camera obscura. Through this it was possible, with the help of mirrors, to obtain a clear view of everything that was happening in the surrounding country for miles around. Unfortunately, however, a local maiden, who happened to glance through the eyepiece of this ingenious device, was rewarded with the sight of her lover, at what he no doubt believed to be a safe distance from home, dallying in the bushes with a Gothic or possibly even a Pecheneg damsel. At which the poor girl was so outraged that she promptly smashed the whole contraption to pieces.

Entering the cathedral through the main door, you find yourself facing a magnificent eleventh-century mosaic of the Virgin. This fills the whole of the upper part of the central apse and conveys an impression of sublime serenity in reassuring contrast to much that was then happening in the world (and has gone on happening ever since). In addition to this and to a number of other mosaics of the same period, the cathedral also contains a large number of fine early frescoes, including an engaging representation of the family of Yaroslav the Wise. On the walls of the turret stair leading to the upper gallery are some unusual frescoes of secular subjects, hunting scenes, games, dances and so on.

Though not utterly destroyed like the ancient Church of the Tithes, which simply collapsed with the weight of the inhabitants who had taken refuge inside it, the Cathedral of St Sophia suffered serious damage during the Mongol invasion of 1240. When its reconstruction and restoration were finally undertaken four hundred years later, it was in the prevailing style of the period, namely Ukrainian baroque, which accounts for its nineteen onion domes (replacing the original flattened domes) and agreeably florid appearance. At the very beginning of the eighteenth century St Sophia was also provided with a fine baroque belfry, just in time to ring out a welcome to Peter the Great as he entered Kiev in triumph after his victory over the Swedes at Poltava in 1709. To its three storeys a fourth, together with a handsome gilded cupola, was added a century and a half after that.

Of the other buildings within the cathedral precincts a refectory, likewise baroque, was built in the 1720s, as was the Metropolitan's Palace. A seminary and the southern and western entrance gates to the precincts were added in the course of the eighteenth century. The cathedral is now a museum and the present Metropolitan, a majestic figure, but also, I should say, a very shrewd one, has his palace in another part of the town. A couple of years back he entertained me most hospitably to a lavish luncheon which included two kinds of caviar and plenty of vodka to go with it. There were certainly no signs that he was short of anything or indeed that he was on anything but the best of terms with the civil power.

In the middle of the square in front of the cathedral stands a statue of the great Ukrainian hero Bogdan Khelmnitski, sitting astride a splendidly prancing horse and clearly preparing to split open the skull of a Polish nobleman with a spiked club which he is whirling menacingly round his head. He it was who led the Ukrainians against the Poles in 1648 and it was largely thanks to him that the reunification of the Ukraine with Russia followed six years later.

A mile or two to the south of St Sophia, strategically sited on the high ground above the river, is the Pecherski Monastery or Monastery of the Caves, its golden cupolas standing out among the surrounding greenery. Founded by two monks in 1051, this is one of the oldest Russian monasteries in existence. It covers a large area of ground, embracing two little hills and the valley between them. Its name, Pecherski, derives from the cells of the early monks – caves carved out of the living rock and honeycombing the smaller and more northerly of the two hills (known as the Hill of the Far Caves), where it stands overlooking the Dnieper.

It was on the Hill of the Far Caves that there was built in the second half of the eleventh century the monastery's first church, the Church of the Assumption, on the site, apparently, of an even earlier wooden church. A characteristic early Russian cruciform church with a single dome, the Church of the Assumption was utterly destroyed during the Second World War and all that now remains of it is a heap of masonry and rubble. Adjoining it was built in due course the Church of St John the Baptist, which still survives. Later more subterranean cells (known as the Near Caves) were dug in the valley between the two hills. Near the entrance to them stands the seventeenth-century Church of the Holy Cross. Above the main entrance to the monastery is the single-domed Church of the Trinity. This was built in 1108, but was heavily restored within and without in the eighteenth century, so that, although it has retained its original walls and form, it today presents the appearance of a typical baroque church.

The Church of the Saviour in the village of Berestovo, just outside the precincts of the monastery to the north-west, was built at approximately the same period by Vladimir Monomakh. It is here that fifty or sixty years later, in 1157, was buried Vladimir's son Yuri Dolgoruki, the founder of Moscow. When the eight hundredth anniversary of the foundation of Moscow was celebrated in 1947, a massive modern granite monument was placed above Yuri's grave in the church. As originally designed, the church was cruciform in shape, with three apses and a single cupola. After being partially destroyed by the Mongols in 1240, it was restored towards the middle of the seventeenth century and the interior decorated in the neo-Byzantine manner by Greek craftsmen from Mount Athos. Of considerable interest are two great slabs of red slate carved in bas-relief and representing Hercules and the Nemean Lion and Cybele in her chariot. Whence they came, nobody knows; possibly, it is thought, from the palace of the Grand Prince.

After its partial destruction by the Mongols in 1240 and the further decline of Kiev as a centre of prosperity and power, the monastery suffered two centuries of neglect and it was not until well into the fifteenth century that any major work of restoration was undertaken. By the end of the seventeenth century, however, after the Ukraine had finally been won back from the Poles, it evidently came into its own again and not long after we hear of its possessing no less than seven small towns, 189 villages, 56,000 serfs, thirteen other monasteries and three glass-works. Within its precincts, a period of intensive building now ensued, one new church following another: the handsome, if strangely named, Church of All Saints over the Economic Gates, the Church and Belfry of St Onufrius, the Church and Belfry of Ivan Kushehnik, the Refectory Church of St Nicholas, the Church of the Holy Cross at the entrance to the Near Caves and a number of other buildings as well, all put up within ten years of each other at the end of the seventeenth and beginning of the eighteenth centuries.

All these churches and belfries, including the magnificent Belfry of the Upper Monastery, built in 1745 by Schädel from St Petersburg, share a certain similarity of style and give the whole monastery a pleasing baroque air not entirely easy to reconcile with its mediaeval origins. But anyone who wants reminding of these has only to spend an hour or two underground among the caves (many of which still contain the mummified bodies of their former inhabitants) to feel himself right back in the Middle Ages. The monastery and its churches have not, in the Soviet phrase, been 'working' for half a century or more, but the caves with their slightly grisly inmates still remain a place of pilgrimage and, while awaiting admission, sightseers and tourists find themselves queuing side by side with genuine pilgrims.

Amongst the mummies I, for one, was glad to be able to identify as an old friend Nestor the Chronicler, upon whom we rely so heavily for any account of early Russian history. It was largely thanks to him and to men like him that Kiev remained through the centuries a centre of Russian culture and civilization. I was, however, unfortunately unable to discover John the Long-suffering, who, determined to live up to his name, had himself buried alive up to the neck with only his head sticking out and is said to have survived in this uncomfortable posture for no less than thirty years, after which his body was preserved in the same position through the centuries, his projecting head, wearing a mitre, being still available for inspection by the devout or curious as recently as 1914.

Of scarcely less importance architecturally than St Sophia and the Monastery of the Caves was the Monastery of St Michael, which until 1934 stood near the statue of St Vladimir on the high ground overlooking the Dnieper. Partly destroyed by the Mongols in 1240, it was painstakingly restored in the baroque manner in about 1700, only to be finally demolished by the Soviet authorities in a fit of militant atheism in 1934. Some of its frescoes, of great artistic merit, were fortunately rescued and are still preserved in St Sophia and in the Tretyakov Gallery in Moscow.

Some way to the south of the Pecherski Monastery and standing like it on the high western bank of the Dnieper in what are now the city's Botanical Gardens is another ancient monastic foundation, the Vidubetski Monastery, with the Churches of St Michael and St George. This was established in about 1070 by Prince Vsevolod but has since been restored and rebuilt so often that it gives very little idea of what the original buildings can have been like. Also on the heights above the Dnieper, but to the north of the Pecherski Monastery, stands a handsome classical rotunda erected in 1810 and said to mark the grave of Askold, the rather shadowy figure who, with his co-prince Dir, was murdered when Oleg seized Kiev in 882.

Towards the middle of the eighteenth century Kiev profited for a time from the presence of Bartolommeo Rastrelli who, temporarily deserting St Petersburg, added two outstanding buildings to the city's rich architectural heritage. The first of these is the Church of St Andrew, which stands overlooking the Dnieper from the heights above Podol, a splendid example of the Russian baroque style of which he was such a master. Above four classical pilastered façades, with clusters of columns at the four corners, rises a large central cupola set on an elegant drum and topped by a secondary onion dome. To meet the five-dome rule of the Orthodox Church, Rastrelli has ingeniously placed at each end of the four corners a little onion-domed steeple like a minaret.

Across the road from the Church of St Andrew, for those who are sufficiently interested, it is still possible to trace the foundations of Kiev's oldest church, the Church of One Tenth, built between 989 and 996 by Prince Vladimir at a cost of one-tenth of his total revenue and destroyed during the Mongol invasion of 1240. It was intended by the newly converted Vladimir to be his capital's principal church and, according to the Chronicler, was a most magnificent building with four bronze horses standing in front of it.

Rastrelli's other masterpiece in Kiev was the two-storeyed Mariinski Palace, which immediately followed the Church of St Andrew and which, with its handsome colonnade, is an almost exact replica of the Razumovski or Anichkov Palace in Leningrad. Partly burnt down and restored in the nineteenth century, it was again largely destroyed in the last war, since when it has once more been restored.

To celebrate the nine hundreth anniversary of the city's conversion to Christianity, a gigantic new cathedral was built near the University in the second half of the last century, appropriately dedicated to St Vladimir. A recent Soviet guidebook to the city describes it in a single telling sentence: 'The architectural style of the seven-cupola cathedral,' it declares, 'is a mixture of the Romanesque, Pseudo-Byzantine and Pseudo-Russian forms,' while a knowing German expert remarks with some justice that *'der eklektische Historismus der Vladimir-Kathedrale bleibt unzufriedigend.'* No more need be said about this monstrous edifice except that it took thirty-four years to build – from 1862 to 1896 – the wrong thirty-four years as far as architectural taste was concerned. One cannot help feeling that it would have furnished a happier target for the iconoclastic zeal of the militant atheists of 1934 than the long-suffering Monastery of St Michael. But other than purely aesthetic considerations doubtless prevailed.

In the course of the nineteenth century Kiev, from a group of scattered monasteries and townships, gradually grew into a great modern city. At the end of the previous century, the Kreshchatik, now the city's principal thoroughfare, had been no more than a wooded valley, to which two of the deeper ravines running into it from either side gave the form of a cross and later its name, the Street of the Cross. A few wooden houses on either side of this were followed, as the century wore on, by more substantial buildings; the valley was filled in; soon shops, banks, business premises, hotels and restaurants made their appearance; other streets and squares were laid out all round it; and by the middle of the century, the Khreshchatik, with chestnut-trees on each side, almost a mile in length and, even by Russian standards, unusually wide, had become Kiev's main street, leading directly from the heights above the Dnieper into the middle of the new part of the town. The chestnut-trees which still line it lend to it and to most of the other streets of Kiev a most agreeable greenness.

For Kiev and indeed for the Ukraine as a whole, the first fifty years of the present century were full of vicissitudes. The city had a strong revolutionary tradition reaching back to the Decembrists and the Revolution of 1905 was the sign for an armed rising of workers and troops from the local garrison. Between 1917 and 1920 the city changed hands several times during some of the worst fighting of the Civil War, in which Bolsheviks, Germans, the Ukrainian Nationalists of Hetman Petliura and the White Army of General Denikin all took an active part.

Barely twenty years later, in the summer of 1941, the Germans were once again threatening Kiev. In September of that year, after holding out for almost three months, the Soviet army withdrew to the left bank of the Dnieper, abandoning the city to the Germans, who held it for more than two years until finally driven out in November 1943 by the troops of the First Ukrainian Front. During their occupation of the city the German forces committed appalling atrocities, one of the most notorious being the mass extermination of a large part of the city's Jewish population in the ravine of Babi Yar, since commemorated in a famous poem by Yevgeni Yevtushenko. They also deliberately destroyed large parts of the city, leaving it virtually in ruins. Since the war it has, however, been restored in the most remarkable way and is now as green and smiling as ever. It is said that the first thing the inhabitants did, once the Germans had gone, was to replant the Kreshchatik and the other streets with chestnut-trees.

Compared with Kiev, Odessa, some three hundred miles to the south-west on the Black Sea coast, is a town of relatively recent origin. During the last 150 years, however, it has steadily increased in importance. Although there had been Greek settlements all along the Black Sea coast since time immemorial, we first hear of what is now Odessa as the Turkish fortress of Hadji Bey, which was stormed by General Suvorov, in 1789. A year or two later Suvorov was authorized by a *ukaz* of Catherine the Great to build a Russian fortress on the same site. Round this nucleus a civilian population gathered which by 1795 amounted to almost 2,500 souls. To the new town was given the name Odessa. Of interest to the classical scholar is the name Ovidopol or Ovidopolis, bestowed at the end of the eighteenth century on a neighbouring township as a tribute to the Roman poet Ovid, exiled to these parts in the year 9 of our era for writing the somewhat lubricious *Ars Amatoria*.

By the beginning of the nineteenth century Odessa was already a flourishing port and a key point in the vast area added to the Empire in the reign of Catherine the Great and known as Novorossiya or New Russia. Indeed it was not long before Odessa succeeded

Grigori Potyomkin's brain-child, Ekaterinoslav (now Kirovgrad), as capital of the province of New Russia. It is from this period that dates the well laid out city we know today. One of its principal architects was the Duc de Richelieu, who, having left France in a hurry at the time of the Revolution, somehow managed to get himself appointed first Governor of Odessa and then Viceroy of New Russia and gave to the new city, with its spacious squares and broad, tree-lined avenues, the orderly, well designed appearance of a typical French town of the period. He also endowed it with the Lycée Richelieu, which, though now used for a different purpose, is still standing, a long, low stucco building forming four sides of a courtyard in the middle of the town, and which was later to become the nucleus of a university.

After the fall of Napoleon, Richelieu returned to France, where he twice served as Prime Minister under Louis XVIII. His good work in Odessa was ably continued by his successor, Prince Michael Vorontsov, a hero of the war against Napoleon who held the post of Governor-General from 1823 to 1854, in which year, though no longer a young man, he was sent to take command in the Caucasus. (See my book *To Caucasus*, chapter 7.) It is from the period of his governorship that the majority of fine early nineteenth- century buildings seem to date, notably the splendid classical palace with colonnaded front which today houses the City Soviet. Here it was that, after numerous vicissitudes, the victory of the Revolution was finally proclaimed by the Bolsheviks in 1920. In front of it stands a British gun taken in 1854 from *HMS Tiger*, a British man-of-war which unfortunately ran ashore while bombarding Odessa during the Crimean campaign. The adjoining building, in the form of a Greek temple, is now a museum. No less successful are the nearby avenue and crescent which provide the background to a classical statue of Richelieu wearing a laurel wreath and a toga and looking out over the port of Odessa. This stands at the top of the great flight of 193 granite steps, immortalized by Eisenstein in his famous film *The Battleship Potyomkin*, in which, with maximum effects, a child's perambulator is sent jolting unevenly down them.

Prince Voronstov, for his part, is commemorated by a handsome contemporary statue which, as befits a distinguished military commander, stands in the middle of the Square of the Soviety Army. Both he and Richelieu are held today in high esteem by the citizens of Odessa, as is also General Suvorov, who, in a sense, was the city's true founder. But most popular of all is the poet Pushkin, who for a time managed to be both Prince Vorontsov's *aide-de-camp* and Princess Vorontsova's lover and who, when he had nothing better to do (which cannot have been often), would sit under a tree in the park which is still proudly pointed out to tourists. He, too, has his monument, which is situated in the public gardens opposite the City Soviet.

As often happens, the original plan to which Odessa was built and the strictly classical style of its early buildings gave it a clearly defined character which it has kept all through its subsequent development, the character of a large French provincial town. To this day it remains a city of wide, tree-lined avenues set at right angles to other wide avenues. For the whole of the nineteenth century the style of its principal buildings continued classical, inclining sometimes to the Italian Renaissance. In the principal streets you find rows of handsome Renaissance palaces, while in the humbler quarters their place is taken by more modest stucco-fronted buildings in a similar style, plentifully hung with vines, which, together with the abundant plane-trees, give the whole city a welcome greenness. Of all the buildings in their city that of which the Odessans themselves are proudest is their great florid, late nineteenth-century Opera House, which for sheer size and magnificence, within and without, rivals the opera house of any capital in the world, including, as one is constantly being reminded, Moscow.

Before the Revolution, Odessa, like many ports, was a cosmopolitan town with a large foreign colony and many of its streets still bear the names of the different nationalities who once lived in them – Greek Street, Italian Street and so on. There was also once a very large Jewish quarter, of which but little now remains. For all this the town still has a surprisingly cosmopolitan atmosphere and one is constantly struck by the olive complexions and aquiline features of many of its citizens.

Both temperamentally and physically Ukrainians are very different from northern Russians and, walking its streets, one is immediately conscious of a southern Mediterranean atmosphere, enhanced by the classical elegance of the buildings, the wide, tree-lined avenues and the recurrent green of the parks and squares. Unlike Moscow, Odessa has a long-standing tradition, lately revived, of bar and café life and, when last there, I visited two or three such establishments, some most lavishly furnished and equipped, where the local citizenry casually congregate to meet their friends and have a drink and something to eat.

Odessa played an active part in the Revolution of 1905 and for a time the mutiny on board the cruiser *Potyomkin* and its savage suppression by the government focussed attention on the city and its inhabitants. Twelve years later, in 1917, the Bolsheviks made a strong bid for power, but this was successfully put down by the Whites with the aid of the Western Allies and it was not until 1920 that the Bolsheviks finally took over.

In 1941 Odessa was one of the first targets of Hitler's armies, who struck at it in strength across the Polish and Romanian frontiers. Although it was not an easy city to defend, the Soviet army somehow managed against overwhelming odds to hold a defence line in the flat country forty miles or so outside the city for more than three months before ultimately evacuating it in good order. During the years that followed Odessa was occupied by an enemy garrison, consisting largely of Romanians who, when the time came, withdrew, no doubt with an eye to the future, as quietly and quickly as they could, doing remarkably little damage in the process.

Until not long ago, the port of Odessa was by far the biggest in the Black Sea. Of recent years, however, a satellite town has developed half an hour's drive to the north with an even larger harbour, Ilichovsk, so called after Lenin, whose patronymic was Ilich and a large statue of whom, with open overcoat, strides boldly into the future from the middle of the main square.

Chugging round the harbour in a launch accompanied by the harbour-master and a rather personable blonde young woman in a trouser-suit, who was introduced as a representative of the local branch of the Communist Party, I could not help being struck by the immense quantity of Soviet and foreign tonnage accommodated by a port of which I, for one, had never even heard. Ilichovsk, which did not exist twenty years ago and whose harbour was hollowed out of the bed of an existing lagoon, now has, it appears, the biggest turn-around of shipping of any port in the Soviet Union. What is more, a third port, designed to complete the complex, is now planned in another neighbouring lagoon, which should make Odessa and its two satellites one of the biggest shipping centres in the world.

My knowledge of the Ukrainian countryside is, I must admit, confined to travelling through it by train or car and to a visit to a not very large collective farm forty miles or so outside Odessa. This I hoped would help to enlighten me on the true agricultural situation in the Ukraine. But, as things turned out, my careful enquiries into output and production figures were suddenly cut short by my somehow becoming involved, as one does, in a village wedding. There I spent the rest of the day, eating, drinking and dancing, being finally asked to propose, in tumblers of home-brewed vodka, the health, not only of the bride and bridegroom, but also of the best man and bridesmaid, who also seemed clearly destined for matrimony. And so I went away, when the time came, with fairly hazy ideas as to Ukrainian agriculture, but with a general impression of an overwhelming abundance of rich food and drink and of a seemingly endless expanse of black earth – the famous *chornozem*, about which one reads so much and which on closer inspection turned out to be every bit as black as it is made out to be.

On my way back to Odessa, I was struck by the sight of several hundred private cars parked higgledy-piggledy by the road-side. What, I wondered, could their drivers all be doing? Scarcely, I imagined, attending a point-to-point or an agricultural show. But that is what it looked like.

The answer I only discovered later. 'Today's Sunday,' said my informant and went on to explain what was happening. In Odessa, as everywhere else in the Soviet Union, anyone who can afford to do so buys a high proportion of their domestic supplies direct from individual peasants, who are allowed by the government to sell the produce of their own personal plots of land for what it will fetch on the open market. In addition to several open markets in Odessa itself, there are more outside the city and it was round one of these that so many worthy citizens of Odessa had congregated. But, being Sunday, it was not only farm produce they were buying. To the port of Odessa come sailors and travellers from all over the world, their kit-bags bulging with smuggled purchases from abroad, watches, cameras, tape-recorders, nylons, scent and so on. On Sundays, as a matter of course, these desirable goods find their way to the food markets and are there sold, side by side with the cabbages and potatoes, to the mutual advantage of all concerned. It was, I thought, an interesting illustration of the various forms taken by human endeavour and of the social and economic effects of the internal combustion engine, now more widely available than ever before to the individual Soviet citizen.

Having visited Kiev (and, for good measure Odessa), my next concern was to refresh my memories of the ancient cities that lie to the north-east of Moscow.

It will be recalled that, with the gradual decline of Kiev, which for some two hundred years had been the temporal and spiritual capital of Russia, power shifted due north to Novgorod and to Rostov-Suzdal in the north-east. Suzdal now took the place of Kiev as a religious centre, rivalling it by the beauty of its palaces and places of worship. Meantime there had been a corresponding movement of population, withdrawing before the onslaught of Pechenegs and Polovtsi into the wooded regions of the north-east, hitherto inhabited by a variety of more or less indigenous Finnish tribes. This was the Zalesye, the Land Beyond the Forests.

Early in the twelfth century, Rostov-Suzdal, already an independent Russian principality, was bestowed by Vladimir Monomakh of Kiev on his son Yuri Dolgoruki, who became its first appanaged prince and gave it his own crest, the white gerfalcon crowned with gold, which to this day remains the symbol of the town of Suzdal. To Suzdal, Rostov and the no less ancient town of Pereslavl Zalesski were added in the course of the twelfth century the new Russian townships of Vladimir, Yaroslavl and Moscow. Together they were to form the nucleus of Muscovy.

On his death in 1157, Yuri Dolgoruki was succeeded by Andrei of Bogolyubovo, his son by a Kipchak princess, who, on becoming Grand Prince, did not take up residence in Kiev but made his capital at Vladimir. Summoning 'master craftsmen from all countries', he endowed the new capital with churches built of the fine white local limestone and fortified it as strongly as he could. After Andrei had been assassinated in 1174 by a group of rebellious boyars in league with his wife Ulita, he was succeeded as Grand Prince by his younger brother Vsevolod III (known, owing to his numerous progeny, as Big Nest), another great warrior, who, like his brother, dominated the Russian scene and, in his turn, contributed greatly to the embellishment of the principality, at the same time restoring the serious damage done to Vladimir by a disastrous fire in 1183. Vsevolod's work was continued by his son Yuri II, who, succeeding

Suzdal

St Sophia, Kiev

him on his death in 1212, reigned until 1238, when he fell in battle against the invading Tartar hordes.

It was thus that, from the accession of Vladimir Monomakh in 1113 to the death of Yuri II in 1238, Vladimir-Suzdal enjoyed a century and a quarter of relative stability and prosperity under princes of unusual ability, intelligence and taste. It was a period marked by an altogether exceptional flowering of Russian art and architecture.

In practice most people setting out to visit the ancient towns of the Zalesye will make Moscow their starting-point. About eighty or ninety miles north-eastwards from Moscow, passing Zagorsk on the way, you come to Pereslavl Zalesski or Pereslavl Beyond the Woods. The indefatigable Yuri Dolgoruki, who founded Moscow, is also generally regarded as the founder of Pereslavl Zalesski. In fact, Pereslavl was a Slav outpost as far back as the tenth century and took its name from Pereyaslavl on the Trubezh near Kiev, the original home-town of its first Russian settlers, who also renamed the nearby river Trubezh, to remind them of their own river back home, which they had forsaken for the comparative security afforded by the forests of the north-east. But it was Yuri who rebuilt the town beyond the river on the shores of Lake Pleshcheyevo, a considerable sheet of water, reputedly rich in fish, two of which figure beneath the golden horn of Vladimir on the town's coat of arms. It was here, incidentally, that several hundred years later, Peter the Great (who had learned to sail here as a boy) built the first ships of his future Baltic Fleet, indeed of the Imperial Russian Navy.

Having fortified his new town and thrown a moat round it, Yuri Dolgoruki started in 1152 to build the little white limestone Cathedral of the Transfiguration which still stands beneath the ramparts of his fortress. In its extreme simplicity, this is perhaps the purest and to many people the most perfect example of early Russian architecture. Each of its walls is divided into three arched panels or *zakomaras*, the central panel being slightly higher than those on either side of it. On the eastern wall a triple apse, with as its only ornament a simple cornice, corresponds to the three arches. A perfectly proportioned drum, fringed by a plain frieze, supports a single onion dome.

In front of the little cathedral stands a Soviet-erected bust of St Alexander Nevski, who was born here and whose summer palace

Bogolyubovo, Church of the Assumption

once stood on a nearby hill which still bears his name. Of the buildings which formerly stood within the walls of the Kremlin, only the sixteenth-century Church of the Metropolitan Peter still survives, a curious galleried structure with a sugar-loaf spire ending in an onion dome, and a free-standing early nineteenth-century bell-tower.

Pereslavl also has three monasteries. The oldest and finest of these is the Goritski Monastery, which, with its massive walls, stands in a commanding position overlooking the lake and is said to have been founded in the reign of Ivan Kalita. Its buildings, however, which include a seven-domed Cathedral of the Assumption built in 1757, date mainly from the seventeenth and eighteenth centuries.

The Danilov Monastery is situated in the south-western part of the town. Its single-domed Cathedral of the Trinity, which contains some interesting frescoes, was built in 1530 in the reign of Vasili III to celebrate the birth of Ivan the Terrible. Next to this is the Church of All Saints, also with only one dome, built 150 years later by Prince Baryatinski, who, tiring of the world, later entered the monastery as a monk.

Most of the Monastery of St Nikita, which lies outside the town on the road to Yaroslavl, was built in three years, between 1561 and 1564. It had been Ivan the Terrible's intention to make it into a stronghold for his *Oprichniki*, but in the event he changed his plans and took them to Alexandrov instead. In 1608 the monastery proved its worth as a fortress by successfully withstanding a two weeks' siege by a Polish force under Jan Sapieha. From the time of Vasili III a little church remains which has been incorporated in the larger cathedral built in his son's day. The monastery also possesses a fine seventeenth-century refectory.

Leaving Lake Pleshcheyevo behind you on the left, you next continue for another forty miles or so to Rostov. Rostov Veliki, Rostov the Great (as distinct from Rostov on the Don, a much larger relatively modern town through which you pass on the way to the Caucasus), is one of the oldest cities in Russia. It is certainly well over a thousand years old and there are indications that, even before the coming of the Slavs, some kind of fortified Finno-Ugrian settlement existed on the same site. We know that from 988 onwards it was ruled over by Yaroslav the Wise and that on his death in 1054 it passed with Suzdal under the sway of his son Vsevolod, who in due course was succeeded by his son Vladimir Monomakh, who, as we have seen, passed it on in his turn to Yuri Dolgoruki.

The only town in Russia besides Novgorod to claim the epithet Great, Rostov is built on the shores of a considerable expanse of water known as Lake Nero. In his *De Architectura* Vitruvius laid down the principle that a town built on the shore of the sea or of a lake, or indeed on the banks of a river, should spread out evenly from that point. There could be no better illustration of this than Rostov, which has developed in a series of concentric circles from its original citadel, firmly placed by its founder on the shores of Lake Nero.

Approaching Rostov from Pereslavl, you get your first view of it from a distance of six or seven miles away, its buildings on a fine day dramatically reflected in the waters of the lake – the city's white limestone walls, the ten round towers of the Kremlin, and half a dozen onion-domed churches. Of these by far the oldest is the Cathedral of the Assumption (Uspenski Sobor), originally built in 1162 by Yuri Dolgoruki's son, Andrei Bogolyubski, but burnt down by the Mongols in 1238 and constantly rebuilt in the intervening centuries. It stands white and four-square at the northern end of the Kremlin enclosure, with four smaller onion domes clustering round a large central cupola. Attached to it is a much lower arcaded belfry with four little domes and a chime of thirteen bells added in the second half of the seventeenth century. For Rostov Veliki, or at any rate for Jona, the Metropolitan of the day, who happened to be an enthusiastic builder, this was a period of considerable prosperity and artistic achievement. It was during these fifty years that the present walls of the Kremlin were built as well as most of the buildings now contained within them. Opposite the Uspenski Cathedral, and not unlike it in size and design, is the Church of the Resurrection, built in 1670 and situated above the main entrance to the monastery. On the west wall of the Kremlin is the graceful Gate-Church of St John the Divine, built a dozen years later. The interiors of these and the neighbouring churches are lavishly frescoed by unusually talented local seventeenth-century painters of whom Guri Nikitin from Kostroma is the best known.

For himself Metropolitan Jona built a handsome palace. This was badly damaged by a sudden hurricane which struck Rostov in August 1953, carrying off its roof as well as the domes of most of the churches. It has now been carefully restored as have the so-called Red and White Palaces, originally built to accommodate the Metropolitan's guests. As his private chapel Jona built the smaller Church of the Redeemer in the Square (Spas na Seniakh), with a plain roof and single golden dome, but a nonetheless magnificent interior. An unusual feature of the Rostov Kremlin is the covered passage-ways which link its various buildings at different levels, enabling one to visit most of them without ever coming out into the open.

Outside the Kremlin walls are the Cathedral of St Gregory the Divine, built on the site of a much older monastery of the same name, the Church of the Saviour in the Market Place and that of St Isidore, built in the time of Ivan the Terrible.

Some way along the shore of Lake Nero is the Church of the Saviour on the Sands, founded by Maria, widow of Prince Vasilko of Rostov, who was tortured to death by the Tartars in 1238. Princess Maria is also famous as the author of a chronicle containing obituary notices of the numerous Russian princes who died fighting the Tartars. Adjoining the Church of the Saviour are a later but nonetheless imposing monastery and church, the Spaso-Yakov-lyevski, founded in the fourteenth but built for the most part in the seventeenth, eighteenth and early nineteenth centuries. Also standing on the shore at about the same distance on the far side of Rostov is the much older Avramyevski Monastery, built on the site of a temple dedicated to Veles, the pagan God of Farm Animals, who after the advent of Christianity quickly reappeared as a Christian saint.

Princess Maria Rostovskaya was not the only great lady from Rostov to win lasting fame. At the battle of Kulikovo in 1380 Princess Daria Rostovskaya and Princess Antonina Puzhbolskaya, both wearing men's clothes and armour, fought bravely against the Tartars. Three hundred years later, in the seventeenth century, Irina, the brilliant young widow of Count Musin-Pushkin, was renowned for her scholarship as far afield as London and Amsterdam and gave much valuable help to Metropolitan Jona when he was building the local Kremlin and its churches. It was she, it appears, who provided the painters of the frescoes with a copy of Piscator's Bible, the illustrations to which clearly had a strong influence on their work. As a girl, Irina came near to being the bride of Tsar Alexei Mikhailovich, but, fortunately for her, was discarded on the grounds that her father, the Boyar Lugovski, was not well enough born. Disappointed at this set-back, not to mention the slur on his nobility, her father then tried to marry her off to a contemporary of his, a rich, elderly and generally unpleasing boyar. But Irina, running away from home, eloped with the handsome young Count Musin-Pushkin, having first sent him the irresistible message, 'If you love me, come and get me.' He did, but did not, it appears, long survive the cultural shock of marriage to this passionate blue-stocking.

In addition to its abundance of churches and monasteries, Rostov can also boast a number of agreeable town houses and secular public buildings, reflecting a period of increased stability and prosperity and a deliberate attempt at town-planning at the end of the eighteenth and beginning of the nineteenth centuries.

On leaving Rostov Veliki, it is well worth turning westwards off the main road and driving as far as Uglich, the scene of the alleged death of the Tsarevich Dmitri in 1591. A dozen miles outside Rostov you come to the Monastery-fortress of St Boris and St Gleb, built as a defensive outpost on a bend of the River Ustye, which protects it on three sides. Its massive fortifications, erected in 1520 on the site of an earlier strong-point, were the work of Grigori Borisov, an outstanding architect from Rostov who also built the Monastery's Cathedral of St Boris and St Gleb (later badly remodelled), the splendid Gate-Church of St Sergius and the Church of the Annunciation, as well as a refectory and various other monastery buildings. A bell-tower and the Church of the Annuciation above the Water-gates were added on the north side in the second half of the seventeenth century. The monastery fortifications served the purpose for which they were designed most effectively when, in the troubled early years of the seventeenth century, an invading Polish army was successfully thrown back from its walls.

A good deal less effective were the defences of the Monastery of St Nicholas on the Uleima, founded in 1400, of which you catch sight through a screen of lime-trees about ten miles before reaching Uglich. It stands on a little hill beyond the river. When Jan Sapieha and his Poles attacked and stormed the monastery in 1608, its defenders barricaded themselves in the Cathedral of St Nicholas, taking the population of the neighbouring villages with them, but the Poles burnt it down with all of them inside. Both the cathedral, which was later restored, and the Church of the Presentation in the Temple, which suffered less, are for the most part of late seventeenth-century construction. The Church of the Trinity above the monastery gate was added in the eighteenth century. The monastery's walls, as the painful events of 1608 showed all too clearly, were never of any great military significance.

In Uglich the oldest buildings are grouped on a kind of little island bounded by the Volga itself on one side and on the others by one of its lesser tributaries which divides it from the remainder of the town. This was the site of the original Kremlin, dating back to the fifteenth century and earlier. And this is where the Tsarina Maria Nagaya, exiled there by Boris Godunov, lived in a palace built a hundred years earlier by Prince Andrew the Big, who, the record tells us, died in a dungeon beneath the Borovitski Gate of the Moscow Kremlin, following a quarrel with his elder brother, Ivan III.

It was here, in the courtyard of the palace, that on 15 May 1591 Maria's son, the little Tsarevich Dmitri, met (or did not meet) his death, possibly at the hands of assassins sent by Boris Godunov or possibly not. What remains of the building is known today as the Palace of the Tsarevich Dmitri. It is a plain, three-storeyed construction of red brick dating from the fifteenth century, but heavily restored in the ancient Russian manner of the mid-nineteenth century and now converted into a museum.

The actual spot where little Dmitri bled to death (or alternatively recovered sufficiently to re-emerge ten years later as a pretender to the throne) is marked by the ornate, five-domed red and white Church of St Dmitri in the Blood, built in 1692 on the site of an earlier shrine and now turned into a museum. It contains a highly dramatic fresco of the death and subsequent canonization of St Dmitri. To this day little Dmitri is still remembered in his home town and the story still told in prose and verse of the miraculous Bell of Uglich, which, having of its own accord rung out to proclaim his murder, was for this publicly flogged with the knout by order of Boris Godunov and then, after its tongue had been torn out, exiled to Tobolsk in Siberia. There it was on view until 1892. It was then returned to Uglich, where it can now be seen in Dmitri's Palace.

Besides little Dmitri's palace and church the Kremlin precincts also contain an eighteenth-century cathedral and bell-tower. But of considerably greater interest architecturally is the handsome Church of the Nativity of St John the Baptist, built at the end of the seventeenth century and standing on the Volga some distance away from the Kremlin buildings. Near it is the Monastery of the Resurrection, built a few years earlier by that enthusiastic builder and patron of the arts, the Metropolitan Jona of Rostov. Seen from the other side of the Volga, the cathedral, bell-tower, refectory and single-domed Church of the Virgin of Smolensk, make, with the nearby Church of St John, an exceptionally handsome group of seventeenth-century buildings.

A considerably older foundation than any of these is the Alekseyevski Monastery. Founded in 1371 by the Metropolitan Aleksei, it was largely destroyed during the Polish invasion of 1608 and rebuilt in the 1620s. Its principal church, the Cathedral of the Assumption, with its blue-green domes poised on slender drums, three sugar-loaf spires and abundance of elegant white tracery and plaster-work on an apricot-coloured ground, is an outstanding example of early seventeenth-century Russian architecture. The monastery stands in the town itself, a little way back from the Volga, but the spires and domes of its cathedral can be seen standing out above the surrounding buildings. To the people of Uglich it has long been a favourite landmark symbolizing their home town and is affectionately known to them as *Divnaya*, the Marvel. Also near the centre of the town are the seventeenth-century Church of St John the Baptist and Monastery of the Resurrection and the Monastery of the Epiphany, which was built at different periods between the seventeenth and nineteenth centuries. In addition to its ecclesiastical buildings, Uglich possesses a number of interesting seventeenth- and eighteenth-century town houses, which once belonged to its rich merchants and other notables, some fine public buildings, a shopping centre and a *Zimin Dvor* or Winter Garden dating from the eighteenth and early nineteenth centuries.

Thirty miles beyond Rostov Veliki (or Yaroslavski, as it is sometimes called), where the little River Kotorosl flows into the mighty stream of the Volga, you come to the ancient town of Yaroslavl, once a key point in the northern defences of Rostov-Suzdal. Yaroslavl is almost a thousand years old, having been founded by Yaroslav the Wise in 1010 at a spot known as Bear's Corner, where he once killed with a battle-axe a bear which had been set on him by the local inhabitants. It is for this reason that Yaroslavl, as the fortified town he built here was subsequently renamed, still has a bear on its coat of arms.

Today Yaroslavl is a flourishing modern city growing steadily bigger year by year, but fortunately it seems as though every effort were being made to preserve the old town and its buildings and restore them, where restoration is needed. Approaching it by road from the south through the pleasantly wooded countryside of the Zalesye, you catch sight first of all of the white walls and towers of the Monastery of the Transfiguration (Spaso-Preobrazhenski Monastir), founded in the twelfth century, and of the shining golden domes of its cathedral, built four centuries later on the site of an earlier church. The bell-tower, Holy Gates and refectory were also built in the sixteenth century, the monastery walls and towers a hundred years later. Immediately outside the precincts of the monastery stands the red-brick Church of the Epiphany, with its five green onion domes, built in the seventeenth century and lavishly decorated with brightly coloured tiles, a local speciality.

Of Yaroslav's original Kremlin no trace remains, but, with the help of a town-plan, it is not difficult to plot its position in the rough triangle between the Volga and the Kotorosl. Thus we know that the massive seventeenth-century Church of the Archangel Michael, which stands on the Kotorosl Embankment on the site of an earlier royal palace, was situated on the boundary between the Kremlin and the Market Place 'where the moat runs beyond the ramparts' and that the Church of the Saviour in the Town (Spas na Gorodu), of approximately the same period and slightly to the south of it, stood on the Market Place itself, having been built, we are told, by the townspeople themselves 'and not by any prince'. The latter church's frescoes, incidentally, depicting a variety of historical subjects, are of a very high standard, as are those, painted in the second half of the seventeenth century by two artists from nearby Kostroma, Guri Nikitin and Sila Savin, which are to be found in the roughly contemporary Church of the Prophet Elijah, a rather pleasing white church on the main square of the town with five green onion domes and two white sugar-loaf spires, one of which serves as a belfry.

Across the square from the Church of the Prophet Elijah are two handsome eighteenth-century buildings which once housed the Law Courts. A little further away, along the street leading to the Monastery of the Transfiguration, one comes to a characteristic early nineteenth-century shopping-centre, provided with lodgings for visiting merchants (Gostini Dvor). Near it and near the seventeenth-century Znamenskaya Tower is a theatre originally built in the middle of the eighteenth century by F. G. Volkov, a local merchant with a talent for acting who can be regarded as one of the founders of the Russian theatre. If you know where to look in the old town you will also find a number of other interesting old buildings besides churches, including a late eighteenth-century inn, a Doctors' Club and some handsome town houses.

For Yaroslavl the seventeenth century (which began with some years of energetic resistance to the Polish invaders) was to become, as trade on the Volga developed, a period of great prosperity. St Nicholas is the patron saint of traders and the town still possesses no less than ten churches bearing his name. On the embankment not far from the Church of the Saviour in the Town is the Church of St Nicholas Rublyeni, meaning St Nicholas in the Wooden Town. (The Wooden Town has, needless to say, long since disappeared.) It is a plain, well proportioned church built in 1695 and almost devoid of ornament. Then there is the Church of St Nicholas the Helpful (Ugodnik), also known as Nadey's St Nicholas, built in 1622 on the banks of the Volga, which had brought him his prosperity, by a certain Nadey Sveteshnikov, a rich merchant whose agents are said to have travelled 'from Pskov to Yakutsk and from Astrakhan to Mangazey'. Its frescoes, painted in the 1650s by Lyubim Ageyev from Kostroma (possibly as a result of a further access of wealth to the good Nadey), are well worth looking at. They include a particularly charming portrait of Noah in his Ark.

Nearby again is the Church of the Nativity, endowed later in the seventeenth century by the Guryevs, another family of merchants who founded and gave their name to the sizeable town and port of Guryev to the east of Astrakhan on the Caspian Sea. The church, like others in Yaroslavl, is lavishly decorated with brightly coloured ceramics. Much of the Guryevs' trade was with Samarkand and Bokhara and it was said at the time that they had used the gold of the Samarkand sun, the green of their emeralds and the turquoise-blue of the mosques and minarets to colour the walls of their church on the banks of the northern Volga. On the Volga Embankment, not far from the Church of the Nativity, is a charming little early nineteenth-century pavilion. To the north of the town, on the banks of the Kotorosl, is the Church of St Nicholas the Wet, adjoining the smaller, warmer 'Winter' Church of the

Virgin of Tikhvin, both dating from the second half of the seven-teenth century and both beautifully decorated with coloured tiles. St Nicholas's also has some fine frescoes.

From Yaroslav's original citadel the town of Yaroslavl spread with the years across the Kotorosl to its west bank and here too are a number of fine seventeenth-century churches. To the north of this part of the town, in the village of Tolchkovo, is the Church of St John the Baptist, built of mellowed brick, splendidly decorated with coloured ceramics topped with green-and-gold-tiled onion domes and somewhat surprisingly balanced by a slightly out-of-the-straight bell-tower resembling a Chinese pagoda.

Walking southwards from Tolchkovo, you next come to the white, five-domed Church of St Theodore (Fyodorovski), with, adjoining it, the Church of St Nicholas Penski. Further south still, on a mound, stands the little single-domed Church of St Paraskeva. In almost all of these churches there are frescoes of varying quality, but possessing, for the enthusiast at any rate, a certain in-definable appeal.

As fine in their way as anything in Yaroslavl itself are two churches in the northern suburb of Korovnikovskaya Sloboda: the Virgin of Vladimir and St John Chrysostom, both built in the second half of the seventeenth century. With their bell-tower and gate-house, they stand on a high cliff above the Volga, to the far side of the Kotorosl, their ten green-tiled domes and sugar-loaf spires standing out strikingly against the sky.

About an hour's drive westwards from Yaroslavl, roughly fol-lowing the line of the Volga, brings you to Kostroma, another key point in the northern defences of Suzdal-Vladimir, strategically sited at the junction of the Volga and the Kostroma River and equally important as a Volga trading post. Founded by Yuri Dol-goruki as a fortress in 1152, Kostroma, like Rostov Veliki, has faith-fully followed the principles of Vitruvius and spread inland from its waterfront on the Volga, in this case in accordance with a plan worked out in the second half of the eighteenth century, the imple-mentation of which was clearly much facilitated by a great fire in 1773, which destroyed almost all the wooden buildings of the old town, leaving nothing but the churches which were practically its only stone buildings.

The principal streets radiate from the main square of Kostroma, which faces the Volga. This was the centre of the city's trade. It is flanked on three sides by single-storeyed shopping arcades, built at the end of the eighteenth or beginning of the nineteenth century and containing the trading stalls or booths of the merchants. These, like the stalls of an eastern bazaar, were grouped according to the merchandise they sold: grain, fish, tobacco, manufactured goods and, in particular, flax, which then, as now, was Kostroma's principal product. (The Lenin Flax Combine is, one in assured, the biggest in the world.)

High above the shopping arcades of the main square and above everything else in Kostroma rises the Fire Tower, an early nineteenth-century tower, rather like a lighthouse, springing a trifle unexpectedly from a handsome, square classical building with a fine Corinthian portico. Across the square is the palace of General Borshchov, a hero of the campaign of 1812, who, having won fame on the battlefield, subsequently built himself this magnificent classical mansion to which to retire. It is only one of a number of fine late eighteenth- or early nineteenth-century town houses and other buildings of the period which adorn the streets leading out of the main market square. Of particular merit is the Town Library, built by the same architect as the Fire Tower and generally regarded as an outstanding example of Russian Classical architecture. Another fine early nineteenth-century building is the Nobles' Club.

Of the older churches which survived the great fire of 1773, one of the most interesting is the Church of the Resurrection in the Valley (Tserkov Voskresenya na Debre), a somewhat ornate five-domed, arcaded, frescoed and much decorated seventeenth-century building standing on the eastern outskirts of the town and bearing over its entrance door a representation in bas-relief of the British Lion and Unicorn. Its story is as follows. In the mid-seventeenth century there was a good deal of trade between Kostroma and the City of London. One day, amongst a cargo of indigo dyes sent out from England in exchange for a cargo of flax, Kiril Isakov, a merchant of Kostroma, found a barrel of gold coins. On his enquiring of his English correspondent what he should do with it, the answer came back, 'Spend it in a good cause.' This gave him the idea of building a church and in 1652 work was begun on the Church of the Resurrection, which he sited not very far from his own wharves, placing the Royal Arms of Great Britain over the door in recognition of British generosity.

The oldest church in Kostroma proper is the sixteenth-century cathedral, which forms part of the Monastery of the Epiphany just off Lenin Square in the centre of the town. There are also two or three more seventeenth-century churches, all interesting in their way. But easily the most striking building in Kostroma is the Ipatiyevski Monastery which stands apart from the remainder of the city on the far bank of the River Kostroma. This was founded in 1332 by the Tartar Prince Zacharias Chet, the founder of the Godunov family, who had fled from the Golden Horde to Kostroma and there been baptized. He built this church, it appears, on the exact spot where the Virgin and St Ipatiyev revealed themselves to him in a vision. For several centuries the Godunovs were the patrons of the monastery and had their family burial vault in th splendidly frescoed Cathedral of the Trinity which they built in 1590.

The monastery's massive walls and towers were built in the reign of Ivan the Terrible. For six months it was in the hands of the Second False Dmitri and later twice seized and held by the Poles. It was from the Ipatiyevski Monastery, too, that in 1613 the young Michael Romanov set out for Moscow to be anointed Tsar, for the Romanovs, like the Godunovs, were big landowners in this area. A mid-nineteenth-century monument in the main square of Kostroma commemorates Ivan Susanin, a peasant hero who was killed by the Poles for refusing to betray Tsar Michael to them, thus giving his 'life for the Tsar' and providing the composer Glinka with a theme and a title for his well known opera of that name.

In 1649 the cathedral, which at the time was being used as a powder-magazine, blew up by mistake, but was quickly restored and some thirty years later adorned with some exceptionally fine frescoes by the well known local painter Guri Nikitin, which, like the magnificent bronze and gold doors, have survived to this day in good condition.

Besides the white limestone cathedral with its five golden domes, the Monastery of the Epiphany possesses a number of other fine sixteenth-century buildings: the Bishop's Palace, the Prior's Residence, the Refectory, the Palace of the Romanovs and a splendid, five-tiered bell-tower commanding a wide view of the town, the Volga and the surrounding countryside. Near the monastery are the Church of St John the Divine, built in the late seventeenth century, and a group of other wooden buildings of various periods brought here from other parts of the country. They include an interesting sixteenth-century Church of the Virgin from the village of Kholm and an unusual mill, but, like all such artificially assembled collections of wooden buildings, do not for me have the same appeal as churches or houses that have remained where they were built.

Unless one is for some reason determined to go back to Moscow by the way one came and then start out again, one's best course, having reached Kostroma, is to return by a rather more easterly route, stopping off at Suzdal and Vladimir, neither of which are more than two or three hours' drive from the capital, and thus completing a fairly comprehensive tour of the ancient principality of Rostov-Suzdal. But, before leaving the Volga valley to turn south in the direction of Moscow, it is worth making a slight detour to visit two villages, both within twenty miles or so of Kostroma: Krasnoye and Plyos; Krasnoye for its marvellous late sixteenth-century sugar-loaf Church of the Epiphany and Plyos, not so much for its two old churches as for its entrancing position, looking out across the Volga from among the surrounding birch-woods. 'I see,' said Chekhov to his friend the painter Levitan, looking at a picture the latter had done of Plyos, 'that a smile has appeared in your pictures.'

From Plyos it is about ninety miles to Suzdal, via the industrial town of Ivanovo. Though once a capital city, Suzdal is now little more than a village. But a village containing more that is worth seeing than most large towns. Suzdal succeeded Kiev as the religious capital of Russia and this is reflected in the surprising number of beautiful churches, convents and monasteries concentrated in so small a space. It was to remain important as a religious centre long after it had lost its political significance.

Approaching from the south, you suddenly see Suzdal with the domes and spires of its churches silhouetted against a background of green fields and woods. It lies on the banks of the Kamenka, a tributary of the Nerl, both of which were once deeper and wider rivers than they are now and of considerable significance as trade routes. The remains of at least one pagan temple show that there were some kind of settlements on the Kamenka in pre-Christian times. These, with the arrival of more Russian settlers in the tenth century, expanded into the town of Suzdal, which its inhabitants claim is older than its neighbour Vladimir. We know that Vladimir Monomakh built a church here, the first stone building to make its appearance in the north-east, and a palace to go with it. In due course his son Yuri Dolgoruki made Suzdal his capital and in 1107 an invading army of Bulgars was thrown back from its walls.

The Kremlin, which, with its palaces and churches and its ring of fortified walls and towers, formed the nucleus of the town, was situated in a loop of the river, while another loop enclosed the merchants' quarter. Though not much remains of the Kremlin's original fortifications, their line is still clearly enough marked. Of the buildings that survive, the oldest and most striking is the Cathedral of the Nativity of the Virgin. This was originally built early in the thirteenth century on the site of an older church, but has been restored and rebuilt at frequent intervals ever since. Today its five onion domes, star-spangled and supported by plain white drums, rise from a square white church, roughly corresponding to the original structure. Of considerable interest are its famous Golden Doors at the western and southern entrances. These date from the early thirteenth century and are of a very high standard of workmanship indeed. Inside the church some of the original frescoes still survive. The cathedral's belfry, with its sugar-loaf spire, was built towards the middle of the seventeenth century. The Bishop's Palace, a rambling, white three-storeyed building, dating from various periods between the fifteenth and eighteenth centuries, takes up most of the remaining space. Nearby are the Church of the Assumption, the Church of St Nicholas and the Church of Christ, all three built in the eighteenth century.

Another eighteenth-century Church of St Nicholas, made entirely from wood, has been transported bodily from elsewhere and re-erected not far from the Kremlin. One is also shown several other transplanted eighteenth-century wooden churches, a peasant's house and a windmill, forming a rather forlorn little group of their own on a convenient bit of ground on the outskirts of the town. Most people are delighted by them, but to me they look like large Swiss musical-boxes and lack any charm they might have possessed if left where they were. Not far away, on Soviet Square, near the approaches to the Kremlin, is an elegant classical shopping centre, known as the Torgovye Ryadi and still used for the same purpose for which it was built in 1811.

There are no less than five monasteries or convents (the Russian word is the same) in and around Suzdal; the largest of these, the Spasski or Spaso-Yevfimiyevski Monastery, first founded in the fourteenth century, stands to the north of the town in a commanding position on the left bank of the Kamenka. It is surrounded by a high fortified wall and twenty massive towers. These date from the troublous times of the sixteenth and seventeenth centuries, when strong fortifications were a necessity and theological arguments were rammed home with the help of siege artillery. Going in through a low arch set in a vast, square entrance-tower, you find yourself in a courtyard immediately facing a second massive gate-tower incorporating the early seventeenth-century Church of the Annunciation. This leads in turn to the onion-domed sixteenth-century Cathedral of the Transfiguration and to the other churches and buildings of the monastery. The Refectory-Church of the Assumption which, with its sugar-loaf spire, resembles the famous Church of the Ascension at Kolomenskoye, is claimed as the earliest church of this design in Russia. A little chapel near the cathedral contains the tomb of Abbot Yevfimi or Euphemius, who founded and gave his name to the monastery. Also buried near the cathedral is Prince Dmitri Pozharski, who, with Kuzma Minin the butcher, led the national rising of 1612 against the Poles. The combined Church and Belfry of St John the Baptist is thought to have been built to celebrate the birth in 1530 of Ivan the Terrible. Not far from the entrance to the monastery, near the south-western corner of its wall, is the majestic early eighteenth-century Church of the Virgin of Smolensk.

At various times the Spasski Monastery was used as a repository for problem prisoners. A number of Pugachov's followers were imprisoned there as was Shakhovskoi, one of the revolutionaries of December 1825. It was also used for disciplining recalcitrant or heretical priests, who could be dealt with arbitrarily and without reference to the Ministry of Justice. Also held prisoner there for a time was the German Field-Marshal von Paulus, who surrendered to the Russians at Stalingrad in 1943.

From the river bank beneath the monastery walls where we sat eating our sandwiches, we looked across the river to the Convent of the Intercession (Pokrovski Monastir). Lying amid the water-meadows that fringe the Kamenka, it was a friendlier-looking place than the ecclesiastical fortress we had just inspected. The Pokrovski Convent was founded in the fourteenth century. The Cathedral and other convent buildings, including a number of wooden houses with their own gardens, are contained by a low white wall broken by occasional towers. Once again, you enter the precinct by way of a gate-tower, topped by the golden dome of the tiny Church of the Annunciation built above it. The austerely beautiful white three-domed sixteenth-century Cathedral of the Intercession, linked by a gallery to its more recent sugar-loaf belfry, looms large above the other buildings. Of interest, too, is the Refectory Church of the Conception, exotic in design and provided with its own bakery, cellar and kitchen.

The Cathedral itself and most of the other convent buildings were built early in the sixteenth century on the orders of Vasili III. It was to the Pokrovski Convent that Vasili relegated his wife, Solomonia, having first, by one means or another, prevailed on the ecclesiastical authorities to let him divorce her in order that he should be free to marry Helen Glinskaya, the beautiful Polish princess who became the mother of Ivan the Terrible. It is said that, when about to take the veil, Solomonia refused to go quietly, but fought and screamed and tore her nun's habit and cursed her faithless husband, until in the end, Ivan Shigonia-Podzhogin, the nobleman who had been put in charge of her, was obliged to get out his whip and give her a good thrashing, after which she proved more docile.

But this was not the end of the story. One of Vasili's excuses for divorcing Solomonia was that, despite his best endeavours, she had not borne him any children. Once in the convent, however, she was found to be pregnant and gave birth to a son. To a number of people this could have been bad news. Clearly the baby's life was at risk. To save him, Solomonia or Sister Sophie, as she was now called, was said to have had him smuggled out of the convent, at the same time announcing that he had died. And there for several centuries the matter rested.

But, strangely enough, confirmation of what had long been regarded as no more than a legend was to come four hundred years later. In 1934, in the course of some excavations a tiny sarcophagus was discovered near Solomonia's own tomb. On being opened this was found to contain, not a body, but a dummy dressed in a little embroidered silk shirt and designed to look like a child. Whose the real baby was and what became of him will in all probability never be known, although it is believed that after his accession Ivan the Terrible did a certain amount of research on the subject. It is of course, not beyond the bounds of possibility that he was in fact Vasili's own son and that his descendants, with a far better claim to the Russian throne than any Romanovs, are today quietly living somewhere near Suzdal. As for Solomonia herself, she was subsequently canonized and, for good measure, miracles are said to have occurred at her grave.

St Solomonia was not the only Tsaritsa to end up in the Pokrovski Convent. Eudoxia, the first wife of Peter the Great, was also despatched there soon after marriage and there, years later, mourned her son Aleksei's judicial murder and the sad fate of his martyred supporters, a list of whose names is kept in the nearby Church of St Peter and St Paul, while in another church an altar is dedicated to the memory of the unfortunate Aleksei.

Immediately across the river from the Pokrovski Convent is the somewhat dilapidated Alexandrovski Monastery, said to have been founded in the thirteenth century by Alexander Nevski. Its surviving buildings date, however, from the seventeenth century: a handsome Cathedral of the Ascension endowed by Natalia Narishkina, the mother of Peter the Great, and a tall bell-tower. Of the Monastery of St Basil, built on another loop of the river to the east of the town, even less remains: a fragment of wall, a small cathedral and a refectory church, all dating from the seventeenth century.

The Convent of the Deposition of the Virgin's Robes (Rizopolozhenski Monastir) is situated nearer to the centre of the town, where Lenin Street joins the local Red Square. The convent is best known for its Holy Gates. These consist of a double arch of brick surmounted by twin sugar-loaf spires topped in turn by tiny cupolas and were completed in 1688. Immediately inside them is a three-domed white early sixteenth-century cathedral, somewhat resembling the Pokrovski cathedral. The later rule, under which all Orthodox churches had to be built with five domes, had at this time not yet been introduced. The cathedral was, it appears, built and endowed by none other than Ivan Shigonia-Podzhogin, the boyar who by vigorous and well timed use of his whip so effectively induced the reluctant St Solomonia to take the veil, thus launching her on an ecclesiastical career eventually to be crowned by canonization, and at the same time preparing the way for the advent of Ivan the Terrible. In the seventeenth century, when the Holy Gates were built, galleries were also added to the cathedral to make it look less austere and more in accordance with the taste of the period. Another church, originally part of the convent and still in existence at the beginning of this century, seems somehow to have disappeared.

Besides its Kremlin and the five remaining convents and monasteries, Suzdal abounds in beautiful churches built for the most part in the late seventeenth and eighteenth centuries. It becomes in the end simply a question of how much time you can spare to look at them or how long it is before your eye becomes bewildered by the profusion of domes and drums and *zakomaras* and sugar-loaf or tent-shaped spires. Many of them, like the great Church of the Resurrection on the Market Place and the little Church of the Virgin of Kazan next to it, were deliberately built in pairs: a big, cool, airy summer church and a smaller, cosier, warmer church for winter. And the same pattern is repeated again and again. Thus, if you walk from the Pokrovski Convent through the meadows along the north bank of the Kamenka, you first pass the Church of the Virgin of Tikhvin and the Church of the Prophet Elijah. Next comes the 'warm' Church of the Nativity, with its beautiful little belfry, paired with the cooler and more spacious Church of the Epiphany. Entering the town from the south by Lenin Street, the Znamenskaya Church is on the right of the road, with the smaller (and warmer) Rizopolozhenskaya adjoining it. Not far away on the banks of the Kamenka, the Church of the Archangel Michael is paired with the Church of Flora and Laura, the former built in the eighteenth and the latter in the early nineteenth century. Nearer the centre of the town, where some of the old fortifications of Suzdal still survive, the Church of the Emperor Constantine is paired with that of the Virgin of Compassion. To the north of the Kamenka in the suburb of Korovniki, on the site of a former pagan temple, stand the Church of St Cosmo and St Damian with its elegant spire and the Church of the Love of God, both built in 1696. Near the Pokrovski Convent are the Churches of St Nicholas and of St Peter and St Paul, the latter built in 1694 and the former in 1712. And so on. Some of the churches, on the other hand, have lost their pair, while some never had one, notably the octagonal Church of St John the Baptist in the centre of the town.

In addition to all its churches and monasteries Suzdal also possesses a considerable number of interesting old houses, mostly built in the eighteenth century, but a few earlier. Some of these bear names well known in one connection or another. At 134 Lenin Street, near the Church of the Virgin of Smolensk, is the House of Father Nikita Pustosviat, a leading Old Believer, who bitterly opposed the reforms of Patriarch Nikon and consequently suffered martyrdom on the Red Square in 1682. The eighteenth-century House of Chicherin presumably once belonged to the noble family from which sprang the famous People's Commissar for Foreign Affairs of that name who in the early 1920s so consistently clashed with the equally aristocratic and equally intransigent Lord Curzon. Finally there are no less than two houses bearing the well-known name of Ustinov.

A mile or so away from Suzdal, due east across the fields, you come to the little village of Kideksha. Here, strategically sited at the junction of the Nerl and the Kamenka, Yuri Dolgoruki, on becoming Prince of Rostov-Suzdal, built himself a stronghold and a palace at a time when Suzdal scarcely existed as a town, and here, earlier still, according to legend, dwelt the martyr-princes St Boris and St Gleb, sons of St Vladimir, murdered in early youth by their elder brother. Of Yuri's palace, which later became a monastery, nothing remains, but it is still possible to trace the line of the ancient fortifications, while the white limestone Cathedral, built in 1152, recalls by its name St Boris and St Gleb. Built within a year or two of the Cathedral of the Transfiguration at Pereslavl Zalesski, which in some respects it resembles, the Cathedral of St Boris and St Gleb is another splendid example of Russian twelfth-century architecture. Once more, tall pilasters divide three of the walls of the plain, square white building into arched panels or *zakomaras* decorated with blind arcading, while the fourth takes the form of a triple apse. A little drum, presumably of later construction, supports a small single cupola. The inside is as austerely beautiful as the outside. Both cathedral and palace were burned by the Tartars in 1238, but the cathedral was restored and reconsecrated the following year. Near the cathedral is a free-standing bell-tower and the little Church of St Stephen, both built in the eighteenth century.

Some thirty miles due west of Suzdal is another small town possessing a connection with Yuri Dolgoruki – Yuryev Polski or Yuri's Town among the Meadows. Looking out across the seemingly endless expanse of meadows stretching away into the distance, it is easy to see why it was so named. Here again Yuri sited his fortress at the junction of two rivers, the Koloksha and its tributary the Gza. Of the ancient ramparts, built, like much of Kideksha, in 1152, enough remains to show how formidable they once were. This is all that has survived from Yuri's time. Today the town's chief glory is the little Cathedral of St George, built in 1234, only three or four years before the Mongol invasions, on the site of an earlier church founded by Yuri. Though parts of the structure collapsed in 1460 and were subsequently rebuilt, the outside of the Cathedral is still decorated with the magnificent carvings which made it famous and which are perhaps the finest of their kind in Russia. They cover a wide range of subjects, both sacred and profane (including Alexander the Great on his way to heaven, a number of saints and a regular menagerie of mythical and other animals) and are of even higher quality than those which adorn the famous Cathedral of St Dmitri at nearby Vladimir. For their survival much of the credit must go to Vasili Yermolin, the architect from Moscow who in 1471 was charged with the rebuilding of the cathedral and managed to preserve much of the work of the original builders and craftsmen. On the other hand, the proportions and lines of the original building were clearly not improved by its collapse and subsequent restoration and a number of the carvings seem to have ended up the wrong way round. Built of limestone, which with the years has turned a strange shade of grey-green, the cathedral has arched entrances on three sides and an apse on the fourth. A rather squat-looking drum supports a single dome of obviously much later construction.

Yuri Dolgoruki's grandson, Prince Sviatoslav, who built the cathedral and lies buried within it, also founded the nearby Monastery of the Archangel Michael, but its surviving churches and monastery buildings, including a typical gate-church, are all of seventeenth-century construction. All these buildings, as well as a massive early twentieth-century cathedral, are contained within what were once the walls of Yuri's fortress or Kremlin.

Returning to the main road and driving southwards from Suzdal, you come after twenty-five miles to Vladimir. From Suzdal the road, roughly following the valley of the River Nerl, carries you through a landscape of woods and meadows typical of the Zalesye. Rather less than half-way, the name of a village, Batyevo, strikes a menacing note. It was here, they say, that in February 1238, Baty or Batu Khan of the Golden Horde pitched his camp before sacking Suzdal and Vladimir and slaughtering their inhabitants.

Having moved the capital of Rus to Vladimir, the city in which he had spent his youth and which he loved best of all, Prince Andrei of Bogolyubovo spared no effort to ensure that it was strongly forti-fied and that its churches and other buildings were as magnificent as those of the former capital, Kiev, which, as though to settle the argument once and for all, he now invaded and sacked.

Just as Kiev is sited on a high bluff overlooking the Dnieper, so Vladimir looks down from the lofty left bank of the Klyazma, once a far more considerable stream than it is today. Here, 150 feet above the river, Vladimir Monomakh had sited the Kremlin which his grandson Andrei set out to strengthen and adorn, build-ing in it a stone church of which today no trace remains.

In 1160, soon after his accession to the throne, Andrei, with the help of master craftsmen whom he had imported from abroad, started work on the Cathedral of the Assumption (Uspenski Sobor), which, when completed, was to be one of the glories of the new town and of all Russia. In it he installed the famous icon which he had brought with him from Kiev and which was to be known henceforth as the *Virgin of Vladimir*. Twenty-five years later, under Vsevelod III, the cathedral was badly damaged by a great fire, which destroyed most of the town. It was, however, quickly rebuilt and restored, this time, as the Chronicler proudly points out, by native Russian builders and craftsmen. The single gold cupola of the original structure was replaced by a group of five domes. At the same time the interior of the cathedral was divided into five parts, the altar apse was broadened and the others apses were enclosed in new walls. The building as it appears today is largely the result of this reconstruction. Apart from the fire of 1185, it has survived numerous other vicissitudes. On capturing Vladimir in 1238, Batu Khan's Tartars, as was their wont, stacked the Cathedral with wood and set it alight with the Royal Family, the Metropolitan and his clergy and most of the leading citizens inside. But, though the congregation died in agony and the interior of the Cathedral suffered serious damage, the structure itself somehow survived this and subsequent lesser conflagrations.

Today, despite the flourishing industrial town which has sprung up all round it, the white and gold Cathedral, standing on its hilltop above the Russian plain, must still look very much as it did in

Vsevolod's day, eight centuries ago. Its austerely beautiful western façade, divided into five tall arched panels, each containing a window and decorated with elegant limestone reliefs, in many ways recalls the mediaeval churches of Georgia and Armenia. This is not really surprising, for, though Kievan influence remained paramount, Yuri I and his sons Andrei and Vsevolod all married eastern princesses, while Yuri, the deplorable younger son of Andrei Bogoliubski, was briefly wedded to the great Queen Tamara of Georgia, so that inevitably Vladimir-Suzdal was open to architectural and stylistic trends from Transcaucasia and the Middle East.

As we have seen, it was this cathedral which three hundred years later served as a model for Fioravanti's Cathedral of the Assumption in Moscow. In it Andrei of Bogolyubovo lies buried. The famous *Virgin of Vladimir*, which he brought from Kiev, remained here until 1395, when it was taken to Moscow to protect the city against Tamerlane's Tartar hordes. The Cathedral still contains some fine frescoes by the great Andrei Rublyov and by Daniel Chorni, though most of the icons by the same painters which originally decorated its iconostasis have now been moved to galleries in Moscow or Leningrad. At the very beginning of the last century a handsome, if somewhat incongruous, free-standing bell-tower in the classical manner was added. The Cathedral is still in use and is so popular that on Sundays and feast days the congregation overflows into the park outside.

Only a few hundred yards from the Cathedral of the Assumption stands the Cathedral of St Dmitri (Dmitryevski Sobor), built by Russian masons in about 1197 in the reign of Vsevolod III, whose Chapel Royal it became. A square building of white limestone with a single golden cupola, it is a particularly fine and well preserved example of the Suzdal-Vladimir style of architecture. In contrast to the more sober style of the Cathedral of the Assumption, its walls, each divided by tall, slender pilasters into three arched compartments, are lavishly decorated with beautiful and also highly enjoyable carvings of Saints, Old Testament Kings and Prophets, and mythological beings covering a wide range of themes. Thus in the central *zakomaras* alone we find no less than three representations of King David. On the south wall Alexander the Great is being carried up to heaven by a team of griffins. On the northern façade Vsevolod Big Nest is depicted proudly presenting his latest-born son to the rest of his numerous brood, while the Labours of Hercules are vividly represented on the west wall.

In the pleasant park where these two ancient cathedrals now stand, looking out across the valley of the Klyazma, there is no longer any trace of the original Kremlin built there by Vladimir Monomakh, though the commanding position clearly suggests the tactical and strategic reasons for which it was sited there. But, strolling along the nearby Street of the Third International, as the main thoroughfare of the old town is now called, you suddenly come to the Golden Gate, originally built in about 1160 by Andrei Bogolyubski as an integral part of the town's defences. This consists of a dazzling white limestone arch, flanked on either side by circular bastions and surmounted by the golden dome of the little Gate-Church of the Rizopolozhenye, built on top of it. Though in the course of the last eight centuries it has doubtless undergone a good deal of reconstruction and restoration, the Golden Gate remains a most impressive structure and still conveys, as you look at it, a feeling of massive strength and preparedness to resist attack.

Meanwhile, I had not entirely abandoned my search for some trace of Vladimir Monomakh's original Kremlin. Glancing from my bedroom window in the Hotel Vladimir, a survival from the Stalin era, which, with its massive corner tower, is itself well on the way to becoming an historical monument, I found that I was looking directly out on the precincts of the ancient walled Monastery of the Nativity, adjoining the Cathedral of St Dmitri on its hilltop and, like it, commanding the valley of the Klyazma. Today it consists of a jumble of buildings of different periods and varying architectural merit, but until the middle of the last century it apparently contained a fine late twelfth-century cathedral, which, however, was first quite gratuitously rebuilt and then apparently demolished. Here for four and a half centuries lay buried the great warrior-saint Alexander Nevski until dug up by Peter the Great and removed to the fine new monastery which Peter, somewhat characteristically, had built for him in St Petersburg.

This in itself was an interesting discovery. No less interesting to me were the massive walls of the monastery and the name of a nearby eighteenth-century church, now the town planetarium and known as St Nicholas-in-the-Kremlin. At last I was getting somewhere. And sure enough, on further investigation, I discovered that

the monastery walls in fact corresponded to the original fortifications of Monomakh's Kremlin and thus constituted a direct link
with the city's founder.

Another interesting ancient monastic foundation is the Princess's Convent, founded by Maria, wife of Vsevolod III, and situated in the north-western part of Vladimir on what were once the
banks of the River Lybed, which originally marked the northern
limit of the old town, but now seems to have disappeared underground. The convent's principal church, another Cathedral of the
Assumption, which served for a time as a burial place for the Grand
Princesses, was originally built in the year 1200. Largely rebuilt
in the sixteenth and seventeenth centuries, it is a pleasant enough
church, typical of the latter period, and surmounted by a single
cupola it contains a number of mid-seventeenth-century frescoes,
including a spirited representation of the Last Judgement. A little
further down the Street of the First of May (on which it stands)
and strongly in contrast with it is the elegant grey and white
baroque Church of St Nikita the Martyr, with its tall bell-tower
and matching spire and dome, built in about 1765.

For anyone with the time to spare the older parts of Vladimir
possess a further abundance of agreeable seventeenth- and eighteenth-century buildings and churches, including yet another
Church of the Assumption, with a cluster of five domes and a graceful bell-tower, built in 1642 by the banks of the Klyazma on the
southern limits of the old town 'by the combined efforts of the
merchants of Vladimir'. That Vladimir was a city of prosperous
merchants is also recalled by two fine matching eighteenth-century
buildings on the Street of the Third International, which originally
housed the town's Torgovlye Ryadi or shopping centre. The
former Gentlemen's Club, a handsome early nineteenth-century
classical building a little way along the same street, has now become
the Officers' Club of the local garrison, so that its social purpose
has undergone no great change.

One way to get a good general view of old Vladimir and see what
it has to offer in the way of antiquities is to climb to the top of
the former Water Tower, which occupies a commanding position
at the western extremity of the old town, not far from the Golden
Gate. On further inspection I found that the little eminence on
which it stands is in fact part of the ancient ramparts which formerly constituted the western defences of the city and date back

to the middle of the twelfth century and to Andrei Bogolyubski. Looking out from the top of the Water Tower, a not very beautiful nineteenth-century structure in red brick, you quickly realize first what a large town Vladimir now is and secondly how many fine old buildings it still possesses which look as though they would repay further investigation. The Water Tower itself, incidentally, houses a kind of local museum containing a strangely assorted collection of faded photographs and other exhibits, mostly relating to the last century, which throw valuable light on life and social conditions in Vladimir before the Revolution. An interesting link with pre-Revolutionary Vladimir is the Jail, built under the Tsars to accommodate political prisoners and still used for the same purpose. From acquaintances who have done time there one gathers that it does not abound in creature comforts.

For his own place of residence Andrei Bogolyubski chose not Vladimir itself but the neighbouring village of Bogolyubovo five or six miles away, from which he took his name and of which, with Vladimir, he had already taken possession in his father's lifetime. Here he built his stronghold on a high bluff overlooking the Klyazma River (which has since receded southward, leaving a little lake behind it) and commanding an extensive view of the surrounding country. Next to it he built a church, connected with his own apartments by a covered passage-way. There was also a stone-paved courtyard with stables, living quarters for his warriors and stores for arms and supplies giving onto it. Round it all he threw a high fortified wall and a moat.

Of Andrei's original palace all that remains today is a stone staircase-tower and part of the passage-way connecting it to the church. These are incorporated in the much later Cathedral of the Resurrection which now stands on the same site.

It was on this staircase that on the night of 29 June 1174 Prince Andrei's assassins, in league with his wife Ulita, finally caught up with him. After murdering him, they looted the palace and treasury. His body they threw to the dogs to eat. But a faithful Court Jester managed at the risk of his life to get it away from the dogs and, having wrapped it up in a rug, carried it to the nearby church. The Prince's murderers did not, it appears, escape the consequences of their crime. They were caught and executed and their bodies, in specially tarred coffins, consigned to the swamps round Bogolyubovo. There they have floated ever since and at night, it is said, can still sometimes be heard moaning and wailing across the marshland.

Though a hard, tyrannical, bloodthirsty man, with no obviously saint-like characteristics except for a certain austere asceticism, Andrei was subsequently canonized. But, saint-like or not, he can certainly be reckoned as one of the creators of the future Great-Russian State who saw in his beloved Zalesye a firm foundation on which to build.

Nor was this Prince Andrei's only bequest to posterity. Barely a mile away across the meadows and easily seen from the palace he had built himself on the hilltop at Bogolyubovo, stands the little Church of the Intercession (Tserkov Pokrova), which he built in 1165 on the banks of the River Nerl in memory of his eldest son killed in battle against the Bulgars. This little white church is one of the glories of early Russian architecture. Over the years, the Nerl, like the Klyazma, has changed its course and Andrei's church, originally built on a man-made stone island in the river, now stands among a group of elm-trees on the edge of a small lake fringed with reeds and water-lilies. Approaching it on foot in spring or summer, you first catch sight of its cupola from a considerable distance away across the fields. As you come nearer, it seems to rise from the tall, flower-sprinkled grass of the meadows and gradually take shape. Everything about it directs the eye upwards. Though this is not apparent, its walls are slightly inclined inwards in order to give an impression of greater height. A single dome set on a slender drum pierced by six lancet windows springs from the graceful four-sided white limestone church. The church itself has three apses and four piers. Slender pilasters divide each of the remaining three walls into three arched panels, corresponding to the apses on the fourth, each framing a narrow lancet window and broken by a line of little vertical columns. Below these in each wall is a doorway with a smaller window on either side of it. Like the churches in Vladimir itself, the Pokrov shows signs of both Eastern and Western influences. The decoration of the exterior, unlike that of St Dmitri, is restrained to the point of austerity, being limited in practice to the surrounds of the windows and doors and to little groups of carved figures under the arches of the *zakomaras*. Here once more we find King David, sitting on his throne, flanked by heraldic birds and beasts. Beneath him are three women's heads, possibly symbolizing the Virgin Mary. The interior of the church, with its soaring piers and arches, is as harmonious and as brilliantly proportioned as the outside. Again the decoration is limited to a few carved ornaments.

After eight hundred years the little church is in remarkable condition. In this there is at least an element of luck. In 1784 the Abbot of the day applied to his ecclesiastical superiors for permission to demolish it, in order to put the stones from which it was built to what he considered better use. In due course permission was granted. But, when it came to the point, the Abbot could not find a contractor prepared to pull it down for a price he was ready to pay. And so the matter lapsed and the little church stayed where it was. According to another version, the men who set out to demolish it found themselves half blinded by a shower of gold dust from the cross on the dome and accordingly desisted.

# 12 *Sixty Years On*

Achieving a greater awareness of the past, we clarify the present; digging deeper into the significance of what has gone before, we discover the meaning of the future; looking backwards, we move forwards.

ALEXANDER IVANOVICH HERZEN

HAVING sought to give some account of Russia past and present, it is tempting, before laying down one's pen, to try for a moment to look into the future, to study, as best one can, current tendencies and trends and hazard a guess at where they may be leading.

At home, the present rulers of the Soviet Union find themselves faced with the same fundamental problem which confronted Khrushchov when he first took over from Stalin a quarter of a century ago: how to satisfy an emergent public opinion and keep abreast of foreign competition in a variety of fields, while at the same time restricting Soviet contacts with the outside world and maintaining adequate political control over every aspect of Soviet life. It is, as we have seen, a perennial problem which, in one form or another and at one time or another, earlier rulers of Russia also had to face.

The task of governing Russia is not a simple one. It never has been. As Sergei Yulyevich Witte put it, speaking from first-hand experience, 'the world should be surprised, not that we have a less than perfect government in Russia, but that we have any government at all . . . the amazing thing is that the country can be held together, even by an autocracy.' Nor is power now concentrated, as it was thirty years ago, in one man's hands, with all the saving of time and trouble that that implied. The system, rather than any one individual, has come to occupy the centre of the stage and within the system there are now signs of varying shades of opinion and a continuing debate on questions of policy, in place of the

330

Marching past

monolithic decisions once so conveniently and decisively imposed from above. A state of affairs which, in the ordinary course of events, is bound to necessitate a measure of political and indeed economic interplay and compromise. As one well qualified observer recently put it, 'Russian totalitarianism is often less than total.'

However much they might want to do so, the present rulers of Russia are no longer in a position to turn the clock right back to where it stood in Stalin's day. The change in atmosphere, the all-round relaxation of pressure have gone too far for that. With the years, Mr Brezhnev has, it is true, emerged as a great deal more than *primus inter pares*. Head of State, Party Secretary, Marshal of the Soviet Union, Supreme Commander of the Armed Forces, holding the Order of Victory and most other Soviet orders and decorations several times over, he occupies a position of very great power. He is above all Secretary of the Party, which by the new constitution of 1977 has been formally enshrined as the source of all power and the supreme authority in the land. But even so the power he wields and that his successors seem likely to wield is altogether different in character from the power once wielded by Stalin. True, from time to time there is a tightening-up. Purges are undertaken, repressive measures reintroduced. But the machine-gun is no longer the answer to everything. It is no longer possible to force the lid right back on to Pandora's box.

For twenty five years and more human nature has been at work, human nature which under Stalin was somehow kept in check, but which, once it is allowed free play, can be one of the most disruptive and subversive forces on earth and, given the chance, can, as Stalin well knew, very quickly make hay of any political or ideological system, especially one which does not take it sufficiently into account. 'I expect you notice a change,' said the man on the park bench when he heard I had known the Soviet Union in Stalin's day. 'I will tell you the biggest change of all: people are beginning to think for themselves.' Apart from this, I had already noticed something else. People were no longer frightened to be seen talking to foreigners in public. This, too, was something new.

Another important development of the past twenty-five years (neatly spanning a new generation of Russians) has been the emergence in Russia of a regular class structure with the usual accompaniment of vested interests, vested interests which now play quite as important a part in Russia as they do anywhere else.

Under Stalin (as under Ivan the Terrible and Peter the Great) there were individuals who for, say, ten or fifteen years enjoyed power and privilege. Some lasted even longer. But in the main the turnover by terror was more rapid; those in power were automatically in danger, and were not given time to dig themselves in as a class.

Now this is no longer so. A man born, say, with the century, who by the age of fifty had managed in any one of a variety of fields to achieve a position of wealth, responsibility and power, would, if still alive today, almost certainly be living in considerable luxury and would have no difficulty in launching his children and grandchildren on careers comparable to his own or at any rate ensuring for them a generous share of the good things of life. (A good start in life makes a difference and so, it may be added, does inherited wealth.) And these children and grandchildren in their turn would confidently expect, when the time came, to do the same for their children and grandchildren. As under Peter the Great, it is still the job you do that matters. But it is a great deal easier to get a good job if your father had a good job before you. In other words, what is emerging sixty years after the Bolshevik Revolution is something of which Russia historically has often felt the lack, a hereditary ruling class. These are the people who earn (and keep) the most money, who, like the nobility under Catherine the Great, are authorized to travel abroad, who possess the finest apartments and *dachas* and drive the fastest cars, who shop, as of right, in special stores and wear the smartest clothes, who occupy the most coveted tables in the smartest restaurants and the best seats in the theatre.

Nor do these class distinctions occur only at the highest level. For practically the first time in Russian history a true middle class is emerging, bringing with them the social stability and all the other bourgeois virtues so sadly lacking under the Tsars, a middle class that can be seen in strength shopping at GUM, disporting themselves at the better Black Sea resorts, spending their evenings at the theatre and ballet and opera, and driving their own medium-sized family cars out into the country on their days off. They are not as rich or as elegant or as self-assured as the upper class, but they know what they want and they have by now a stake in society. Meanwhile, of course, as in Victorian Britain, there are plentiful opportunities for the working class, the proletariat, if sufficiently

333

shrewd and industrious, to better themselves, to improve their position and, given time and opportunity, to climb to who knows what heights on the social ladder.

From personal observation, from chance glimpses behind the scenes, one very quickly comes to realize that throughout this whole elaborate structure a complicated social life is in progress, regulated, here as elsewhere, by good or bad luck, by every kind of human motive and emotion, virtue and weakness, by good judgement and bad, by ambition, success or failure, by intrigue or corruption, by poverty or wealth, by idleness, envy or greed. None of which important human factors seem so far to have been eliminated by the changes which have taken place in the Russian political, social and economic system which once used to aim, amongst other things, at the creation of a New Soviet Man.

While in many respects beneficially, this stratification of society must inevitably complicate the task of government. What it amounts to is that there are today in Russia, not to mention the other Republics, any number of people who have a considerable stake in the country, who know their own minds and whose views and requirements have to be taken into account by those in power, who constitute, in other words, an embryonic public opinion.

There is another thing. To anyone who, like myself, knew the Soviet Union of forty or even twenty years ago, the improvement that has taken place in the Soviet standard of living, in the availability of consumer goods, in housing conditions and in amenities generally, is positively startling. But this does not prevent all these significant people, many of whom have by now enjoyed power and privilege for a couple of generations, from demanding a greater improvement still, and going on demanding it. Their wives see to that. The deep-seated desire of Soviet womanhood, especially in the higher social echelons, for greater luxury and glamour and more and better consumer goods is something which the Ministers concerned cannot afford to ignore.

The Consumer Revolution (though this, too, has had its setbacks and its reverses) has come to stay. To meet the ever more insistent demand for a better standard of living, the whole balance of the Soviet economy is gradually being altered. Profitability and the laws of supply and demand, so long denounced as wicked capitalist inventions, are now gradually being taken more into account. Today in certain fields something approaching a market economy is coming into operation. Goods are now, quite often, produced because people want them and not, as at one time, simply to fulfil some theoretical norm.

And with the Consumer Revolution have come its various by-products – such, for example, as the proliferation of the private motor-car, with all the complications which that involves in a country where tight control is of paramount importance. (Did not the great Duke of Wellington, after all, oppose the railways on the ground that they increased the mobility of the working class, which he, for one, evidently considered a dangerous thing to do?) In the same way, better living accommodation, the resulting increase in privacy, a wider choice of goods and other amenities, more contact, if only indirect, with the outside world, all make it easier for the Soviet citizen who feels so inclined to abstract himself, to escape, at least in spirit, from the suffocating centralization, standardization and collectivization of the system and above all from that un-avoidable conformity which is such an essential part of any totali-tarian or authoritarian regime.

In the short term, it would probably be possible to spend two or three years in the Soviet Union and still take the view that no progress was being made in any of these directions or even that things were getting worse. But, looking back over a much longer period and allowing for periodic set-backs and reversals, it is hard to resist the conclusion that, long term, progress is being made, that, however slowly, a gradual evolution is taking place, that, to para-phrase Lenin, it is a case of three steps forwards and two back. What is more, the motive force behind this evolution (or should one perhaps call it revolution?) is the pursuit not of any vague, abstract ideas or ideals, but, as Burke preferred to see happen, of solid material advantage for those concerned.

In other fields, too, things are moving. Under Stalin there was no 'internal emigration'. Dangerous thoughts were dealt with by a bullet in the back of the neck, almost before they had taken shape. Only the utterly reckless indulged in poor-taste jokes at the expense of the regime. The intelligentsia, like every other section of Soviet society, were kept strictly under control and channelled in whatever direction the Party chose. Now this is no longer so. To a limited extent the intelligentsia (with much the same attachment to abstract ideals as their nineteenth-century predecessors) have reverted to their historic role as critics of the regime and proponents

335

of Utopian counter-theories. Poor-taste jokes proliferate and, from a revolutionary creed, Marxism-Leninism has been relegated to the role of an Established Church, to which lip-service must be paid and obeisance made, if advancement is to be obtained. 'What,' one citizen asks another, 'is the difference between capitalism and communism?' 'Under capitalism,' comes the reply, 'man exploits man. Under communism it is the other way round.'

It is, of course, true that if this or that intellectual oversteps the mark he is often savagely disciplined. Indeed by their treatment of dissidents the Soviet authorities do infinite harm to their public image, drawing muted criticism even from some of the less abject Western Communist Parties. Even so, there is all the difference in the world between a couple of years in a lunatic asylum or in Siberia and actually facing a firing squad.

And so the old struggle between progressives and reactionaries, between Westerners and Slavophiles, or whatever you like to call it, goes on. Despite the difficulties (and they should not be under-estimated), dissidents hold press-conferences, banned books and secret news sheets continue to circulate, contact is maintained with the outside world, people listen to foreign broadcasts, protests are made, pictures are painted and ideas expressed, at any rate in private, which, if not openly subversive, certainly do not conform to the precepts of the Party Line. There is even, unbelievably, an independent, unofficial trade-union movement. For the authorities the dilemma is fast becoming an awkward one and policy is delicately balanced between what can still be safely withheld and what must now be grudgingly granted. But, for all that, it seems probable that change, when it comes, will spring first and foremost from class and other vested interests, vigorously pursued, from what Burke called 'human wants', rather than from the abstract ideas of the intelligentsia.

Meanwhile, in Russia as elsewhere, a new generation is growing up, as cynical as elsewhere and no more amenable, born when Stalin was already long since dead and buried, disinclined to accept at its face value anything they are told by their elders, clearly providing fertile ground for any dangerous thoughts that happen to be floating about, and as likely as any one else to stand up for what they conceive to be their own interests.

Nor, by a long chalk, are these the regime's only problems. Like other countries, the Soviet Union, more than sixty years after the

Revolution, still has serious economic difficulties to contend with. Economic growth, bedevilled by the side-effects of Bureaucratic Centralism, is apt to be disappointing. An American industrial worker still produces twice as much and an American farm-hand ten times as much as his Soviet counterpart. Soviet agriculture, owing partly to the less than brilliant success of collectivization, partly to old-fashioned farming methods and partly to climatic conditions, is all too often in trouble. Year after year the Government has had to spend valuable currency on importing grain. What is more, about thirty per cent of all agricultural produce comes from the private plots of individual peasants, totalling not more than two or three per cent of the available agricultural land, and is sold by them for what it will fetch on the free market – in itself a terrifying indictment of the system.

Nor is the international outlook very much simpler. Directly or indirectly the Soviet Government now holds sway over a vaster empire than the Tsars. Soviet interests and aspirations extend to every quarter of the globe. This brings its rewards, but also its responsibilities and problems. Within the frontiers of the Soviet Union, the task of ruling over a varied assortment of subject races has not always proved an easy one. Outside its frontiers, the carefully constituted *cordon sanitaire* of Soviet satellites, stretching from the Baltic to the Black Sea, has for the last thirty years been a source of constant concern. During this period recurrent signs of undue liberalism or independence have at frequent intervals made it necessary for the Kremlin to bring pressure to bear on individual satellite governments or even, as in Hungary and Czechoslovakia, to intervene directly by force of arms. Bulgaria alone has shown scarcely wavering docility and loyalty. Of the rest, following Jugoslavia's defection in 1948, East Germany, Poland, Hungary, Czechoslovakia and Romania have all at one time or another caused trouble and all, in their different ways, still give proof of a greater measure of non-conformity than is altogether acceptable. Even the communist parties of the West have shown disquieting signs of independence. Fear of contagion, of undesirable tendencies and trends, led to the formulation of the Brezhnev Doctrine, designed to explain Soviet intervention in Czechoslovakia in 1968 and retained thereafter as justification for any future action of this kind which might prove necessary elsewhere. Whether by formally recognizing the existing international frontiers at Helsinki in 1975, and no less formally undertaking to abstain from all intervention in the internal affairs of other countries, the Soviet government was in fact renouncing this doctrine, remains to be seen. One somehow doubts it.

Meanwhile, for the Russians an even more serious problem and one to which there seems at the moment to be no immediate solution, is that of China, Russia's fellow-communist colossus and former satellite, looming up on its eastern frontier with what will soon be a population of a thousand million brave, dedicated, hard-working, intelligent citizens, looking for somewhere to expand into and meanwhile missing no opportunity of denouncing, in the most insulting terms, Russia's fall from grace and cynical betrayal of the Revolution. Tito's defection back in 1948 was bad enough; a first crack had appeared in the monolith. The rift with China, widening and deepening with the years, now effectively splits the communist world in two. From every point of view, racial, military, economic and ideological, China remains a menace, a perpetual reminder of all the unpleasant things which, in Russia's long history, have come at her out of the East, a constant threat which, whatever the situation elsewhere, can never for one single instant be left out of sight.

On a wider horizon, the outlook for the Soviet Union, though complicated, is not altogether discouraging. By and large, the capitalist world has, as predicted by the prophets of Marxism, managed to get itself into a mess, thereby at first sight lending substance to the old Marxist theory that capitalism carries within it the seeds of its own destruction and encouraging the Soviet hard-liners and proponents of world revolution under Soviet auspices in their conviction that they are right. The developing, uncommitted countries are for the most part in a state of equal confusion and therefore, in theory at any rate, equally open to penetration and subversion, though here it is noteworthy that in Africa and the Middle East Soviet experiments in this field, though plentiful, have not been uniformly successful. In a number of countries there has been a swing to what is still known as the Left (though not always the right Left from a Soviet angle). In others, there has been a swing to the Right (by now an almost equally ambiguous term).

Which brings us to the well-worn but nonetheless important question of East–West relations, which, in one guise or another, has for more than thirty years held the centre of the international stage. During this period we have experienced, one after the other, cold war, coexistence, and, more recently, détente, none of them in practice very readily distinguishable from the others. And here, once again, one is tempted to try to look into the future.

In practice, as in theory, everyone must clearly be in favour of détente, if only because the alternative does not bear thinking about. To condemn the two halves of the world light-heartedly to perpetual tension or, worse still, to mutual extinction, is scarcely a very constructive proposition. What is absolutely essential, how-ever, is to determine, right at the start, exactly what, in present circumstances, is meant by détente.

For this purpose it is necessary to take a long, hard and above all realistic look at the basis and motivation of Soviet policy. Win-ston Churchill once said that Russia was a riddle wrapped in a mys-tery inside an enigma. In my view he exaggerated the problem. The Russians have, of course, always enjoyed keeping the rest of the world guessing. 'Russia,' wrote the Marquis de Custine in 1839, 'is a country where everyone is part of a conspiracy to mystify [*enguirlander*] the foreigner.' But in fact, there is nothing very mys-terious or very hard to understand about the underlying motives of Soviet policy. Like that of most countries, it is based on more or less enlightened self-interest, the self-interest, in this case, of a super-power, with, as its immediate aim, the safeguarding of its own security and, as its ultimate, theoretical purpose, world domi-nation or, to put it in another way, world revolution.

There is nothing very new about this. The Bolshevik Revolution, it is true, gave a new dimension to Russian policy. But the idea of the Third Rome, of Russia's Imperial destiny, of Holy Russia enlightening and, by extension, dominating the world, has been there all along. Indeed in some ways the Revolution only served to accentuate existing tendencies and increase this very Russian sense of mission.

At the time of writing, more than sixty years after the Revolution, there are signs that the Russians are anxious for a measure of détente, for a relaxation of tension in their relations with the West and in particular with the United States. Nor is it particularly sur-prising that they should be. Things are not going uniformly well for them. They are, we know, worried about China. They also have domestic problems: problems with their satellites, with their own national minorities, with agriculture, with the economy, with the intelligentsia. For all these reasons they would no doubt welcome a respite, a period of peace and quiet, in which to mend their fences and recover their equilibrium and, most important of all, to obtain from the West the financial, economic and technical assistance which at this stage of their development they still require and in return for which they are now even prepared to accept a certain measure of dependence on the West.

From a Soviet point of view these are perfectly sufficient reasons for wanting détente. What, from a Western point of view, would be entirely erroneous would be to imagine that this desire for détente springs from some sudden feeling of benevolence towards the capitalist world. On the contrary, the Russians are still in theory pledged to the overthrow of capitalism everywhere. And this they demonstrate in practice by the rate at which they continue to build up their armaments, both nuclear and conventional. 'Soviet sea power,' wrote Admiral Gorshkov recently, 'has become the optimum means to defeat the imperialist enemy and the most important element in the Soviet arsenal to prepare the way for a Communist world.' Nothing, surely, could be clearer than that.

The purpose of these vast and increasing armaments and in particular of the recent enormous increase in Soviet naval strength is, of course, in one sense military. But in another very important sense it is political and ideological. They are not just intended for use in case of war. They are primarily intended for constant use in peacetime as a political weapon, a means of bringing pressure, designed to further Soviet interests in any and every part of the world. The Soviet government makes no bones about this. 'The actions of the Warsaw Pact', to quote Mr Gromyko, 'are having a major influence in shaping the situation, not only in Europe, but far beyond Europe.' Of late this tendency has been more in evidence than ever, particularly in Africa. It would, therefore, be very foolish to ignore it especially when the Russians keep telling us, quite frankly, that their present policy of co-operation with the West does not mean that they are abandoning their efforts to change what they call 'the balance of social-political forces' in the world. This, we may be sure, is an aim which – détente or no détente – they will continue to pursue for the foreseeable future, sometimes by subversion, sometimes by financial or economic means, sometimes by the use of Cuban or other mercenaries and sometimes by more or less direct intervention or confrontation, in the hope, no doubt, that, if they keep it up, if they persevere, the West, and much else besides, will eventually fall into their lap like a ripe plum, as foretold by the prophets of Marxism. For us in the West, their attitude should certainly not come as a surprise. Nor should we allow ourselves to be lulled into thinking that, because there is so much talk of détente, we can safely sit back and relax. Nor, in all seriousness, can we afford to ignore the danger that, if, as seems all too probable, we allow the balance of power to shift too drastically to our disadvantage, the Soviet Government or its military advisers could consider this a sufficient reason for seeking to settle with us once and for all, though here we should be clear that in the Russians we are contending with cautious realists rather than power-crazed maniacs.

What then should be the Western attitude towards détente? It seems clear that we should not reject the idea of détente as such. But to my mind it is no less clear that we should approach it with great wariness and even greater realism. In the ultimate analysis the Soviet Union still needs détente at least as much as the West. The Western powers are therefore in a position to insist on terms which would make it worth while for them. Quite obviously, for example, it must be ridiculous for the Americans to provide the Russians with all the grain and advanced industrial plant and technological know-how they need and get nothing worth having in return. Nor could it make sense for them to bolster up the Soviet economy, simply in order to help the Russians spend even more on armaments.

What could we hope to gain from détente? Clearly the most worth-while thing of all would be to secure a measure of genuine disarmament on the part of the Soviet Union. This could help remove what is at present a very real threat to world peace and stability and perhaps in due course make possible a corresponding reduction in armaments on the part of the West. Without at least equivalent reductions on the Soviet side, any unilateral disarmament on the part of the West would of course be sheer lunacy. Indeed, so long as the Russians maintain their present level of armaments, it is obviously essential that the Western powers should at all costs maintain, or better still, increase, their present somewhat inadequate armed capacity, especially in the field of conventional weapons. Nor should they simply accept as inevitable any further Soviet encroachment world-wide. For the West the Soviet take-over of Angola, meekly accepted by the Western powers, was an unmitigated disaster. Since then an equally disturbing situation has arisen in the Horn of Africa. It will no doubt be followed by other threats to our interests elsewhere. But this does not mean that we have to put up with them. So long as the balance of power is not too heavily weighted against us, such conflicts of interest are, as history has shown, perfectly capable of solution by international negotiation and agreement. It is simply a question of knowing where to draw the line and being able to draw it. As Lord Palmerston put it more than a century ago, 'the policy and practice of the Russian Government has always been to push forward its encroachments as far and as fast as the apathy or want of firmness of other Governments would allow it to go, but always to stop and retire when it met with decided resistance'. The Russians, it should be remembered did not reach Constantinople in 1878. Nor did they retain their rockets in Cuba for long in 1962.

There are also, I believe, numerous advantages to be gained by the West in other fields. The Helsinki Agreement of 1975, to which the Soviet Union most surprisingly and, in my view, mistakenly subscribed, provided, amongst other things, for the freer exchange of ideas, for greater freedom of movement between East and West and for better safeguards in the field of human rights. These, I am convinced, we should press for most vigorously and keep on pressing for at every level, whether the prospect of gaining satisfaction be good or bad.

Stalin, who certainly gave the matter considerable thought, was clearly convinced that, to maintain adequate control over the peoples of the Soviet Union, it was necessary to keep them as far as possible protected from contact with the outside world. Since his day the barriers between East and West have to some extent been broken down. So have the pressures designed to prevent the Soviet peoples from thinking for themselves. As I have sought to show, other influences, notably human nature, have been at work in a rather more favourable atmosphere, influences calculated in the long run to transform the Soviet Union into something a little less difficult to live with. And nothing, I believe, will accelerate this process more than freer contact of all kinds between East and West.

Over the last twenty-five years the Soviet people, or some of them, have come – indirectly – to have a little more say in the running of their own affairs. Their rulers have, in some contexts, been obliged to take their wishes into account, to make more concessions to them. Though proud of their country and prepared to fight bravely in defence of it, the Soviet people certainly do not want war. How could they after the sufferings they have endured in two world wars? And it therefore seems possible that, as time goes on and they come to have even more say in the conduct of their affairs and even more contacts with the outside world, the pressures on the Soviet government in favour of peace and of genuine détente with the West will increase rather than diminish.

The conflict between East and West is first and foremost a conflict of ideas. The Russians are taught to believe as absolute dogma that our system carries within it the seeds of its own decay and is therefore doomed. Personally, I believe that, on the contrary, our Western democratic ideas are infinitely better and stronger than theirs and that, if given the chance, they are bound to prevail in the end. In fact in many parts of the world, including Russia itself, one can see signs that this is already happening. Which is why détente and the greater freedom of intercourse it should bring with it is a challenge from which we in the West cannot flinch, because to do so would show lack of confidence in ourselves and our values.

What is vitally important is that, in pursuing this policy, the West should never weaken, whether militarily or politically, economically or ideologically, that we should have confidence in ourselves and the courage of our own convictions, that we should keep our wits about us and on no account lower our guard. In other words that we should be as tough and as resilient as the Russians are, if not tougher. So long as we do this, we need have nothing to fear from détente or, for that matter, from confrontation.

Weakness is something the Russians despise. Strength they understand and admire. It was Hitler's strength and the apparent weakness of the West that led them (mistakenly, as it turned out) into an accommodation with him in 1939. Any sign of weakness on our part directly nurtures Soviet aggressiveness, increasing the danger of power passing to men hellbent on war. A more robust attitude would on the other hand win respect, shake any belief in our decline and improve the prospects of genuine understanding.

And here it is useful to recall that there have been other apparently insoluble conflicts and confrontations in history and that, with the passing of time, the original causes of conflict have as often as not disappeared and been in the end forgotten. Without being unduly optimistic, there seems to me at any rate a chance that this could happen in the present instance. With time, experience has shown, the steam goes out of crusades, but never out of human nature.

# Select Bibliography

ALIOSHIN, DMITRI, *Asian Odyssey* (London 1941)

ALLEN, W. E. D., *A History of the Georgian People* (London 1932)

ASCHER, A., *The Kremlin* (New York 1972)

AURORA (Leningrad), *Pamyatniki Arkhitekturi Gruzii* (1973) *Pamyatniki Arkhitekturi Armenii*

BADDELEY, J. F., *The Russian Conquest of the Caucasus* (London 1908)

BAEDEKER, KARL, *Russia: A Handbook for Travellers* (London 1914)

BANIGE, V., *Kreml Rostova Velikogo* (Moscow 1976)

BEHRENS, EWALD, *Kunst in Russland* (Cologne 1969)

BERTON, K., *Moscow: An Architectural History* (London 1977)

BILLINGTON, J. H., *The Icon and the Axe* (London 1966)

BLANCH, LESLEY *The Sabres of Paradise* (London 1960)

BREMNER, ROBERT, *Excursions in the Interior of Russia* (London 1839)

BRYCE, J., *Transcaucasia and Ararat* (London 1877)

BURNABY, FRED, *A Ride to Khiva* (London 1877)

CAMERON, G. P., *Adventures in Georgia, Circassia and Russia* (London 1845)

CARR, E.H., *The Bolshevik Revolution* (London 1950)

CATHERINE II, *Memoirs* (Paris 1953; London 1955)

CHARQUES, RICHARD, *A Short History of Russia* (London 1956)

CLARKE, E. D., *Travels*, Part I, *Russia, Tartary and Turkey* (London 1810)

CONQUEST, ROBERT, *The Great Terror* (London 1968)

COXE, WILLIAM, *Travels Into Poland, Russia, Sweden and Denmark* (London 1784)

CRANKSHAW, EDWARD, *Russia and the Russians* (London 1947) *Russia by Daylight* (London 1951) *Russia Without Stalin* (London 1956) *Khrushchev's Russia* (London 1959) *Khrushchev* (London 1966) *The Shadow of the Winter Palace* (London 1976)

CRONIN, VINCENT, *Catherine, Empress of All the Russias* (London 1978)

CUNYNGHAME, A. T., *Travels in the Eastern Caucasus* (London 1872)

CUSTINE, MARQUIS DE, *La Russie en 1839* (Paris 1843)

DEUTSCHER, I., *Stalin: A Political Biography* (London 1949) *The Prophet Armed: Trotsky 1879–1924* (London 1954)

DISBROWE, C. A. A., *Original Letters from Russia (1825–28)* (London 1878)

DRANCEY, A., *Les Princesses Russes prisonnières au Caucase: Souvenirs d'une Française* (Paris 1857)

FITZLYON, K., AND BROWNING, T., *Before the Revolution* (London 1977)
FLETCHER, G., *Of the Russe Commonwealth* (London 1591)
FLETCHER, G., AND HORSEY, J. *Russia at the Close of the Sixteenth Century*, ed. E. A. Bond, Hakluyt Society (London 1856)
FORBATH AND GELETA, *The New Mongolia* (London 1936)
FORTIA DE PILES, A. DE, *Voyages de deux Français dans le Nord de l'Europe* (Paris 1796)

GAUTIER, THÉOPHILE, *Voyage en Russie* (Paris 1866)
GNEDOVSKI, *Yaroslavl, Tutayev* (Leningrad 1970)
GOSLING, NIGEL, *Leningrad* (London 1965)
GROUSSET, R., *L'Empire Mongol* (Paris 1941)
*L'Empire des Steppes* (Paris 1952)
GRANVILLE, A. B., *St Petersburg* (London 1828)
GRIMM, BARON F. M., *Correspondence artistique avec Catherine II* (Paris 1932)

HAMBLY, GAVIN, *Central Asia* (London 1969)
HAMILTON, G. H., *The Art and Architectuure of Russia* (London 1954)
HASLIP, JOAN, *Catherine the Great* (London 1977)
HAUTECOEUR, L., *Architecture classique à St Pétersbourg à la fin du XVIIIᵉ siècle* (St Petersburg 1912)

HEBERSTEIN, S., *Rerum Moscoviticerum Commentarii* (Basle 1571)
HINGLEY, RONALD, *The Tsars* (London 1968)
*A Concise History of Russia* (London 1972)
HOETZCH, O., *The Evolution of Russia* (London 1966)
HOOKHAM, HILDA, *Tamburlaine the Conqueror* (London 1962)

ILIN, M., *Moskva: Pamyatniki Arkhitekturi XIV–XVII Vekov* (1973)
*Moskva: Pamyatniki Arkhitekturi XVIII–XIX Vekov* (1975)
*Podmoskovye* (1974)
*Moskva* (1970)
IVANOV, B., *Rostov, Uglich* (1975)

KAISER, ROBERT G., *Russia* (London 1976)
KARGER, M. K., *Novgorod Veliki* (Moscow 1973)
KENNETT, V. AND A., *The Palaces of Leningrad* (London 1973)
KHALPAKHIAN, O., *Sanain* (1973)
KHRUSHCHEV, N. I., *Khrushchev Remembers* (London 1971)
KLYUCHEVSKI, V. O., *A History of Russia* (London 1911–26)
KOCHAN, L., *The Making of Modern Russia* (London 1962)
*Russia in Revolution* (London 1966)
KOCHAN, M., *The Last Days of Imperial Russia* (London 1976)
KOSTOCHKIN, V., *Drevnerusskie Goroda* (Moscow 1972)
KUDRIAVSTEV, F., *Zolotoye Koltso* (Moscow 1974)

LANG, DAVID MARSHALL, *A Modern History of Georgia* (London 1962)
*The Georgians* (London 1966)

LAWRENCE, JOHN, *Russia in the Making* (London 1978)

LOGVIN, H., *Hagia Sofia* (Kiev 1971)

LOUIS, V. AND J., *The Complete Guide to the Soviet Union* (London 1976)

LOUKOMSKI, G., *Charles Cameron* (London 1943)

LUKE, H. C., *Cities and Men* (London 1953–56)

MACLEAN, F., *A Person from England* (London 1958)
*To the Back of Beyond* (London 1974)
*To Caucasus* (London 1976)

MAKMAYEVSKI, M. A., AND PAMTOV, Y. D., *Kreml Rostova Velikogo* (1976)

MASSON, C. F. P., *Secret Memoirs of the Court of St Petersburg* (London 1800)

MILLER, MARGARET, *The Rise of the Russian Consumer* (London 1965)

MILLER, WRIGHT, *The Russians as People* (London 1960)

MOLEVA, N., *The Moscow Kremlin* (Moscow 1975)

MURARKA, DEV, *The Soviet Union* (London 1971)

NERESSIAN, S. D., *The Armenians* (London 1969)

OSSENDOWSKI, F., *Tiere, Menschen und Götter* (Munich 1955)

PEREIRA, M., *Across the Caucasus* (London 1973)

PHILLIPS, E. D., *The Mongols* (London 1969)

PIPES, R., *Russia under the Old Regime* (London 1974)

PLATONOV, S. F., *History of Russia* (New York 1925)

POLUNIN, K., *Pamyatniki Arkhitekturi Vladimira, Suzdalya, Yuryeva, Polskogo* (1974)

RIASANOVSKY, N. V., *A History of Russia* (London 1969)

SCHUYLER, E., *Turkestan* (London 1876)

SETON-WATSON, H., *The Decline of Imperial Russia* (London 1952)

SMITH, HEDRICK, *The Russians* (London 1976)
*Spencer's Travels in Circassia* (London 1839)

STORCH, H. F. VON, *Picture of Petersburg* (London 1801)

SUMMER, B. H., *A Survey of Russian History* (London 1948)

TELFER, J. B., *The Crimea and Transcaucasia* (London 1876)

TROTSKY, LEON, *The History of the Russian Revolution* (London 1934)

VERDEREVSKY, M., *The Captivity of Two Russian Princesses* (London 1857)

VOEIKOVO, I. N., AND MITROFANOV, V. P., *Iskusstvo Drevnego Yaroslavlya* (Moscow 1973)

VOLOGOV, A. A., *Pskov* (Leningrad 1974)

VORONIN, N., *Vladimir, Bogolyubovo, Suzdal, Yuryev Polskoi* (1974)

WALLACE, DONALD MACKENZIE, *Russia* (London 1905)

WARD, MRS, *Letters from a Lady who resided some years in Russia* (London 1775)

WHEELER, G., *A Modern History of Soviet Central Asia* (London 1964)

# SELECT BIBLIOGRAPHY

WILBRAHAM, R., *Travels in the Transcaucasian Provinces of Russia* (London 1834)

WILMOT, M. AND C., *Russian Journals 1803–08* (London 1934)

WITTRAM, R., *Russia and Europe* (London 1973)

# Index